STRENGTH COACHING
IN AMERICA

TERRY AND JAN TODD SERIES
ON PHYSICAL CULTURE AND SPORTS

Edited by Sarah K. Fields, Thomas Hunt,
Daniel A. Nathan, and Patricia Vertinsky

Also in the series:

Thomas Hunt, *Drug Games: The International Olympic Committee
and the Politics of Doping*, 1960–2008

John D. Fair, *Mr. America: The Tragic History of a Bodybuilding Icon*

John Hoberman, *Dopers in Uniform: The Hidden World
of Police on Steroids*

Kevin Robbins, *Harvey Penick: The Life and Wisdom of the Man
Who Wrote the Book on Golf*

Andrew R. M. Smith, *No Way but to Fight: George Foreman
and the Business of Boxing*

STRENGTH COACHING
— IN —
AMERICA

A History of the Innovation
That Transformed Sports

JASON P. SHURLEY

JAN TODD

TERRY TODD

UNIVERSITY OF TEXAS PRESS

AUSTIN

"In Memoriam: Dr. Terry Todd (1938–2018): Pioneering Powerlifter, Writer, Sport Promoter, and Historian Who Changed the Cultural Paradigm for Strength" originally appeared in the *Journal of Strength and Conditioning Research* 23.11 (November 2018): 2995–3003. Copyright © National Strength and Conditioning Association; used by permission.

∞ The paper used in this book meets the minimum requirements of ANSI/NISO Z39.48-1992 (R1997) (Permanence of Paper).

LIBRARY OF CONGRESS CATALOGING-IN-PUBLICATION DATA

Names: Shurley, Jason P., author. | Todd, Jan, author. | Todd, Terry, author.
Title: Strength coaching in America : a history of the innovation that transformed sports / Jason P. Shurley, Jan Todd, Terry Todd.
Other titles: Terry and Jan Todd series on physical culture and sports.
Description: First edition. | Austin : University of Texas Press, 2019. | Series: Terry and Jan Todd series on physical culture and sports | Includes bibliographical references and index.
Identifiers: LCCN 2019013062 |
ISBN 978-1-4773-1979-6 (cloth : alk. paper) |
ISBN 978-1-4773-1980-2 (library e-book) |
ISBN 978-1-4773-1981-9 (nonlibrary e-book)
Subjects: LCSH: Physical education and training—United States—History. | Physical fitness—United States—History. | Weight training—United States. | Coaching (Athletics)—United States.
Classification: LCC GV223 .S48 2019 | DDC 613.7/13—dc23
LC record available at https://lccn.loc.gov/2019013062

doi:10.7560/319796

CONTENTS

ABBREVIATIONS

AAP	American Academy of Pediatrics
AAU	Amateur Athletic Union
ACSM	American College of Sports Medicine
ACWLA	American Continental Weight-Lifters Association
AED	automated external defibrillation
AFL	American Football League
AMA	American Medical Association
BAWLA	British Amateur Weight Lifters Association
CPR	cardiopulmonary resuscitation
CSCCa	Collegiate Strength and Conditioning Coaches Association
CSCS	Certified Strength and Conditioning Specialist
HIIT	High-Intensity Interval Training
IDEA	International Dance-Exercise Association
IGH	*Iron Game History: The Journal of Physical Culture*
JASSR	*Journal of Applied Sport Science Research*
JSCR	*Journal of Strength and Conditioning Research*
NCAA	National Collegiate Athletic Association
NFL	National Football League
NSCA	National Strength and Conditioning Association
NSCAJ	*National Strength and Conditioning Association Journal*
PRE	progressive resistance exercise
RM	repitition maximum
SCCC	Strength and Conditioning Coach Certified
SCJ	*Strength and Conditioning Journal*
T and C	Training and Conditioning

USTFCCCA	United States Track and Field and Cross Country Coaches' Association
YMCA	Young Men's Christian Association
YMHA	Young Men's Hebrew Association

STRENGTH COACHING

IN

AMERICA

INTRODUCTION

Modern college football is big business. In fiscal year 2017 the two largest universities in Texas led the nation in revenue generation for major college athletic departments, with each generating more than $210 million. The University of Texas at Austin was the standard-bearer, pulling in $214.8 million, while Texas A&M's haul was $212 million. Other top earners include the Ohio State University, the University of Alabama, the University of Michigan, the University of Georgia, and the University of Oklahoma, each of which counted between $155 million and $185 million in revenue during 2017.[1] In order to generate these hefty sums, teams rely on sales of broadcast rights, tickets, merchandise, and more.[2] Each of those things is more valuable if the team is successful on the field, which is often contingent upon having the biggest, strongest, and fastest players, along with the best coaches. Teams have spared no expense to secure the hottest commodities in coaching. In 2016 the University of Michigan paid head coach Jim Harbaugh just over $9 million to run their program. In 2017–2018 Alabama's Nick Saban earned $8.3 million from his regular salary and was eligible for $1.1 million more in bonuses.[3] Ohio State's Urban Meyer pulled in $7.6 million in 2017.[4] In 2016 seventy-two football coaches in Division I of the National Collegiate Athletic Association (NCAA) made more than $1 million per year, half of them making more than $3 million and seven making more than $5 million.[5] In 2018 the number of Division I head college football coaches earning more than $5 million a year stood at thirteen, with fifteen assistant coaches earning more than $1 million per year.[6]

In order to attract the best players, schools have also invested in extravagant facilities. Clemson University, winner of the 2016 national championship, recently completed its new football complex at a total cost of $55 million.[7] The facility includes expansive locker rooms, meeting rooms, dining facilities, a bowling alley, a golf simulator, a barber shop, a nap room, a movie theater, a two-story slide, a sports medicine center, an "outdoor village" that features basketball courts, a mini-putt golf course, a sand volleyball court, a fire pit, a whiffle ball diamond with artificial turf, and a 23,000-square-foot weight room.

The University of Oregon finished its Hatfield-Dowlin complex, described by the university's student newspaper as "a mecca built for the football team," in 2013. Though it was originally expected to cost $68 million, the final estimates for the total cost exceeded $130 million. That is only an estimate, however, as the facility was privately funded, keeping the final tally out of the public record.[8] Like Clemson's complex, the Oregon facility includes ornate locker rooms, sports medicine and dining facilities, a barbershop, and various lounges. The lounges even have chairs upholstered with the same leather used for the seats of Ferrari sports cars.[9] The Ducks' 25,000-square-foot weight room has floors of Brazilian Ipe wood and a forty-yard "electronic track" with sensors in the floor to analyze speed and force production and cameras to provide feedback on a player's mechanics and energy efficiency.[10] Prior to the 2017 season, the University of Texas upgraded its football locker room by installing new lockers, each of which cost $10,000 and includes a 43-inch television screen displaying the individual player's highlights and biography, rather than a simple nameplate to identify the locker.[11]

While locker rooms and lounges are key features of opulent football complexes, no less important is the weight room. Lockers with televisions might attract top-level talent, but that talent must be developed in order to win championships. To that end, any modern top-level football facility features a grand weight room. Amenities of top-tier weight rooms frequently include 20,000 or more square feet of floor space, indoor fifty- to seventy-yard sprint tracks, plyometric areas lined with artificial turf, rows of lifting stations that each cost several thousand dollars, and specialized strength machines and cardiovascular equipment.[12] In 2013 the University of Alabama spent $9 million on its weight room.[13] The 37,000-square-foot facility includes two floors, one for weights and another for cardio equipment, as well as a nutrition bar. The Anderson Center at the University of Kansas boasts a twenty-yard indoor hill divided into a ramp, stadium steps, and plyometric steps filled with shredded tires.[14] At the University of Nebraska and other Division I universities, lifting stations are equipped with a small touch-screen computer. Athletes sign into the computer and then see their daily workout on the screen. Workouts are tailored for individual athletes by the strength coaches and include specific weights for each set of the workout. Once the athletes have loaded the bar with the specified weight, they tap a "start" button on the screen to commence lifting. After the exercise is completed, they tap the "stop" button that starts a preset timer, again tailored by the strength coach, to regulate the athletes' rest time based on the intensity of the set. While the athletes rest, they can peruse the touch screen to see bar velocities for each repetition of their previous set as well as a video playback to monitor their form. Strength coaches also have access to the videos and information about bar velocities and weight lifted, allowing them to be far more accurate in monitoring the athletes' progress and setting goals for the next workout.[15]

The salaries of some of the top strength and conditioning coaches are almost as large as the facilities they oversee. America's highest paid collegiate strength coach is the University of Iowa's Chris Doyle, whose base salary in 2018 was $725,000.[16] In 2017, when Doyle's total compensation package was $717,800, he ranked as the seventeenth highest-paid employee at the university. Of the eight academics who earned more than Doyle at Iowa that year, seven were medical doctors and one was a dentist; all taught in the medical school. Three university administrators earned more than Doyle, although that number does not include the university's president, Bruce Harreld. The other top salary holders at Iowa all worked in the university's athletic department and included head football coach Kirk Ferentz, men's basketball coach Fran McCaffery, and athletic director Gary Barta.[17]

In college sport, Doyle is followed by Tennessee's Craig Fitzgerald, listed by *USA Today* as earning $625,000 for 2018, Alabama's Scott Cochran at $585,000, Clemson's Joey Batson at $500,000, Oklahoma State's Rob Glass at $500,000, and Michigan's Ben Herbert at $450,000.[18] These hefty salaries give some indication of the status of the modern collegiate strength and conditioning coach and demonstrate the changed perception of the importance of strength coaches in college athletics. In contrast, when Boyd Epley, who is considered the first full-time college strength coach, was hired in 1969 to oversee the football training program at the University of Nebraska, he earned two dollars an hour.[19]

It is worth noting that in 2016–2017 the average salary for American strength coaches was only $40,000.[20] Despite the high salaries paid to coaches like Doyle and Fitzgerald, hundreds of strength coaches, particularly assistant coaches, make well under $100,000 in the college ranks. At UT-Austin and Iowa, for example, twelve full-time strength and conditioning coaches are working to prepare athletes for competition.[21]

The rationale for such high head-coach salaries and the large number of far less well paid assistant strength coaches on team rosters is that these individuals have the greatest access to players under National Collegiate Athletic

Association (NCAA) rules, in addition to playing a key role in developing the athletes' physical capacity for sport. During the off-season, athletes have little, if any, contact with their sport coaches. Moreover, coaches typically interact only with their specific position players or units during the season. Strength coaches interact with all of the players during the majority of the year and thus play a key role in determining the atmosphere of an athletic program.[22] Common justifications for lavish strength complexes include their utility as a recruiting tool and source of motivation. These gigantic facilities, often with floor-to-ceiling windows overlooking the football field, are meant to impress potential recruits. In addition, their size and the variety of equipment allow entire teams to work out simultaneously, which coaches hope enhances camaraderie. Some believe that the high-dollar aesthetics are not only impressive but also inviting, presumably encouraging athletes to stay and work out longer.[23]

These investments in strength facilities and personnel are relatively recent developments in the arms race of college sports. Since the earliest days of intercollegiate competition, however, teams have consistently searched for any edge that might give them an advantage over their competition.[24] In the second half of the twentieth century teams increasingly found that edge through a new type of professional emerging within the ranks of collegiate (and professional) sports. The fundamental responsibility of these individuals, called strength coaches, was, and is, to improve the physiological parameters associated with a sport, such as strength, speed, power, and agility. They do not coach the actual techniques of the sport like blocking or tackling in football. Rather, they attempt to improve players' physical capacity so that they will be able to perform their sport skills more effectively and efficiently. In this book we use the term "strength coach" to describe a person whose primary job duties are to "assess, motivate, educate, and train athletes for the primary goal of improving sport performance."[25]

We define strength the same way as exercise physiologists Steven Fleck and William Kraemer do: as "the maximal force a muscle or muscle group can generate in a specified movement pattern at a specified velocity."[26] Another way to conceptualize it is Vladimir Zatsiorsky's description of strength as "the ability to generate maximum external force."[27] To increase strength, muscles must be subjected to an overload stimulus, meaning that they are required to generate more force than they are habitually accustomed to, in order to adapt and grow stronger. One of the primary modes of muscular adaptation is an increase in the size of the muscle. Equally important, however, is the nervous system's synergistic recruitment of more muscle fibers, allowing for the generation of more force in response to the training stimulus. Exposing a muscle to weight training or some other form of overload stimulus therefore causes both muscle and the central nervous system to adapt in ways that lead to greater speed, strength, and power. Strength coaches are experts in designing programs that create this adaptation. Common methods of overloading muscles include using free weights (like barbells, dumbbells, and kettlebells) as well as training on various kinds of resistance-based machines and even lifting one's own body weight.

To avoid excessive repetition, "resistance training" and "weight training" are used synonymously with "strength training" in this book and all imply the use of some form of external loading of the muscle in order to create physiological adaptations in muscle function. The terms "weightlifting" and "powerlifting," in contrast, refer to sports in which lifts are performed competitively. Weightlifting is the sport included in the Olympic Games. Its lifts are the snatch and the clean-and-jerk. Powerlifting is a non-Olympic sport in which the squat, the bench press, and the deadlift are contested: the athlete's highest squat, bench press, and deadlift are added together to determine the "total."

Our aim in writing this book is to explore the historical, social, and scientific factors that led to the development of the strength and conditioning profession. Because the modern strength-coaching profession first began with a meeting of university practitioners in 1978, our focus is largely on events that occurred in the twentieth century. We also cover the evolution of the profession inside collegiate athletics more than we discuss strength coaching inside pro sports, high schools, or the popular private sport academies and "strength and speed" camps of the twenty-first century. We do cover some aspects of the wider field of modern strength coaching, of course. But the profession began and was first nourished by men with aspirations to be recognized as academic professionals at the college level, in much the same way that athletic trainers fought for academic and medical recognition for their field, so we focus more on these important formative years of the profession.

In any discussion of the social and scientific forces that impacted strength and elite performance in the twentieth century, the subject of anabolic drugs must of course be acknowledged. However, in our opinion, their influence on modern sport is far less significant in the rise of sport performance in the twentieth century than the development of strength coaching and the rise of strength science. The history of the use of anabolic steroids, human growth hormone, and other substances believed to enhance athletic performance has been covered extensively elsewhere. Examples include

John Hoberman's seminal work *Mortal Engines* as well as his more recent *Testosterone Dreams*, Daniel Rosen's *Dope*, Thomas Hunt's *Drug Games*, Matt Chaney's *Spiral of Denial*, Shaun Assael's *Steroid Nation*, and many more.[28] While it is undeniable that some athletes—especially in the last five decades of the twentieth century—used anabolic drugs to help them gain size and increase their strength and speed, the vast majority of athletes did not. However, Olympic, national, and collegiate records have still climbed, and the overall fitness and performance of athletes have reached unprecedented levels. Even casual observers now recognize that contemporary athletes in nearly all sports are bigger, faster, and stronger than their predecessors in the first five decades of the twentieth century. Those differences cannot be explained solely by anabolic substance use.

We believe that the real explanation for the modern athlete's greater physicality relates to (1) better methods of strength training in general; (2) weight training during the adolescent years; and (3) improved nutrition that allows for greater muscle building. We further believe that these changes represent a paradigm shift in our understanding of the ability of the body to be transformed by regular, progressive exercise. This book explores this paradigm shift, its construction by specialized coaches and sport scientists, and the impact of research on training methodologies. By focusing primarily on strength training (not performance-enhancing drugs), our aim is to give credit to the still underappreciated impact that strength training and strength coaches have had in shaping athletic performance in the latter half of the twentieth century and beyond.

In a keynote address at the annual conference of the North American Society for Sport History in 2008, Jan Todd explained, in essence, why we believe that strength coaching actually is the most important sport innovation of the twentieth century:

> Granted, there are now approximately 350 NFL players weighing over 300 pounds, and granted, we now see more home runs hit than we did in Babe Ruth's or even Roger Maris' era. However, weight training for football now begins in junior high school . . . and baseball players who used to fear that weight training would lessen their flexibility and make them muscle-bound are now weighing well over 200 pounds, hiring personal trainers, and bragging about their bench presses. While anabolic drugs *are* a contributing factor to the larger size and greater power of some athletes, historians must help the public understand that we are in the midst of a paradigm shift in the training of athletes. We have entered an era in which, for the first time in history, athletes are employing scientifically-organized strength training *throughout their entire sporting careers.*[29]

The history of strength training is contained in a relatively small body of literature, authored by a handful of individuals, including the three authors of this book. Jan and Terry Todd have written extensively about all facets of strength training, including the history of strength implements, pioneering figures in the "Iron Game," the history of competitive lifting, and the impact of anabolic steroids.[30] Moreover, the Todds founded the academic journal *Iron Game History: The Journal of Physical Culture* (*IGH*), which has served as an important resource on the history of strength training. One of *IGH*'s frequent contributors, John Fair, has covered the development of competitive weightlifting, the rise of bodybuilding, and the relationship between strength training and masculinity.[31] Similarly, Kimberly Beckwith, currently *IGH*'s associate editor, has written about the evolution of barbells, early "muscle magazines," and strongmen.[32] Eugen Sandow authority David Chapman and Scotland's David P. Webster, author of *The Iron Game: An Illustrated History of Weight-Lifting*, have also played significant roles in unpacking the history of weight training and strength.[33]

The history of bodybuilding and the intersection of strength training, gender, and identity have also been examined. Randy Roach's two-volume *Muscle, Smoke, and Mirrors* meticulously describes the origins and growth of bodybuilding as well as the dietary practices of bodybuilders.[34] David Chapman's *Sandow the Magnificent* details the career and impact of legendary strongman Eugen Sandow. Chapman credits Sandow with a key role in the development of bodybuilding as a stand-alone sport, demonstrating that physical perfection could be developed, revolutionizing standards for the male physique, and enticing an entire generation to take up weight training. The construction of masculinity is also explored in Kenneth Dutton's *The Perfectible Body*. Historian John Kasson examines similar ideas in his chapter on Sandow in *Houdini, Tarzan, and the Perfect Man*.[35] The construction of gender identity through physique development is not limited to males, of course, and solid work on the relationships of exercise, strength, and femininity has been done by historians Jan Todd, Patricia Vertinsky, and Roberta Park.[36]

Other works touching on strength training more tangentially as part of an overall history of fitness include Harvey Green's *Fit for America*, which covers various health and exercise movements from the early nineteenth century until World War II, and Shelly McKenzie's *Getting Physical*, which picks up the fitness story after the war.[37] Like Green, McKenzie covers strength training, particularly in her discussion of the emphasis on physical strength during the Ronald Reagan years. They both treat strength training only as part of a multifaceted history of fitness. Jonathan Black's *Making the American Body* focuses on fitness more broadly during the twentieth century, with a particular emphasis on the people who drove various fitness trends.[38] Daniel Kunitz's *Lift* covers a wide swath of history, from the ancient Greeks through America in the twenty-first century. His focus is more philosophical, and he emphasizes a type of functional training that he terms "New Frontier Fitness" rather than honing in specifically on the history of strength training.[39]

As a subset of a relatively small discipline, even less work has been done on the history of the strength and conditioning profession. Scott McQuilkin's master's thesis details the history of the first and largest organization of strength coaches, the National Strength and Conditioning Association (NSCA), from 1978 to 1993.[40] As an organizational history, however, it includes only a brief discussion of the precipitating factors leading to the development of the profession. Instead, the majority of McQuilkin's work focuses on governance and expansion of the organization. John Fair's *Muscletown USA* discusses the efforts of Bob Hoffman of York Barbell to advocate the use of strength training in athletic preparation.[41] The true focus of his book, however, is on Hoffman himself and the rise and fall of American Olympic weightlifting; only three pages examine the use of weights to enhance sport performance. Similarly, a thesis on the US Olympic weightlifting team by Mark Kodya explores the impact of social and political events on the team but does not discuss the impact of competitive lifting or of Bob Hoffman on sport training.[42] A 1979 dissertation by William Kutzer is even less helpful, being primarily a catalog of major competitions and results without a discussion of the broader influence of Olympic lifting.[43] Nicholas Bourne's dissertation, "Fast Science," is a thorough treatment of the evolution of training for track and field through the latter twentieth century.[44] Bourne's work includes a discussion of the addition of weight training to track programs as well as the development of periodization and its diffusion to the United States, which is of particular relevance for this project. Jan Todd discusses the use of dumbbells, Indian clubs, and heavy-weight health lifting in her book *Physical Culture and the Body Beautiful*. She has also written about the history of weight training for female athletes and about the pioneers of strength-training research in a series of articles co-authored with her husband, Terry Todd, and Jason Shurley.[45] Perhaps the most significant author in this area, however, is Terry Todd, whose work on muscle-binding, analysis of the role of strength training at colleges and universities, and profile of the first recognized strength coach, Al Roy, are foundational to this book's exploration of the evolution of the modern strength and conditioning profession.[46] Sadly, Terry Todd passed away on July 7, 2018, just as this manuscript entered its final stages. The memorial tribute to Terry Todd published in the *Journal of Strength and Conditioning Research* is reprinted at the back of this book.[47]

The authors of this work have lived through different eras in the evolution of the strength-coaching profession and therefore bring different personal experiences to the writing of this book.

Terry Todd grew up in the era when it was widely believed that lifting would hurt athletic performance. As an avid tennis player, Terry began barbell training in the summer before he started college to increase the size of his left arm, which was smaller than his racquet-wielding right arm. Liking the strength and added muscle that the barbells provided, he continued lifting as a varsity tennis player at the University of Texas in the late 1950s, despite his coach's advice to the contrary. Although highly successful as a tennis player, Todd eventually got tired of his coach's admonitions, gave up his tennis scholarship, and turned full-time to lifting, going on to win national-level titles in both Olympic weightlifting and powerlifting and setting numerous records. In the early 1980s, while a professor at Auburn University, Todd also worked one winter with the Auburn football team as their strength coach.

Jan Todd began weight training after she married Terry Todd in 1973 at a time when there were no official competitions for women in powerlifting, weightlifting, or bodybuilding. Jan was already in college when Title IX—the legislation requiring equal access to sport for women—became law, so she had had only limited sport experiences in high school or college before she began weight training. Once she began lifting, however, she became interested in pursuing strength for its own sake and realized not only that women could respond to strength training in ways similar to men's responses but that they could also find joy in strength and competition. Described as the "World's Strongest Woman" by *Sports Illustrated* in 1977 and listed in the *Guinness Book of Records* for more than a decade, Jan set records in five weight classes during her competitive powerlifting career, including a personal best of 545 pounds in the squat. In 1980–1981 Jan was hired by Auburn University to oversee the strength and conditioning program for its women's teams, making her one of the first women in America officially to hold the title "strength coach."[48]

Unlike the Todds, Jason Shurley was not warned by anyone to avoid strength training. As a Texas schoolboy growing up in the 1990s, his experience was like that of many contemporary male athletes. He began lifting under a coach's direction in seventh grade as an adjunct to football and continued training primarily for sport through high school. In college he turned to competitive powerlifting, winning several national-level medals while lifting for the Longhorn Powerlifting Team. A life-long weight trainer, Shurley then went on to graduate school, becoming a certified athletic trainer (ATC), and worked with both professional and collegiate sport teams. Now an associate professor at the University of Wisconsin–Whitewater, Shurley holds the Certified Strength and Conditioning Specialist (CSCS) certification from the National Strength and Conditioning Association and conducts research on both applied and historical aspects of strength and conditioning.

CHAPTER 1

BEFORE BARBELLS

Strength Training, Athletes, Physicians,
and Physical Educators from the First Olympic Games
to the Twentieth Century

On June 1, 1892, the Medical Society of Berlin opened a conference on medical anomalies. Along with an infantile tumor and a distorted face, the day's topics included a man with excessive muscularity. Although the man's large muscles seemed to convey health, according to the physician Hans Virchow, they revealed quite the opposite. The "muscle-man" suffered from breathing difficulties and vertigo, which the physician attributed to the patient's well-developed chest musculature. The enlarged muscles, Virchow explained, pressed down upon the man's ribcage, preventing it from expanding and causing the patient's symptoms.[1]

That the physicians listening to Virchow did not protest this assertion and instead regarded it as a sound medical diagnosis seems curious from a modern perspective. However, theories about the negative impact of muscularity on vital energy were widely accepted in the late nineteenth and early twentieth centuries. Even professional strongmen like the great Arthur (Hennig) Saxon sometimes denigrated the possession of "too much muscle" in the training guides that they sold to the public. In *The Development of Physical Power*, for example, Saxon explained that he felt muscular endurance was far more important for health than great strength or muscle size. "The man capable of long feats of endurance should live longest," Saxon wrote, "and such a man will find his powers of more avail in everyday life than the man who has sacrificed vital strength for an extra few eighths of an inch of muscle, and perhaps the ability to raise a few pounds more in a certain position in a weightlifting contest."[2] Such a statement from the man regarded as the strongest man in the world at the fin de siècle requires explanation. In the Western world the origin of the medical and popular concern over "too much muscle" can be traced back to the rise of sport in ancient Greece.

"STRENGTH IS HEALTH": WEIGHT TRAINING THROUGH THE 1870S

Resistance training was practiced in cultures across the ancient world, including Egypt, China, and India as well as Greece, before the Common Era. Because we have so many more surviving narrative materials from ancient Greece, however, most strength historians begin with the Greeks and link resistance training to the rising importance of victory in the Panhellenic Games. The prestige that flowed from triumph at Olympia was particularly coveted and helped spur crude forms of resistance training among athletes as early as the fifth century BCE. The most famous story regarding strength training in these early times is the apocryphal tale of Milo of Crotona, who is often described in modern weight-training texts as the "father of progressive resistance exercise." According to the legend, Milo began lifting and carrying a young bull calf every day: as the calf grew larger, Milo grew stronger. His lifting of the calf, the legend holds, represented the first attempt at progressive training and helped Milo win six consecutive Olympic wrestling competitions.[3]

As in the case of many early tales, however, there is little solid evidence that it ever happened. The legend did not begin to circulate until several hundred years after Milo's death, when the Greek essayist Athenaeus wrote that Milo had once walked a set distance in the main arena at Olympia carrying a young bull across his shoulders. Athenaeus went on to report that Milo killed the bull and ate it all in a single day, so simple common sense suggests that skepticism may be in order about this story of Milo carrying a fully grown bull on a regular basis.[4]

It is undoubtedly true, however, that a man with the strength of Milo could have trained with rocks and logs and other kinds of weights, as was common in the ancient period. In 708 BCE, when the pentathlon was added to the Olympic schedule of footraces and wrestling, strength and power became increasingly important to the early athletes.[5] The events of the initial pentathlon included the *stadion* race (approximately 200 meters), wrestling, the discus throw, the long jump, and the javelin throw. The earliest version of the long jump included holding *halteres* (jumping weights) to increase the distance. By the fifth century BCE these forerunners of the dumbbell were also being used in a variety of drills to strengthen the upper and lower body.[6]

Concerns about the muscular bodies created by such training began to surface in the fourth and fifth centuries BCE in the writings of the Greek physician Hippocrates, who is regarded as the founder of Western scientific medicine. Hippocrates discussed the relationship between food consumption and exercise, advocating moderation in each and promoting the idea of the "balanced" body. The Roman physician Galen, who lived from 120 CE to approximately 200 CE, was heavily influenced by Hippocrates and identified six elements of the body, which he termed "non-naturals," that required proper balance in order to have good health. These non-innate components of health included air and environment, food and drink, motion and rest, sleep and wake, excretions and retentions, and emotions. While Galen advocated exercise for all ages, he specifically warned against excessive exercise. Both Galen and his predecessor Hippocrates saw the development of athletes as a dangerous extreme. Galen contended that the health of most athletes was "far from being highly desirable" and that it was right to be critical of their physical condition. Athletic development was worthy of condemnation, Galen argued, because athletes sought "the acquisition not only of good mixture, but also of physical mass—which cannot take place without an ill-balanced type of filling. And thus the state is rendered both dangerous, and from the point of view of public service, valueless."[7]

Not everyone agreed. Philostratus, born approximately fifty years after Galen, argued that the training of athletes should be regarded as a science. His text *Concerning Gymnastics* discussed training methods and coaching techniques for endurance and strength athletes, suggesting that those who need endurance should run against horses and hares. Those who need strength, Philostratus advised, should train by bending and straightening iron, lifting heavy loads, and even wrestling lions and bulls.[8] Philostratus also understood the concept of sport specialization and even recommended a simple form of periodization using a four-day training. According to historian Jack Berryman, the treatise of Philostratus was "one of the earliest recommendations of weight lifting and resistance training to develop strength beyond normal use."[9] Recognition of the value of heavy training persisted in the Roman era, as Roman gladiators and legionnaires trained with heavier swords than were actually used in combat, in order to strengthen their muscles for battle.[10] There is even evidence that some women may have trained during Roman times. On the wall of a Roman general's summer home from the second century CE, for example, there is a mosaic panel showing a group of women who appear to be athletes, with one woman holding a pair of dumbbells in her hands.[11] The Roman satirist Juvenal also discussed with some contempt the fad of society matrons who took up gladiator training as exercise, asking rhetorically, "What modesty can you expect in a woman who wears a helmet, abjures her own sex, and delights in feats of strength?"[12]

After the fall of the Roman Empire, the church discouraged sport as spectacle, and the training that accompanied it largely vanished as a result.[13] A revival of interest in physical training occurred during the Renaissance, following the rediscovery of ancient Greek texts on health and exercise. Sir Thomas Elyot became one of the first of this era to discuss lifting weights: based on Galen's *De Sanite Tuenda* (On Hygiene), Elyot specifically recommended the lifting of "alteres" as well as heavy stones or bars in 1531.[14] Three decades later, the Italian physician Hieronymus Mercurialis published *De Arte Gymnastica* (The Art of Gymnastics), a manuscript largely composed of ancient Greek ideas on exercise and medicine. The text included copious drawings of different exercise methods, went through five editions in the following century, and proved influential well into the nineteenth century.[15] Shortly after the publication of *Gymnastica*, the French essayist Michel de Montaigne described how his father used wooden canes filled with lead and shoes with leaden soles to improve his ability to run, leap, throw, and fence.[16]

In the late eighteenth century German physical educator Johann Friedrich GutsMuths oversaw a program of required manual labor and gymnastics at the Schnepfenthal Philanthropic School. As one of western Europe's earliest physical educators, GutsMuths sought to restore interest in the ancient Greek methods of training. His gymnastics program included climbing ropes and poles, discus throwing, and swinging weighted implements. The program gained extensive influence after the publication of his widely read *Gymnastics for Youth or a Practical Guide to Healthful and Amusing Exercises for the Use of Schools: An Essay toward the Necessary Improvement of Education; Chiefly as It Relates to the Body* in 1793. The first English translation appeared in London in 1800 and an American edition appeared in Philadelphia in 1802. Another German educator and follower of GutsMuths, Friedrich Ludwig Jahn, expanded the gymnastics program at Johann Ernst Plamann's school beginning in 1809. Two afternoons each week Jahn taught students to perform a series of gymnastics and strengthening exercises that he developed, using equipment that he built. While GutsMuths was interested in improving the individual, Jahn's training program had a strong element of nationalism. He intended his program to both foster German identity and physically prepare the Germans to resist their Napoleonic occupiers. In his 1810 book *Deutsches Volksthum* (German Folk) Jahn deliberately avoided referring to the exercises as "gymnastics," a term of Greek origin, choosing instead to call his system *Turnen* in an attempt to establish a uniquely German system. Three years later, in 1813, Jahn and his students were among the Prussian troops that ousted the French forces. Despite his support for German independence, the new government worried that Jahn's Turner Movement was becoming too powerful in its own right and officially banned *Turnen* in 1819.[17]

Jahn was placed under house arrest. Several of his most important disciples left Germany, fearing that they would also be imprisoned. Among those disciples were Charles Follen and Karl Beck, who made their way to Massachusetts and introduced Jahn's system, which was soon called "German Gymnastics." Beck took a position at the prestigious Round Hill School for Boys in Northampton, Massachusetts, in 1825, where he built an outdoor gymnasium and taught the *Turnen* system of exercises to his young students. Three years later, he also published *A Treatise on Gymnastics*, a translation of Jahn's 1816 book *Die Deutsche Turnkunst*, which played a large role in introducing the German system to the United States.[18] Follen joined the Harvard faculty in 1826 and began teaching gymnastics shortly thereafter. His introduction of gymnastics to the students at Harvard led to a subscription campaign to create a public gym (near the Boston Commons), which had more than 400 members by 1827.[19] As German-style gymnastics was introduced in New England in the 1820s and became a popular form of school physical education, dumbbell training became increasingly familiar to Americans. Wooden and lightweight dumbbells were used in many such nineteenth-century exercise regimens, including those specifically designed for women.[20] In 1828 Beck wrote of dumbbells that "these hand-held appliances are too well known to require a particular description."[21] He was right. Well before the German experts arrived, Ben Franklin was using dumbbells as part of his own training routine, writing in a 1772 letter to his son that the dumbbell was a great indoor training implement: "by the use of it, I have in forty swings quickened my pulse from sixty to one hundred beats in a minute counted by a second watch."[22]

By the mid-nineteenth century, then, there was a burgeoning interest in the United States in physical training for health and athletic performance. This interest was due in part to the influence of the Second Great Awakening and preachers like Charles Finney who sermonized about human perfectibility. As Protestant church membership soared in the first half of the nineteenth century, the inspired faithful sought to bring God's kingdom to earth through good works and striving for personal perfection. The Great Awakening spawned a host of reform movements advocating temperance, abolition, education reform, and prison reform.[23] In addition to improving society, many sought to improve themselves, including physically. The drive toward physical improvement received a spark in the late 1850s when a host of foreign visitors derided the poor physical condition of Americans. British consul Thomas C. Grattan charged that a lack of exercise and sports resulted in American men whose "physical powers are subdued and their mental capability cribbed into narrow limits."[24]

The call to remedy Americans' poor health was heard in a variety of quarters in the years after the Civil War. According to historians Elliott Gorn and Warren Goldstein, "before the Civil War, a handful of influential doctors, educators, reformers, and clergymen advocated sports and recreations. During the next generation, these occasional voices merged into a chorus."[25] For their part, many physicians and health reformers sought to remedy the poor condition of Americans by rekindling interest in Galen's non-naturals in the antebellum era.[26] Health, they explained, could be maintained by obeying "natural laws" and maintaining balance and moderation, with particular attention paid to food consumption, fresh air, and a proper amount of physical activity. The idea of health through moderation was reinforced by the understanding of physiology in the 1860s. The body's physiological systems were viewed as operating under the restrictions of the first law of thermodynamics: as a closed system where the amount of energy available was finite.[27] This fixed amount of energy was often referred to as vitality or vital force. With energy fixed, excessive activity by any one part of the organism took away from other parts and systems and exposed the individual to possible ill health. As Randolph Faires, a physician and instructor of physical education at the University of Pennsylvania in the 1890s, warned, "overdevelopment of one part is always accompanied by a corresponding weakness."[28]

Of particular concern to many in the mid- and late nineteenth century was a condition called "neurasthenia," with nebulous symptoms ranging from headaches to fatigue and hypertension. It was believed to be caused by the "exhaustion of the brain and nervous system," from too much "brain work" that allowed the body to get out of balance.[29] Too much physical activity, however, could also be considered pathological.[30] Heavy exercise such as weight training was to be avoided because it built muscle. Some physicians argued that hypertrophied muscles were actually "parasitic," because they "impose[d] a severe strain on the rest of the organism."[31] Larger muscles not only required greater amounts of nutrition for hypertrophy but, once built, continued to draw blood and nutrients away from other parts of the body.[32]

In spite of these concerns, by the middle of the nineteenth century a number of gymnasiums existed in America's major urban centers. Many of them contained some form of resistance training equipment. In 1861, for example, *Atlantic Monthly* author Thomas Wentworth Higginson described a gym near his home in Massachusetts that had calisthenics classes for women; a gymnastics area with ladders, rings, ropes, pommel horses, and parallel bars; and another area filled with a "row of Indian clubs or scepters . . . giants of fifteen pounds to dwarfs of four" and dumbbells or "masses of iron," as he called them, ranging from four to one hundred pounds.[33]

William Wood of New York was perhaps America's first gym owner. A native New Yorker, Wood began competing as an athlete at age eighteen, excelling in rowing. He would have a distinguished career and coached the Yale crew to many victories. In 1835 he opened a gym on Crosby Street in lower Manhattan called Wood's and Ottignon's Gym. He was then twenty years old.[34] Wood was the first of a number of American gym owners who were not only serious weightlifters but also great all-round athletic competitors. During his long life, Wood competed in at least fifty-eight different sporting competitions—rowing contests, races, and wrestling matches—and reportedly lost only four times. Wood's performance as an athlete helped people understand that strength aided athletic performance and could be enhanced through training. His gymnasium became central to the emerging sport scene in New York City and was populated by wrestlers, boxers, baseball players, and many competitive rowers who did dumbbell training and other forms of resistance exercise. When he died in 1900, his obituary in the *New York Times* referred to him as the "Grandfather of Athletics in the United States."[35]

By the early 1850s, Charles Ottignon was instructing pupils in boxing and gymnastics at a second gym, on Canal Street, as well as the Crosby Street location.[36] His brother and business partner, Hubert Ottignon, was an all-around athlete in the mold of Wood and put on exhibitions that demonstrated his strength and versatility. For example, during February and March 1856, he displayed his muscular endurance by pulling down a cable machine with thirty pounds of resistance 5,000 times in sixty-five minutes, won a sprint race of just over one-third of a mile against twelve competitors, and gave a weightlifting exhibition. The Ottignons' New York gyms were so successful that they opened another gym in Chicago in 1854. In 1860 management of the Chicago branch was transferred to one of Hubert's protégés, William Buckingham Curtis. Like Wood and Ottignon, Curtis successfully competed in a variety of athletic events that included rowing, sprinting, shot put, hammer throw, and a fifty-six-pound weight throw for height.

These commercial public gyms became particularly popular in the 1850s and 1860s as a new wave of European immigrants, including many Germans, settled along the Eastern Seaboard. Many of these Europeans were familiar with the idea of weight training before their immigration to America because of the Turner Movement in Germany and the existence of European gyms in which resistance training was common practice by the 1850s. Historian Louis Moore suggests that several African American "professors of pugilism" also ran commercial gyms in New England during this era. Although their clients were generally white, these men were viewed as experts on the basis of their own sporting achievements. Aaron Molyneaux Hewlett, for example, opened a gymnasium in Worcester, Massachusetts, in 1855. Four years later, he was hired by Harvard University as its first gymnasium director.[37] An 1865 photo shows Hewlett surrounded by the tools of his trade: boxing gloves, a wooden wand, a medicine ball, heavy and light Indian clubs, and two iron dumbbells of significant size.[38]

One of the least known but most important figures in this early history is James L. Montgomery, a member of the New York Knickerbocker Baseball Club, who may well be the first American to pursue strength for its own sake.[39] As a teenager Montgomery began hanging out at Charles Ottignon's New York gymnasium. A surviving lithograph of Ottignon's gym from 1845 shows men fencing, sparring, doing one-legged squats, and climbing ropes and ladders. On the left of the faded image a single man can be seen training with a pair of pulley weights. On the floor below him are several ring weights, but no large dumbbells or barbells.[40] By 1852, however, when Montgomery first came to the public's attention for winning a dumbbell-lifting contest, Ottignon had found some heavy dumbbells for his clients. "Great dumbbells were handled with perfect ease" by Montgomery in his victory, reported the *New York Times*, while men of twice his size failed.[41]

Although little is known of his early life, Montgomery's lifting exhibitions at Ottignon's gym had turned him into a sports celebrity by the mid-1850s. The *New York Clipper* wrote in 1856 that Montgomery "may now be considered as one of the greatest gymnasts the world ever produced." That same year the newspaper published several drawings of Montgomery and presented him as America's answer to Britain's famed club-swinging champion, Professor (Henry Thomas) Harrison, whose bare, muscular torso had been featured several months earlier. The *Clipper* wrote beneath the engraving of Montgomery lifting a dumbbell overhead that the image "represents a specimen of Young America . . . the strength displayed by him in his feats with his 101 lb. bell are truly astonishing, and should be witnessed by all fond of such exercises."[42]

Although most strength historians have credited George Barker Windship and his lectures as the cause of the enthusiasm for heavy lifting that occurred in the 1860s and 1870s, in reality Montgomery had already gotten the ball rolling. The *New York Daily Reformer*, for example, described Montgomery as a man of "prodigious power," who was responsible for "introducing the fashion of using dumbbells" to America. Montgomery's great feat was that he could curl and then press overhead a 101-pound dumbbell. The *Reformer* article further strengthened Montgomery's claim: while other men could now lift more overhead than Montgomery had done, no one—not even Windship—had been able to curl a hundred-pound dumbbell except him.[43]

As heavy dumbbell lifting spread to other gymnasiums, Higginson claimed that "a good many persons in different parts of the country" could "now handle one hundred and twenty-five," after being inspired by Montgomery.[44] Higginson went on to explain in that 1861 article that Boston's George Barker Windship now held the greatest records in overhead lifting. He could press a 141-pound dumbbell overhead without bending his knees, wrote Higginson, but with a dip and a rapid jerk he could manage 180.[45] The same year, 1861, Windship was invited by William Buckingham Curtis to demonstrate his strength and speak on the health value of heavy training at a gymnastics competition in Chicago. The event was intended to promote the Metropolitan Athletic Club, which Curtis managed.[46]

By the time of the invitation, Windship was well known, having been a touring lecturer on the benefits of strength training since 1859. Unlike other health reformers, Windship did not advocate light training or vegetarianism.[47] The path to health, he claimed, was not moderate exercise—it was to be as strong as possible. He claimed to have "discovered" through his own training that with increased strength came increased resistance to disease. This revelation led to his oft-repeated dictum "Strength Is Health." Windship began training shortly after entering Harvard as a five-foot-tall freshman of sixteen years who barely tipped the scales at one hundred pounds. The diminutive freshman was jeered by his classmates and resolved to build his body through training.[48]

Windship spent part of most evenings in the Harvard gymnasium doing bodyweight gymnastics exercises. By the time he graduated, his body had transformed and he was known as the strongest man at Harvard.[49] In spite of that reputation, when he tested his strength in 1854 on one of the lifting machines that had begun to appear on street corners as novelties, the result was underwhelming. The twenty-year-old Windship failed to impress a gathered crowd when he was able to raise a mere 420 pounds in a partial deadlift-type movement on the machine. The disappointment caused him to alter his training: instead of concentrating on gymnastic movements, he focused on lifting heavy weights. More specifically, Windship began training on the very lift at which he had failed.

Windship built a small platform that stood over a hole into which he had sunk a barrel filled with sand and rocks. A rope, attached to the barrel, extended through a hole in the platform and attached to a strong handle. Windship would stand on the platform and then pull upward to lift the barrel. Though he moved the weight only a few inches, Windship was thrilled by the amount he could move in this manner and reveled in his increasing strength and muscularity. By 1860 Windship was able to raise 1,208 pounds using this method, which would come to be known generically as the "Health Lift."[50] He then began experimenting with harness arrangements and built a special yoke to wear over his shoulders that eventually allowed him to lift more than 3,000 pounds, according to contemporary reports.[51]

To demonstrate his belief in the importance of strength, Windship typically performed lifting exhibitions after his lectures on health. At the gymnastics extravaganza hosted by William Curtis in 1861, an offer of $200 to any man who could outlift Windship added drama to the performance. William Thompson of the Metropolitan Athletic Club was the only man to take up the challenge. In America's first weightlifting contest, the men competed in two events: the partial deadlift and a harness lift.[52] Windship won the partial deadlift with a pull of 1,100 pounds when Thompson failed to budge the same weight. In the second lift Windship used a yoke and chains that fit around his shoulders to lift 1,500 pounds. With a personal best of 1,934 pounds in the lift, the 1,500 was effectively a warm-up. Unfortunately for Windship, the first attempt broke his lifting harness. Thompson then got out his own leather harness, which fit around his hips. The implement offered a clear mechanical advantage over Windship's apparatus by taking out the spinal column and resting the weight on the pelvis. Accordingly, Thompson easily bested Windship's previous record with a lift of 2,106 pounds. With the first event won by Windship and the second by Thompson, the first public weightlifting contest was judged a tie.

In spite of the mixed outcome, Windship and his theories received important validation and exposure. Although he never weighed more than 155 pounds and hence was an unprepossessing strongman, Windship's Boston Brahmin heritage, his visibly muscular body, his lectures, and his ability to lift such enormous poundages—even though he did not move them very far—inspired dozens of other men to try heavy lifting in the years ahead. His training methods began to be discussed in athletic training literature like Ed James's book *Practical Training* (1877). Before long dozens of boxers, wrestlers, and all forms of athletes were adding dumbbell training and "Health Lifting" to their training regimen.[53] Following the Civil War, Windship opened a gym in Boston, connected to his medical office. Men and women practiced the health lift there, on machines that he invented, and they also trained with dumbbells and weighted pulley machines.

In addition to providing publicity for Windship, the contest in Chicago also served as an important exemplar of premodern sport. Historian Melvin Adelman has identified six key differences between premodern and modern sport: organization, rules, competition, role differentiation, public information, and statistics and records. In premodern sport the rules are "simple, unwritten, and based upon local customs and traditions," whereas modern sport is marked by "formal, standard, and written" rules.[54] In this first weightlifting contest, there was clearly some agreement on the lifts to be performed, though the specifics were not laid out (which gave a significant advantage to Thompson, even if Windship's harness had not broken).

Competitive weightlifting was in good company in its premodern state during this era. Baseball, the sport that Gorn and Goldstein contend "may well have been the most important sport of the antebellum era," was also in the early stages of its evolution toward modernity.[55] Dozens of clubs formed in the 1850s and became increasingly standardized in the 1860s and 1870s as a result of the Civil War. Soldiers from different regions, accustomed to playing by different conventions, would work to develop common rules as they played baseball in camp between battles. When the war was over, the game went home with them in a sporting diaspora that helped make it America's game. As America rebuilt itself after the Civil War, the game grew ever more popular as sporting goods began being mass-produced for the new national market.

In order to secure a foothold in the market, manufacturers like Albert G. Spalding also produced "guidebooks" for sports like baseball. The books served multiple purposes: they promoted the sport and informed readers how to use the company's products but also functioned to standardize the rules of games as companies vied to produce "official" books for leagues and games. According to Stephen Hardy, sporting goods manufacturers "became the first line of promoters and educators during the great sports surge of the late nineteenth century . . . teaching not only the use of equipment but the value of physical activity."[56] The push to promote and standardize sport came from many fronts, of course. William Buckingham Curtis played an important role when he helped found the New York Athletic Club in 1866 and the Amateur Athletic Union in 1888. Both organizations worked to sponsor and promote a variety of sports as well as establish records and rules.[57]

By the 1870s weight training as a component of sport training had become "widely accepted on the American sporting landscape."[58] Athletes like Curtis had successfully demonstrated that strength and superior athletic ability went hand in hand. Like sporting goods manufacturers, purveyors of weight-training equipment explained the benefits of strength training and their products. Sim Kehoe, a manufacturer of Indian clubs, published *The Indian Club Exercise* in 1866. In addition to explaining the benefits of using his products, it also contained the endorsement of famed boxer John C. "Benecia Boy" Heenan. Kehoe's advertisements listed other top boxers as well as well-known rowers and long distance walkers/runners, known as "pedestrians," who followed his methods.[59] Other instructional manuals included *Athletic Exercises for Health and Strength* by Robert DeWitt as well as a series guides published by Ed James, including *How to Acquire Strength and Muscle*, and *Practical Training*.[60]

At the same time, the "muscular Christianity" movement was starting to garner more widespread attention. This movement was an English import and vestige of the perfectionism and millennialism of the first half of the century. Proponents of muscular Christianity "contended that bodily strength built character and righteousness and usefulness for God's (and the nation's) work."[61] Physical weakness, according to psychologist and professor G. Stanley Hall, was "dangerously near" wickedness. A primary cause of both weakness and wickedness was urbanization. Proponents of muscular Christianity worried that life in the cities led to "stiff-jointed, soft-muscled, paste-complexioned youth" and feminized men.[62] This was particularly troublesome in an era when the Lamarckian concept of evolution, in which characteristics acquired over the span of a lifetime could be passed on, had still not been discredited.[63] In this view physical degeneration in the current generation would portend degeneration in the next. Inherited debility would presage disaster, as more robust nations would inevitably surpass the United States, industrially or militarily.[64] The cure for this physical and many believed inextricably linked moral malaise was to engage in a "strenuous life" through a combination of out-of-doors pursuits, sports, and exercise.[65]

To facilitate this vigorous activity churches opened gyms to "save citified children" and "ensure healthfulness."[66] Another site for exercise and evangelism was the Young Men's Christian Association (YMCA). Founded by London dry-goods clerk George Williams in 1844, the organization first established itself in the United States with a Boston location in 1851. It grew rapidly, expanding from Boston to 20 locations by 1853, 56 in 1856, and 205 by 1860. The earliest YMCAs included reading rooms, libraries, and Bible classes. When the YMCA modified its mission to provide for the "improvement of the spiritual, mental, social, and physical condition of young men" in 1866, many locations added gyms, which often included weight-training implements.[67] According to historian Clifford Putney, "there existed no greater place for physical exercise in the Progressive Era than YMCA gymnasia."[68]

By the 1870s, then, serious strength training was becoming increasingly common, as a means of both improving health and augmenting sport performance. This was to change with the untimely death of George Barker Windship in 1876.

WINDSHIP'S DEATH AND THE PUSHBACK AGAINST WEIGHT TRAINING

On September 12, 1876, George Barker Windship died of an apparent aneurysm at his home at only forty-two years of age. Detractors of heavy strength training were quick to blame the methods that he so ardently advocated as a factor in his untimely demise. Prior to his death, Lewis Janes cautioned against the training advocated by Windship, pointing to "the pernicious effects of forcing abnormal muscular development."[69] In a paper presented before the Philadelphia Medical Society, Benjamin Lee, a physician, asserted that Windship's untimely passing had been the result of his strenuous training.[70] Assertions such as Dr. Lee's implicitly validated the opinion held by many in the medical and physical education communities that heavy strength training was deleterious to health. These groups often held views similar to Galen's: that too much added mass violated "nature's laws" and would lead to ill health.

Exercise pundit Dioclesian (Dio) Lewis also disparaged the type of heavy training that Windship recommended. Lewis began developing his own exercise program in the late 1850s. He intended the system to be practiced by women, men, and schoolchildren to ensure "all-sided development" that could not be provided by "one game or set of games."[71] Lewis's system was based in part on the Swedish "movement cure" system of gymnastics, which sought to correct ailments through specific exercise prescriptions. Lewis felt that the therapeutic exercises practiced in the United States placed too much emphasis on the development of strength and not enough on flexibility and speed of movement.[72] Lewis referred to his system as the "New Gymnastics" and like Windship also opened a gym in Boston. With an August 1860 resolution by the American Institute of Instruction, Lewis's system became the first exercise curriculum to receive the endorsement of a national group of educators.[73] As other Lewis-type gyms for adults opened in the 1860s, the New Gymnastics began to compete directly with heavy strength-training methods for devotees. Lewis directed a component of the 1864 edition of his text *The New Gymnastics* toward discrediting other systems. Lewis contended that heavy strength training would make a man too large and slow: in his words, "lifting great weights affects him as drawing heavy loads affects the horse." Practicing the brisk movements of the New Gymnastics, by extension, would result in the agility of a smaller carriage horse. It should be noted, however, that the larger body and muscularity of a draft horse are the result of selective breeding, not training.[74] Nonetheless, iterations of this argument would prove tenacious, as evidenced by advocates of strength training still attempting to refute it into the 1950s.[75]

One of the most prominent physicians and physical educators to decry heavy training was Dudley Allen Sargent, who was appointed as an assistant professor of physical training at Harvard University in 1879.[76] Sargent had become interested in physical training at age fourteen, after seeing an image of Professor Harrison swinging heavy Indian clubs in a text called *The Family Gymnasium*. The adolescent Sargent "regarded this man Harrison's physique with envy" and crafted his own Indian clubs in an attempt to build a physique similar to the Englishman's. By sixteen Sargent also engaged in boxing and systematic heavy gymnastics, becoming so enthusiastic about the training that he organized a group of gymnasts who trained with him in a barn equipped with parallel bars, a pommel horse, and rings, among other apparatus. In 1867 Sargent joined a traveling circus. But by the fall of 1868 he had grown weary of the "tawdry trappings, the inevitable company of loafers, and the artificiality of the show life" and sought a way to advance his education while fostering his interest in training.[77]

To that end, Sargent accepted a position as director of gymnastics at Bowdoin College in 1869. In the antiquated Bowdoin gym Sargent found the standard gymnastic equipment, similar to the items in the barn in which his group trained in Belfast, Maine. Students generally avoided the gymnasium, in part because the gymnastic apparatus took a significant amount of strength to use. The few weights that were found in the gym were also too heavy for most students to lift, owing to their lack of training experience.[78] In order to work around this impediment, Sargent invested in light dumbbells, Indian clubs, and adjustable pulley machines that would accommodate varying levels of strength and training experience among the student body. With the new apparatus, students saw significant results in a relatively short time. The faculty at Bowdoin was sufficiently impressed and made the training compulsory for all students in 1872.[79]

His experience at Bowdoin caused Sargent to shift his view of training, from emphasizing strength to democratizing exercise and focusing on balanced physical development rather than maximizing ability at any one skill.[80] Sargent left Bowdoin in 1875 to pursue his medical doctorate from Yale, which he attained in 1878. After failing to convince the Yale faculty of the necessity of a department of physical education, Sargent took a position at Harvard in 1879.[81] There he employed anthropometrical measurements similar to those performed by Edward Hitchcock, who supervised the Department of Physical Culture at Amherst College in Massachusetts from 1861 to 1911.[82]

Sargent utilized girth measurements to create a hypothetical perfect form. Students were then given an exercise prescription to help them attain that form by improving deficient aspects of their physiques. This view of balanced development was also promoted by William Blaikie in his 1879 text *How to Get Strong and Stay So*, which helped expose Sargent's ideas to a much wider audience.[83] Blaikie, a member of the Harvard crew before his graduation, was an influential associate of Sargent. Targeting specific skills instead of focusing on balance meant the athlete was "rendered weak": his ability to excel in only a few tasks was problematic and, in fact, marked his lack of development.[84] Heavy strength training tended to lead to imbalance between physique and psyche as the muscles grew out of proportion with Sargent's ideal form and was therefore contraindicated.[85]

This view of training became widespread among physicians and physical educators, as Sargent spread his theories through summer institutes at Harvard. Among the attendees of these programs were Edward Hartwell, William Anderson, and R. Tait McKenzie, who brought similar programs to Johns Hopkins University, Yale University, and the University of Pennsylvania, respectively.[86] Luther Gulick, a dominant figure in the YMCA, also attended the institute.[87] As an example of the influence of Sargent and the balanced physical development philosophy, R. Tait McKenzie, a physician and the first professor of physical therapy in the United States, warned as late as 1924 that overdeveloped muscles were "parasites" of vitality. On the same page as this assertion was a photograph of an impressively muscled man with a caption that read "extreme muscular development without a corresponding increase in heart and lung power." The caption noted that "this man could not float in sea water and died prematurely." Though McKenzie implied that the man's density and his premature death were related, no further explanation was given.[88] Some physiologists and physicians took the attacks on strength training a step farther by attributing to it a host of fanciful negative outcomes ranging from impotence to insanity to an early grave.[89]

In his widely read *How to Get Strong*, Blaikie specifically cautioned that heavy weight training would result in movements that were "stiff and ungainly." Echoing Dio Lewis, he contended that "he who does work of the grade suited to a truck-horse is far more likely to acquire the heavy and ponderous ways of that worthy animal." This case was seemingly cemented in humans by professional strongmen, many of whom were very large men moving very large weights.[90] While the nervous system is undeniably important in feats of strength, the primary limitation on force production is the cross-sectional area of the muscles.[91] Bigger men were and are usually capable of lifting more weight than smaller men. The men who astonished audiences with their feats of strength thus tended to be very large. Because they made their living lifting large weights, they primarily devoted their time to maximizing this skill and chose not to also work on quick movements or agility.

As such, many professional strongmen were "ponderous men performing their feats by brute strength," rather than exemplars of athletic prowess that budding athletes might seek to emulate.[92] The combination of seemingly commonsense criticisms of heavy lifting and the corpulent performers that many associated with great strength helped cement the notion of a "muscle-bound" condition in the minds of many people. The popular understanding of the condition was a combination of decreased speed and coordination that resulted from heavy lifting.

Physicians suspected that danger was closely associated with strenuous athletic participation well into the twentieth century.[93] In addition to muscle-binding, one of the most common charges against heavy strength training as well as other high-intensity anaerobic exercises was that they might produce a sudden and excessive strain on the heart. Physical educators and physicians alike were disturbed by the obvious strain, redness, and distension of neck veins that accompanied heavy lifting. Regarding the effect on the heart, some warned against the damage likely to result due to the rapid increase in intrathoracic pressure that results when lifters hold their breath while lifting. Physician and physical educator Percy Dawson pointed to "bed pan death" as evidence that weak hearts, in particular, were not up to such stress.[94] It was recognized that the increased intrathoracic pressure caused by expelling air against a closed glottis resulted in decreased return of blood to the heart.[95] Dawson explained that "the flooding of the heart which occurs as soon as the subject desists from his effort, by the damned back venous blood, has been regarded as favoring acute dilation of heart which has been weakened by the previous coronary anemia."[96] Following a similar discussion, R. Tait McKenzie remarked that exercises of strength and speed produced the greatest strain on the heart and blood vessels.[97]

Many endurance sports also prompted medical doctors to warn participants of the danger of developing such maladies as athlete's heart and "bicycle face."[98] Any activity performed in a competitive setting was particularly dangerous because it might cause the athletes to overextend themselves as they sought the approval of spectators. "The intense emotional appeal of competition," said physician A. M. Kerr, could carry a "boy on to feats of strength and endurance he would otherwise find impossible."[99] In his 1914 book on training for track and field events, Olympic and University of Pennsylvania track coach Michael Murphy noted, "Although we hear it less about it now than we once did, nearly every athlete will be told at one time or another that participation in athletics is likely to shorten his life—that it will give him the 'athletic heart.'"[100]

Though it could affect weightlifters, athletic heart was primarily a disease thought to afflict rowers, runners, and bicyclists. The heart could be adversely affected in two ways: hypertrophy or dilation. Hypertrophy of the heart resulted in a heart that was so strong that it pounded the arterial system with blood, weakening the vessels. This could be particularly problematic as one aged when the overdeveloped heart continued to wear away at the increasingly weak tissue after the cessation of regular training. The association of high blood pressure, heart valve defects, and cardiac hypertrophy was well known. As a result, many believed that any degree of hypertrophy was pathological.[101]

Dilation could be caused by a sudden or persistent overfilling of the heart with blood. The increased volume of venous blood returning to the heart during exercise was thought to overfill and stretch the vessel, resulting in distension and weakening of the heart's walls.[102] A major problem with diagnosing either condition was that the tools of measurement were imprecise at best. Initial investigations were carried out by percussing the chest to find the outline of the heart, determining heart size based on the locations of its sounds, or using radiographs. Radiographs are much more sensitive at depicting hard tissue such as bone, not soft and moving structures like the heart.

Nonetheless, medical doctors proceeded to identify individuals afflicted by the condition. One physician, T. Abutt, even diagnosed the condition in himself while mountain climbing in 1875. "During the ascent Abutt was suddenly seized with air hunger and a feeling of stretching in the epigastrium. He had to lie down, and he confirmed upon himself an evident enlargement of the heart dullness to the right."[103]

Perhaps the largest study was performed by Felix Deutsch and Emil Kauf, who examined more than 1,700 athletes at the Vienna Heart Station. The athletes came from a wide variety of sports, including swimming, track, soccer, rowing, weightlifting, wrestling, boxing, skiing, and several others. The doctors used orthodiagrams, a specialized type of radiograph, to record the transverse diameter of the heart. From their imaging, the authors concluded that the athletes did have larger hearts than a group who engaged in similar activities for fun. The resultant enlargement "cannot be looked upon as harmless" and resulted from dilation, though they suggested that the condition could be reversed with rest.[104]

Notably, in the weightlifters there was "no marked influence upon the heart." Deutsch and Kauf mentioned that several champion weightlifters tended to have larger hearts but could not determine that the size was due to their training. As a confounding factor, they noted that "the mode of life of this class of men must be given consideration. They are all worshippers of

Bacchus."[105] The finding that strength training had little impact on heart size presumably played a role in the assessment that weight training actually did not work the heart enough.[106]

A PHYSICAL CULTURE REVOLUTION

As many physicians wrung their hands over the effects of strenuous exercise and vigorous athletic participation, a nascent "physical culture revolution" was beginning in 1893.[107] The exhibition of strongman Eugen Sandow as part of the Chicago World's Fair served as the primary spark. Unlike other strongmen, who (in the words of David Chapman) were typically "huge mountains of flesh and sinew," Sandow was both exceptionally muscular and exceptionally lean. In addition to his pleasing appearance, Sandow's strength equaled or surpassed that of his more rotund counterparts. According to historian John Kasson, his unique combination of muscularity and definition "represented a new standard of male fitness, beauty, strength, and potency": "physical fitness experts and journalists alike hailed him as the 'perfect man.'"[108]

In his formative years Sandow trained as an acrobat and gymnast, which laid the foundation for his physique. This training made him remarkably lean and symmetrical but did not develop the size for which he would later become famous. That size developed after Sandow began training with Louis Durlacher, a notable strongman better known as Professor Atilla. While heavy strength training had fallen out of favor in the late 1800s, Atilla insisted that it was integral to producing both size and strength. He introduced Sandow to the progressive strength training that developed his physique.[109] In addition to playing a key role in Sandow's development, Atilla helped train world heavyweight champion boxer "Gentleman" Jim Corbett and numerous other athletes at his gym in New York City that opened in 1893.[110]

Two weeks prior to the opening of Sandow's shows, historian Frederick Jackson Turner asserted that the American frontier had closed, as of the 1890 census. Turner argued that this event was significant because the progression of American civilization westward had been integral in shaping American history. Men were transformed by the wilderness from something European into "a new product that is American."[111] The frontier offered a space for the exercise of individualism, fostered egalitarianism, and, though not explicitly stated, developed manly self-reliance. With the disappearance of the frontier, a certain brand of American masculinity was also passing. In this context, men were willing to embrace the new standard of masculinity set by Sandow.

During his stay in Chicago for the World's Fair, thousands streamed to the Trocadero Theater to see Sandow. The desire to see this "new standard of male fitness" was so great that his shows were sold out throughout his tenancy. Many of those who witnessed the German's superbly developed muscles desired to build a body like his and became, in the words of historian Kimberly Beckwith, "Sandow's ripples."[112] One of those ripples was health re-former Bernarr Macfadden. Just one year younger than the twenty-six-year-old Sandow, Macfadden had already been a fervent believer in the power of exercise and strength training for ten years. Macfadden had been a "weak and sickly" child who contracted a variety of diseases and recovered slowly. One particularly debilitating bout with illness came after being vaccinated for smallpox, which resulted in "blood poisoning" and required six months of convalescence.[113]

The experience left Macfadden with the deep mistrust of physicians and traditional medicine that would color his later health crusade. In addition to his own illness, Macfadden's alcoholic father died when he was five and his mother succumbed to tuberculosis when he was nine. Shortly after inform-ing the boy of his mother's death, the relatives who were caring for him declared that he would likely be "going the same way soon."[114] Following his mother's death, Macfadden was sent to live on a farm, where he did a great deal of manual labor and ate a variety of fresh foods.

Life on the farm made Macfadden feel stronger and healthier and helped establish his fervent beliefs in the importance of diet and exercise. After watching gymnasts and weightlifters at a St. Louis gym in 1883, Macfadden's life was changed: "thereafter," he declared, "I had but one object in view. . . . I would not be satisfied until I was a strong man." To that end he began lifting dumbbells and reading incessantly about diet and exercise programs, which included reading Blaikie's *How to Get Strong*.[115] By the time of the Chicago World's Fair, Macfadden was well on his way to becoming the "one-hundred percent, do-as-I-do health crusader . . . a zealot, body and soul" for which he would be remembered.[116] His stay in Chicago was financed by serving as a pitch man for the Whitely wall mounted exerciser, a pulley machine mar-keted to businessmen. Like others who saw Sandow, Macfadden was suit-ably impressed by his physique, particularly when Sandow, dusted in white powder, assumed the poses of classical statuary against a black backdrop. Macfadden later copied this technique for some of his own photographs.[117]

Both Sandow and Macfadden began publishing physical culture maga-zines in 1898. Though Macfadden's *Physical Culture* started out as "an exercise catalog at best," hocking equipment and exercise books, he quickly moved to make it a more legitimate publication: in just over three years the magazine's circulation reached more than 100,000.[118] Macfadden used the magazine to rail against corsets, drugs, alcohol, sexual ignorance, muscular inactivity, overeating, and physicians.

In addition to their magazines, both men put on massive physique competitions. Sandow's "Great Competition," held in London in 1901, was "the world's first major bodybuilding contest."[119] Macfadden followed with his own Physical Culture Exhibition in New York City in 1903, at which he named Al Treloar and Emma Newkirk the most perfectly developed physical specimens for their genders. It is worth noting that Treloar was another of Sandow's "ripples," having worked as an apprentice under him during the World's Fair.[120]

Macfadden's 1903 show was followed by another massive exhibition in 1905 at Madison Square Garden. The second Physical Culture Exhibition garnered extra attention after Anthony Comstock, the head of the Society for the Suppression of Vice, attempted to shut the show down for obscenity because of the white union suits worn by the female physique competitors.[121] The additional publicity that resulted from the clash between Macfadden and Comstock resulted in a massive crowd for the exhibition: on opening night 20,000 people thronged to Madison Square Garden, which only held 15,000. The event marked only the third time in the venue's history that paying customers had to be turned away.[122] The second exhibition also differed from the first in that the contest included an evaluation of both the competitors' physiques and their athletic ability in a series of races and weightlifting events. The capacity crowd was able to see clearly that a well-developed physique and athletic ability were not mutually exclusive.[123]

While both men made monumental impacts on the physical culture movement, it is important to note that both publicly eschewed heavy strength training. In spite of the heavy weights that developed his physique, Sandow's course recommended light weights and high repetitions.[124] Macfadden recommended exercising the muscular system to fatigue but to avoid straining or exhaustion. As Clifford Waugh noted, "some [of the workouts authored by Macfadden in *Physical Culture*] included specialized movements for particularly weak areas of the body such as the upper-legs and calves, arms, shoulders, forearms and abdomen, but most were general over-all routines utilizing for resistance chairs, stools, light weights (but never heavy weights) and even one's own muscles."[125] Moreover, from the first issue Macfadden urged his readers to avoid using heavy weights, asserting that they were "of no value to a man who desires simply superabundant health."[126] Like many of the physicians he railed against, Macfadden viewed heavy weight training through the lens of energy conservation and believed that it would drain vitality and decrease longevity.

Nonetheless, *Physical Culture* did feature occasional articles that melded resistance training and sport performance. A 1926 article by Earl Gregory included the contention that better-developed muscles would lead to better swimming ability. To that end, Gregory discussed an exercise program to strengthen the muscles. The program was largely a series of bodyweight exercises and stretches, though the author mentioned that "if one has done these exercises without the desired results, then weights may be held" to make them more difficult.[127] Another 1926 article detailed how Babe Ruth had resurrected his career through "physical culture." Suffering from a variety of ailments, including an abscess, poor eyesight, constipation, indigestion, obesity, and muscular weakness, the prolific slugger had a disappointing 1925 season. After being put on a rigid schedule by trainer Art McGovern that included more sleep, elimination of caffeine and alcohol, long walks, manual labor, and some light resistance exercise, Ruth reported to spring training nearly twenty pounds lighter than he had been at the end of the previous season.[128] The improvement in his performance was dramatic: during the 1926 season Ruth played in an additional fifty-four games, improved his batting average from .290 to .372, and nearly doubled his previous year's home-run total.[129]

Another of Sandow's ripples, Alan Calvert, did believe in heavy strength training and actively worked to promote it. Like Macfadden, Calvert had read Blaikie's *How to Get Strong* and done some of his own training during his teenage years. He followed the advice of Blaikie and other high-repetition, low-weight proponents but was ultimately disappointed with the results. After seeing Sandow in Chicago he realized that heavy weights were the key to developing significant muscularity and attempted to secure the tools that would help him develop his own physique. Calvert quickly found, however, that there were no commercially available barbells in the United States.[130] To remedy the situation, he designed his own.

Calvert's father, Pehrson Butler Calvert, had owned a tinplating business since Alan's birth. As a result, Alan was familiar with metal working, which facilitated his ability to design and make barbells.[131] He applied for his first barbell patent in January 1902 and opened the Milo Barbell Company in April of the same year. According to David P. Willoughby, the opening of Milo was "the greatest single impetus ever given to weight-lifting in this country."[132] Barbells with a standard design could now be acquired relatively easily by prospective lifters and gyms. To advertise his new product, Calvert took out advertisements in Macfadden's *Physical Culture* and Richard K. Fox's *National Police Gazette*. As noted, heavy strength training was not something that Macfadden advocated, so readers of his magazine were not overly eager to procure Calvert's barbells. Fox's *Police Gazette* contained stories about and challenges between strongmen, but it was primarily a sports magazine, not a strength magazine.[133] Like Albert Spalding and the sporting goods manufacturers in the mid-nineteenth century, Calvert needed to create a market for his product by teaching people about its proper use. So, like those manufacturers, he created his own "guidebook" in the form of *Strength* magazine in 1914.

In the new magazine Calvert mocked programs that called for light weight training: "If there were anything in light dumbbell exercise, the United States by this time would be the finest developed nation in the world; you would meet Samsons and Apollos in every block, for I suppose almost every man has, in his time, practiced light dumbbell exercises to some extent."[134] Calvert ridiculed light training with the same conviction that Lewis, Blaikie, and others had when they dismissed heavy training. He vigorously rejected the notion that heavy weights produced muscle-binding. As an example, in his March 1915 article "What Does Muscle-Bound Mean?" he pointed to boxers James J. Jeffries and Stanley Ketchel as being both strong and quick. He also asserted that if weights were lifted through the full range of motion, they could actually increase, not lessen, flexibility.[135]

In addition to refuting muscle-binding, Calvert played a key role in making weight training respectable by calling for standardization. As a competitive sport, weightlifting had progressed some since the competition between Windship and Thompson in 1861. A supervisory body to establish rules had been created in Germany in 1891. Weightlifting was also contested at the Olympic Games in 1896, 1904, and 1908. The first world championship meet had been held in Vienna in 1898.[136] While lifting weights was becoming more reputable as a competitive endeavor overseas, in the United States it was still considered questionable, owing to the shenanigans of strongmen who used a variety of tricks to market themselves as the strongest in the world.[137]

Calvert criticized the "very foolish and short-sighted attitude of professional lifters in this country" who were more interested in their own finances than in their impact on weightlifting. To remedy the situation, he called for the use of tested scales, standardization of the performance of lifts, establishment of weight classes, and an "American Board of Control" to oversee competitive lifting.[138] Calvert's call was taken up by Ottley Coulter, George Jowett, and David Willoughby, who worked to transform weightlifting into an organized sport in the United States during the 1920s.[139] As a result of Calvert's efforts, according to Kimberly Beckwith, weightlifting "evolved in the early twentieth century into a respectable, modern sport and into an accepted training method to enhance one's general fitness and appearance."[140]

A PHYSIOLOGY REVOLUTION

Another revolution was taking place alongside the physical culture revolution of the early twentieth century. That revolution would be a shift in the understanding of physiology away from the notion of conservation of energy and toward a more contemporary understanding of the ability to enhance one's physical capacity through specific training. One of the earliest refutations of the conservation theory of physiology was put forth by a physician who had trained with weights, Austin Flint, who contested this view as early as 1878. Flint was a professor of physiology at Bellevue Hospital Medical College in New York and a Fellow in the New York Academy of Medicine. In *On the Source of Muscular Power* Flint pointed out that, with training, a man "becomes capable of greater and prolonged muscular effort, with precisely the same food than the same man out of training." The idea that the body simply burns the food without alterations in the muscular system was untenable. The body's capacity to perform work, then, must be enhanced.[141]

At the time of Flint's writing, of course, there was only rudimentary knowledge of muscular function. Microscopists, starting with Antonie van Leeuwenhoek in 1682, had described the striated nature of skeletal muscles and the A-band of each sarcomere.[142] Due to the limitations of the wavelength of visible light, however, little more could be gleaned about the microscopic makeup of muscle. The electron microscope, which would ultimately reveal the sliding filament action involved in muscular contraction, was invented in the 1930s. It was not until 1954, with the advance of specimen preparation techniques that two sets of researchers working independently laid out the sliding filament theory of muscular contraction.[143] In the interim between reaching the limits of the light microscope and the use of the electron microscope, scientists filled in the gaps through gross and chemical observations of the neuromuscular system. They also learned more about the function of the cardiovascular system, paving the way for the notion of expanded capacities by the 1930s.

While those discoveries were being made, researchers and physical educators alike largely focused on improving efficiency, not expanding capacities. As discussed by historians Rob Beamish and Ian Richie, "training" at this time was synonymous with repetition of specific sports skills.[144] Athletes and coaches did not emphasize improving the antecedents of performance but instead sought to refine the performance itself. For example, Norman Bingham's 1895 coaching text advocates only repetition of football skills to prepare for the sport. Bingham used the example of Everett Lake, Harvard halfback, who spent his summer practicing holding tacklers at arm's length.

"When Autumn came, he was one of the most difficult halves in the country to stop, because, in addition to his great weight and strength, the tackler was nearly always kept at arm's length." In a later chapter on rowing Bingham did recommend a combination of walking, running, gymnastics, and weight training. Regarding weight training, he called for the use of wrist weights, "arm and chest weights," and the "setting up" exercise, which resembled a deep squat on the toes. Bingham recommended up to forty minutes of gymnasium exercise, which decreased to ten to fifteen minutes after the rowing season had begun.[145]

It is important to point out, however, that this type of training had been practiced by college crews since the 1860s.[146] In his 1914 text on training for track, Michael Murphy discussed the importance of strength for sprinters, but his training recommendations consisted largely of practicing one's technique in starting the race. For quarter-mile training, the coach recommended jogging distances up to 600 yards and sprints of 200–300 yards, with occasional "trial" runs of the full distance.[147]

This type of training was in keeping with Fredrick Winslow Taylor's principles of scientific management, which sought to increase worker productivity by decreasing the number of movements that workers had to perform and then perfecting those movements.[148] Taylor's ideas would have a profound impact on the study of exercise physiology: early research sought to identify the causes of fatigue, not for sports purposes but to maximize efficiency. For example, the Harvard Fatigue Laboratory, an entity that Andrea Johnson has called "the single most important laboratory in the history of American exercise physiology," was housed in the basement of Harvard's business school. The lab was initially funded by the Rockefeller Foundation for Research in Industrial Hazards.[149] The interest in work and fatigue led physiologists to use athletes, including themselves, as their experimental subjects. Archibald Vivian (A. V.) Hill, "the father of exercise physiology," was a runner himself and based some of his theories on energy production on his own experiences. Furthermore, Hill utilized athletes in many of his studies because they "can be experimented on without danger and can repeat their performances again and again."[150] The experiments on fatigue led to a series of important developments regarding the function of muscles and the adaptations of the neuromuscular and cardiovascular systems to exercise.

As early as 1807 lactic acid, a by-product of intramuscular anaerobic energy production, was discovered in hunted stags.[151] Glycogen, the muscles' storage form of carbohydrate, was identified in 1859.[152] Nearly five decades later Walter Fletcher and Frederick Gowland Hopkins of Cambridge University were the first to demonstrate that lactic acid was produced by muscular contraction.[153] In 1920 Otto Meyerhoff in Heidelberg, Germany, provided the first experimental evidence that the acid was produced from glycogen.[154] This led to the erroneous theory, advanced by A. V. Hill, that muscle contraction was fueled directly by lactic acid. By 1929 Karl Lohmann, Cyrus Fiske, and Yellapragada Subbarow had identified both adenosine triphosphate (ATP), the molecule whose hydrolysis fuels muscle contraction, and phosphocreatine, the molecule that most directly replenishes ATP, though their roles were not yet understood.[155]

Hill's theory would be disproven by Bruce Dill, H. Edwards, and Rodolfo Margaria of the Harvard Fatigue lab, whose work pointed to the importance of "phosphagen" in muscle contraction. Their theory of excess postexercise oxygen consumption to resynthesize phosphates was in agreement with the work of Einar Lundsgaard, whose 1930 and 1932 experiments demonstrated that muscle contraction could occur in the absence of lactic acid production.[156] It was not until 1943 and the work of Hungarian biochemist Albert Szent-Györgyi that the role of ATP was fully understood. Szent-Györgyi soaked a muscle cell in glycerin, dissolving nearly everything except the contractile proteins, actin and myosin. What was left of the cell shortened when those proteins were bathed in ATP, clarifying ATP's role in muscle contraction.[157]

In addition to gaining insight into the process of muscle contraction, Sir Charles Sherrington of Oxford first described a "motor unit" in 1929.[158] Sherrington realized that one motor nerve supplied many muscle cells and that different muscles showed motor units of varying sizes. In the same year one of Sherrington's contemporaries at Oxford, Derek Denny-Brown, demonstrated that cat muscle also had different muscle types, red and white, which had different contraction times.[159] Between 1926 and 1932, according to A. V. Hill, a "revolution" had taken place in the understanding of muscle physiology.[160]

In addition to sowing the seeds for the contemporary understanding of muscle contraction, scientists were also beginning to understand how the muscles and cardiovascular system changed with training. Experimenting on dogs and rabbits, scientists in Germany showed that training increased the volume of intramuscular glycogen and phosphocreatine.[161] As early as 1897 the work of German physiologist B. Morpurgo had shown that individual muscle cells increase in size (hypertrophy), rather than increasing in number (hyperplasia), to account for muscle growth in dogs trained by running.[162] In 1899 C. Hirsch noted a direct relationship between the size of skeletal musculature and the size of the heart. W. Roux made the connection between chronic exertion and muscular size in 1905, and in 1928 W. Siebert found that muscular growth in rats was increased when they ran at higher speeds.[163] In addition to intramuscular changes in response to exercise, adaptations made by the heart became more apparent by the early 1930s. One of the key advances was the identification of what would become known as the Frank-Starling Law of the Heart.

In a 1926 article E. H. Starling and M. B. Visscher showed that, rather than becoming dilated by the excessive blood flow returning to the heart during endurance exercise, the ventricles actually responded to the stretch with a stronger contraction.[164] Instead of damaging the heart, the increased venous return strengthened it. This finding was discussed in exercise physiology texts by the early 1930s. For example, in a 1931 text by two researchers at the Harvard Fatigue Lab, Arlie V. Bock and David B. Dill, Starling's work was cited along with the assertion that the dilation of the heart during exercise was a "strictly physiological process" that enabled the heart to pump more blood per beat during exercise.[165]

Similarly, Adrian Gould and Joseph Dye, professors of hygiene and physiology, respectively, at Cornell University noted that a heart stretched by increased blood volume responded with a more forceful contraction.[166] Not only was dilation of the heart an important adaptation that allowed for increased performance, but the hypertrophy that resulted from exercise also came to be viewed as physiological, not pathological. Arthur Steinhaus affirmed that the heart hypertrophied by exercise resulted in a "more efficient" heart that was "not to be considered pathological in any sense of the word."[167] Bock and Dill called the notion that cardiac hypertrophy was pathological "entirely erroneous" and said that "opinion is now essentially unanimous that the condition [athletic heart] does not exist."[168]

During the revolution in understanding muscular physiology and the effects of exercise on the heart, there was little discussion of strength or how to produce it. For example, while Bock and Dill noted that a highly developed muscular system was a necessity for an athlete, their chapter on the effects of training did not discuss methods to develop that system.[169] Gould and Dye stated that running speed was in part dependent upon the strength of the muscles, which in turn depended upon the muscles' cross-sectional area. However, they did not mention performing strength training to improve cross-sectional area and thereby running speed.

In a later chapter on the effects of training on the muscular system, Gould and Dye mentioned that progressive training increased the size and power of the muscles, though strength training was not specifically discussed. The section went on to say that training reduced the oxygen requirement for a given workload, hinting that the training they were referring to was endurance rather than resistance training.[170] Arthur Steinhaus remarked that "the amount of work done in a unit of time, not the total work done, is the decisive factor in calling out these muscle changes [hypertrophy]." He further mentioned that "apparatus work and wrestling" resulted in greater hypertrophy than track and field but made no connection between the two or comments on the utility of that hypertrophy.[171]

The lack of interest in the production of strength explains the response received by Ohio State undergraduate physical education major John Capretta to a mailed survey on "the condition called muscle-bound." Of twenty-two responses received from "leading physiologists," only seven ventured an opinion, while the remainder knew nothing of the subject.[172] Of those who offered a theory on the condition, some speculated that it was caused by an overgrowth of connective tissue that resulted in a strain on the muscles. Perhaps the physiologists were making the observation voiced later by *Strength & Health* writer Jim Murray that cheap cuts of beef are the toughest and most fibrous and come from the muscles accustomed to doing the most work.[173] W. O. Fenn, chair of the Department of Physiology at the University of Rochester and future president of the American Physiological Society, speculated that the muscles became overdeveloped relative to their connection to the nervous system. Such a condition could result in decreased coordination, though Fenn's speculation rested on an increase in the number of muscle fibers, which, based on animal experiments, appeared not to be the primary cause of muscle growth.[174]

CONCLUSION

By the 1930s the groundwork had been laid for the incorporation of heavy resistance exercise into sport training programs. Physiologists successfully refuted the notion of an "athletic heart" as a detrimental effect of athletic participation and training. Moreover, the adaptations of skeletal muscle to various training methods became increasingly clear. Few researchers, however, showed much interest in specifically investigating strength training. Nonetheless, weight training had its own dedicated publication in *Strength* magazine and received periodic discussions in other health related publications like *Physical Culture*. These magazines and the commercial availability of barbells produced many new converts to weight training in the first three decades of the twentieth century. Old beliefs die hard, however, and many still avoided weight training out of fear that it would damage their heart or result in muscle-binding.

As posited by Thomas Kuhn, it takes a generation or more for new paradigms to be fully accepted as hold-outs argue against the new position.[175] Modern notions of muscular and cardiovascular adaptations to exercise were not fully incorporated into physiology texts until the early 1930s. As a result, men who had been trained under the old paradigm of energy conservation and balance held sway in the first half of the twentieth century. By 1940, however, strength training had added two spectacularly fervent adherents. These men, Bob Hoffman and Joe Weider, railed against opponents of weight training at every opportunity and played a major role in hastening the paradigm shift.

CHAPTER 2

BUILDING THE BARBELL ATHLETE

Bob Hoffman, Joe Weider,
and the Promotion of Strength Training
for Sport, 1932–1969

I n April 1934 Arthur Steinhaus, a physiologist and professor at George Williams College, presented a paper titled "Why Exercise?" to the Central District Physical Education Association in Saint Paul, Minnesota. The talk was intended to demonstrate all of the scientifically verified benefits of exercise, including increased efficiency of the heart, decreased fatigue, weight control, increased strength, and fun. While Steinhaus marveled at the increased functionality of the trained heart, he was more skeptical of developed strength. He explained in the most straightforward terms that "any exercise which is heavy enough to tax a muscle to its limit will stimulate the muscle to grow larger, and with this hypertrophy there comes greater strength." He continued: "But, let us ask ourselves, is strength a desirable goal? Does modern man need large muscles?" Answering his own question, Steinhaus asserted that "the ideal muscular development is that which has just enough margin of strength and power to maintain posture without effort, to do the day's work easily and to handle one's body weight readily." "Beyond this point," he announced to the audience, "it is wise to observe the maxims: 'Truck horse muscles are out of place on a buggy-horse job,' and 'Why bang around with a five-ton truck when a run-about will do?'"[1]

Four years later, Peter Karpovich, a medical doctor and professor at Springfield College in Massachusetts, echoed Steinhaus's earlier position. "In principle," Karpovich began, "heavy weight-lifting is a thing of the past. It is a relic of the idea that big muscles are essential for man's success in life. It was correct in primitive society. Now the place for a strong man is in a circus." Karpovich went on to caution that lifting excessively heavy weights caused "great strain" and could lead to being "muscle bound."[2]

The sentiment that large muscles were superfluous in the twentieth century, expressed by Steinhaus and Karpovich, arose in part from the Industrial

Revolution of the late nineteenth century and more recent technological innovations of the 1920s. Heavy construction machinery that included steam turbines and shovels, belt and bucket conveyors, and electric motors was becoming common at work sites in this decade, replacing an estimated 200,000 workers annually and leading to a new phrase: "technological unemployment." As the economy shifted from a production economy to an economy of consumption, a variety of affordable labor-saving devices also became available. Automobile production boomed during the 1920s, with an increase from 10 million cars on the road in 1920 to 26 million by 1929. The availability of cars changed the face of cities, as residents no longer had to live close to their work sites. This rapid proliferation of labor-saving commercial products and industrial machinery seemed to render physical strength gratuitous, rather than being seen as a marketable asset.

By 1925 even Alan Calvert, founder of the Milo Barbell Company, had turned against weight training, though his conversion took almost everyone by surprise. Calvert sold his company to Daniel Redmond, son of the treasurer of Fairmont Foundry in 1919. The foundry supplied Milo's weights, and Calvert became deeply indebted to it during late 1910s.[3] Calvert sold his company to settle his debt and "agreed never again to re-enter the Bar Bell business," though he continued to write for *Strength* magazine, which he had also started, through 1924.[4] After he cut ties with Milo, Calvert published two booklets criticizing weight training.[5] Calvert said that he lost faith in the system he had promoted for more than two decades because of the possibility that overexertion from lifting weights could lead to rupture (hernia), heart damage, blood vessel ruptures, and generally drained vitality. Instead of heavy lifting, Calvert promoted the system of Edwin Checkley, which involved no equipment at all. This system, he claimed, developed "natural" strength, the practical variety that enabled a man to perform daily tasks better. Barbells, he asserted, developed "made" strength, which was showy and impractical. He went on to warn parents that heavy weight training was more dangerous than football. His censure gave support to the medical doctors and physical educators who opposed weight training.[6]

Efforts to unify competitive weightlifting also faltered in the 1920s. Along with Ottley Coulter and Bernard Bernard, George Jowett established the fledgling American Continental Weight-Lifters Association (ACWLA) in 1922. The organization was modeled after the British Amateur Weight Lifters Association (BAWLA). Both groups aimed to standardize lifts and rules, establish records, and certify referees. When Jowett served as the editor of *Strength* between 1924 and 1927, he promoted the organization—and himself—with some success.[7] Milo owner Daniel Redmond replaced Jowett as editor with Mark Berry in 1927, however. Berry quickly formed a rival Association of Bar-Bell Men (ABBM). The German-American Athletic Club, a legacy of the Turner Movement, was also trying to sanction weightlifting contests, which weakened recognition of American interests in relation to the Olympic Games until the Amateur Athletic Union began running national championships in 1929.[8]

Though the sport of weightlifting was still trying to find its way, athletic endeavors as a whole flourished during the 1920s "Golden Age of Sport." One of the primary causes of this upsurge in athletic participation and interest, according to Mark Dyreson, was that between 1876 and 1919 "a critical mass of American thinkers began to argue that modern sport is one of the most important tools for shaping human societies."[9] Sport came to be viewed as a social technology that could build a sense of community and social values. The result was that "unprecedented numbers of Americans threw themselves into sports, games, and organized play." World War I played an important role in sparking the new interest in sport. Though soldiers had played sports informally during their down time in previous conflicts, World War I marked "the first time in American history [that] sports were formally linked to military preparedness."[10] Athletic competitions were used to boost troop morale and fitness—and to keep soldiers from pursuing more unsavory activities during their free time. Fitness became an even greater concern following passage of the Selective Service Act in May 1917.

The size and fitness of American soldiers had been a subject of concern since at least the Mexican-American War, when measurements revealed that American-born recruits weighed less than their European counterparts and were much more likely to be rejected for being too slender or having "contracted chests."[11]
The first million draftees for the Great War had almost exactly the same measurements as their Civil War counterparts, in fact, with an average height of 67.5 inches and average weight of 141.5 pounds, they were actually almost half a pound lighter than the soldiers who had fought more than fifty years earlier.[12] In light of these disheartening statistics, physical fitness and athleticism became patriotic virtues, laying the groundwork for physical education and scholastic sports programs in the decades that followed.[13]

In addition to the war, changes in working conditions and the rise of newspapers, radio, and print magazines also contributed to the growth of spectator sports. The average time that workers spent on the job decreased from just over forty-seven hours per week in 1920 to forty-two hours by 1930. The shorter work week paired with a 20 percent increase in real wages over the same span meant that consumers had the time and the disposable income to enjoy sports.[14] The accessibility of news about sports changed as radio broadcasts brought boxing, baseball, and college football into peoples' homes on a regular basis. If consumers wanted to go to the games, plenty of seats were still available, particularly for college football, which experienced an explosion of stadium construction and expansion. A prime example is found in the Big Ten Conference, in which every member institution built a stadium in the 1920s. Ohio Stadium, home of the Ohio State University Buckeyes, was one of seven stadiums constructed during the decade that could hold more than seventy thousand spectators.[15] The portrayal of the athletes who played in these and other stadiums also changed during the Golden Age, as what some have called "Gee-Whiz" journalism mythologized prominent athletes and hyped games.[16] Sportswriters became hero makers in the 1920s; they created the legend of Notre Dame's "Four Horsemen," lionized Knute Rockne, made Babe Ruth, Bill Tilden, Gertrude Ederle, and Red Grange into true sport celebrities, and raised the public's appreciation for professional sports.[17] Bob Hoffman would follow a similar journalistic path in *Strength & Health*.

In the early years of the Depression, weightlifting found its most powerful twentieth-century advocate in the bombastic, egoistic, indefatigable marketing genius Robert "Bob" Hoffman.[18] Though a mediocre lifter at best, Hoffman revered strength and worked to promote the competitive sport of weightlifting, the idea of weight training for fitness, and especially the idea of using weights to train for sport. Though men like William Wood, George Barker Windship, and Professor Louis Attila in the nineteenth century and Bernarr Macfadden and even Alan Calvert in the early years of the twentieth had all proselytized in favor of strength training for sport, it was Hoffman who most consistently hammered home the point to Americans that barbell training made better athletes. To do this and, equally importantly, to promote the barbells he manufactured, Hoffman started his own magazine, *Strength & Health*, in December 1932. Hoffman initially focused on the connection between weight training and sport performance, based on his own experiences with barbell training. Without a doubt, however, he was also aware that pro sports, college sports, and particularly high school sports were rapidly growing in popularity and participation.

Canadian-born Joe Weider followed in Hoffman's footsteps nearly a decade later. While chiefly associated with weight training for bodybuilding, not athletics, Weider also made important contributions to strength training as an adjunct to sports performances through his magazines. Weider began publishing *Your Physique* in 1940. He used it and subsequent publications like *Muscle Builder* and *All American Athlete* to promote weight training and undermine the charges against heavy lifting.

In the following pages we examine the important role played by Hoffman and Weider in helping to dispel the idea that weight training was detrimental to athletic performance. Neither man could ever have been called a scientist or even a trained physical educator, but their consistent advocacy of strength training for sport in the pages of their widely circulated magazines may have been more influential in changing the public's ideas about "muscle-binding" than any other single force of the twentieth century.

STRENGTH FOR SPORT: HOFFMAN'S EARLY YEARS

In the first issue of *Strength & Health*, editor, publisher, and author Bob Hoffman claimed that "graded barbell work and dumbbell exercises taught by our methods will improve any man at his chosen sport."[19] This claim was at odds with most sport training advice of the time, which generally called for repetitive performance of the sport itself as conditioning or on occasion recommended light calisthenics or some form of manual labor to get in shape for competition.[20] Beginning with the first issue of his magazine, Hoffman specifically refuted these ideas and claimed that systematic barbell training would produce greater gains in strength, speed, endurance, and coordination—and do it more rapidly—than the methods then commonly employed. In a refrain borrowed from Alan Calvert, Hoffman pointed out that "a good big man is still better than a good little man" and advised readers that, if they trained for strength, athletic success would follow.[21]

In addition to his claim that barbell training would produce better athletes, Hoffman wrote an editorial in the first issue that outlined the purpose for the magazine. *Strength & Health*'s primary goal was to "keep our country physically equal to or superior to all other nations." This would be done by encouraging people of all ages to lift weights and by advocating for compulsory training for children and adolescents. Much of the encouragement to train with weights was couched in the rhetoric of national decline. In Hoffman's estimation, *Strength & Health* was necessary because other nations were "outstripping us physically."[22] Hoffman's goals for the magazine were therefore rooted in nationalism. He would provide information on how to train with barbells so that the United States would not be physically embarrassed by stronger nations. Strength training to improve athletic performance and strength training to stave off national decline were two of the primary themes of the magazine throughout its run and were well established in the first issue. These prominent themes were based on Hoffman's view of the utility of strength, his own introduction to weight training, and the conflation of fitness and patriotism that had engulfed the nation during Hoffman's formative years.

Much of what is known about Hoffman's early years come from Hoffman himself. Like other prominent, self-promoting physical culturists, Hoffman often shaped his autobiography to suit his needs. In his case that included telling a variety of tales about his precocious physicality.[23] What is certain is that Robert Collins Hoffman, born in 1898, was the fourth of five children following his sister Florence, two brothers, Charles (Chuck) and Jack, and preceding his sister Eleanor.[24] Hoffman claimed that he was "born with a desire to be athletic and strong" and that he was trying to outdo his playmates as soon as he could walk.[25] For example, he said that he ran repeatedly around a double tennis court at age four, for reasons that are never explained. In most versions of this story he did 200 laps around the court, but in other accounts the laps vary from 100 to 250.[26] Another oft-cited story of Hoffman's athletic prowess as a child was his claim that he had run a ten-mile race at the age of ten. The young Hoffman had supposedly been asked to hold some clothes for two older boys during the race. Knowing that they would need their clothes at the end, Hoffman ran the race himself to ensure their delivery and finished next to the winner "fresh as [he] could be."[27] By the age of thirteen, Hoffman had supposedly completed several full (twenty-six-mile) marathons in Pittsburgh.[28] Although these early stories cannot be verified, Hoffman did participate in a variety of aquatic competitions after joining the Pittsburgh Aquatic club when he was sixteen.[29] His two older brothers also participated in swimming and canoeing contests and consistently bested the teenaged Bob in the earliest competitions, especially Jack. He resented being known as "Chuck's brother" or "Jack's brother" and began training to beat them, hoping that they would come to be known as "Bob's brothers." During the winter after his seventeenth birthday Bob began using some light dumbbells, pulleys, and a rowing machine as part of his training. Never one to give credit to others that he could claim for himself, his inspiration for beginning such training is noticeably missing from his various biographies. He did admit to doing some "train you by mail" exercises when he was ten, though these consisted simply of agonist-antagonist co-contraction exercises recommended by Charles Atlas.[30] Hoffman said that he trained for hours on end in his winter program until the floor was soaked with his perspiration.[31] The training apparently paid off, as he reportedly "won everything in sight" the following aquatic season.[32]

Shortly after the United States entered World War I in 1917, Hoffman enlisted in the Pennsylvania National Guard.[33] Descriptions of his wartime experiences were published in *Strength & Health* and in his book *I Remember the Last War*. Both accounts are full of bravado and tales of heroism, some of which are as improbable as his tales of childhood athleticism. Hoffman claimed to have enlisted in order to stop the atrocities that the Germans and their allies had been committing. He did so "expecting to get killed, but hoping to have done more than my part before I got mine."[34] Among his more improbable tales of heroism, Hoffman maintained that he had been sent on five patrols in one day, that he was the only soldier to survive three of them, and that he survived a bomb blast "right in my face" that killed all of those near him. Such was his gallantry that his superior officers were eventually "ashamed" to send him out on any more "certain death missions."[35] While these tales may be embellished, Hoffman was cited by General John "Black Jack" Pershing for "gallantry in action" and awarded the Belgian Order of Leopold and Croix de Guerre.[36]

In keeping with his persona, Hoffman emphasized that his physical prowess was integral to his survival. In a story titled "*Strength & Health*'s Boys" in 1934 Hoffman told of being pinned behind German lines and surrounded. His only flank not hemmed in by German troops was cut off by barbed wire. In a feat of tumbling prowess, Hoffman somersaulted over the wire and safely returned to his unit. The message of Hoffman's tale was that his young readers needed to participate in all forms of physical exercise because they never knew when it might pay dividends.[37] Similarly, Hoffman claimed in other articles that his physical competence enabled him to be a "champion digger," a record-holding marksman in speed and accuracy, and impervious to disease. Hoffman credited his fitness with helping him to survive the war: "I owe much of the fact that I am here to careful training, superb physical condition, and being as careful as I can be."[38]

Shortly after returning from the war Hoffman went into business with his brother Chuck in York, Pennsylvania, selling oil burners. While this business was only marginally successful, Hoffman did learn quite a bit about foundry work, machine work, and pattern making during this venture.[39] He eventually partnered with a man named Ed Kraber and established a successful oil-burner company.[40] While selling oil burners, Hoffman again began to compete in a variety of athletic events and trained as he had before the war, with the addition of some weights that he made at the shop. Hoffman also began reading *Strength* magazine and "became convinced that barbell training was the way to gain the strength and muscle [he] desired." By placing a "swear jar" in the oil burner factory he was able to raise the forty dollars necessary to purchase one of Calvert's Milo Barbells and in short order began training with the new weights. Following a year of intermittent training due to his travel schedule, Hoffman claimed that he had added twenty-one pounds to his frame and improved his performance at a variety of sports and athletic events, including handball, the standing broad jump, the high jump, the shot put, and even the 60- and 160-yard potato race. Moreover, he claimed to have won the "International YMCA Hexathlon" championship and to have added an astounding ten inches to his high jump and eighteen inches to his broad jump in the span of twelve months.[41] These sudden improvements, as much as anything else, confirmed Hoffman's belief that heavy resistance training could benefit athletic performance.

Hoffman shifted his focus to competitive weightlifting in the late 1920s. He began manufacturing barbells in his oil-burner factory in 1929 and organized a competitive weightlifting club in 1931. While other muscle entrepreneurs struggled during the Depression, Hoffman's physical culture ventures were supported by his oil-burner business, which remained enormously profitable.[42] Following the 1932 Olympic Games in Los Angeles, Hoffman began publishing *Strength & Health* with strongman and physical culturist George Jowett. For the next fifty-three years, until his death in 1985, the magazine served as a megaphone for Hoffman's ideas, helped satisfy his need for celebrity, and publicized his barbells.

Hoffman's athletic success after strength training profoundly affected his view of the utility of barbells, so he used enhancement of athletic performance as a primary selling point for his new products. Additionally, Hoffman truly felt that being strong and fit contributed to his survival and supposedly heroic deeds in World War I. Despite its status as the first modern war with a variety of technological advances in killing machinery, the war that Hoffman experienced was decidedly primal. Hoffman's worst fear, he claimed, was being impaled by a bayonet: he reportedly spent a great deal of time training on his own during the war to avoid this gruesome fate.[43] Being able to overpower an enemy soldier physically was crucial to his goal. As a result, Hoffman consistently admonished readers to be strong to avoid being conquered by other countries. "Many people think that physical strength is not necessary in this age," he claimed in 1933. "Yet physical strength is more necessary now than ever before."[44] For Hoffman, weight training was functional: it developed strength and improved health, both of which would then enable people to succeed in other endeavors.[45] Weight training also developed a person's physique, but he viewed this as a by-product of training, not the overarching goal.

JOE WEIDER'S INTRODUCTION TO WEIGHT TRAINING

Hoffman's publishing rival was Joseph Weider. Weider was born in 1920 in Montreal, Quebec, to Louis and Anna Weider, who had emigrated from Poland only ten years earlier.[46] Joe was the sixth child born to the couple, the third in Canada, and only the second to survive past infancy. Ben, his younger brother and eventual business partner, was born in 1923. As members of Montreal's Jewish community, the boys were subject to harassment by their classmates and around town. After years of taking "a lot of crap" and periodically getting into fights, Joe sought a way to make trouble avoid him. He initially turned to wrestling but claimed that the local coach would not let him try out because he feared the gangly teenager would get hurt. Dejected, Weider happened upon an old issue of *Strength* magazine while at the library. The magazine contained photos of weight-trained men as well as articles on how to train with weights to gain muscle and strength. One particular image of a man walking out of a lake struck the teenager. The photo was of a young man whose relaxed muscularity conveyed both strength and power to Weider. The text next to the photo said that his impressive physique had been built by lifting weights. Weider claimed that this was his call to take up weight training.[47] If such muscularity and implicit power could be manufactured, he could transform himself into a man who would be respected.

To that end, then thirteen-year-old Weider attempted to acquire the type of weights that he had seen in *Strength*. Unable to find them commercially available, he convinced a foreman at a scrap yard to make him a makeshift set from some small flywheels and a rusted iron shaft. The "barbell" was carted back to a shed behind the Weider home, where Joe lifted it religiously until his strength improved to the point that more resistance was needed. A proper weight set was beyond the teenager's means, however, and he petitioned George Jowett, whose side business included weight equipment sales, to let him buy a set on a layaway plan.[48] Jowett agreed, and Weider mailed him fifty cents each week until he had paid off the seven-dollar price of the barbell set. With his new adjustable set, Weider was able to make additional gains in muscle mass and strength. The culmination of Joe's transformation from a lanky waif to a muscular man came when a local bully followed Ben home to challenge Joe. Ben had attempted to avoid a beating by telling the man that his brother would retaliate if he got hurt. The man apparently took it as a challenge and went to the Weider home to confront the elder brother. While he deplored violence, Joe claimed that his weight-trained muscles allowed him to punch the man so hard that he was bloodied and knocked unconscious in a single blow.[49]

Joe Weider's physical transformation would color his view of the utility of weight training. His appearance had changed, which altered the way he was perceived by women and other men. He apparently actually asserted his physicality over another man only once: the rest of the time the appearance of strength was sufficient. As a result, increased size and the appearance of power, implicit in enhanced muscularity, were paramount for him.

Weider began publishing his first magazine, *Your Physique*, in August 1940, subtitled the "National Health and Physical Culture Magazine." His first editorial was nationalistic like Hoffman's first article. Weider warned that Canada had once been a land known for producing some of the strongest men in the world but had fallen far behind other countries physically.[50] He diverged from Hoffman, however, in making clear that his magazine would contain information on competitive weightlifting *and* building a better physique. He urged the readers of his original publication: "We must preach body-building, so as to get our youth to build up their bodies, and who knows produce championship material, of which we can never have too much." In keeping with the view that building the body was inherently valuable, Weider and the other writers in his magazines were deliberate in separating the practice of lifting for size and appearance from lifting for competition.[51] Their view, summed up in a maxim that has become part of the arcana of bodybuilding, was that one should "train for shape and strength [would] follow."[52]

Weight training had made Joe a man. His added muscularity caused bullies to steer clear, and those who did not paid the price. An additional benefit of this brand of hypertrophic masculinity was that he received extra attention from women and more respect from adults. "Bodybuilding changed me—body, mind, and soul," Joe claimed, "and altered my circumstances."[53]

Both Hoffman and Weider's tales are examples of the oft-told tale of the transformative power of weight training.[54] The story was first used in America by George Barker Windship in an article for the *Atlantic Monthly* in 1862.[55] Professional strongman Eugen Sandow and *Physical Culture* magazine publisher Bernarr Macfadden told similar tales at the turn of the twentieth century.[56] And then Charles Atlas (born Angelo Siciliano) marketed his mail-order training course "Dynamic Tension," based on the idea that manhood (and concomitant strength and courage and success) could be achieved by developing muscles. Atlas's advertising campaign is regarded as the most successful print advertising campaign of all time.[57] First run in 1929, the advertisement titled "The Insult That Made a Man Out of Mac" showed a skinny teenaged boy and an attractive young woman sunbathing at the beach when a bully comes along and kicks sand in their faces. Afraid to respond, and embarrassed to be seen as a coward in the eyes of the young woman, the boy sends away for Atlas's Dynamic Tension course. In the next frame of the ad, a newly muscular young man returns to the beach several months later, fells the bully with a single punch, and then walks out of frame with an adoring girlfriend on his arm.[58]

The idea that manhood could be "achieved" through a tangible, physical transformation was a common component of "masculine conversion narratives" in the late nineteenth and early twentieth centuries.[59] The man of this era was being converted, not necessarily from a child, but instead by setting himself apart from femininity.[60] In a cultural milieu where men searched for identity, autonomy, and personal fulfillment, they could be more easily persuaded to take up weight training. Sociologist Kenneth R. Dutton, building on the work of zoologist Desmond Morris, has discussed the weight-trained male body as a type of "super normal" stimulus. The increase in muscularity, particularly of the upper extremities, serves as a physical signifier that a young male is reaching physical maturity. Moreover, the muscularity helps set the male apart both from the more androgynous shape of the child and from females. The amplified muscularity that results from strength training is thus an exaggerated signifier of masculinity as opposed to the physiques of both a child and a woman.[61] Heightened muscularity can therefore be viewed as a means of gaining gender capital. As sociologist Michael Kimmel put it, in the absence of landownership and workplace autonomy, American manhood has to be proven in the modern world.[62] Physicality became an important avenue through which to express manhood. The hard, muscular body was, and is, associated with warriors and physical dominance.[63] The strength implicit in manufactured muscular size, Dutton contends, is part of a "dominance display" in which men may seek to assert authority over other men based on their size.[64]

In addition to securing gender capital, muscularity could also convey a type of American morality. Achieving noticeable hypertrophy of muscles requires regular, planned, and progressive resistance training. The wearer of the muscles, in a sense, is showing his fitness for capitalist society: he is a man of discipline, a worker who, in Hoffman's words, showed that he had "graduated from the college of strength and health."[65]

Tales of such muscular "Ragged Dicks" and other Horatio Alger–type characters filled thousands of pages in muscle magazines in the twentieth century. Competitive weightlifters and bodybuilders were heroically portrayed as men who had achieved success through consistent, hard work that helped them in humankind's battle for the survival of the fittest.[66] Joe Weider also stressed the Alger-like qualities of his own narrative. He commissioned Frederick Tilney to write an article recounting how he transformed himself by "demand[ing] for himself a well-developed body" and then started the highly successful *Your Physique* magazine in his parents' kitchen "with a paltry twenty dollars!"[67] In addition to having the gumption to start such an ambitious venture, Weider further proved his capitalistic piety by eschewing drinking or carousing so that he could work. In his retelling, "I didn't drink or go wild like other young people. I had to be sharp for work in the morning, and I had to save my money."[68] Much like Alger's "Ragged Dick," Weider succeeded through temperance, hard work, and frugality.[69]

While Hoffman was not loath to brag about his own accomplishments, he and other *Strength & Health* authors also focused their tales of success on members of the Olympic weightlifting team, legendary strongmen, and readers.[70] The stories generally revolved around the common trope that these tremendously strong or well-developed men had overcome debility through dogged determination and arduous physical training, often against the advice of physicians.[71] Hoffman even went so far as to claim that "the majority of men who are the strength champions of today were inferior physically in the beginning."[72] One example of this type of feature appeared in the first issue of *Strength & Health*. Joe Miller, author of the piece and a member of the York Barbell Athletic Club and Olympic weightlifting team, recounted how he had not been expected to live past infancy and had been a weak child. Tired of debility, he sent away for a physical culture course. In a story that predates Weider's by almost fifteen years, Miller claimed that he began to train with equipment fashioned from inner tubes, doorknobs, buckets, and an auto axle.[73] *Strength & Health* author and professional weightlifting champion Harry Good in 1934 reiterated Hoffman's claim that nearly all strongmen had to overcome handicaps or debility and then posed a question: "if these men succeeded so greatly, starting so heavily handicapped, what excuse can the normal person offer not to take the best care of the body that God gave them and to exercise to help it reach its maximum strength and health?"[74]

Good's query exemplified the goal of the Alger-type tales in both the Hoffman and Weider publications. Readers had to be convinced that they could be like the men shown in the magazines. They must truly believe that they could redefine their masculinity through the training that both publishers offered. Furthermore, they had to be convinced that the masculinity conferred by muscularity would bestow social benefits. Before they could be convinced of the benefits of strength training, however, they had to be dissuaded from the view that strength training could be harmful.

BATTLING IN THE COURT OF PUBLIC OPINION

Despite their opposing views on the purpose of strength training, both Hoffman and Weider in the pages of their magazines waged war with the notion that weight training was dangerous and fought their war on multiple fronts simultaneously. Their objective was to change the public's and the scientific community's ideas related to weight training and its supposed relationship to such negative outcomes as "athlete's heart," diminished vitality, rupture (hernia), stunted growth, and—most significant of all for the future of strength coaching—the theoretical condition known as being "muscle-bound."

The earliest feature article to refute the idea of athlete's heart appeared in the March 1935 issue of *Strength & Health*. Author Dr. Walter Laberge contended that there was "no such thing" as athletic heart and that his position was "backed by the foremost heart specialists of America and Europe."[75] As evidence for this statement Laberge cited medical doctor Thomas Lewis of Brigham Hospital in Boston, who observed that enlargement of the heart in athletes did not constitute disease. *Strength & Health* writer Harry Good had observed in an article just two months earlier that the heart is a muscle and must adapt to training similarly to the other muscles. "An 'enlarged' heart is no more dangerous than an enlarged biceps," Good asserted, "and I know that many thousands of you are striving to get one of them."[76] Later in the same year New York gym owner and weight-training advocate Siegmund Klein made the important observation that the heart, as a muscle itself, adapts to strenuous exercise in a manner similar to skeletal muscle.[77] Hoffman used the same analogy in March 1936: "Exercise builds a strong arm muscle and also a strong heart."[78] The notion of athlete's heart being caused by strength training proved tenacious, however, and as late as 1959 *Strength & Health* continued to feature articles debating the topic. Physician A. M. Gibson, for example, expressly denied the existence of the condition in two articles that year and echoed Hoffman by asserting that the heart adapted to training like the other muscles of the body.[79]

The first issue of Joe Weider's *Your Physique* included an article credited to Canadian strongman Arthur Dandurand, in which the long-time strength athlete claimed that he had been told in his youth that heavy lifting would result in being "muscle-bound, a weak heart, high blood pressure, rupture, and so on." In spite of these dire warnings, he assured readers, "a lifetime spent in strenuous sports did not have ill effects" on him. His health was purportedly verified by a physician whose findings accompanied the article, who reported, "Heart—Regular beat; no murmurs."[80] In the fourth issue of *Your Physique* Olympic weightlifting coach Mark Berry explicitly denied the existence of athlete's heart as a pathological condition. He quoted physician Irvin Cutter, who asserted that there was "probably no such thing as athlete's heart" in his defense of weightlifting and assured readers that there was "practically no danger" of heart damage occurring as a result of training with weights.[81]

While many in the medical community continued to warn of athlete's heart, coaches and physical educators were actually more concerned with the far more difficult-to-diagnose condition known as being "muscle-bound." Hoffman, Weider, and their various writers focused most of their energy on dispelling this particular myth, in part by attacking its origins. Both publishers argued that the idea that someone could become muscle-bound from lifting heavy weights was an outmoded belief. Harry Good pointed out in 1933 that the concept was probably due to strongmen who had "plenty of adipose tissue" and created the impression that it was necessary to be rotund to be strong. Moreover, their lifting style was slow because "the present science [of progressive training] was not applied."[82] Hoffman repeated this claim in 1936, and it was reiterated by *Muscle Power* writer W. A. Pullum in 1946.[83] Another York writer, Alan Carse, blamed "train-you-by-mail" entrepreneurs for perpetuating the myth in order to sell their mail-order courses that required little to no equipment.[84] Hoffman also discussed the idea of becoming bulky and potentially awkward, like a draft horse, correctly pointing out that their size was due to selective breeding, not "training."[85]

MAKING IT PERSONAL: BARBELLS MAKE BETTER ATHLETES

Research examining the effect of strength training on speed and range of motion did not begin until the late 1940s and began to be published in the early 1950s (see chapter 3).[86] With no experimental evidence to refute the existence of the condition called muscle-binding, Hoffman, Weider, and their writers found their most powerful weapons to be the personal stories of successful athletes who had used barbells to prepare for competition.

Hoffman tended to provide personal testimonials of how weight training had improved his athletic ability, but this was not his only tactic.[87] In many articles he simply appealed to the readers' logic, for example, in asserting that "a good big man is better than a good little man." To football players he emphasized that additional size and strength would allow them to smash through blockers and overpower ball carriers. "Read about those selected for the All-American teams and see how few, if any, weigh less than 200 pounds," he suggested.[88] To a reader who wanted to lift weights for football but feared becoming muscle-bound, Hoffman highlighted the similar power requirements in football and the Olympic lifts. For those familiar with rowing he noted that the heavier crews almost always beat the lighter groups, because while "they have more weight to pull . . . they have more power to pull it."[89] The power conferred by weight training would allow a baseball or tennis player or golfer to hit the ball harder: as Hoffman pointed out, "hitting power is the difference between a star and an ordinary player."

That same power would allow track athletes to run faster, jump higher, and throw farther.[90]

Logic and boosterism freely mingled in Hoffman's appeals to take up weight training for sport. In an attempt to provide evidence for his claims, Hoffman first showcased the York weightlifters and later used a wide variety of athletes as examples. He claimed that competitive weightlifters had as much speed, power, coordination, endurance, and flexibility as any athlete. "Weight lifters are never muscle bound," he claimed, noting that "they must be terrifically fast and powerful to succeed in the lifting of a heavy weight." He hyperbolically claimed that while only 1 percent of the population could likely touch the floor with their hands while bending at the waist with their knees locked, all weightlifters could perform such a feat.[91] He also pointed to York lifters like Gordon Venables, "champion swimmer, sprinter, runner, jumper, boxer, a star at a host of games," to verify that weightlifters were successful in other sports.[92]

In the first issue of *Strength & Health*, Hoffman's "How to Improve at Your Chosen Sport" article included the pledge that each issue would include examples of athletes "in every line of sport" who used weights. Other than Hoffman and the York lifters, however, concrete examples were not immediately provided. Hoffman mentioned in April 1938 that the York Barbell Club was being represented in boxing and that the pugilists had been trained with weights, to prove that weight training would not adversely affect their punching speed, but provided few specifics on the team's workouts or success.[93] In 1941 *Strength & Health* tried a new tactic in "Mr. America" Jules Bacon's column, with a direct appeal to readers to share their own stories about how weight training had improved their athletic performance. To help spur readers, Bacon provided a few examples of his own, including the story of celebrated amateur golfer Frank Stranahan. Stranahan had placed second in a 1941 golf championship and purportedly credited "his strength and skill to the unusual muscles which weight lifting built."[94] The inclusion of a successful golfer is important because it is not a traditional power sport like football or throwing the shot put. While the ability to generate powerful trunk rotation is undeniably important in a successful golf drive, just as important is the fine motor control to keep the club head properly aligned with the ball. The fact that a highly successful golfer would credit weights with enhancing his performance and not detracting from his coordination was a significant endorsement.

Bacon continued his column with the story of Sidney Gold, a high school football player in Los Angeles who had been cut from his school's team. After spending the winter and spring hefting his York barbell, Gold gained twenty pounds and made the varsity roster. "Weight training," Bacon contended, "is the best out of season activity for football players."[95] This tale echoed Hoffman's contention in a 1933 article that weight training should be practiced in the off-season to allow boys who did not make the team to secure a roster spot the following season.[96] The October 1941 issue featured another "What Can You Do?" column, this one telling the story of Bill Robush, a former college track athlete and friend of the author. Robush took up weight training after college, which allowed him to maintain his power in the pole vault and high jump despite having gained twenty-five pounds and aged nearly twenty years.[97] In the decades ahead these athletic Horatio Alger–type stories of strong or well-developed men who had overcome some infirmity to achieve success in sport became a mainstay of the magazine. Time and again Hoffman and his authors reminded readers that they might not have been born with athletic ability but could build it with weights and thereby achieve success on the athletic field and in life as men.[98]

As football grew in importance in the 1940s, features on football players and/or the importance of strength training for football began to appear more frequently in *Strength & Health*. Frank Schofro, a national champion in weightlifting, described how weight training had been integral to his success in football and track and enabled him to secure several athletic scholarship offers in 1939.[99] York Barbell Club member and national champion Steve Stanko told how he had trained with legendary bodybuilder John Grimek while he was in high school. In the first off-season of training Stanko, at five feet, ten inches, had gone from 120 pounds up to 170 pounds. After another year of training, his body weight had increased to 200 pounds, and he was offered a scholarship to play football in college. Though he turned it down to pursue competitive weightlifting, he assured readers that "scores of thousands of high school students are making their teams this fall and building for themselves a football reputation which will mean scholarships at higher institutions, laying the foundation for happy, successful lives through training with weights."[100] W. J. McClanahan, then a lieutenant in the Air Corps, told how the discovery of barbell training in the military had made him a better football player for his unit's team than when he had played for the Ohio State Buckeyes before the war. Furthermore, he asserted that J. C. Wetsel, All-American guard for Southern Methodist University's national championship football team in 1935, "owed a great share of his grid success to training with weights."[101] The legendary "strongman priest" Father Bernard Lange of Notre Dame, who had helped football players and track athletes train with weights since Knute Rockne's days as a player, authored an important article on football training in December 1947. "Every boy, deep in his being somewhere, loves to play football," he wrote, "yet every boy . . . does not play because he cannot, and he cannot simply because his physique, his build, will not permit it." Weight training, claimed Lange, was the secret needed for these boys to attain their heart's desire by developing the strength that "Mother Nature" had *not* given them.[102]

BARBELLS IN THE SERVICE

Lack of strength was not only a limitation in gaining access to the playing field but also a hindrance to making it onto the battlefield. Writing under the pseudonym D. A. Downing, Hoffman authored an article in January 1943 that purportedly consisted of letters received from American servicemen. One of the letters, attributed to navy yeoman Charles Mendoza, lamented that less than 20 percent of the men trying to enlist at his naval station were in sufficiently good physical shape for service. The condition could be easily rectified, Mendoza asserted, if only those rejected would follow his advice and pick up a copy of *Strength & Health*.[103] If they had started reading the magazine they would know that it featured a series that ultimately came to be titled "Barbell Men in the Service" and ran in one form or another from 1941 to 1946.

One of the most important aspects of the "Barbell Men" series was the way in which it chronicled the spread of strength training to tens of thousands of men who had previously not been exposed. This was done in both formal and informal capacities by those who were barbell men before the war. Frank Thompson, for example, had been the chair of the Kansas weightlifting organization in peacetime and was chosen to oversee physical training for 15,000 men at a camp in Norman, Oklahoma.[104] Less formally Peter Delgado used his experience with competitive lifts to teach other airmen in his unit, eventually staging a weightlifting contest at an unnamed air base in the South Pacific.[105] Many of the men who regularly lifted weights at Muscle Beach—Jack LaLanne, Les Stockton, and Harold Zinkin, for example—were turned into physical training instructors during World War II and taught hundreds of men the basics of weight training in boot camp as they worked to get them into shape for war.[106] Though slowed by material shortages, York churned out as many barbell sets as possible during the war years, shipping more than 4,000 sets by 1943 to installations across the continental United States, in Alaska, Hawaii, throughout the South Pacific, in Cuba, Panama, Newfoundland, and aboard a handful of navy ships.[107] By the end of the war, Hoffman claimed to be selling more than seven thousand sets per year.

To some extent this claim was borne out in a typical letter received near the end of the series in which a soldier asserted that he had seen so many people lifting weights and reading *Strength & Health* during the war that Hoffman would have to open additional factories and printing facilities to handle all of the barbell orders and new magazine subscriptions when the soldiers returned home. While new facilities for York Barbell were not required in the 1950s, John Fair has documented the rapid growth of York sales in the late 1940s and 1950s after tens of thousands of servicemen were exposed to barbell training in the service. Their familiarity with the basic benefits of strength training would be instrumental in the acceptance of weight training in the decades after the war.[108]

"BARBELLES"

As a savvy businessman, Bob Hoffman did not restrict his appeals about the benefits of barbell training to male audiences. Beginning in January 1934, Hoffman featured his first wife, Rosetta, holding what was purported to be a 100-pound barbell overhead with one arm. Three months later "Strength, Health, and Beauty for the Ladies," authored by Harry Good, claimed that lifting would improve the health, well-being, and motherhood capacity of trained women. Articles attributed to Rosetta herself began to appear regularly in the magazine by the end of the year. The pieces included beauty tips, recipes, and of course advice on lifting weights. In addition to discussing strength training for aesthetic reasons, some of the articles included references to the utility of lifting weights for sport. "Training with weights makes it possible for me to enjoy other games and sports," Rosetta reported in 1937, noting that "the secret of barbell training is to use comparatively heavy weights for a few repetitions." As a result of lifting heavy weights only a few times, she asserted that the training would build strength, energy, and "vital power."[109]

Just as Hoffman was not the first barbell entrepreneur to use a magazine to sell his weights, he also was not the first to recommend strength training for women in order to improve their health, maternal fitness, and athletic performance. As Jan Todd has discussed extensively, other publishers, particularly Bernarr Macfadden, had been using their magazines to urge women to strength train several decades earlier. At Macfadden's second "Physical Culture Extravaganza" in 1905, for example, the winner of the physique contest was based on points awarded in a series of athletic contests, including a weightlifting competition, as well as a contest for the most symmetrically developed female physique. In 1911 Macfadden's magazine, *Physical Culture*, featured a letter to the editor in which a female diver discussed training with dumbbells, Indian clubs, and a series of gymnastic exercises to help her become more proficient at her sport.[110] In the 1920s a competing publication, *Strength*, actively promoted both the development of women's sports and training for them. For example, a 1926 article by Dana Hamilton declared that "the female athlete personifies the highest type of womanhood," while an article the following year claimed that both women and men could "cash in on trained muscles" and make their favorite sport a profession.[111]

In spite of Hoffman's divorce from Rosetta in late 1938, he continued to feature strength-trained women (including his romantic partners Gracy Bard, Alda Ketterman, and Dorcas Lehman) and non-Hoffman-affiliated females in his magazine.[112] Abbye "Pudgy" Eville Stockton, born and raised in Santa Monica, California, was the most important woman athlete to appear in *Strength & Health* magazine and played the major role in Hoffman's crusade to encourage weight training for women. Stockton's first appearance in the magazine was just a single photograph in September 1940: the caption claimed that, despite her small size, she had strength equal to or better than a much heavier man and was "proof that heavy exercise, weightlifting, handbalancing, and acrobatics will produce the ideal development for the ladies too."[113] In addition to her appearances in *Strength & Health*, Stockton also appeared in many mainstream magazines, including *Life*, *Pic*, and *Laff*, which garnered attention beyond those already interested in strength training.[114] By 1944 she had her own column in *Strength & Health* called "Barbelles," featuring other women who shared her qualities of strength, physical attractiveness, and athleticism. These included track athletes Alyce Yarick and Edith Roeder and gymnast Maria Blumer, all of whom trained seriously with barbells and attributed their sporting success to that training.[115]

WEIDER JOINS THE CAUSE

Once Weider's *Your Physique* began to take off in the 1940s he, like Hoffman, peppered it and his other magazines that followed with articles and captions attacking the idea of muscle-binding. The articles were similarly anecdotal in nature, and most discussed champion athletes who practiced one form of weight training or another. One of the earliest examples was provided by Bill Pullum, who cited a British boxer, Joe Wakeling, a multiclass champion and "one of the fastest men of his weight ever seen in the ring." Pullum claimed to have trained the boxer personally and wrote that Wakeling "himself used to say that the using of weights had actually made him faster."[116] References to boxers and wrestlers dominated *Your Physique* in its first decade. A three-part article appeared on heavyweight champion Jack Johnson in 1948. The

Indian wrestler known as the Great Gama made his first appearance in 1947. Another wrestler, known as the "Terrible Turk," appeared in 1949.[117] Writer Martin Franklin quoted strongman Arthur Saxon in *Muscle Power* magazine as stating that many boxers and wrestlers were in fact doing resistance training, though not with barbells. Saxon asserted that weight training had made boxer Tommy Burns faster and that boxers Tommy Sayers and Tom Cribb had both used more primitive forms of resistance that included heaving bricks and lifting sacks of coal. Even the spectacular boxer Jack Johnson, Saxon claimed, "occasionally performed the wrestler's bridge while handling heavy weight."[118]

In 1950 Joe Weider responded to a reported deluge of reader letters inquiring about the advisability of weight training for athletes by providing a laundry list of prominent boxers who had trained with weights. Though he did not discuss their specific programs or provide evidence, Weider asserted that such champions as Joe Louis, Primo Carnera, and Max Baer were weight-trained athletes and made the blanket statement that it was a known fact that "at least 99 percent of all the great wrestlers used weights."[119] In that same issue George Russell Weaver also offered as evidence a number of weight-trained athletes: "Frank Strafaci is a barbell trained man who has won golf championships. Joe Walcott was a circus strong-man before he became one of the greatest boxers . . . Emile Maitrot, a wrestler and weight-lifter, won a world's championship in speed-cycling." Continuing his list, Weaver claimed that "Eugen Sandow, the professional strongman, surpassed Mike Donovan, one of the most agile boxers in a special test of speed in response to a signal. James Hudson, a barbell trained man, broke the Georgia State record in the 100-yard breast-stroke swim . . . Charles Steinman, an active weight-lifter, was also captain of the Ohio State University tennis team." He concluded: "Such facts as these show the remarkable versatility of weight-lifters."[120]

The first active athlete who was not a boxer or wrestler featured in a major article in a Weider magazine was golfer Frank Stranahan.[121] Stranahan was one of the best golfers in the world in the 1940s and early 1950s, winning more than seventy amateur tournaments, including the 1948 and 1950 British Amateur Championships. He also played (and placed) in many pro events but retained his amateur standing by refusing to take the prize money. To the surprise of many, Stranahan appeared regularly in weightlifting competitions during his golf career, a fact that caused some sportswriters to begin calling him the "Toledo Strongman" after his hometown.[122] A 1949 article by Earle Liederman argued that weight training had made Stranahan a longer and more accurate hitter and, most importantly, that "barbells do not conflict with the delicate sense of touch" necessary for golf.[123] Two years later, Barton Horvath profiled Stranahan again for *Your Physique* and explained how Stranahan had begun lifting weights for football in high school then found that it also made him a better golfer. When Horvath asked Stranahan about the theory of muscle-binding, "Frank replied with a curt, 'rubbish.'" Many coaches and other golfers had warned him that weight training would only be detrimental to his game, Stranahan explained, but he had just ignored them and followed his own path.[124]

The inclusion of Stranahan in *Your Physique* was especially important because he was one of the most famous athletes of the mid-twentieth century to be open about his barbell training.[125] Although Stranahan is briefly mentioned in a column by Jules Bacon in *Strength & Health* in 1941 and is touched on again in an editorial by Hoffman in 1947, the article by Liederman more fully introduced this remarkable athlete to barbell fans.[126] As a role model for strength training for sport, the fact that Stranahan won the 1950 British Amateur Championship and entered the Ohio State Weightlifting Championship that same year sent a powerful message to readers. And his lifts were excellent: he pressed 225 pounds, snatched 220 pounds, and cleaned and jerked 300 pounds. According to Horvath, he could also "squat with over 400 and deadlift over 500 pounds."[127] A realist about training, Stranahan told Liederman that one "cannot expect weight training alone to make you a champion athlete." Being a champion, he explained, also required "many long hours of practice at the sport you are trying to improve."[128]

THE POWER OF ROLE MODELS

Both Hoffman and Weider continued peppering their magazines with powerful athletic role models in the years ahead. Track and field athletes were a natural choice for these kinds of athletic profiles, of course (especially those who threw the shot, discus, javelin, and hammer), as they were some of the earliest discoverers of the power of weight training. John Davis, for example, profiled Olympic decathlete Irving Mondschein in 1948, explaining that Mondschein credited weight training with improving his athletic performance.[129] Hoffman quoted from a letter sent by shot-putter Otis Chandler in 1945, who affirmed that weight training did not "tie you up," which once again gave Hoffman the chance to urge young athletes to take up weight training.[130] Female shot-putter Jackie MacDonald, a member of the Canadian Olympic team, made the magazine in 1955, and American throwers Parry O'Brien, Bobbie Gross, and Bill Nieder were also featured.[131] British sprinter McDonald Bailey, high jumper Ernie Shelton, and pole-vaulter

Don Bragg were similarly used to exemplify the benefits of weight training for athletes.[132] Perhaps the most notable of all was the 1952 cover story on Olympic Gold medalist Bob Richards, who won the pole vault in the 1952 and 1956 Olympic Games.[133]

Other sports were also included in these athletic profiles in the 1950s. Profiles of Jackie Jensen, outfielder for the Boston Red Sox, and Ohio State University swimmer Al Wiggins also had an impact. Jensen credited weight training with saving his career after an arm injury in high school. Following a stint in the navy, Jensen starred as a fullback and pitcher at the University of California in the late 1940s, winning All-American honors in both sports. The "bull-necked" Jensen was the "best right fielder in the American league" through the mid-1950s and a multiple All-Star and American League MVP (Most Valuable Player) by 1958.[134] Al Wiggins was a very good, but not great, swimmer in his freshman year. Prior to his second season at Ohio State, Wiggins took up weight training after record-holding sprint swimmer Dick Cleveland spoke enthusiastically about how weight training had improved his performance. The training paid dividends in the pool: Wiggins played a role in eight team or individual national championships for the Buckeyes between 1955 and 1957, set three world records in butterfly events, and competed at the 1956 Olympic Games in Melbourne.[135] Wiggins explained: "There is one factor which deserves more credit than all the others for my sudden improvement in swimming ability, and that is my training with weights."[136]

STRENGTH-TRAINING PROGRAMS IN THE 1940S AND 1950S

During the 1930s and 1940s, *Strength & Health* articles on strength training for sport were largely aimed at disproving the notion that weight training would harm athletic performance. Little guidance was provided on how weight training for football might differ from weight training for golf or pole-vaulting. In lauding the success of shot-putter Otis Chandler, for example, Hoffman claimed Chandler had simply followed the basic York Barbell courses.[137] This would change in the early and mid-1950s as athlete profiles began to more specifically discuss programming.[138] Most 1950s training regimens still largely resembled the total body programs of the general York courses, but readers began to notice that the program employed by the Istrouma (Louisiana) High School football team differed from the program that Harry Paschall suggested for basketball, which, among other alterations, omitted the bench press and included a plyometric lunge jump.[139]

Weider's approach to training diverged from Hoffman's. This is not surprising considering that Weider viewed bodybuilding as an important sport in its own right—and one that he wanted to grow.[140] Consequently, many of the early articles encouraged bodybuilders to take up a "second choice" sport.[141] Weider's rather convoluted idea was that bodybuilders would serve as ambassadors for strength training by demonstrating that their built physiques were at least as "useful" and athletic on the field as those of men who had not weight trained. Summarizing this view, Bob Leigh urged readers: "Build the bodies and then take them to other activities."[142] This desire to show the utility of the muscles created by bodybuilding was due in part to attacks from the Hoffman camp. Hoffman portrayed the "lumps" created by the bodybuilders as useless muscles. In his view they were created through deliberate high-repetition, moderate-weight exercises, intended primarily to cause muscle growth. To Hoffman, the physiques of bodybuilders were not useful and were simply "mirror" muscles, bred by vanity.[143]

It should be noted that some of the training ideas of both men have been incorporated into modern sport training. In one contemporary model of periodization, strength training for sport begins with the "anatomical adaptation" or "hypertrophy" phase.[144] This phase is essentially bodybuilding training, based on the belief that larger muscles are stronger muscles.[145] The third phase of the periodization model is intended to improve the rate of muscular force production and often includes the snatch and the clean-and-jerk. These Olympic lifts are included because they mimic the powerful hip, knee, and ankle extension required in explosive jumping and running movements.

ALL AMERICAN ATHLETE: BRIDGING THE GAP

Both Hoffman and Weider continued increasing the amount of coverage devoted to strength training for sport as the 1950s gave way to the 1960s. In 1959 Hoffman added a new column, called "Barbells on Campus," which helped to demonstrate the growing use of barbells by athletes at various American universities.[146] Each article featured a different college or university and discussed young men who competed in Olympic weightlifting, trained for sport, or both.[147] In 1958 Weider had shuffled magazine titles and changed *Muscle Power* to *Mr. America: The Magazine of Champions*.[148] This title change accompanied a gradual increase in the number of articles stressing strength training for sport that culminated in 1962 with the launch of a special series of sport-specific instructional articles.[149]

Weider's "Barbells and [name a sport]" series was a particularly important development in the evolution of strength coaching, marking the first time a mainstream magazine systematically addressed the important concept of sport specificity.[150] In our modern era the idea that sport training must mimic the energy systems used while playing, as well as the movements of the sport itself, is well understood and considered by most authorities to be fundamental to successful training.[151] However, until Jim Murray and Peter Karpovich published their landmark book *Weight Training in Athletics* in 1956, little attention was paid to the fact that different sports needed different kinds of strength-training regimens. Murray and Karpovich included individualized routines for football, baseball, and track and field and provided limited advice for what they called the "minor sports" of wrestling, swimming, boxing, rowing, tennis, golf, and fencing.[152]

The new Weider series began with a jointly published article by E. M. Orlick and Joe Weider called "Barbells and Baseball" in June 1962. It was followed the next month by "Barbells and Swimming," and in succeeding months with articles on running, football, shot-putting, basketball, bowling, boxing, wrestling, and the decathlon.[153] The one on bowling, one of America's most popular recreational sports in the 1960s, is a good example of the level of detail to be found in these articles. The cover graphic showed a bowler, covered in numbers, releasing the ball.

The numbers corresponded to the exercises pictured at the left of the page, which strengthened all aspects of the movement. The article even included instructions for practicing the actual bowling motion with a dumbbell.[154] Similarly, a running workout incorporated such novel resistance movements as running in water, running with ankle weights, and running stadium steps. These were performed in addition to more traditional bodybuilding movements such as squats, calf raises, and leg presses.[155]

By August 1963 *Mr. America* featured the subtitle *All American Athlete*. The number of sport training articles inside the magazine dramatically increased. Surviving letters between E. M. Orlick and both Joe and Ben Weider report that plans were being laid in the summer of 1963 to start a new kind of magazine. Orlick, who had been a university faculty member and had affiliations with professional coaching and physical education associations, wrote to Ben Weider outlining steps that needed to be taken to assure that the new magazine would reach the right hands. "Canada is ripe for our new magazine and all that goes with it," he explained, before cautioning that the readership for *All American Athlete* would be different than for other Weider publications. "The 'intellectuals' will have to be treated a little different than the musclemen," he explained to Ben. "We've got to reach them thru their own thinking and language." Orlick then told Ben to get the addresses of high school coaches, college coaches, and physical educators by contacting their professional associations and asking for a list of members so that they could be informed of the new magazine. He told Ben that they also needed to write all Young Men's Christian Associations (YMCAs), Young Men's Hebrew Associations (YMHAs), the Canadian Olympic Committee, and the National Fitness Council to get the word out. "Mention my name," wrote Orlick, "and some of the Universities I was at—McMaster, Western, Sir George Williams, McGill—it might still help to open up some sticky doors. Also, I was on the Olympic Committee, Pan Am Games Committee, British Empire Games Committee, was Vice President of the AAU of C[anada]."[156] Ben Weider wrote back the following week reporting that he was "following through with this immediately." He added that he felt "All American Athlete will be a smashing success, and we will do everything we can in Canada to promote it."[157]

All American Athlete: The Magazine That Builds Champions was finally launched in November 1963 with E. M. Orlick as editor.[158] The first issue included two lengthy articles on strength training for football: an article by Orlick on dietary advice for athletes; a feature story on sprinter Frank Budd, described as the world's fastest human; a primitive biomechanical analysis of the football punt; several medical and scientific reports gleaned from a variety of research publications; and an article by former *Strength & Health* editor Jim Murray, entitled "Added Resistance for Overload."[159]

In the months that followed, *All American Athlete* continued to feature strength programs for various sports as well as coaching and technique tips, discussions of strategy, and information on nutrition. The second issue of the magazine, for example, was primarily dedicated to training for track and field and included another Jim Murray article, this one detailing a step-by-step training routine for the decathlon, along with six articles discussing coaching techniques for different track and field events written by prominent coaches.[160] The early issues of the magazine were more than one hundred pages in length. The expansive format created room for training programs for a wider variety of sports (including surfing, Olympic paddling, and other nontraditional sports). The concept of sport-specific training was increasingly refined in these and other articles.[161]

In addition to recommending exercises based on the actual muscles used during various sporting activities, Weider's new magazine also addressed the need to think about speed of movement as a facet of barbell training. An important aspect of the application of strength training to sport is that it has to require the athlete to contract certain muscles quickly and simultaneously. Consistent heavy training does not necessarily do this, because maximal lifts require incredibly forceful but slow contractions. It is generally agreed that to teach the rapid muscle recruitment required in quick sport movements the movements must periodically be performed rapidly.[162] This is an adaptation on the part of the nervous system, not the muscular system per se, but it is nonetheless an important training adaptation. George Jowett had recognized this basic idea at least as early as the 1930s, when he wrote about it in *Strength & Health*.[163] He advocated a similar program in 1962 in *Muscle Builder*, which called for light-weight, low-repetition exercises performed as rapidly as possible to "coordinat[e] the nervous forces with the muscular."[164] In 1965 Ben Weider also advised a fast training program in *All American Athlete*, which called for first using heavy weight then reducing it 20 percent and deliberately attempting to move it faster.[165]

Throughout 1964 *All American Athlete* appeared on a monthly basis and continued to bring science and sport into the homes of thousands of individuals around the globe.[166] In that Olympic year, to no one's surprise, the magazine was filled with Cold War concerns that begin with Orlick's "Let's Answer the Communist Sports Challenge" in March 1964. That article was followed by cover stories in May and June discussing the need for America to adopt a national sport program in order to combat the rise of Communist sport.[167] In October 1964 editor Orlick announced that *All American Athlete* was taking on an even larger role in the Olympic movement and that the magazine was actually helping to design strength-training programs for some of America's Olympic teams. According to Orlick, at the request of the Olympic canoeing coach, he and other experts "took into consideration the anatomy, physiology and kinesiology involved. And, after weeks of intensive study, backed by a lifetime of training and experience . . . we developed a scientific strength building program . . . one of the first such scientific programs for USA athletes in any sport."[168] He noted: "There exists a big gap between scientific knowledge and its practical application, especially with respect to sports . . . we have taken a big step to bridge this gap."[169]

Despite the important role that *All American Athlete* apparently hoped to play in advancing the cause of sport training, the magazine ultimately failed to catch on as Weider and Orlick had hoped. In an appeal to advertisers in 1963 Orlick's son Ronald, who served as advertising manager, claimed that the magazine had a circulation of more than 81,000, made up of 26,000 coaches, 1,200 gym owners, 48,000 individual athletes, 1,700 department of recreation officials, 1,800 athletic directors, and 3,200 athletic trainers.[170] Despite those numbers—which may or may not be real—Ron Orlick wrote that even though he was working his "guts off," he just was not finding advertisers.[171] By April 1965 the magazine fell to only sixty-six pages in length, and Weider stopped producing it as a stand-alone magazine. Although "we all want to keep AAA going," he wrote in January 1965, he had already lost $50,000 on the magazine, which had only developed a circulation of 23,000 subscribers.[172]

Although the first iteration of *All American Athlete* was over, Weider's interest in marketing a sport-training magazine remained. According to writer Jim Murray, Weider even approached him about coming to work for him on a full-time basis in the late 1960s so he could run a new version of the magazine. Murray, who played football and threw javelin at Rutgers University at the same time he lifted weights, always believed that a magazine such as *All American Athlete* was needed and could succeed. However, he reported, "by the time Joe approached me, I was working for Johnson and Johnson, and I really didn't want to give up the security that that job offered."[173] So, Murray explained, he worked for Joe Weider as a freelancer and helped during 1968 and 1969 when *All American Athlete* once again appeared on American newsstands. The last two issues list Murray as the editor.[174] "After writing the book with Dr. Karpovich, I knew how important it was to bring science and sport together," he said.[175]

The 1960s also saw the publication of another magazine that included articles on weight training for sport in nearly every issue. Walter Marcyan's *Physical Power* attempted to appeal to a variety of constituencies, with regular articles on bodybuilding, weightlifting, training for women, and strength training for sport. Like Hoffman and Weider, Marcyan sold barbells, but he also sold an innovative multistation "universal" gym that historian Terry Todd credited with making gyms friendlier to the average person who wanted to take up weight training.[176] Like Hoffman and Weider, Marcyan was a competitive lifter and bodybuilder himself, who intended to use his magazine to promote his products and his California gyms. Among *Physical Power*'s regular contributors were Stan Burnham and Jim Murray.[177] Burnham was a professor of physical education at the University of Texas and has been credited with playing a key role in bringing strength training to the Texas Longhorns football team.[178] In his articles Burnham discussed research related to strength training for sport and sport-specific strength-training programs.[179] The training articles covered a variety of sports, although (as with the magazines of Hoffman and Weider) football, shot put, and discus were most heavily featured.[180] Marcyan's *Physical Power*, however, failed to attract advertisers. The magazine peaked at fifty pages in late 1963 and ceased publication in 1965.

CONCLUSION

By 1965 the dozens of articles published by Weider and Hoffman and Marcyan had provided a powerful case for the efficacy of weight training for athletes. Across North America men (and women) were beginning to experiment with weight training for sport. Furthermore, a more sophisticated understanding of the best methods for strength training was beginning to evolve, furthered by new scientific research (see chapter 3). It is clear that Bob Hoffman and Joe Weider played a key role in the development of strength training for sport and difficult to imagine that the modern world of strength training would have emerged as it has without them. The efforts of both men to dispel the myths of the damaging effects of weight training proved crucial in convincing many to take up barbell training. Once they had been converted, the new lifters often excelled in sports and became living role models who were strength training's best advertisements.

While anecdotal evidence for the benefits of strength training was valuable, what was truly needed was scientific proof of the effectiveness and relative safety of strength training in order to dissuade its detractors. This proof had already begun to emerge (see chapter 3). Like many scientific ideas, however, it would require "nurturing" to reach the point where it became accepted as immutable fact and a person could say without caveats that weight training was known by scientists, doctors, physical educators, coaches, and average Americans as the best way to improve overall sport performance.

•

CHAPTER 3

THE SCIENCE CONNECTION

Thomas DeLorme, Progressive Resistance Exercise,
and the Emergence of Strength-Training Research: 1940–1970

A lthough most of us now regard the Young Men's Christian Association (YMCA) as an agency supportive of weight training, in the early twentieth century, the YMCA movement had a far more ambivalent attitude toward strength and muscle. While most YMCAs in that era had at least some barbells, the men running those facilities often received their academic training at YMCA-sponsored Springfield College in Massachusetts, the preeminent university in America in the field of physical education during the first half of the twentieth century. At Springfield the use of heavy weight training was viewed unfavorably by the faculty. As Springfield College student and *Strength & Health* magazine subscriber Fraysher Ferguson put it, "I went to Springfield because I wanted to study physical education and I knew . . . that Springfield College was the best place in the country. But when I got there everyone seemed to be against weightlifting and I began to feel ostracized because I believed in it. . . . Professors would say negative things about it in class all the time, and it used to burn me up. I knew they'd never touched a barbell and had no way to know whether it worked or not."[1]

The disparaging views of strength training held by many of the Springfield faculty were, of course, primarily fueled by the medical and scientific myths discussed in chapter 2. Also at play, however, was Springfield's desire to turn out "professional" physical educators, which meant that most of the faculty looked askance at nonacademic physical culture entrepreneurs like Bernarr Macfadden and Bob Hoffman and professional strongmen who sold training courses like Eugen Sandow. A Springfield College newsreel from the late 1930s, ironically titled *Men of Muscle*, speaks directly to this antipathy. The announcer declares early in the film that "the burnt-out or musclebound athlete is not found at Springfield" and later explains that the school's physical training goal is not to create the "the bar-bending brute strength of the Vaudeville athlete": "Springfield does not aspire to develop biceps-bulging supermen."[2]

The problem for Springfield College, however, was that after Hoffman began publishing *Strength & Health* young men were increasingly interested in becoming "biceps-bulging supermen." Evidence of this can be found in a series of surveys conducted through program directors at YMCAs. Knowing little about the effects or practice of weight training, however, some physical educators continued to fret about its popularity in their professional publications. In a 1937 article in the *Journal of Physical Education*, Harvey Allen polled forty-five YMCAs by mail on whether they permitted the activity. Thirty-six of the thirty-nine replies permitted weight training, though seventeen physical directors said that they felt "coerced" into allowing it and eight said they did not favor the activity. One of the physical directors wrote that he had consulted doctors and other physical directors and "was not surprised upon finding that the unanimous opinion in regard to the activity was decidedly unfavorable." Others commented that lifting weights had "no place in our program" and was "the finest builder of athletic glass arms I know of." The end of the article, however, quoted an anonymous director who said that he had "never heard a sound physiological argument against it" and that most of the criticisms were hearsay.[3]

Two issues later, Howard Wilson of the Boston YMCA came to the defense of weight training. He pointed out that large muscles were openly admired and that replicas of muscular Greek statuary were included on medals and plaques awarded by some YMCAs. He pointed to the illogic of venerating the physique but deriding the most efficient way to build it. Wilson went on to discuss the most prominent arguments against lifting: that large muscles were "unnecessary in this day and age" (even citing the examples of plow horses and race horses) and that weight training was likely to be injurious. The argument that muscles were not necessary was fallacious, because "so are a great many other things unnecessary which are included in a program of physical education." Moreover, if there was so much hand wringing over the injuries caused by weight training, what about other activities sponsored by YMCAs, such as football, basketball, and wrestling? Wilson suggested that they were at least equally injurious if not more so. If physical directors opposed lifting weights, he asserted, they must develop "scientific reasons" for their objection to the activity. Otherwise they would not be able to "offset the quackery of magazine articles written attractively by men with little or no training in physical education; but who themselves are good business men and build muscles for *commercial* gain." In closing Wilson asked a rhetorical question: if a boy wanted to gain recognition through a powerfully developed physique, "who are you, who am I, or who is anyone else that we should discourage him?"[4]

The July–August 1938 issue of the *Journal of Physical Education* included a letter from C. F. Benninghoff, associate physical director of the New Haven (Connecticut) YMCA. Benninghoff advocated a "sane" approach to weight training: if young men were going to lift weights, YMCAs should do everything they could to obtain "scientific" information to advise them how to perform the activity properly.[5] Other YMCA directors were less accommodating. Several national YMCA officials advocated a ban on the activity at all facilities during the 1930s.[6] There was a great deal of enthusiasm for weight training in the late 1930s regardless of how much physical directors knew about or were willing to tolerate it. In a survey by Ted Krause from the northeastern branch of the Detroit YMCA nearly two-thirds of 297 respondents reported "much interest" in lifting weights, while another 17 percent reported "moderate" interest.[7]

In spite of burgeoning interest in weight training, many physiologists and physical educators still had little interest in studying the activity. A case in point can be found in the text published the same year as Krause's study by Professors James McCurdy and Leonard Larsen of Springfield (Massachusetts) College. The book was directed at students of physical education but contained scant discussion of weight training. One section (of three) was dedicated to discussing the effects of various games and activities on the body. Included among the sports and activities were gymnastics, track, American football, basketball, golf, rowing, swimming, and even marathon running. Strength training was not specifically mentioned in this section. The scarce discussion of strength training mentioned the relationship between a muscle's size and its force development but little else, with no mention of the implications of force development on other activities or how to train to increase a muscle's size.[8] Howard Knuttgen, president of the American College of Sports Medicine in 1972–1973, commented that during this time most researchers had a negative impression of weightlifters. "If someone came to the American Physiological Society and was going to give a paper on strength training," he explained, "people would have raised their eyebrows and asked 'what the heck is going on here?'"[9]

The academic community's lack of interest in the development of strength would change during World War II. Hoffman, Weider, other prominent strength entrepreneurs had helped to create substantial interest in strength training in the 1930s and early 1940s. As weight-trained athletes joined the service, they proselytized about the advantages of strength training and were able to make new converts. Owing to advances in the understanding of physiology by the early 1930s, physical educators, physiologists, and medical doctors became less obstinate in their opposition to strength training. Some, like physical educator C. H. McCloy, were exposed to barbells through the military training facilities set up at universities across the country. Finally, when the War Manpower Commission limited the army's access to recruits through the draft in 1943, the army began to search for more efficient and effective methods to return injured soldiers to the battlefield. The confluence of these factors precipitated a growing academic interest in strength training beginning in the 1940s.

WORLD WAR II, THOMAS DELORME, C. H. MCCLOY, AND INITIAL INVESTIGATIONS OF STRENGTH TRAINING IN THE POSTWAR YEARS

World War II would prove to be pivotal in shifting the perception of weight training.[10] Many had previously argued that strength was unnecessary in modern civilization, but the brutal reality of combat prompted calls to promote strength training. While the United States did not officially enter the war until December 1941, the country had been mobilizing and preparing for conflict since at least the summer of 1940.[11] Bob Hoffman took advantage of the early stages of the European war to urge his readers to be fit for their role in the impending struggle. He pointed to America's official neutrality: "Our leaders will struggle hard to keep us out . . . [but] it will be hard to avoid. . . . It will be more than difficult not to be pushed in." He continued, "When they need you, and I hope they won't, they'll come for you and you'll have to carry a rifle." As a result, Hoffman advised, "You have a far better chance of surviving the fighting of the war and recovering from wounds, should it be your fate to receive them, if you are physically fit than if you are not."[12]

The call to prepare for war with strength training was also taken up by physical educators. As an example, Robert Edwards, a physical educator at the University of Illinois, declared in a 1940 article in the *Journal of Health and Physical Education*, "We have been living too luxurious lives. To survive, we must turn our energies toward strength and away from comfort." He advised performing arm curls, deep knee bends, prone presses, and abdominal raises for the regions of the body "heavily taxed by the rigid army life." Edwards suggested that the exercises must be progressive and, closely following the progression recommended by Bob Hoffman and other weight-training advocates, directed readers to increase the weight once ten repetitions could be performed.[13]

In March 1941 Wilbur McCandless of the Saint Paul (Minnesota) YMCA also alluded to a soft life that necessitated strength training. "Modern civilization as a rule does not demand vigorous physical activity. Quite generally, therefore, we are deprived of the opportunity of developing a reserve of vitality and strength which is so valuable in times of physical and mental crisis." McCandless went on to dispute the idea that strength training would damage the heart and advocated "progressive weight lifting" that worked the muscles to near their capacity.[14] He advised the lifter to choose a weight that could be lifted without undue strain for eight to twelve repetitions for the arms and fourteen to twenty for the trunk. Once the maximal number was performed, the weight was increased and the repetitions decreased accordingly.

The utility of heavy strength training was not fully embraced, however, until the latter stages of World War II, as large numbers of injured soldiers began to overwhelm military hospitals. The backlog was created by the combined effects of the sheer number of fighting men involved in the war effort, advances in surgery and medicine that allowed more men to survive increasingly severe injuries, and rehabilitation protocols that often required six to nine months of postoperative therapy.[15] Rehabilitative programs at the time emphasized rest and incorporated a high number of repetitions with little weight when they called for resistive exercise.[16] According to army physical therapist Dorothy Hoag, "good results have been obtained [following that program], usually over a long period of time, but often the patient left the hospital with considerably less muscle bulk in the affected extremity than in the normal one."[17] The program with light weights was a cautious, seemingly commonsense approach: in a system already taxed by debility, further stress should be minimized. This idea was rooted in first-law notions of a depletion of vitality.

For example, the 1923 edition of R. Tait McKenzie's *Exercise in Education and Medicine* warned that "if the entire muscular system be developed to its physiological limit a very considerable drain on vitality is inevitable."[18] In light of this, in the 1917 edition he had advised that exercises should include maximum contractions but "should never be continued beyond the point of moderate fatigue, and some of them should be given with resistance," though this advice was dropped by the 1923 edition. Most exercises, however, were range-of-motion and isometric contractions performed up to twenty-three times, three times daily.[19] A program that includes such little resistance and so many repetitions is more likely to produce muscular endurance than strength or hypertrophy.

Similarly, *Physical Therapeutic Technic* (1932) by Frank Butler Granger, who once served as director of physical therapy for the US Army, included only the most cursory discussion of therapeutic exercise. The vast majority of the text was focused on therapeutic modalities such as electrical stimulating currents, hydrotherapy, and diathermy. When muscle contractions were discussed, they were often electrically induced, presumably to limit the pain caused by volitional muscle contraction. Butler warned practitioners that, "in all treatment, care should be taken not to overtire weakened muscles."[20] In the early 1940s physicians still warned that asking patients to lift weights that were too heavy could result in "chronic sprains," especially in the knees.[21] As a result of these protocols, patients gained little strength and tended to be reinjured when they were advanced to the next phase of their rehabilitation—games.[22] To solve this problem, "the literature was thoroughly combed; the brains of the best visiting dignitaries, who were many, were picked dry; with disappointing results."[23]

Thus a backlog of patients welcomed Dr. Thomas DeLorme at Chicago's Gardiner General Hospital when he began there in February 1944. By the time he joined the army, DeLorme had been an avid weight trainer for many years. As a teen he had been stricken with rheumatic fever, a bacterial infection that could lead to permanent heart damage.[24] After proffering the diagnosis, the physician attending him recommended only rest and advised that he avoid strenuous activity in perpetuity. While he lay wasting away in bed, DeLorme read books on medicine and Bob Hoffman's *Strength & Health* magazine. He became convinced that he would "prove the medicos wrong" by building a strong, powerful and healthy body through weight training.[25] To that end, DeLorme crafted his own weight set from train wheels and other small mechanical parts that he was able to scrounge. He lifted the makeshift weight set regularly and even competed in weightlifting contests, registering a personal-best 250-pound clean and jerk. By the age of twenty-two he had deadlifted 503 pounds and even performed a lifting demonstration at half-time of a University of Alabama football game, raising or deadlifting the front end of a truck off the ground.[26] After completing his medical degree at New York University, DeLorme joined the army in January 1944.[27]

Shortly after his arrival at Gardiner, DeLorme ran into Sgt. Thaddeus Kawalek, who had suffered a noncombat knee injury. Kawalek had also lifted weights extensively before the war, which he credited with allowing him to throw the shot, wrestle, and run track in college. During their conversations the men discussed their histories with strength training, causing DeLorme to speculate that a lack of strength was a major factor in the length of convalescence and frequent recurrence of injury. After mulling over DeLorme's theory, Kawalek volunteered to let DeLorme try a program of heavy resistance exercises on his injured knee. The improvised program of heavy knee extensions with a weighted iron boot and a series of lighter pulley exercises proved successful, as Kawalek recovered more quickly than typical Gardiner patients and had better function.[28]

Shortly thereafter, a paratrooper from Louisiana sought DeLorme's help. The patient, Walter Easley, had torn both the anterior cruciate and medial (tibial) collateral ligaments in one of his knees during an awkward landing from a parachute jump. Easley had been at Gardiner for six months but still had swelling and pain in the knee after following the standard rehabilitation protocol. A farmer by trade who had been told he might have to wear a restrictive brace to stabilize the knee for the remainder of his life, Easley came to DeLorme out of desperation. DeLorme noted Easley's still severely atrophied quadriceps muscles and offered him the opportunity to perform a program of heavy knee extension and flexion exercises. The program was a sort of middle ground between the standard protocols and the programs employed by competitive lifters. DeLorme supervised Easley as he performed seven sets of ten repetitions with the maximum weight he could lift for each set. In less than a month the size of the paratrooper's quadriceps had increased substantially, as had the function of the knee. The pain and swelling had resolved and "for all activities, even 'jitterbugging,' the knee was normal."[29]

The tremendous gains made by Kawalek and Easley were noted both by other patients and by DeLorme's commanding officer, Col. John Hall. The clamor of patients wanting to try the new program allowed DeLorme to set up a true clinical trial of his method. The findings of that trial were published in a 1945 article in the *Journal of Bone and Joint Surgery*. The article discussed the application of the "seven sets of ten" protocol to a variety of knee injuries, including sprains, fractures of the femur or patella, and meniscus injuries. The cases of instability caused by ligament sprains produced the most dramatic results, with patients acquiring sufficient stability even to return to demanding sports. Though less dramatically, patients with a variety of other knee injuries also improved more than their counterparts who performed the standard protocol. DeLorme asserted that the weakness of the standard protocol was its focus on muscular endurance rather than power. The heavy resistance program induced hypertrophy, which was well known at the time to be associated with strength. Moreover, since hypertrophy was related to the loading of the muscle, it was important that muscles be exercised intensely. As DeLorme put it, "in order to obtain rapid hypertrophy in weakened, atrophied muscle, the muscle should be subjected to strenuous exercise and, at regular intervals, to the point of maximum exertion."[30] DeLorme reiterated this point the following year in an article in the *Archives of Physical Medicine*, saying that, "on the basis of 300 cases in which this program of exercise was used, I firmly believe that even extremely atrophied muscles should exert their maximum effort at regular intervals."[31]

News of the success of the new heavy resistance program spread quickly. Medical doctor E. H. Anderson explained late in 1946 that since the publication of DeLorme's "brilliant" article "the answer to the knee problem has been solved, and all our previous mistakes have become crystal clear."[32] Other investigators tested the high-intensity method and found similar impressive results including doubling of strength in as little as four weeks.[33] In late 1945 representatives of the Surgeon's General Office issued an order for all therapists to use the new protocol with their orthopedic patients, with naval hospitals quickly following suit.[34] DeLorme's method was regarded as so significant that he was awarded the army's Legion of Merit award.[35]

Thomas DeLorme left Gardiner hospital on August 28, 1945, but continued to publish important articles on strength training into the early 1950s, when his research interests shifted to polio and then to arm and spine injuries and the survivability of amputated limbs.[36] His strength-training articles included "Technics of Progressive Resistance Exercise" (PRE) in 1948, in which weight training was called "progressive resistance" for the first time and a new "blueprint" for training was described. The new program called for only three sets of ten repetitions, with 50, 75, and 100 percent of an individual's ten-repetition maximum (10RM) lifted in each set, respectively. The change was made because fewer sets were more conducive to lifting a heavier weight, thereby producing more extensive and rapid hypertrophy than in the seven-set program. Additionally, the name was changed to reflect the idea that muscles must simply be increasingly challenged, not required to lift a weight that was "heavy."[37]

The progressive resistance program was also applied to polio patients with good results.[38] In a 1949 article J. Roswell Gallagher and DeLorme reported on the gains made by applying the PRE program to adolescents with knee, lower back, or shoulder injuries.[39] The description of the twenty-five knee patients included six case reports about the injuries sustained and their previous treatments. Half of the patients had been told simply to rest, in spite of their significant injuries, which compromised the stability of the joint. Those who were given exercises were typically prescribed only quad-setting and straight leg raises, both of which involved isometric contractions unlikely to induce significant hypertrophy or strength in the injured limb. Several of the boys had attempted to return to sports only to reinjure the previously damaged knee. The PRE protocol for this study included eight weeks of strength training on knee extension and a combination knee and hip extension exercise. At the end of the program the boys reported much more confidence in the stability of their knees and in a six-month follow-up had not incurred additional knee injuries in spite of their return to athletic competition. As a result, DeLorme and Gallagher emphasized the importance of strength in injury prevention as well as rehabilitation. Moreover, they pointed out that stronger muscles would fatigue later because each individual contraction represented a lower percentage of the muscle's maximum capacity.

The same observation had been made by C. H. McCloy in *Physical Educator* the previous year. McCloy was an influential physical educator who had served as president of the American Association for Health and Physical Education and would be a charter member of the American College of Sports Medicine (ACSM).[40] Early in his career McCloy had not been one of weight training's detractors, but he had not been particularly interested in the activity either, at least not in barbell training.[41] As a child growing up in western North Dakota in the late 1800s, McCloy was called a variety of unflattering nicknames by classmates, including Pipe-Stems, Spindleshanks, and Splinters, due to his slight build. The unflattering monikers made him self-conscious about his undersized frame and inspired a desire to learn more about physical training. On train trips through Minneapolis in his early teens, McCloy purchased copies of Macfadden's *Physical Culture* magazines and a book by A. G. Spalding on track and field. In short order he was running through the hills around his home and tossing rocks, which served as stand-ins for shot. The young McCloy also ordered dumbbells, Indian clubs, a punching bag, and trapeze rings through the hardware store owned by his family and transformed his attic into a mini-gymnasium.[42] "At age fifteen," McCloy recalled, "I had decided to become a physical educator."[43]

McCloy went on to earn both his bachelor's and master's degrees from Marietta (Ohio) College. He then worked for the YMCA in various capacities, from physical director to director of physical education, earned a physical education certificate from one of Dudley Sargent's summer courses, and spent thirteen years in China directing teacher education. In 1930 he was hired as a research associate professor at the University of Iowa (at the time the State University of Iowa), where he specialized in physical education and anthropometry and spent the rest of his career. Coinciding with his academic appointment, McCloy earned his PhD in physical education at Columbia University in 1932.[44]

During World War II a naval pre-flight school moved into the field house at the University of Iowa, where McCloy was also engaged as a consultant for the War Department on matters related to physical fitness training and testing. McCloy's students watched as the servicemen lifted weights and inquired whether he thought it would be bad for athletes. Not familiar with the impact of weight training on sport performance, McCloy sought out academic literature on the subject and quickly found that there was "almost nothing." McCloy could not accept popular literature as scientific evidence, so he decided that experimentation was necessary. Like A. V. Hill and other exercise scientists, McCloy used himself as a test subject, reasoning that if he became "muscle-bound," it would not hamper his athletic prospects, as he was already fifty-five years old. Quite the contrary: after his training program McCloy found that he was stronger than he had been at twenty-one, using the same tests, and no slower than when he had initiated his training.[45]

The experiment led McCloy to encourage several master's theses on the effects of strength training. McCloy's 1948 "Endurance" article was heavily cited due to his observation, like DeLorme's, that a muscle made stronger by strength training must exert a lower percentage of its force with each contraction, enabling it to work for longer periods before fatiguing. As such, he recommended, "it would seem wise for physical educators to promote the development of more than 'just enough' strength."[46] In order to develop significant strength, McCloy advocated barbell training: "contrary to popular physical education opinion, exercises such as pull-ups, push-ups, sit-ups and squat jumps, and some of the stiffer callisthenic drills do not develop really large amounts of strength."[47]

Graduate students at the University of Iowa in the late 1940s and early 1950s, thanks to McCloy's influence, became keenly interested in the production of strength and its effect on athletic performance. Edward Chui's 1948 master's thesis compared the effects on muscle power of a total-body strength-training program, using each individual's eight- to twelve-repetition maximum, with the traditional physical education program required at the University of Iowa. Chui's introduction specifically mentioned the belief that strength training would produce "muscle boundness," although there was "no scientific evidence" to support that belief. Muscular power was measured by performance on vertical and broad jumps, shot-put throws, and a sixty-yard dash. The results showed that the weight-trained group consistently increased power output, while the physical education group did not.[48]

Similarly, the introduction to Edward Capen's work mentioned the claims of Hoffman, the notions of deleterious effects of strength training, and the lack of scientific studies to validate either position. Capen's study compared the effects on muscular strength, endurance, power, and cardiorespiratory endurance of a total-body weight-training course with those of a conditioning course that included sprints, bodyweight exercises, and gymnastics. The weight-trained group excelled, scoring better than the conditioning group in all of the performance measures, leading Capen to conclude that strength training likely did not result in muscular tightness or reduce speed.[49]

The master's thesis of Bernard Walters in 1949 examined the effects on muscular strength and endurance of performing a set of ten to twelve repetitions or a set of twenty to twenty-two repetitions. Walters found that the lower-repetition, higher-intensity program was more effective at producing both muscular strength and endurance.[50] Clayton Henry compared DeLorme's PRE method to a slightly altered variation calling for the use of 10RM for one set of ten, one set to fatigue, and a third set utilizing 75 percent of 10RM for twenty repetitions. No difference was found between the two methods in the development of strength.[51] Everett Faulkner tested the effects of altering the order of the sets in the PRE program, performing the first set with 50 percent 10RM, the second with 100 percent, and the final set with 75 percent. The results were similar, regardless of the order of the sets.[52] William Teufel compared the PRE program with five sets of ten repetitions at 10RM and found that DeLorme's program produced better strength gains.[53]

In addition to the growing research interest in strength training, physical educators and medical doctors increasingly came to the defense of weights by the late 1940s. For his part, Arthur Steinhaus began to advocate strength training that was "much harder" than required by daily activities, although only for men.[54] John Thune, physical director of the central Oakland (California) YMCA, disputed the idea that strength training was bad for athletes, noting that "some weight men have the finest bodily flexibility I have ever seen."[55] D. E. Strain, physical director at the Winnipeg (Canada) YMCA, documented an increase in membership of the bodybuilding group at his branch from 20 to 127 lifters between 1943 and 1945. Strain went on to describe the program followed by the club, which utilized the same progression scheme advocated by Hoffman.[56]

Physician J. L. Rudd authored two 1949 articles in the *Journal of Physical Education* that defended weight training. The first lamented the "loose talk" about lifting on the part of "empiricists, theorists, and not infrequently by faddists." In spite of all of the unfounded theories on the subject, Rudd assured readers that muscle-boundness need not develop if knowledge of the muscles and methods of proper development were utilized. Though he was an advocate of strength training, Rudd mocked the stories of Hoffman and others who claimed that weights had allowed them to overcome a physician's prognosis that they had little time to live. "It appears that such a prognosis lengthens the life of the patient and shortens the life of the doctor," he joked.[57] Rudd's second article asserted that weight training was no more injurious than football, basketball, or running and specifically cited DeLorme's work as evidence for its utility even in the infirm.[58]

Similarly, medical doctor Joseph Wolffe published two journal articles in 1949 refuting the existence of athlete's heart. Wolffe and his co-authors suggested that no relationship was observed between sport participation and an increased risk of heart disease. They suggested that the term caught on when doctors "guess-o-metrically" recorded heart size by auscultation and percussion and that it was a relic from the time when doctors treated all heart conditions with "the three Rs: rest, more rest, and more rest."[59]

As heavy strength training gained legitimacy in the eyes of the medical and physical education communities, competitive American weightlifting was enjoying its "Golden Age."[60] Owing in part to the devastation throughout Europe following the war, the United States won the World Championships every year between 1946 and 1952 with the exception of 1949, which was won by Egypt.[61] In their first foray into international competition in 1946 a full Russian team of ten men was bested by a short-handed American team consisting of only six lifters.[62] So embarrassed were the Russians by this defeat that they "bought a duplicate [trophy] from a Parisian silversmith to take home as proof of their 'victory.'"[63] The Russians did not compete in the World Championships again until 1950 and also declined to enter a team, instead sending observers for the 1948 London Olympics.[64]

Though the initial meetings had gone well for the Americans, the Soviets started to allocate significant resources toward domination of international athletics shortly after the end of the war.[65] While the Soviets initially expressed reticence about involvement in internationally competitive athletics and disliked the class implications of amateur athletics, the struggle against the United States to gain spheres of influence following the war caused them to reevaluate the utility of sports.[66] In the Cold War sports became "a weapon in the fight for peace" in the words of Peter Soboleve, secretary-general of the Russian Olympic Committee in the early 1950s.[67] One former medical advisor for the Soviet All-Union Physical Culture Council commented that victories on the athletic fields were seen as propaganda not only for foreign audiences but for domestic ones as well. "The average Russian thinks 'If Dinamo [Soviet sport society] can beat a French team, obviously the French have even less bread and meat than we do,'" he explained, adding that "this is exactly what the Soviets wish people to think as a sort of justification for their hunger and a consolation for the evils of the system."[68] To that end, the Soviets began offering cash incentives in late 1945 for the top three places at national championship meets as well as broken records.[69] The Soviet government also established "sport schools" to facilitate the training of promising young talent.[70] After receiving pressure against their monetary inducements for athletic performance, the government officially awarded medals instead of cash.

In another step taken to make it appear that they were abiding by the formal code of amateurism, "proficient sportsmen" were assigned one of three jobs: "student, serviceman, or physical education instructor, under the sponsorship of a trade union or other (such as the army) sports society."[71] The assigned employment status allowed the athletes to train as de facto professionals, without actually needing to perform any job duties, and allowed the Soviet sports program to maintain a façade of amateurism. In addition to recruiting and training athletes beginning in childhood, the government sponsored research on training programs and athletic performance and employed researchers who worked "hand-in-hand" with sport coaches.[72] Like athletes, coaches were incentivized to produce top performances and garnered awards corresponding to the achievements of athletes under their tutelage.[73] This concerted effort at achieving dominance in international sport would begin to pay off when Russia reentered the world athletic stage in 1952.

THE 1950S: INVESTIGATING THE CHARGES AGAINST WEIGHT TRAINING

While the Soviets focused on melding sport training and research, there was no such connection in the United States. According to sport historian Nicholas Bourne, American coaches "often had to *extrapolate* how certain conditions would affect training from articles on military fitness or medical rehabilitation," which caused significant lag time between discoveries that could enhance sport performance and their actual implementation in sport programs. Researchers were only beginning to disprove the criticisms of weight training by 1950. Professional journals read largely by coaches and physical educators still featured articles on sport training that did not suggest weight training.[74]

As an example, Dale Lewis's 1950 article on conditioning for collegiate tennis emphasized the importance of training outside of the playing season but recommended only calisthenics and running to prepare for playing.[75] Evelyn Loewendahl, writing that same year, highlighted the importance of strength of the lower leg musculature in the powerful takeoff required for basketball, hockey, and track, among others. In order to condition the muscles to produce that power, however, Loewendahl recommended only bodyweight exercises or running and walking barefoot in sand or grass.[76] In May 1950 Edward Capen published the results of his thesis in *Research*

Quarterly, showing that weights increased muscular strength, power, and endurance.[77] Edward Chui's findings of increased power with strength training were published in the same journal in October.[78] Thomas DeLorme continued to emphasize that "passive and light resistance exercises are of little or no value" in maximizing muscle strength and hypertrophy. George Wackenhut reemphasized that training produced a stronger heart not a pathological one, though he did allege that strength training actually did not tax the heart enough.[79]

As researchers began to investigate the charges against weight training more systematically, mainstream interest in strength in the United States increased. The warnings about soft living and weak citizens appeared not to come to fruition during World War II, as American soldiers held their own in barbaric hand-to-hand combat. When the North Korean forces invaded South Korea, however, the fear of a citizenry made soft by decadence returned to the fore as the ill-prepared and poorly equipped American forces were nearly pushed off the peninsula by Communist forces.[80] The poor performance of American troops in the early stages of the Korean War seemed to substantiate the softness of the soldiers and those eligible to serve. To make matters worse, writer Eugene Kinkaid reported that one-third of American prisoners of war had collaborated with the enemy in some way. In addition, more than 38 percent of Americans who were taken prisoner died during the war, more than in any previous conflict, leading to the charge that Americans were both physically and mentally soft.[81]

The physical weakness of American children was confirmed in a 1953 study by Hans Kraus and Ruth Hirschland. The researchers administered a series of flexibility and strength tests that included examination of back and abdominal muscular endurance and hamstring and back flexibility. Kraus and Hirschland noted that nearly 57 percent of American children between the ages of six and nineteen years failed at least one of the tests, while only 8 percent of European children did. The reason for this disparity, they asserted, was that "European children do not have the benefit of a highly mechanized society."[82] Concern over the fitness of American youth reached President Dwight Eisenhower, who established the President's Council on Youth Fitness in 1956. It had little funding but maintained a high media presence in the late 1950s and early 1960s, working to portray fitness as a civic duty of children and their parents.[83]

In this context researchers sought to determine the safety and efficacy of strength training. One of the most important studies of the early 1950s was published in the May 1951 issue of *Research Quarterly*. The frequently cited study by William Zorbas and Peter Karpovich investigated the impact of strength training on the speed of limb movement.[84] Karpovich undertook this study, and follow-up strength research, due to the efforts of Fraysher Ferguson, the undergraduate student quoted earlier. In 1940 Ferguson had the opportunity to organize a student assembly at Springfield College, which he audaciously used to invite Bob Hoffman, "Mr. America" John Grimek, and World Weightlifting Champion John Davis to give an exhibition on weight training. Karpovich had been a staunch member of the "anti-weight-training camp," telling a reporter in February 1940 that it was important "to fight these muscle builders," who were no better than "quacks" and "faddists," and that some of them apparently believed that heavy training could do "anything—just develop big muscles and . . . [even] all your illness will go [away]."[85] As Jan and Terry Todd documented, after a truly historic demonstration in which Grimek demonstrated his flexibility by doing a full split and Davis did a back flip holding a pair of fifty-pound dumbbells, Karpovich had a "conversion" experience and began investigating the concept of muscle-binding through scientific research.[86]

In the article that he co-authored with William Zorbas, Karpovich noted, as Chui had, that coaches and physical educators often believed that strength training would slow the athlete down, while barbell enthusiasts claimed the opposite: neither had any scientific proof for their claim. Their study compared the speed of 300 nonweightlifters to 300 men who had lifted for at least six months and were still actively doing so. In order to assess speed of movement, each group was asked to attempt two trials of twenty-four clockwise revolutions with an arm crank. Time to complete the revolutions was recorded: the weightlifters turned out to be, on average, nearly two-tenths of a second faster. Zorbas and Karpovich concluded that "the findings of this study appear contrary to the common opinion of coaches, trainers, and others associated with physical education who believe that weight lifting will slow down the athlete."[87]

Earlier in the same year Karpovich had published a study on the incidence of injuries suffered by weightlifters. The impetus for the study was the "common belief among physical educators and physicians that weightlifting is a harmful sport." Karpovich remarked that he had shared this belief until very recently. Data for his study included surveys of over 31,702 participants in regular but not necessarily competitive weightlifting. Those surveyed reported no cases of injury to the heart, and the prevalence of hernias was actually lower than the population average. The most frequently cited injuries were bruises and muscle strains, which led Karpovich to conclude that "weight lifting is a safe sport."[88]

An important text by Thomas DeLorme and Arthur Watkins, *Progressive*

Resistance Exercise: Technic and Medical Application, intended for use by physicians and physical therapists, was also published in 1951. In the foreword the chief of the orthopedic department at Massachusetts General Hospital, Joseph Barr, described the significance of their work: rehabilitation had been transformed from an art into a system that rested on a "sound physiological basis."[89] Lawrence Morehouse and John Cooper's *Kinesiology* was targeted toward physical educators and, like DeLorme's work, emphasized the importance of overload. Morehouse and Cooper stressed that simply practicing a sport would have little effect on maximizing the strength or endurance that would allow for optimal performance in the sport. Instead of repetitive practice, the coach must find a way to incorporate overload, whether through weighted implements or specific sprint or endurance training. The physical education professors from the University of Southern California also instructed readers that specific sport skills had little crossover between sports. To maximize performance, then, athletes needed to emphasize both the movements and physiological systems required by the primary sport.[90]

Research into the charges against weight training continued appearing in physical education journals, most notably *Research Quarterly*, throughout the 1950s. Bruce Wilkin found in 1952 that weight training did not result in decreased speed of arm movement on an apparatus similar to the one employed by Zorbas and Karpovich. It is important to note, however, that he also concluded that weight training did not result in any faster movement in untrained college students than did a semester-long swimming or golf class.[91] DeLorme also investigated the effect of the PRE program on muscle contraction time, saying that the work was of interest to coaches and trainers who believed that "heavy exercise 'slows down,' 'throws timing off,' and makes athletes 'muscle bound.'" After already having shown that the PRE program produced an increase in range of motion in a 1950 study, he was able to demonstrate that the program did not adversely affect the speed of contraction.[92] Physical educators John Masley, Ara Hairabedian, and Donald Donaldson investigated the effects of six weeks of strength training on muscular speed and coordination. Speed was assessed using the same protocol as in the Zorbas and Karpovich study, while muscular coordination was measured by accuracy of hitting a target with a fencing foil. After six weeks of training, the members of the group that lifted weights had increased both their speed of movement and coordination more than a group that had participated in a volleyball course.[93]

Physiologist Philip Rasch, however, was unable to establish a relationship between arm strength and speed of movement. It is important to note that he measured strength by using a dynamometer.[94] Due to different motor recruitment patterns, studies in the 1950s and 1960s that compared strength measured isometrically with speed of movement often found no relationship. Studies that examined the association between isotonic strength and speed of movement typically concluded that the two were related.

Based on the favorable results of previous studies in using weight training to improve speed and power, University of Iowa graduate student Richard Garth was able to convince athletic administrators to allow him to implement a strength program for the basketball team prior to the 1954–1955 season as part of his research for his master's thesis. The Hawkeyes had finished second in the Big Ten conference in 1953–1954 and were looking to compete for the title. Garth put the players through a series of exercises that included walking lunges, the clean and press, shoulder raises, and arm curls for six weeks prior to the season. The players were 15 to 25 percent stronger after the completion of the program, and their vertical jump increased an average of two and two-thirds inches. The Hawkeyes went on to win the Big Ten title that year and continued their weight training prior to the 1955–1956 season, when they again were conference champions.[95] Another 1954 master's thesis evaluated the effect of six weeks of upper-body strength training on fine motor skills, including picking up toothpicks, assembling nuts and bolts, threading small beads, and placing washers on pegs. At the end of his study Frank Buckiewicz concluded that the weight program improved grip strength and performance of the fine motor tasks.[96]

Owing largely to the validity of strength training indicated by DeLorme's work, its techniques received closer examination by the medical community in a 1954 article in the *British Medical Journal*. University of Sheffield anatomy researcher I. J. MacQueen detailed the typical programs performed by those interested in maximizing strength or hypertrophy. The "bulk" program, he noted, involved more sets and higher repetitions than the power program, which entailed the use of maximal weights and lower repetitions. Both programs nonetheless had their place in rehabilitation, as the muscles could only regain their former strength if they returned to their preinjury size, and strength could only be maximized with heavy training. Importantly, MacQueen mentioned almost in passing that weight training improves performance in other sports and that the nations that had performed the best at the most recent Olympic Games were those that "widely and intensely" practiced strength training.[97]

In 1955 renowned physical educator James Counsilman posed a question in the *Journal of Health, Physical Education, and Recreation*: "Does weight training belong in the program?" "Most persons will readily agree that weight training is the fastest way to build strength and muscle size," Counsilman explained, adding that "the question seems to be whether the person can use these muscles as well." To address the issue of muscle-binding, Counsilman cited the recently published literature on strength training as well as an investigation that he had performed at Cortland (New York) State Teachers' College. Weightlifters including Jim Parks (1952 "Mr. America") proved to be above average in flexibility. Furthermore, he cited the work of Zorbas and Karpovich, Chui, Capen, and Wilkin to prove that strength training did not result in decreased speed of movement and also mentioned DeLorme's work on atrophied muscles. In conclusion, Counsilman asserted that there was "little evidence to show that weight training causes muscle boundness or slows the athlete." As a result, "weight training has a place in the physical education program."[98]

While most of the research in the mid- to late 1950s was still focused on determining whether weight training had any deleterious effects, some researchers began to explore the best method to maximize strength, a trend that would pick up in the 1960s. A study by Edward Capen in 1956 attempted to determine the optimal number of sets and repetitions to produce strength gains. His experimental groups included participants doing one to three sets performed with loads of one to eight repetition maximums with groups further subdivided into those lifting three or five times weekly. Capen concluded that heavier loads (five repetition maximum or less) performed three times weekly appeared to optimize strength gains.[99]

Other researchers were not satisfied that the case could be closed on the possibility of detrimental effects of weight training. Benjamin Massey and Norman Chaudet studied the effects of six months of strength training on muscular size, strength, and flexibility. Their results showed that, while both strength and size of the muscles had improved, range of motion was not reduced.[100] A 1957 literature review by the University of Michigan's Paul Hunsicker and George Greey concluded that increased strength did not necessarily slow down the motion of the joint.[101] Ivan Kusinitz and Clifford Keeney compared the effects of a two-month weight training program to those produced by an equivalent period in a regular physical education class. The groups were evaluated before and after for muscular size, strength, endurance, and flexibility as well as overall agility and cardiorespiratory endurance. While both groups improved after the training, the weight-trained boys exceeded the physical education group in every testing category. Additionally, medical examination showed that the members of the weight group did not experience any negative health consequences as a result of their training.[102]

A similar study performed by Sidney Calvin on high school boys in Baltimore showed that four months of weight training not only did not decrease coordination but actually appeared to enhance it when compared to the results of a standard physical education program. Calvin commented that, in spite of weight training's "controversial" standing, it was becoming increasingly popular and more prevalent as a conditioning tool for other sports by "leading universities and numerous high schools."[103] Researchers Hugh Thompson and G. Alan Stull substantiated this claim by examining the effect on sprint swim performance of a combination of swimming and weight training or either performed in isolation. Of the groups tested, the exclusively weight-trained group was the only one that did not show an improved performance. The rest of the groups improved similarly, which included the combination swim and strength-training group.[104]

In *Physical Educator* Stratton Caldwell cited the work of Steinhaus, Capen, Morehouse and Cooper, and Counsilman as he asserted that strength training should enhance performance in track and field. Connecting the dots, he pointed out that muscular strength was related to muscular size and speed was dependent upon the ability to produce force, so an "increase in strength should bring about an increase in speed."[105] YMCA program director Rembert Garris more explicitly refuted the idea of muscle-binding, saying the "misconception is formed by persons who know nothing about sport." Garris, like Hoffman and Weider, discussed successful athletes, such as Frank Stranahan and Bob Richards, who trained with weights as validation for his claim. He also asserted that Bud Wilkinson, head football coach at the University of Oklahoma, had "required bar bell exercises for his football team for years." Regardless of one's opinion on muscle-binding he suggested that "weightlifting is taking the country by storm" as evidenced by the dramatic rise in participation in the activity at several YMCAs in the Carolinas.[106] Writing in *Physical Educator*, F. A. Schmidt reaffirmed that exercise made the heart stronger and more efficient. Admonitions to stay away from sports or exercise were "well-intended but wholly unfounded warnings."[107]

The middle and late 1950s also saw the publication of three important texts regarding the application of strength training to sport. *Weight Training in Athletics*, authored by Jim Murray and Peter Karpovich, refuted the existence of the muscle-bound condition and cited the different adaptations of endurance and strength training as a rationale for the necessity of training programs specific to the demands of a particular sport. They pointed out a common fallacy in the muscle-bound argument: when discussing the impact of weights on speed and flexibility, men of the heavyweight classes were most commonly used as examples of potential negative effects of strength training.

Dr. Karpovich told of how he had come to believe in muscle-binding, saying that he had been told as a boy that a professional wrestler or strongman could not reach between his shoulder blades to scratch and had to pay a boy pennies to do his scratching for him. After seeing champion lifters and physique stars John Davis and John Grimek perform feats of strength and agility at Springfield College in the spring of 1940, however, his mind was changed. "Both men had huge muscles and therefore should have been muscle-bound," Karpovich explained, "but they were like the bumblebee who flies, although expert aviation engineers have proved mathematically that a bumblebee cannot fly."[108] After reaffirming the positive adaptations made to strength training and emphasizing the importance of overload in eliciting those adaptations, the text concluded with a series of sport-specific strength programs. In the preface to the football program Murray pointed out the logical inconsistency of coaches who panned weight training:

> There are probably many football coaches who insist that their players not use weight training, because to work against heavy resistance would make their charges "muscle-bound." These same coaches are probably the ones who work their boys hardest on the charging sled, with their heaviest line coach along for the ride. No, they wouldn't want their men practicing resistance exercises![109]

Physical educators Benjamin Massey, Harold Freeman, Frank Manson, and Janet Wessel were no less dismissive in their assessment of muscle-binding, which they described as a prejudice that resulted from ignorance.[110] They pointed to the work of Karpovich, Capen, Chui, Masley, Murray, Wilkin, and others as evidence that no such condition could be shown to exist. More importantly, Massey and his co-authors described eight principles of athletic conditioning that are still largely adhered to in designing weight programs for sports, including that a conditioning program should be based on an analysis of the sport, should be tailored to the demands of that sport, should incorporate overload, and should be year-round. "A good conditioning program," they asserted, "like a suit, must be tailored to the situation."[111] Peter Karpovich's *Physiology of Muscular Exercise*, also published in 1959, included less applied information regarding strength training than found in his earlier text co-authored with Murray. It did go into more detail, however, regarding specific adaptations to different training stimuli, including muscular hypertrophy, capillarization, changes in intramuscular fuel stores, and motor unit recruitment with training.[112]

At the close of the 1950s, then, the opinion of most scientific researchers was nearly unanimous that weight training did not decrease range of motion, coordination, or muscle contraction time. For their part, coaches were slow to embrace this information. A primary reason for this was that few would have taken the time to read journals like *Research Quarterly* and people probably had not been exposed to the new consensus unless they were made aware of it during their college coursework. Additionally, since the late nineteenth century coaches had been creating their own programs based on personal experience and discussions with other coaches. With no governmental or sport authority to sponsor or translate research, many coaches viewed their profession as much as an art as a science.[113] The reticence to embrace the new research was exemplified in a farcical 1958 article for *Physical Educator*. Walter Kroll explained that "after coaching for a number of years I thought I was doing a pretty good job in my chosen profession." He added that "after returning to do advanced graduate work, I saw the error of my ways." Kroll then told a fanciful story in which he worked a host of scientific terminology into a half-time speech to a basketball team. After his jargon-laced pep talk, Kroll declared that he now understood the true meaning of the relationship between science and philosophy. He ended by saying: "P.S. Any school needing such a coach please contact me. I lost my job."[114]

The appearance of research-based articles examining strength training in the most important academic journals of the day had a profound impact. However, the general public learned about most of these new findings through muscle magazines. The findings of DeLorme's research, for example, were featured in a 1949 *Muscle Power* article authored by Philip Rasch, who made his own significant contributions to the study of strength. Rasch discussed both the unconventionality and effectiveness of DeLorme's approach, noting that it had been validated by several other studies. He wrote with obvious satisfaction that "this must bring a wry smile to the older weight trainers," adding: "For the last quarter of a century, we have been trying to pound these exact facts into the medical fraternity . . . at long last the medical profession has caught up with the weight trainers."[115] DeLorme was also the subject of a lengthy biographical profile in *Strength & Health* in 1959.[116]

Karpovich's research was discussed and applauded in an article by "Mr. America" George Eiferman. After citing weight-trained athletic champions, including Frank Stranahan and Mickey Mantle, Eiferman noted that Karpovich "definitely proved that weight training in no way detracted from muscular speed or accuracy."[117] Some sport scientists were unafraid to submit their own articles to these popular magazines. Exercise scientist Jack Leighton, for example, refuted the muscle-bound hypothesis in "Are Weight Lifters Muscle Bound?" in *Strength & Health* in 1956. C. H. McCloy also wrote for *Strength & Health* under his own name, pointing out to men like Weider and Hoffman that they should not be upset that the scientific community had taken so long to understand what they had been preaching. McCloy explained that their lack of academic credentials allowed people to ignore their anecdotal evidence. But as America moved into the 1960s with this new group of academically trained advocates for strength training—McCloy, DeLorme, Karpovich, and Rasch—to help spread the message, not only was the popular muscle press validated, but the field of strength-training research itself continued to grow larger.[118]

THE 1960S: THE SPECIFICS OF STRENGTH AND APPLYING STRENGTH TO SPORT

The Russians, of course, did not share the reticence of Kroll's fictional coach or like-minded coaches in conflating sports and science. By 1960 the combination had produced dramatic results. The Soviets sent observers to the 1948 Olympic Games in London and made their Olympic debut at the 1952 Games in Helsinki, Finland. Though few of the Russian athletes had competed against world-class competition prior to the Helsinki Games, their inexperience was not reflected in the medal count. While they won only twenty-two gold medals to the United States' forty, the Soviets captured thirty silver medals and nineteen bronze, more than the Americans' nineteen and seventeen, respectively. According to one scoring system that allocated points for top six finishes, the Russians and Americans tied in their first Olympic contest.[119] In the 1956 Games in Melbourne, Australia, and the 1960 Games in Rome, Italy, the Russians proceeded to "trounce" the United States, in the words of an article in the *Saturday Evening Post.*[120]

At the Rome Games the two countries attempted to send a political message through their choice of flag-bearer for the opening ceremony. The United States chose Rafer Johnson, an African American decathlete who was the student-body president at the University of California–Los Angeles (UCLA). Johnson was the first African American to carry the American flag and lead the team into the stadium during an opening ceremony. He was respected and well-liked by his teammates, but his selection was due in part to the official desire to counteract propaganda from the Soviets about racial inequality in the United States.[121] The Russian delegation was headed by heavyweight lifter Yuri Vlasov, "a national hero in a culture that worshipped strength above other physical attributes." To underscore his tremendous strength, Vlasov carried the Soviet flag bearing the hammer and sickle around the track using one arm.[122]

The disappointing Olympic performances coupled with the losses in the early stages of the Korean War and the results of the physical ability tests administered by Kraus and Hirschland caused a great deal of concern among American policy makers.[123] In December 1960 John F. Kennedy specifically referenced the latter two factors, as well as a high rate of Selective Service rejections, warning that "softness on the part of individual citizens can help destroy the vitality of a nation."[124] Other allegations that Americans were "soft," following the poor Olympic showing, came from Arthur Daily at the *New York Times*, International Olympic Committee president Avery Brundage, and Australian Olympic miler Herb Elliott.[125] In the months before the 1964 Tokyo Games Robert Kennedy explicitly stated that "part of a nation's prestige in the cold war is won in the Olympic Games." He continued: "In this quadrennial conflict the U.S. has skidded steadily for 16 years."[126] As a result, Robert, like his brother John before him, called for a concerted effort to enhance youth fitness and athletic skill.

Physical educators and coaches who viewed their profession as much as an art as a science were shaken not only by the dominating performances of the Russians but also by two stinging criticisms about a lack of academic rigor in the early 1960s. The first and more damning criticism was leveled by James B. Conant, president of Harvard University, who shuttered the Harvard Fatigue Lab in 1946 after failing to see any value in it.[127] In 1961 Conant was hired by the Carnegie Foundation to evaluate teacher education in the United States. His 1963 book *The Education of American Teachers* contained a scathing indictment of physical education, which Conant said left him "far from impressed." He said that if he "wished to portray the education of teachers in the worst terms," he would "quote from some graduate courses in physical education." He closed by asserting that, to his mind, "a university should cancel graduate programs in this area."[128] Conant's assessment was buttressed by Franklin Henry, a physical educator at the University of California at Berkeley, who voiced doubt about the academic merit of many of the courses in the physical education curriculum at his school. In the face of this public criticism, physical educators and university administrators pushed for a reorganization of the field and more emphasis on scientific research. Strength training was one beneficiary of this new effort at "scientization" of physical education, as research on strength-training methodology blossomed in the 1960s.[129]

With consensus on the nonexistence of muscle-binding largely achieved, researchers in the 1960s shifted their attention to the application of strength training. The three primary themes of strength-training research in the 1960s were examining the effect of strength training on the speed of movement, comparing the effects of different strength-training programs, and applying strength training to sport preparation.

The focus on the effect of strength training upon speed was largely the result of studies that showed an inconsistent relationship between speed of movement and muscular strength. As previously discussed, the primary reason for this disparity was the method of measurement of muscular strength. Studies commonly employed a static measure of muscle strength with a necessarily dynamic measure of speed. Due to the different motor recruitment patterns and joint angles involved in isometric and concentric muscle actions, the relationship between strength and speed was often low. Follow-up studies by the same authors produced different results.[130] By altering the testing position from lying to standing or moving the measured joint to the beginning of its range of motion rather than the middle, researchers in the middle of the decade concluded that there was a relationship between muscular strength and speed of movement.[131] Physical educators Jim Whitley and Leon Smith concluded in 1966 that "it now seems quite apparent that, regardless of the type of strength increase program employed, a faster movement will be affected."[132] It seems that other researchers agreed that the relationship was apparent, as the interaction between strength and speed was simply a component of other studies, not the focus, in the latter part of the decade.

One of the most influential researchers with regard to the specific sets and repetitions to maximize strength was Richard Berger. He had been introduced to weight training by a high school friend, John Hagen, following their service as marines. The two men began to train together in an old chicken coop on the Hagen family farm, in order to prepare to try out for the Michigan State University football team. Berger made the team as a running back and continued to train with weights when football was out of season. Upon hearing that Berger had been seen lifting weights, head coach Clarence "Biggie" Munn advised him: "I don't want to hear about you doing any of that lifting. It's bad for you. I want you to get a summer job doing heavy construction work. That's what you need, not those weights."[133] Berger left the team after his second year for reasons unrelated to Munn's suggestion. He continued to lift weights and was an able competitor at the National Weightlifting Championships in the late 1950s and early 1960s.

Following completion of his master's degree at Michigan State and doctorate at the University of Illinois, Berger took a position at Texas Technological Institute in Lubbock, Texas, where he performed much of his research.[134] Using weight-training classes at Illinois and Texas Tech for his subjects, Berger put the men through a variety of programs that altered sets and repetitions to determine the optimal means of producing strength. Subjects performed one to three sets of two, six, or ten repetitions; single sets of two, four, six, eight, or ten repetitions; six sets with their two-repetition maximum or three sets with their ten-repetition maximum; or one repetition with various percentages of their one-repetition maximum.[135] The results of each program indicated that the most effective program for optimizing strength included multiple sets with between four and eight repetitions. Another study compared the effects of performing a set with a person's ten-repetition maximum to performing ten consecutive maximal contractions with a constantly decreasing load. Although it would be nearly impossible to implement such a protocol from a practical standpoint, the ten consecutive maximal contractions were found to be superior at maximizing strength.[136] Berger also studied the effects of isometric and isotonic strength programs on vertical jump, finding that isotonic programs were superior at improving jump height.[137] His other work in the 1960s included the creation of a formula to compare lifting ability between weightlifters in different weight classes, description and study of the effects of isometric training, and analysis of the relationship between static and dynamic leg strength and leg power.[138]

While Richard Berger was the most prolific researcher in the area of determining the programmatic specifics that would maximize strength gains, he was not the only researcher investigating the matter. Patrick O'Shea, an exercise physiologist and fellow competitive weightlifter, also examined the effect of different set and repetition plans on strength and found, like Berger, that multiple sets performed with five to six repetitions appeared to maximize strength.[139] Vermon Barney and Blauer Bangerter of Brigham Young University compared two iterations of DeLorme's PRE program with two groups performing a hypertrophy or strength program, respectively. The authors concluded that the PRE program that incorporated 50, 75, and 100 percent of an individual's ten repetition maximum (10RM) spread over three sets was superior for producing both hypertrophy and strength. The most significant aspect of their study, however, was the recommendation that "all athletic teams such as football, basketball, track, etc., could benefit greatly from specifically organized programs of PRE for increased performance and the prevention of athletic injuries."[140]

Another group of researchers from the University of British Columbia, led by J. D. Dennison, compared the effect of an eight-week program of isometric or isotonic exercises. While both increased muscular endurance and strength, isotonic exercises produced better results.[141] Two of the same researchers, M. L. Howell and W. R. Morford, performed a similar study the following year that yielded no significant differences in muscular endurance between the isotonic and isometric groups.[142] Jerry Ball, George Rich, and Earl Wallis found in 1964, as Berger had the previous year, that isometric training was not effective at improving vertical jump performance.[143] When comparing isometric to traditional isotonic or high-velocity isotonic training, Lynn McCraw and Stan Burnham of the University of Texas found that isometric and isotonic training produced similar strength gains, while repeated high-velocity contractions improved endurance.[144]

A final group of studies in the 1960s sought to examine the impact of strength training on sport performance more directly. Robert Campbell of Winona (Minnesota) State University studied the effects of strength training in the first or second half of the competitive season on muscular strength, endurance, and power. His subjects included collegiate football, basketball, and track athletes. The rationale for Campbell's study design was that coaches tended to utilize weight training in the preseason and then discontinue it once the season had started. He found, not surprisingly, that the group that trained early in the season and then stopped showed a decline in their fitness scores. As a result, Campbell stated that "weight training should be started well before the competitive season and continued throughout the season."[145]

Clayne Jensen of Utah State University investigated the impact of five different combinations of swimming and weight training on sprint swim times. He found no significant differences between the groups, who all improved their times.[146] Similarly, George Dintiman assessed the outcomes of different combinations of sprint, strength, and flexibility training on running speed, finding that the addition of strength and flexibility training increased sprint speed more than running alone.[147] John Alexander and his colleagues found that five weeks of isometric training increased the speed of both slap shots and wrist shots in collegiate hockey players.[148] Donald Brose and Dale Hanson utilized weighted baseballs and pulley weights to investigate the impact of overloaded pitching movements on throwing velocity. After six weeks of overload training, both groups improved throwing velocity with no decrease in accuracy.[149] Gordon Schultz analyzed the results of six different training programs on sprinting and jumping ability, shot-put distance, and a timed zigzag. The training programs included a combination of direct practice of the skills, weights, and sprinting or each in isolation. The results indicated that strength training only improved performance when combined with direct practice.[150] Weight training thus clearly had to be a component of a larger overall program in order to enhance performance.

Unfortunately for American athletes, especially Olympic athletes, a great deal of work had already been done in this area in the Soviet Union. Beginning in 1917 with the publication of the text *Olympic Sport* by Boris Kotov, Russian physical culturists initiated an exploration of year-round training for sport with differentiated phases.[151] In Kotov's case, training was broken into general, preparatory, and specific phases. This was followed by V. Gorinewsky's *Scientific Foundations of Training* in 1922 and Birsin's *The Basics of Training* in 1925, both of which presented ideas similar to those in the earlier work.[152] Grantyn's "Contents and General Foundations of Training Preparation" included a "transition" phase that called for training in sports other than one's primary specialty in order to develop performance components in other contexts. In 1949 N. G. Ozolin's *Training the Athlete* called for a differentiated program of training that took account of the competitive calendar and annual climate. The following year S. P. Letunow laid out the importance of individual characteristics of an athlete in *Reflections of the Systematic Formulation of Training*, arguing that one should account for achievement of specific performance parameters before progressing to the next phase of training.[153]

The culmination of these theories came in 1965 with publication of Professor Leo Pavlovic Matveyev's *Periodization of Sports Training*, which described a multiyear, year-round approach to training taken by Soviet athletes. The text was based on previous theories, Matveyev's work coaching both gymnasts and weightlifters, and analyses of the performances of thousands of athletes in track and field, swimming, and weightlifting.[154] In the book Matveyev discussed the parameters of training, including the balance between an optimal training load and rest, and further broke down training load into its component parts of volume and intensity. The two components generally had an inverse relationship. As the intensity of training increased, volume decreased.

The final section of the book, which would earn Matveyev the title of "The Father of Periodization," discussed the organization of training in cycles of different lengths. The largest cycle was the "macrocycle," which may have included a full year or half-year segments. Macrocycles were further divided into "mesocycles" of three to six months. Each mesocycle included smaller "microcycles," which were typically one month in length. Each microcycle had specific goals to prepare athletes for competition. Microcycles included "general preparatory" to get the athletes generally conditioned for sport, "specific preparatory" to work on skills relevant to their particular sport, and "competition" to ensure physiological peaking during a certain part of the competitive calendar. Other microcycles included "rehabilitation" and "shock," which included a high intensity and volume of training.[155]

Training of Soviet athletes, then, took a long view. A team of individuals worked to create goals for the athlete years in advance. Coaches working in combination with exercise scientists manipulated the variables of training volume and intensity over the course of the year so that athletes would

achieve their physiological peak at the time of one or two major competitions. As Matveyev himself noted in 2001, Soviet athletes achieved peak
performances at Olympic or other world championships 18 percent of the
time, while non-Soviet athletes only did so 7 to 10 percent of the time.[156] The
results of these differences were evident in the final medal counts: the Soviets won six of the eight Summer and Winter Games in which they competed
directly against the United States.[157]

TRAINING OF FEMALE ATHLETES

It is worth noting that a significant reason for the Soviets' success was their
concentration on excellence in sports that might be weak points for their
competitors. A prime example is their emphasis on elite female sport. As
noted by Riordan, the Soviets won twice as many world championships as
the Americans in a variety of sports during the 1960s. In thirteen dual meets
between the United States and the USSR between 1958 and 1975, the United
States came out victorious only twice. In those eleven victories, however, the
Soviet men won only three times, while the women lost only once.[158]

During the same era, many more women in the United States also began
to take up sports. After seeing what women were able to accomplish in factories, driving trucks, welding, and more during World War II, many of those
who warned women that sport participation could be injurious found their
position increasingly untenable.[159] While girls were increasingly encouraged
to participate in sports, participating and training to reach an elite level of
performance are two very different things. As discussed by Welch Suggs,
leaders of the female sporting movement, primarily educators by training,
were wary of adopting the high-performance model of male sports.[160] Moreover, while Americans were impressed with the performances of Eastern
Bloc athletes, there was still a deep concern that such performances implied
a certain level of masculinity. Avery Brundage, president of the International
Olympic Committee from 1952 to 1972, voiced his distaste for the muscularity of women in certain sports in 1949, even going so far as to argue for
elimination of the shot put from the Olympic program.[161]

Brundage's aversion to high levels of muscularity in female athletes was
far from unique, as the American press tended to describe Soviet athletes as
unfeminine, "Amazons," lesbians, or outright men. Educators were warned
that they would have to work actively to discourage lesbian tendencies in
female athletes.[162] The fear of the masculinizing effect of certain sports and
training regimens was so great that "sex testing" or, more euphemistically,
"femininity control" was instituted in 1968 and continued until the 2000

Olympic Games. In light of these concerns, it is hardly surprising that the research that was being done on the effects of strength training focused on male participants. One of the few scientific works that discussed strength training for women was Theodor Hettinger's *Physiology of Strength*. Based on a survey of research performed up to that time, as well as experiments that he had performed on men and women at hospitals in Germany and Philadelphia, Hettinger concluded that women were generally only two-thirds as strong as men and only 50 percent as responsive to training.[163] Beyond Hettinger's work, the preoccupation with success in male sports, concern about fitness of an all-male fighting force, and anxiety about muscularity in females combined to put off most research on strength training in women until the 1970s.

However, a male reader of *Strength & Health* magazine decided to try what Hoffman had been preaching after he was named the US women's swimming coach for the 1952 Olympic Games. While not a scientific study, it was an experiment of sorts for Walter Schlueter, then the head coach of the Town Club Swimming Team in Chicago. He decided to place his twenty-five women swimmers on a weight-training program beginning in September 1951. The swimmers included several women from previous Pan American and national teams. During their three-month cycle, they did squats, curls, military presses, bench presses, and pullovers. At the end of the program Schleuter reported that he was very happy with the results and that the women had more stamina and greater speed. As far as we can determine, the 1951 Town Club swimmers were the first American women's team to use a progressive resistance program.[164]

CONCLUSION

In a 1967 article John Piscapo declared that "research evidence is abundant to advocate the desirability of strength improvement as one essential for many activities and sport skills."[165] Writing in the same publication two years earlier, John Jesse quoted Gene O'Connell of the University of California–Los Angeles (UCLA) as saying that "most coaches and trainers are in favor of a weight training program, but knowledge of appropriate programs is not readily available."[166] Some of the information, of course, was available. Thanks to the work of Thomas DeLorme, Peter Karpovich, Jim Murray, Richard Berger, Patrick O'Shea, and others, pioneering coaches had access to experimental evidence on the most effective methods to improve strength. Unfortunately the "clearing house" called for by Emmanuel Orlick, to disseminate that research to the coaches who might use it, did not yet exist.[167]

Moreover, information was lacking in overall program design: how best to incorporate strength training into a *comprehensive, year-round* training program for sport that included both resistance training and conditioning.

As Robert Campbell's 1962 study showed, coaches who did include weight training tended to discard it during the actual season.[168] This is consistent with Nicholas Bourne's discussion of the different training approaches taken by Western and Soviet bloc countries in the 1960s. Whereas American and other Western coaches tended to break training periods into fairly simplistic preparation and competition phases, the Soviets developed training cycles that ran the course of several years with smaller cycles built in. The multi-year programs accounted for all aspects of training and allowed athletes to peak for a handful of events annually or at the end of the macrocycle. This sophisticated program development resulted from the combined efforts of coaches, athletes, physicians, and scientists. The more simplistic Western approach was usually the result of planning only by coaches and athletes.

A few articles on the mechanics of multiyear programs began to filter into American coaching literature in the early 1960s, but many more appeared in the closing years of the decade. The mechanics of a year-round, multiphase program were not fully explained in the United States until Frank Dick published "Periodization: An Approach to the Training Year" in 1975.[169] In the interim a few coaches began to embrace strength training in the 1950s, but the practice did not really catch on until the 1960s. The sport programs that included weight training during this era were often initiated by athletes, younger coaches, or younger faculty members who had trained on their own and served as evidence of the effects of strength training.

FIGURE 1. Training in an ancient Greek/Roman gymnasium using dumbbells, heavy plates, and "plummets." Illustrations from Hieronymus Mercurialis's *De Arte Gymnastica* (1577).

MR. HARRISON,

ONE OF THE STRONGEST MEN IN THE WORLD.

FIGURE 2. Professor Henry Thomas Harrison, 1852 exhibition. Courtesy of the H. J. Lutcher Stark Center for Physical Culture and Sports.

FIGURE 3. In 1835, William Wood opened one of the first gyms in the United States. Wood trained rowers, boxers, pedestrians, and businessmen and was also known for his rugged physique and great strength. This image was created in response to an engraving of Professor Harrison, the club-swinging champion of England. *New York Clipper*, February 16, 1861.

FIGURE 4. Charles Ottignon's Sparring Academy and Gymnasium in New York City, 1845—note the pulley weights and ring weights on the floor. T. Dwight Booth and William Wade (active 1844–1852), from the Collections of the Museum of the City of New York, 57.300.602.

FIGURE 5. Illustration from an 1854 program for an exhibition at Ottignon's gym. Note the pulley weights and dumbbells. From the Collections of the Museum of the City of New York, 36.409.60.

FIGURE 6. Surrounded by the tools of his trade, former professional boxer Aaron Molyneux Hewlett, ca. 1860, served as director of the gymnasium at Harvard in the 1860s. HUP Hewlett, A. Molyneaux (3a), olvwork173667. Harvard University Archives.

FIGURE 7. "Strength is Health" advocate Dr. George Barker Windship posed for one of America's first physique photographs in 1862. Carte de visite in the personal collection of Jan Todd.

FIGURE 8. The burly Canadian strongman Louis Cyr was probably the strongest man of the fin-de-siècle era, but his thick physique caused many to fear weight training would make one muscle-bound. Courtesy of the H. J. Lutcher Stark Center for Physical Culture and Sports.

FIGURE 9. The 1922 University of Texas men's wrestling team shows off the muscles they built by weight training with coach Roy J. McLean. McLean is in the top right of this rare photo. Courtesy of the H. J. Lutcher Stark Center for Physical Culture and Sports.

FIGURE 10. From left to right: John Terpak, Professor Edmond Desbonnet, Bob Hoffman, and Al Roy in Paris, where Roy was first exposed to the benefits of strength training. Robert Hoffman and Alda Ketterman Collection, the H. J. Lutcher Stark Center for Physical Culture and Sports.

FIGURE 11. Nearly every issue of *Strength & Health* discussed weight training for sport. In July 1952, the Olympic gold medalist pole-vaulter Bob Richards was featured on the cover. Courtesy of the York Barbell Co., York, Pennsylvania.

BARBELLS
AID OLYMPIC SWIMMING ASPIRANTS
TOWN CLUB COACH TRAINS GIRL SWIMMERS WITH WEIGHTS

Prepared with the cooperation of the Chicago Town Club and Harry McLaughlin, York (Pa.) Dispatch Sportswriter, a leading national swimming authority.

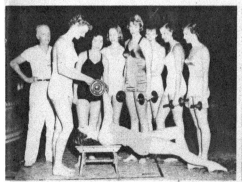

Town Club of Chicago Trainer Frank Klees supervises as Jody Alderson, 16-year-old Olympic team contender, hands a barbell to Alice Deimling (on bench). Looking on (left to right) are Barbara Jensen Reeves, Barbara Grow, Mary Kostelyn, Marlene Cahill, Ann Bockwinkle and Marge Hulton. Jody Alderson ranks as the nation's number two freestyler as this is written, and, at 16, has good prospects to take over the top position by Olympic time. (Cliff Oettinger photo)

Alice Deimling performs one-arm dumbell presses and Barbara Jensen Reeves practices curls under the direction of Frank Klees, Town Club trainer who works with Olympic Swimming Coach Walter Schlueter. Barbara Jensen Reeves was a member of the 1948 Olympic team, and in 1949, as a backstroker, was named among the U.S.A.'s number one swimmers. (Cliff Oettinger photo)

FIGURE 12. The first women's team to lift weights was the Town Club swim team, based out of Chicago. The lifting program was implemented by coach Walter Schlueter, who also served as coach of the US Olympic women's swimming team for the 1952 Games. Courtesy of the York Barbell Co., York, Pennsylvania.

FIGURE 13. Al Roy, kneeling, is generally regarded as the first true strength coach in the United States. He is shown here supervising the training of Billy Cannon, who would go on to win the 1959 Heisman Trophy for Louisiana State University. Courtesy of the York Barbell Co., York, Pennsylvania.

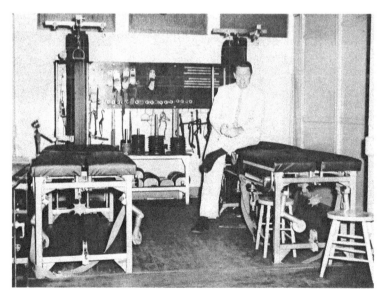

FIGURE 14. Thomas DeLorme with his Elgin Benches as pictured in the June 1959 issue of *Strength & Health*. Courtesy of the York Barbell Co., York, Pennsylvania.

FIGURE 15. Amateur golf champion Frank Stranahan was a particularly important role model in the fight against the theory of muscle-binding. Terry and Jan Todd Collection, the H. J. Lutcher Stark Center for Physical Culture and Sports.

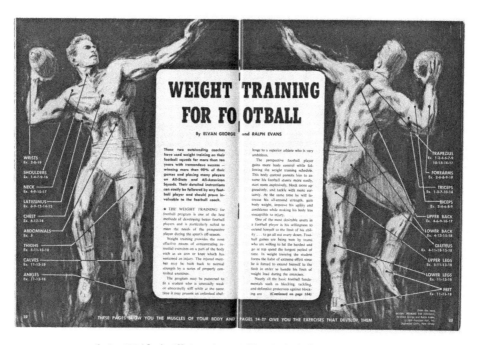

FIGURE 16. Joe Weider's *All American Athlete* included sport-specific training programs for a host of sports, ranging from swimming to decathlon to bowling to football.

FIGURE 17. 1960: "Barbells on Campus" in *Strength & Health*. The imposing Father Lange is shown posing at the lower left and deadlifting at the
lower right. Courtesy of the York Barbell Co., York, Pennsylvania.

FIGURE 18. Universal gym training with University of Texas football
players Olen Underwood, Ernie Koy, Pete Lammons, and two unidentified
players, ca. 1968. Photographer unknown. Department of Kinesiology
Collection, the H. J. Lutcher Stark Center for Physical Culture and Sports.

FIGURE 19. Cindy Wyatt, shown here with her husband, the world powerlifting champion Don Reinhoudt, in 1976, deserves far greater recognition than she has received for her pioneering role in opening strength training to female athletes. As a field event specialist in the early 1960s, Wyatt was virtually the only American woman lifting heavy weights. Photo by Doug White. Courtesy of Jan Todd.

FIGURE 20. Boyd Epley with his early assistant strength coaches at Nebraska. Pictured from left to right: Randy Gobel, Jon Jost, Boyd Epley, Bryan Bailey, and Mike Arthur. Photo courtesy of Boyd Epley and the University of Nebraska.

FIGURE 21. A selection of Bruce Algra's early 1980s biomechanical covers from the *National Strength and Conditioning* journal. Photo by Ryan Blake. Courtesy of the H. J. Lutcher Stark Center for Physical Culture and Sports.

FIGURE 22. The 20,000-square-foot Dr. Nasser Al-Rashid Strength and Training Center features customized training equipment and special weight platforms and exemplifies what can be built when a university and its donors want to compete for the best talent in the country. Photo by Patrick Meredith. Courtesy of Texas Athletics.

FIGURE 23. Jeff Madden, associate athletic director for strength and conditioning at the University of Texas from 1998 to 2011, was a founding member and past president of the CSCCa. He continues to serve on its board. Courtesy of Texas Athletics.

•

CHAPTER 4

PIONEERS OF POWER

Strength Training for College Sports before 1969

A
fter the passage of the Servicemen's Readjustment Act (more commonly known as the GI Bill) in 1944, millions of former service
members flooded America's colleges. By 1947 veterans constituted 49
percent of college admissions; by 1956 nearly 8 million of the 16 million World War II veterans had attended college or occupational programs.[1]
This influx strained college facilities and resulted in a building boom on
campuses across the country. San Jose State College, for example, grew from
a student population of 10,000 in the early 1950s to nearly 20,000 by 1963.
Despite the college's enrollment, the weight room, created by moving lockers
out of an old dressing room and used by both the physical education and
athletics departments, consisted of less than 500 square feet.[2]

The physical education facilities at Michigan State University were
designed when enrollment hovered around 8,000, but 20,000 students attended the university by 1959, and many of them wanted to lift weights. The
earliest weight trainers at Michigan State lifted a barbell owned by forestry
student Jim Newman, who was allowed to train in a basement alcove behind
the gymnasium swimming pool.[3] Weight training at Eastern Carolina College began when an undergraduate asked if he could bring his weight set
to the gym so others could join him in training. Hoping that interest in the
activity would quickly wane, the head of the Physical Education Department
gave permission but limited the lifters to a corner in a small storage room.[4]
They came anyway. Eventually Eastern Carolina, like other universities, realized that it needed to make more space for barbells.

Many of the new college men, often former GIs, had learned about weight
training from fellow soldiers or in boot camp when mass weight training
was frequently done with homemade barbells constructed of pipe, paint
cans, and concrete.[5] Others were introduced by enthusiastic teammates or

coaches during their high school careers.[6] Regardless of their introduction to the iron game, it was increasingly apparent by the 1950s that both former GIs and many traditional students wanted to continue their lifting while they attended school. At Louisiana State University (LSU) students often lifted their own weight sets in their dorm rooms when the facilities or hours proved insufficient at the campus weight room. The hefting of weights in such a confined space sometimes resulted in dented floors and broken furniture and led to fines for damaging university property. The practice and fines became so widespread that graduate student Sam Lyle suggested that each dormitory set aside some space for a weight room. For a dollar a semester students could lift in the weight room of their residence hall and avoid the fees associated with damaged furniture or floors.[7] At the University of Iowa the weight room was initially available for recreational use from 3:30 to 5:30 P.M. on three days and from 7:30 to 9:30 on the other two school nights. Students apparently found the hours insufficient, however, as the weight room door was smashed from its hinges twice after hours during the 1959–1960 academic year.[8]

The new passion for lifting displayed by the students at LSU and Iowa was perhaps one answer to the Cold War concern over the softness of American youth in the 1950s. Historian Donald Mrozek described the creation of a "cult of toughness" during the Cold War that played out in the lives of teen-aged males through fast cars and street racing, leather jackets, slicked-back hair, and, of course, participating in masculine, aggressive forms of sport. According to Mrozek, "various figures in government, organized athletics, and physical education used sport and physical training in increasingly ritualized forms to generate a tough and winning attitude in the Cold War." Distinct from fitness, toughness was more "aggressive" and "action-oriented."[9] Football was a primary conduit of toughness, as it was the sport most prominently associated with physical punishment, suffering, discipline, and aggression. According to President Eisenhower, "football, almost more than any other sport, tends to instill in men the feeling that victory comes through hard—almost slavish—work."[10] This drive for toughness altered training programs for a variety of sports, many of which became tests of mental as much as physical strength.[11]

Some of the most venerated coaches of this era were men associated with painfully long "almost slavish" training sessions. Immortalized in the book *The Junction Boys*, Paul "Bear" Bryant took one hundred Texas A&M football players through a hellish 1954 preseason camp in a desolate west Texas town.[12] When the camp ended, only twenty-seven players remained. In 1962 University of Kentucky coach Charlie Bradshaw similarly winnowed a group of eighty-eight players down to a "thin thirty" by the start of the season. University of Texas coach Darrell Royal also relied on brutal drills and grueling conditioning routines to run off less talented players. The players who endured such workouts referred to them scornfully as "shit drills."[13]

This new cult of toughness, World War II, the promotion of barbell training in fitness magazines, and burgeoning scientific research on strength training worked synergistically to cause a massive expansion of weight training on college campuses at midcentury. Weight training gained momentum not only because of fears of falling behind the Soviets but also because of an increasingly competitive environment within college sports—and especially in football—after the NCAA allowed scholarships in 1956. This move away from amateurism had a significant impact on the level of professionalism overall and created expectations that players would fully commit themselves to training year-round.[14] By allowing scholarships, the NCAA tacitly acknowledged that many of the players enrolled in "big-time" universities were there for their athletic, not scholastic, abilities. At the end of the 1960s, *Sports Illustrated* writer John Underwood put it best: "from the moment the outstanding athlete arrives on campus there is an unspoken understanding that he is majoring in professional sport."[15]

This massive expansion of weight training on college campuses was documented in a series of articles in *Strength & Health* called "Barbells on Campus," beginning in 1959. A few articles in the series were written by *Strength & Health* staff writers, but more were authored by students, coaches, or faculty members at the universities described. The articles detailed participation in strength training at the time of writing as well as the history of weight training at many of the schools. While most of the articles discussed strength-training programs with relatively short histories, a handful of colleges were trailblazers in making weight training available to their students and athletes.

STRENGTH TRAINING AT COLLEGES AND UNIVERSITIES, 1919–1945

One of the first colleges to embrace weight training was the University of Texas at Austin. The tradition began in 1913, when athletic booster and Board of Regents member H. J. Lutcher Stark decided to learn about weight training. Stark had enjoyed too much food and too little activity since his graduation from UT in 1910 and weighed a soft 230 pounds at the height of five feet, seven inches when he decided to become fitter. To slim down, he traveled to Philadelphia to train with weights under the tutelage of Alan Calvert of the Milo Barbell Company. After two months, Stark was down to a muscular 180 pounds and become a fervent advocate of heavy strength training.

The following year Stark convinced Houston YMCA director Theo Bellmont to take a position as the first athletic director at the University of Texas. Bellmont had been introduced to weights while working at the YMCA and was also a believer in weight training. Stark traveled to Austin almost weekly during 1913 and brought his Milo set with him. The two men lifted the barbell together and used some dumbbells that Bellmont had brought from Houston for their training sessions outside the "Old Main" administration building. They were joined in 1914 by freshman Roy J. McLean, who thought the weights might help him in wrestling. After finishing his undergraduate degree, McLean was hired by Bellmont as an instructor of physical training and secured permission from the university to teach what may have been the first credit-carrying weight-training class in a United States college.[16]

McLean taught his first section of the weight-training course in 1919 while still working on his master's degree. With meager equipment, consisting of only two Milo Barbells and several pairs of ten- and fifteen-pound dumbbells owned by McLean and Bellmont, McLean took eleven freshmen who had never seen barbells through the mechanics of a strength program. At the beginning and again near the end of the course McLean put the freshmen though a series of tests to assess their size, speed, and power. After finishing the semester, the men had added muscle, could jump higher, could run faster, and were all so impressed with the results of their class that they told their friends, many of whom enrolled the next semester. By 1929, ten years after McLean's first section of the course, a complete weight room had been designed as part of the newly constructed Gregory Gymnasium to accommodate McLean's ten sections of weight-training classes offered each semester.[17] What McLean began continues to this day: 2019 marks the one-hundredth anniversary of that first weight-training class taught at Texas. What is now called the Department of Kinesiology and Health Education still offers more than twenty sections of weight training every semester.

In addition to his weight-training courses, McLean accepted coaching duties for the newly formed cross-country team in 1920 and the wrestling team in 1923. To the surprise of many, he encouraged his athletes in both sports to lift weights, a practice that was far from common in the 1920s. For thirteen consecutive years, until he stepped down as head coach in 1933, McLean's barbell-trained runners won every Southwest Conference championship. The wrestlers were also quite successful during the program's short four-year run, winning several conference championships. One wrestler, Ralph Hammond, even placed fourth at the 1928 Olympic Games, losing the bronze medal on a technicality.[18] In spite of the success of weight-trained athletes under McLean's tutelage, other coaches at Texas were slow to incorporate weight training because of the entrenched fear of muscle-binding.[19] Other varsity teams at Texas did not begin systematic training to increase strength until the late 1960s or 1970s.

Father Bernard Lange began operating a weight room in the University of Notre Dame's old natatorium in 1935.[20] Born in 1888 in Prussia, Lange immigrated to the United States as a young boy, ending up in Oil City, Pennsylvania, with relatives.[21] He worked for a time in the oil fields of western Pennsylvania before enrolling at Notre Dame's preparatory school as a teenager.[22] Lange was almost expelled from the school after scaling Notre Dame's famous "Golden Dome" and waving to awestruck classmates below, but he was allowed to finish his undergraduate degree in 1912. He enrolled in seminary the following year and was ordained as a priest in 1917.[23] Lange began to train with weights at age nineteen and found both his body and his career aspirations transformed. When he first picked up a barbell, Lange, who was five feet, eight inches tall, had a chest that measured only thirty inches in circumference, an upper arm of ten inches, and a thigh of a mere nineteen. By 1923, at the age of thirty-five, Lange tipped the scale at well over two hundred pounds, had added twenty inches to his chest, almost doubled the size of his upper arm, and added eight inches to his thigh.

At the time, Lange was employed as the physical director at Notre Dame. He would remain there until 1927, when he moved to Saint Edward's University in Austin, Texas, to serve as the director of the physical education department and pursue a PhD degree in biology.[24] After completing the degree, Lange returned to Notre Dame in 1934, where he no longer claimed the title of physical director but instead taught science courses. Shortly after his return, however, his failing eyesight—a complication of diabetes—forced Lange to leave the classroom. With his career redirected, Lange set up a workshop in the university's old natatorium, where he used the woodworking skills that he had learned in his father's shop as a boy to make altars, crosses, and other ornaments for worship. Lange's workshop also housed a jumble of strength-training equipment and a door adorned with a "KEEP OUT" sign in order to ward off all but the most serious trainees.[25]

For those not dissuaded by the sign, lifting in the workshop required approval from Lange himself and was decided on a case-by-case basis, seemingly arbitrarily.[26] Those who were selected paid annual dues of five dollars and had their names recorded in Lange's ledger. Despite his gruff demeanor, the priest ultimately did not turn away many: he claimed to have trained over 6,000 students by 1960 in a twenty-five-year span.[27] The number is particularly impressive when we consider that Lange's gym had no official connection with either the physical education department or athletics and no school support. Weights for the facility were purchased by Lange or donated to him.[28] The priest even built much of the equipment himself, including platforms, benches, and various lifting machines.

In spite of the lack of any official connection to the athletic department, many of Lange's trainees included Notre Dame athletes who lifted on a voluntary basis. Some athletes were encouraged by coaches to work with Lange, but many just sought him out for assistance. Legendary coach Knute Rockne, an undergraduate classmate of Lange's, purportedly recommended weight training for some of his track and football men in the early 1920s. As in Texas, however, lifting would not truly be embraced until the 1960s, when football coach Ara Parseghian sought Lange's advice in creating a team-wide strength program for the 1966 football season.[29] That year the Irish would finish undefeated and tied once, marking their first national championship since 1949.[30]

University of Southern California (USC) quarterback and tailback Russ Saunders used barbells to improve his football performance between 1927 and 1929. Owing to the weights, Saunders stood five feet, seven inches tall and weighed a stout 180 pounds. The versatile and hard-nosed player was a key member of USC's 1928 national championship team and was named an All-American in 1929 as well as the player of the game in the 1930 Rose Bowl. So impressive was Saunders's weight-trained physique that he served as the primary model for USC's famous Tommy Trojan statue, which was unveiled in 1930. Southern California's head football coach, Howard Jones, was sufficiently impressed with the effects of weight training that he recommended it to his players throughout the 1930s as an excellent conditioner for football.[31] As was the case at Texas and Notre Dame, however, weight training was not systematically employed for varsity sport at USC until the early 1960s.[32]

Following a demonstration by Bob Hoffman and some of the York lifters in nearby "Muscletown," Pennsylvania State University began including weight training as part of their required physical education program for all male students by 1942. The curriculum for the classes was essentially the York Simplified System of Barbell Training. The male students performed the program during regular class meetings, with some lifting after hours as well. Writing in January 1943, Alan Carse claimed that the weights were responsible for the Penn State football team's success in 1942.[33]

THE POSTWAR YEARS AND AL ROY

After World War II weight training began to expand at colleges and universities, but the expansion would not truly take off until the mid-1950s. Schools that initiated weight-training classes quickly found them filled to capacity due to a lack of facilities and tremendous student interest. At the University of Georgia, for example, the first weight-training course was offered in the fall quarter of 1948. Enrollment had more than doubled by the next quarter, and students had to be turned away. The course was introduced through the work of physical education major and former merchant marine Richard Burks, a competitive bodybuilder who had begun lifting weights in high school. After discovering that the campus had no weight room, Burks put on a strength show in order to generate interest in lifting weights and to raise funds for a facility. The show included strongman acts, tumbling, muscle control, and competitive weightlifting and drummed up sufficient interest and money for the university to set aside a room for weight training. Burks was even offered a teaching position as a weight-training specialist for the physical education department. Following the course's initial success, the university appropriated funding for an additional 2,000 pounds of weights to accommodate larger classes.[34]

Weight training at Stanford University and Michigan State University began in 1948 and 1949, respectively. Both programs, like Georgia's, were the result of student-led initiatives. The Stanford program began through the efforts of shot-putter and weightlifter Otis Chandler, with help from two other lifters, Charles Coker and John Nourse. Chandler would captain the Stanford track team in 1950, winning the Pacific Coast Conference championship that year and placing second at the national meet. Chandler, the heir to a publishing fortune, found an identity in sports when he was sent far from his Los Angeles home to Phillips Academy in Andover, Massachusetts. Highly competitive and desirous of more strength and size, he had taken up weight training after graduating from high school and bulked up from 155 pounds to 220 in his senior year of college. His achievements in the shot put were crucial to dispelling the myth of muscle-binding: many later track stars would point to his success as proof of the efficacy of strength training.[35] The track team at Stanford had its own weight room by 1956. Barbell training was adopted by the Cardinal basketball team in 1958; baseball followed suit in 1959, though weight training was still optional for football players in 1960. Due to a lack of space, physical education classes were limited to thirteen students in 1960. With seven sections offered, only ninety-one students could take weight training in a given semester, though the weight room was kept open extra hours three days each week to accommodate recreational training.[36]

The weightlifters at Michigan State were not discouraged by a lack of facilities and lifted in an alcove behind the school's swimming pool from the barbell club's inception in 1949 until a new facility was provided in the Men's Intramural Building in 1959. The facility was fashioned with input from head football coach and later athletic director Clarence "Biggie" Munn. After construction, Munn spoke with pride of the 1,400-square-foot weight room, citing his membership in President Eisenhower's Physical Fitness Program and his understanding of the importance of strength in total fitness. The new weight room had so much space allotted for strength training that it was subdivided into space for beginners' weight-training classes, bodybuilding, and competitive weightlifting. The room was kept open seven days each week for recreational or competitive lifting. By 1959 members of the Spartan swim team had begun lifting as part of their regular workouts, though weight training for other sports continued to be voluntary and unsupervised in 1962.[37]

The year before Michigan State unveiled its new facility, weight training at Louisiana State University (LSU) was sparked when its weight-trained football team captured the 1958 national championship. The preceding season the Tigers had garnered the pedestrian record of five wins and five losses, having lost four in a row and only salvaging a .500 record by beating Tulane in the final game. Prior to the Tulane game, LSU coach Paul Dietzel told a friend, "If I don't win this game, I'm through as a football coach."[38] He had good reason to fear for his job, having finished with just three wins and losing records in the 1955 and 1956 seasons.[39] Shortly after the 1957 season, Dietzel was visited by Baton Rouge gym owner Alvin Roy, who offered to set up a weight-training program for the team. Dietzel was hesitant, because he had been taught that large muscles were synonymous with slowness. After disappointing results in his only three seasons at LSU, however, he was willing to listen to Roy's offer. Roy was not completely unknown to Dietzel: his two star running backs, Billy Cannon and Jimmy Taylor, both trained under Roy's tutelage.

Roy had shared Dietzel's belief that weight training caused muscle-binding before being assigned to work as the aide de camp for the American weightlifting team in France while he was serving in the army in 1946. After witnessing the speed and power of the world champion weightlifting team and visiting with Bob Hoffman, Roy became a believer in barbells.[40] Roy was doubly confident in what he was proposing to Dietzel, because this was not the first time he had made such an offer to a desperate football coach. In

November 1954 Roy had visited James "Big Fuzzy" Brown, coach of the Istrouma Indians, under similar circumstances. Istrouma High School, located in Baton Rouge, Louisiana, was Roy's alma mater. The school's football team closed out the 1954 season with a crushing defeat by cross-town rival Baton Rouge High School. Though the Indians had a respectable 9–2 record, the loss had kept them out of the state playoffs. Roy had made a similar pitch to Brown several years earlier, but Brown was willing to listen after the 1954 setback. After Roy brought weight equipment to the school, the team began required training with weights during spring football practice in the first week of January. Though required to lift only during spring practice, most of the team members continued to lift three times each week throughout the spring and into the summer. When fall football practice started, only one member of the forty-man roster had failed to gain at least nine pounds. Fullback Billy Cannon had increased his size from 172 to 196 pounds, while tackle Luther Fortenberry and tight end Billy Castilaw had added fifteen and thirty-two pounds, respectively. In addition to size, many of the players had doubled or tripled their strength after eight months of training. The results were remarkable. Istrouma went undefeated in 1955, scored more points than any team in Louisiana history, and easily outpaced Fair Park High School of Shreveport in the championship game, 40–6. The margin of victory was the largest ever in a state championship game. Additionally, the Indians placed four players, including Cannon and Fortenberry, on the "all-state" team, the first time a school had ever done so. After his stellar football season, Cannon went on to excel in track, where he won three gold medals at the state meet between the 100-yard and 220-yard dashes and the shot put.[41] Cannon was recruited heavily by Dietzel and chose to attend LSU that fall.

Thus the results of Roy's handiwork were not completely unknown to Dietzel. In addition to Cannon, halfback and weight trainer Jimmy Taylor also excelled for the Tigers. Dietzel described Taylor as "bull strong" and "hard as a rock" but still possessing soft hands.[42] In describing how he overcame his trepidation about weight training, Dietzel explained: "all I can say is that after seeing what Taylor and Cannon could do and after listening to Al, I was sold."[43] As he had done for Istrouma three years earlier, Roy brought weights to campus and put the team through a weight-training program. The program was basic, consisting of ten to fifteen repetitions and two sets of seven exercises: squats, rows, deadlifts, stiff-legged deadlifts, calf raises, bench presses, and overhead dumbbell presses. The players lifted throughout the spring and summer of 1958. Before the season began, the Tigers had been picked to finish ninth in their conference. By season's end, however, they were the only untied and undefeated team in the country.[44] Billy Cannon led the way, finishing as a unanimous "All-America" selection and the player of the year in the Southeastern Conference (SEC). He was joined on the All-American list by two-way lineman Max Fugler; two other backs, Johnny Robinson and Warren Rabb, were named to the All-Conference team. The national championship was LSU's first and garnered SEC "Coach of the Year" honors for Paul Dietzel. Billy Cannon would go on to win the Heisman Trophy in 1959 and is still hailed as "the greatest football player ever to don the purple and gold."[45]

By 1960 all athletic teams at LSU were training with weights in a dedicated weight room at Tiger Stadium, while the rest of the student body had access to a physical education weight room as well as facilities in the dormitories.[46] For his part, Al Roy moved on to San Diego to begin serving as the strength coach of the to San Diego Chargers of the American Football League (AFL) in 1963. Roy's program produced similar results in professional football, with the Chargers capturing the 1963 AFL championship after having gone 4-10 the season before.[47] Roy's work as a coach who oversaw only the strength-training aspect of the players' development led Terry Todd to label him the "first modern strength coach."[48]

A "DISTINCT ADVANTAGE" IN THE MID- AND LATE 1950S

Louisiana teams were not the only teams to experience dramatic turn-arounds in the mid- and late 1950s after beginning strength training. The University of Washington Huskies experienced a similar turnaround the following year after coach Jim Owens mandated weight training before the 1959 season. The 1958 Husky squad had gone 3–7. The weight-trained 1959 group went 10–1 and smashed Wisconsin in the Rose Bowl, 44–8, finishing as the eighth-ranked team in the country according to the Associated Press.[49] The "Flying L's" of Fort Lauderdale, Florida participated in a weight-training program in preparation for the 1955 high school football season. Twenty-eight boys took part in a voluntary training program created by local gym owner Al Christensen. He offered to train the boys at the high school some afternoons and during the evenings at his gym three times each week for eight weeks. The training program was similar to Roy's, employing two sets of ten to fifteen repetitions on eleven different exercises. The team's coach, Bill Armstrong, commented that the boys reported for fall camp with more confidence and a new attitude. Both were on display that season as the L's went 9–1, winning their conference championship and recording the best record in school history. After the season coach Armstrong commented that he was "sold on weight training."[50]

At Southeastern Missouri State University (SEMO), weight training for football started after one of the team's best players petitioned the coach, Kenneth Knox, to make the training team-wide and mandatory. The player, Marvin Rosengarten, was an outstanding lineman and competitive weightlifter who would go on to be a Missouri state champion in weightlifting. Rosengarten crafted the weight program with assistance from line coach Jim Hamby, a former Notre Dame football player, and physical education instructor Joe Uhls. The program consisted of two sets of seven exercises, with the first set performed for twelve repetitions and the other for five. The program was performed in the off-season and utilized two to three days weekly. Following implementation of the weight program before the 1955 season, the SEMO Indians went on to smashing success, winning five conference championships in the following eight years and twice placing second.[51] The basketball players at SEMO also began training with weights in 1959, though their results were less dramatic than those of their football counterparts.[52]

Not every team could boast a dramatic turnaround, but the increase in the number of athletes training with weights in the mid-1950s was dramatic. At tiny Catholic Stonehill College in Easton, Massachusetts, many of the varsity athletes began to train with weights after Brother Joseph Faul established a weightlifting club in 1952.[53] Similarly, athletes at Eastern Washington College began to lift after physical education professor Jack Leighton brought his own weights to the school in 1954.[54] The weight program at Temple University in Philadelphia started when physical education professor Joseph Carroll was able to secure funding for barbells in 1955. The new facility was used for physical education classes, general recreation, and athletic teams. By 1960 all Temple athletes were encouraged to lift.[55] The track team at another Philadelphia-area school, Villanova University, also began to lift weights in the mid-1950s. Assistant track coach James Tuppeny admitted to having been biased against weights in his younger years; but after seeing the results of Otis Chandler, Irving Mondschein, Bob Richards, and others, he could no longer believe that strength training would hamper performance. By 1959 all of the Villanova track men went through a three-phase weight workout leading up to the competitive season. The first phase was performed by all athletes and included training three times each week. The second phase reduced the volume and frequency of lifting for runners, while increasing volume for athletes in field events. By the third phase all athletes had decreased the frequency and volume of their training in preparation for the season.[56] Springfield (Massachusetts) College's track coach, Vern Cox, similarly recommended progressive weight training for all of his athletes, with particular emphasis on its importance for shot-putters and other throwers. The basketball team at Springfield began team-wide preseason training in 1957. The football and wrestling teams were also spending time in the weight room to prepare for their seasons by 1959.[57] The first athletes to train with weights at New York University (NYU) were the "weight men" of the track team. Shot-putter Jerry Monkofsky convinced coach Joe Haley of the value of the exercises, which were soon used by men in a variety of events. Within two years weight training was recommended by coaches of the NYU baseball, basketball, wrestling, and swimming teams.[58] The athletic department at the University of Illinois also supported weight training, though on a voluntary basis, for all athletes by 1960.[59]

A "NECESSITY" BY THE 1960S

In 1962 the football line coach for the University of California Golden Bears, John Neumann, declared that, "up until a short time ago, it was a distinct advantage for a coach to utilize weight training methods in conditioning and developing his athletes." In the early 1960s things changed, however, and strength training became "absolutely necessary if a team is to compete on par with its opponents." Required, rather than encouraged, weight training became more prevalent in many major college programs. Neumann went on to assert that "almost without exception, every track and football team on the West Coast makes use of weight training in one form or another in its total program. The school that does not is rare indeed."[60] Neumann's Golden Bears trained with weights in the off-season. The program included testing to evaluate players' specific strengths and weaknesses, such as muscular power, strength, or endurance. Individual lifting programs would be tailored according to those results. Neumann stressed the importance of specificity both in training the muscles used in football and in training them to contract either forcefully or quickly depending on the goals of a training session. The thrice weekly training program consisted of light, medium, and heavy days, with the medium day modeled after Thomas DeLorme's PRE protocol.[61] The strength program for football players at California started in 1960 when new head coach Marv Levy hired Neumann away from the University of New Mexico. Unfortunately for the Golden Bears, the results of the weight program were not equal to those experienced by LSU or Washington. After having gone 2–8 prior to Levy's hiring, California proceeded to go 2–7–1, 1–8–1, 1–9, and 4–5 in Levy's four seasons as head coach.[62]

Newly appointed Wake Forest head football coach Bill Hildebrand implemented team-wide weight training in the spring of 1960. The program was crafted with significant input from baseball coach Gene Hooks. Hooks was chosen because he had implemented weight training for all of the baseball players the previous season with great success, forcing a playoff against Clemson to decide the Atlantic Coast Conference (ACC) championship in 1959. Hooks was a professor in the physical education department and had done research for his doctoral dissertation on the impact of strength on base-ball skills.[63] The spring weight program for football resulted in "probably one of the best springs in the school's history." Many players did not continue their training over the summer, however, so the results did not translate to the fall season: the "Demon Deacons" managed to win only two games, while losing eight. Hildebrand's record at Wake Forest was not unlike Levy's at California, and the team won only seven games out of forty played in his four-season tenure at Winston-Salem. In spite of football's lack of success, other coaches at the school adopted off-season strength training, including swimming coach Leo Ellison and track coach Bill Jordan. The basketball team still trained on a voluntary basis in the early 1960s, but coach Horace "Bones" McKinney had gone from a "die-hard opposer of weight training" to heartily endorsing it.[64]

While weight training did not work out for the California or Wake Forest football teams, its success at LSU forced at least one other football power-house to adopt off-season weight training. After being shut out by the weight-trained Tigers in the 1963 Cotton Bowl, coach Darrell Royal instructed his staff to implement a program of heavy weight training.[65] The Longhorns had done quite well under Royal, never finishing with a losing record in his first six seasons in Austin. In fact, they were ranked as the top team in the country by the Associated Press during both the 1961 and 1962 seasons but were unable to finish the seasons unblemished and fell out of the top spot both years. The Longhorns had done some weight training during those seasons, following a program designed by athletic trainer Frank Medina. Medina's view of weight training was shaped by a film of the training employed by the Northwestern University football team, which used light weights and high repetitions in the 1950s. "A pair of twenty or twenty-five pound dumbbells is enough for anybody, no matter how big and strong he is," Medina claimed.[66]

In keeping with this philosophy, Medina put the players through grueling workouts with light ankle weights, wrist weights, weighted vests, and dumb-bells. The players referred to the workouts as "Medina sessions" and regu-larly performed hundreds of repetitions in a heated locker room. In keeping with the "cult of toughness," the goal of the training was as much mental toughness as it was physical performance. To enhance the players' physical strength, however, a four-phase program was designed and implemented by physical education professor Stan Burnham in the spring of 1963. The first phase consisted of circuit training with progressively heavier weights performed in less time. This type of lifting was done in the lead-up to spring football. After spring football ended, the players lifted heavy weights for two sets of five to ten repetitions until school ended. Over the summer the players trained on their own with heavy weights, if available, or by doing various bodyweight drills if they were not. As the summer proceeded, more and more running was practiced to prepare for the season. During the season, only a handful of players deemed to have "special needs" were required to lift, and then only once weekly.[67] Burnham's program apparently succeeded in getting the Longhorns over the hump: they went undefeated in 1963, handily defeated the second-ranked Navy Midshipmen in the Cotton Bowl, 28–6, and claimed the school's first football national championship.[68]

Many of the Midshipmen in that Cotton Bowl were also weight trained, though weight training had been implemented at the Naval Academy for a very different reason. According to Lt. Joe Fournier, "with the advent of Presidents Eisenhower and Kennedy's report on the unfavorable condition of American youth and subsequent Navy Fitness Program, the weight training program and facilities were given closer and much needed attention." In the fall of 1961 Fournier instituted "Operation Shape Up," a voluntary weight program performed by thirty Midshipmen. Prior to this trial, weight training had been limited at the academy because of the presumed negative effects. After six weeks, the strength gains made by Fournier's charges were dramatic enough to convince the administration to purchase several thousand pounds of additional weights and bars. The small Naval Academy weight room was quickly overcrowded. The members of the track team were given their own training space shortly thereafter. By 1964 all Midshipmen had to take part in weight training as a component of a required "personal conditioning" course.[69]

In the early 1960s many small colleges also took up weight training. Marist College, a Catholic school with just over a thousand students and a tight budget, added weight training in 1961 and established a weightlifting team. Coach Frank Swetz set up training programs for most sports and kept the weight room open for recreational use seven days each week.[70] Another small Catholic college, Mt. Saint Mary's in Emmitsburg, Maryland, first organized a barbell club at the beginning of the spring semester of 1963. The handful of lifters there grew to well over 150 and attracted mostly men with little or no previous experience in weight training.[71] Administrators at Bloomsburg State College in Pennsylvania believed that athletic success would lead to increased applicants to the rural college. Strength training was strongly supported by the university president, Harvey Andruss, who declared that physical fitness was a requirement for graduation from the school. As a result, all athletic programs lifted weights in the preseason or off-season at the school. In writing about weightlifting at the school, Joseph Figliolino specifically cited John F. Kennedy as having "increased this country's interest in physical fitness" and having "instilled in its citizens the importance of a physically fit America." The interest generated by Kennedy "has spread into our intramural programs, our competitive weightlifting, and affected our varsity teams."[72]

At Gordon Military College in Barnesville, Georgia, weight training was introduced in 1963 by football coach Joe Windham. The coach had trained during his college career at Middle Tennessee State and felt that this was crucial to his having been named a "Little All-American" in football. Windham brought weight training to Gordon because the athletes from the small military school regularly took on football powerhouses like the University of South Carolina and Miami University. In order to stay on the field with those teams, the Gordon men would have to maximize their talent and physical fitness, which meant training with weights.[73]

At Wesleyan College in Middletown, Connecticut, all athletes were encouraged to lift by 1965 and many did, including outstanding athletes in football, track, baseball, basketball, and soccer. The training largely involved circuit workouts performed up to three months before the competitive season.[74] The track men at Abilene (Texas) Christian College began team-wide weight training in 1965, as did the football team at Ithaca (New York) College.[75] By 1968 the football, track, and swimming teams at Franklin and Marshall College in Lancaster, Pennsylvania, were all encouraged to train with weights, while Kendall College in Chicago became the only college in the Midwest to sponsor weightlifting as a varsity sport.[76]

WEIGHT-TRAINED WOMEN?

To do justice to any discussion of collegiate women in America using weight training in the 1960s, we must start with the obvious fact that no truly unified sport system for American girls and women existed until the passage of Title IX in 1972. While some universities had collegiate teams—often in swimming, tennis, basketball, and track and field—many colleges and many, many high schools had no varsity sports for women. For this reason, *Strength & Health* had no "Barbells on Campus" articles that showcased collegiate women's teams using weights. If a woman became interested enough in training for her own sake to begin lifting, it was usually done in the presence of a supportive male, like her father or husband, because women had very few role models to emulate.

As mentioned in chapter 2, during these two decades *Strength & Health* did include profiles on a few individual women athletes, ran Pudgy Stockton's "Barbelles" column, and showcased one team with its article on the Town Club Swim Team. It also frequently included articles on figure shaping through barbell use and generally aimed recipes and nutritional articles at their women readers. *Strength & Health* was the most dominant voice in favor of weight training in this era, so it should not come as a surprise that almost no women in America were seriously lifting weights for sport before 1972.

The one notable exception was the American track athlete Cindy Wyatt, who was featured in *Strength & Health* in 1962 in an article written by Olympic gold medalist Tommy Kono, with photos showing her doing an overhead jerk of more than 220 pounds.[77] A native of Williamsville, New York, Cindy began competing at the age of eleven years in the local Junior Olympics. At age fourteen, she won the shot put, won the discus, and finished third in the javelin at the Junior Nationals in track and field. Over the next decade or so Wyatt had an enormously successful track and field career: she was on five All-America track and field teams (1958–1959 and 1961–1963), earned a scholarship to attend the University of Hawaii (nearly unheard of for a woman in the 1960s), and was invited to throw in a number of USA versus USSR track meets that exposed her to the strength and power of the Soviet women athletes.[78]

According to Wyatt, though it was widely believed that Soviet women athletes used weight training before the 1952 Helsinki Games, the conversion of American women to barbell training came slowly. In a 1988 interview Wyatt asserted that if not for her weight training she would never have been able to compete as successfully as she did in track and field. "I was always the smallest competitor, by far, at the national meets. For a number of years, Earlene Brown was number one, and I was number two in the United States. But Earlene outweighed me by nearly a hundred pounds. Internationally, I was up against Galena Zabyna and Tamara Press from the Soviet Union. They had the advantage of being not only a lot taller and heavier than I was, but they weight trained too." The sad thing, Cindy continued, was that for a long time, "none of the other American women on the track team seemed to care."[79]

Wyatt had been exposed to barbell training by her brother when she was twelve, and she credited that weight work with helping her to overcome her small stature and win multiple national championships in the early 1960s. The incredible success of Wyatt, who stood only five feet, six inches tall and generally weighed 165 pounds, inspired other athletes to begin seeking her out for training advice as the 1960s moved forward. In many ways Wyatt is America's first internationally successful weight-trained female athlete. She deserves to be considered both the "godmother" of women's strength training and the match that lit the twigs and grass that blazed into a "movement" after Title IX passed in 1972. Wyatt's story was frequently used to motivate female athletes by the new coaches who began working with female athletes in the early 1970s. Her power as a role model was that she was not only truly strong but had wholesome good looks and a smaller stature that helped allay many a young female athlete's fears about getting "too strong," "too big," or muscle-bound.

There were, of course, other women pioneers as well. Gym owner Jerri Lee and her husband, Bob Lee, respectively held the women's and men's world records for the Mount Whitney Marathon—a twenty-six-mile race to the mountain's 14,496-foot summit. The Lees had done the Whitney marathon several times and generally used a combination of running and weight training in their training. But in 1959, as an experiment, they decided to do all their training in the gym—with weights—and did no running at all. Their workouts consisted of twenty sets of 100 repetitions (with weight) in the quarter squat, set after set of 50 repetitions in the leg curl and leg extension, and sets of 500 in the leg raise, day after day. On the day of the race, both set new records for the twenty-six-mile all-uphill course: 4:56:33 for Bob and 7:56:58.78 for Jerri.[80]

Over the course of the 1960s other women also joined the Iron Game. Britain's Stella Jacobs pioneered the way for women long jumpers; American Audrey McElmury led the way in women's cycling; and Canadian Nancy Greene won the World Cup downhill ski championships in 1967 after a training program that included sets of forty repetitions in the squat with 170 pounds.[81] By the 1968 Olympic Games, weight training had become commonplace among women throwers at the international levels of the sport; by the 1972 Games other track athletes, swimmers, cyclists, and skiers followed suit.

North American women athletes came slowly to the use of weight training for athletic enhancement because of a variety of societal taboos surrounding women, strength, and femininity. Until Title IX passed, women were generally denied access to collegiate weight rooms. Likewise, most commercial gyms did not permit men and women to train at the same time. When Jan Todd wanted to begin training with weights in 1973, for example, she had to petition the physical education department at Mercer University even to walk into Mercer's tiny weight room. When she and Terry later began training at a far nicer commercial gym called Powerbuilders in downtown

Macon, Georgia, she was the only woman permitted to train there. She was welcomed with the caveat that the facility had no place for her to dress or shower and no restroom for women only. As Jan Todd freely acknowledges, without her husband, Terry, to help her navigate this all-masculine terrain in those nascent years of her powerlifting career, she is not sure she would have continued to strength train.

CONCLUSION

By the close of the 1960s weight training had, in Patrick O'Shea's words, "emerged from the dark ages," at least for male athletes.[82] Weight training had spread across the country's colleges and was used by major college athletic departments as well as departments of physical education at small private colleges. Barbells had also worked their way into the official curriculum on many campuses with the 1962 publication of *Weight Training in Sports and Physical Education* by the American Association for Health, Physical Education, and Recreation (AAHPER).

With increasing exposure to the effects of weight training on the field and in the classroom, coaches began not only to encourage training but often to mandate it, based on the belief that it was necessary to stay competitive.[83] As coaches became more comfortable with weight training, it also began to move from being practiced only in the off-season to being carried on throughout the year—including during the season.[84] The programs were often monitored by line coaches, like John Neumann at California, or athletic trainers, like Frank Medina and then Charles Craven at Texas. As weight training proliferated and programs became more elaborate, however, a need was created for individuals who specialized in training. Football coaches and athletic trainers oversaw conditioning as a side job, not as their primary responsibility. While Al Roy was the first "modern" strength coach, designing programs for high school, college, and professional teams, it is important to note that he continued running his gymnasium business and was not solely employed as a strength coach. The first true specialist would emerge in 1969 when the University of Nebraska hired Boyd Epley, who was exclusively tasked with oversight of strength training for football.

The timing of the hiring was surprising, as it coincided with widespread revolts by athletes across the country. While the 1960s was an era of increasing competitiveness in college and professional sports, sport historian David Zang has noted that it also marked the end of the consensus that sports built character. Furthermore, many began to question "the very nature of that character and the methods used to build it."[85] Students initiated protests for a variety of reasons: some protested against racial inequality, some for political reasons, but many athletes protested against what they perceived as tyrannical and brutal treatment by their coaches.[86] In early 1969 members of the University of Maryland football team successfully called for the removal of their coach Bob Ward who, they charged, abused them mentally and physically. Football players at Oregon State University also initiated a protest in February 1969. Their grievance was the suspension of black linebacker Fred Milton by head coach Dee Andros. Milton was suspended because he refused to shave his beard and mustache, which were against official athletic department policy. As a result of the suspension, members of the football team boycotted classes and games throughout the following semester. In light of this rising resentment against the authority of the coach, it was peculiar timing for head Nebraska football coach Bob Devaney to extend the reach of the athletic department by hiring a conditioning specialist.

CHAPTER 5

•

AN EMERGING PROFESSION

Boyd Epley and the Founding of the National Strength and Conditioning Association

n a 1960 article in *Strength & Health* magazine, Al Roy, the man that Terry Todd called "the first modern strength coach," was interviewed about his legacy.[1] Specifically, the authors of the article asked Roy how strength coaching had become his passion and reported:

> In his typical adroit manner, the man responsible for this genesis in train-
> ing recalls those who inspired him. He acknowledges the fact that the
> father of American weightlifting, Bob Hoffman, and the brilliant weight-
> lifting technician, John Terpak, laid the foundation for his own system
> and are exemplars for those who will follow. *And others will follow*, for he
> emphatically states that the surface has just been scratched in creating a
> need for vital young men in the field of developing strength for athletics.[2]

Once again *Strength & Health* proved prophetic: the 1960s closed with the hiring of a young man who would eventually mold strength coaching into the autonomous profession we recognize today—and he was still an undergraduate when it all started.

As discussed in the preceding chapters, strength training for athletics underwent a cultural and pedagogical shift in the United States in the 1950s and 1960s. Into the 1950s most athletes and coaches still avoided weight training because they had been warned by coaches, doctors, or sports scien-tists that weight training would make a person muscle-bound.[3] In the 1960s, however, many athletes and coaches embraced weight training, though they were still experimenting with program design. By the end of the 1970s it was much less likely for an athlete to compete for a championship in any sport without having spent the requisite time in the weight room and doing sport-specific conditioning drills. So pervasive had preparation for sports become that in 1978 Boyd Epley, the first collegiate strength coach, was able to convince others to join him and form a national organization, the National Strength Coaches' Association (NSCA). The group's formation signaled that the older paradigms for weight training had finally begun to wane.[4]

"IF ANYONE GETS SLOWER, YOU'RE FIRED"

In September 1969 Epley, a junior pole-vaulter at the University of Nebraska, was performing his daily rehabilitation exercises in the tiny Schulte Field House "weight room" when he was summoned by an assistant athletic trainer who said, "You've got a phone call." Epley was surprised to be receiving a call; he had only been a student-athlete at Nebraska for less than a year and certainly did not expect to get a call at the athletic complex. His contemplation of who might be on the line was interrupted by the athletic trainer, who impatiently shouted, "Get in here! It's Tom Osborne." Osborne, who would later become the most successful head coach in Nebraska history, was at that time coaching the receivers and calling the offensive plays for the team. Epley recalls that he was taken aback when he heard that it was Osborne and wondered if he had somehow gotten into trouble with the football coaches.[5]

First, some background. Epley had chosen to include heavy resistance training as a part of his rehabilitation program for a back injury. While the meager selection of weights and machines in Schulte Field House limited his options, Epley drew upon his previous exposure to bodybuilding and Olympic weightlifting to craft a program to improve his overall strength while recovering from his training injury. Other injured athletes, also unable to practice, were frequently in the weight room during Epley's workouts. A number of them became intrigued by his training program and began following him around and performing the same exercises. At the time, none of the Nebraska athletic teams engaged in organized, heavy resistance training. The prevailing belief at Nebraska in this era, according to Epley, was still that heavy strength training would result in decreased speed and range of motion for athletes. Consequently, heavy resistance training was excluded from nearly all sport-training programs. So Epley was worried that Osborne's call would be a rebuke for allowing some of the injured football players to lift with him. His heart sank as Osborne asked, "Are you the guy who's been showing these guys how to lift weights?" Somewhat reluctantly, Epley affirmed that he had been working with the players and that some of them had been following his routine. Then, to his surprise, Osborne said, "I've noticed that they come back to practice healthier and stronger and I'm interested to know what you're doing in there. Would you be interested in coming over and talking to me?"[6] With a sigh of relief, Epley said that he would be happy to come right over.[7]

Osborne and the other Nebraska football coaches had no doubt seen the well-muscled 180-pound Epley around the athletic complex, but they could not have known that he was already a serious student of strength and conditioning practices along with his athleticism and exceptional muscular development. One freshman on the 1972 football team, George Mills, described Epley as looking like "Mr. America, yet he wasn't bulky; he looked like an athlete." At 215 pounds Epley could bench press more than 400, "so he really was an example of what weight training could do."[8] By the time Epley arrived at Nebraska, he was familiar with the training methods of bodybuilding, powerlifting, and Olympic weightlifting and had learned to borrow from all three systems for his own training.

Epley's involvement with strength training began in the seventh grade when his father purchased one of Bob Hoffman's York barbell sets for him. The set included a sheet with instructions on how to perform the Olympic lifts, so he began his career by doing presses, snatches, cleans, and jerks. Although he practiced these lifts faithfully for a time, he gradually lost interest in training at home. When Epley entered Alhambra High School in Phoenix, Arizona, he tried barbell training again, this time as part of a physical education class. Again, however, he did not stick with it. According to Epley, it just "didn't really make sense" to him at that time. However, following the end of the football season in his junior year in high school, he decided that he had to be bigger and stronger: he began training more seriously in order to gain weight.[9] During the summer between his junior and senior years he worked out at a local health club with a classmate, Pat Neve, who would go on to win the Mr. USA bodybuilding title in 1974.[10]

Neve, who was already interested in bodybuilding, taught Epley how to train. By the end of the summer Boyd had gone from 160 pounds to 180 pounds and had learned a great deal about the training methods of bodybuilders and powerlifters. When he reported for football practice in the fall, his newly added size came as a surprise to his coaches.[11] At linebacker, Boyd went from a self-described nonfactor in his junior year to the defensive player of the year as a senior. His newfound strength also translated well to his spring sport, track, where he garnered track athlete of the year honors as a pole-vaulter. After graduation, Epley took a track scholarship to attend Phoenix College, the local junior college. There he continued lifting and soon caught the eye of the Nebraska track coach Dean Brittenham, who in 1968 offered Epley a scholarship to join the track team at the University of Nebraska. Epley set a new Nebraska record in the indoor pole vault at fifteen feet. During his preparation for the spring 1969 track season, however, he suffered the back injury that inadvertently put him on the path to shaping the future of Nebraska athletics and creating the profession of strength coaching.

AN UNDERGRADUATE STRENGTH COACH

We can only imagine what must have been going through Epley's undergraduate mind as he abandoned his workout and walked to Osborne's office after the phone call. To his great surprise, however, Osborne did not just want to talk: he had a proposition for Epley. Osborne told Epley that he was interested in having the entire Cornhusker football team begin a weight-training program and asked what Epley would need in order to direct such a program.

Epley's response to that question tells a lot about the man that he eventually became. Rather than just suggesting that he could get by with only a few extra weights, Epley informed Osborne that the current weight room was too small to accommodate an entire team's workout and that a significant amount of additional equipment would be needed. After talking about space and what would be ordered, Osborne decided to place his faith in the self-assured twenty-two-year-old and told him that he would have a wall moved to create a larger space. Osborne then asked Epley to write out a shopping list of new equipment that they would need for training the entire team.[12]

Epley returned the next day with a list of the basic equipment needed for such a program.[13] The initial list was fairly conservative, because Epley was not sure how much Osborne intended to spend on the nascent program.[14] According to Epley, Osborne took the list from him, gave it only the most cursory glance, and handed it to the football secretary, instructing her to "order this." According to Epley, that moment opened his eyes to the power of football on campus, so he shrewdly said, "Coach! I forgot the second page," feigning distress. Osborne gave him a wry smile and said, "Alright, bring me the second page tomorrow."[15]

Osborne then turned to Epley and told him, "Now we've got to go in and see Bob." The comment jolted Epley. Bob Devaney was Nebraska's head football coach and athletic director and therefore one of the most powerful men in the state of Nebraska. "What do you mean?" Epley asked incredulously. Osborne responded, "We've got to go get permission to do what we just did." And with that the men headed up to Devaney's office. Epley recalls how unnerved he was to see Devaney sitting behind his massive desk in an imposing red leather chair and claims that he has a hard time remembering all he said to convince Devaney to support Osborne's project. While Devaney was interested in the idea, he was not at all sold on it. "Why," he wanted to know, "should we [lift weights]? No one else is doing it. My good friend Duffy Daugherty at Michigan State isn't doing it. Why should we?"[16] The only real evidence for the efficacy of a strength program that Epley was aware of was anecdotal, in the form of his own success through strength training.[17] He groped for an answer and eventually informed Devaney that weight training would help him win more games because his players would be faster. Devaney told Osborne and Epley that they could go ahead. Looking Epley square in the eye, he told the new strength coach, "If anyone gets slower, you're fired."[18] Epley's career as a strength coach had formally begun.

Devaney's apprehension was based on received knowledge. He had been told by his coaches that strength training hindered athletic performance and had carried that belief deep into his coaching career. In an interview with Terry Todd, Epley commented that "people are victims of their coaches. What their coaches did to them is what they know; whether it's right or wrong."[19] Given that Bob Devaney played his collegiate football in the 1930s, it seems quite likely that his approach to preparation for football was guided by what his coaches "did to him," which almost certainly did not include weight training.[20] Additionally, after coaching at the high-school level for fourteen years, Devaney's first collegiate coaching job was at Michigan State University under Clarence "Biggie" Munn from 1953 to 1956. Though Munn softened on weight training in his later years, in the mid-1950s he was strongly against weights.[21] Duffy Daugherty was the head football coach at Michigan State from 1955 to 1973 and had served with Devaney as an assistant under Munn. Given their coaching lineage, it is hardly surprising that neither man would employ weight training, especially given Munn's success at Michigan State without it.[22] The sample size that Devaney used to claim that "no one" was lifting weights was extremely limited, of course, but he was not the only coach who felt that way.

The attitude of many coaches who thought like Devaney did at that time was epitomized by Harry Paschall in a 1956 issue of *Strength & Health* magazine: "One Midwestern University Coach, whose teams have played in the Rose Bowl, once told us, 'I don't want any musclebound weightlifters on my team.'" Paschall went on to say, "The coach is no longer with this University because, while he was a smart strategist and knew football, he didn't know men and didn't know proper methods of conditioning. He belonged in the Past and that is where he is now spending his future."[23]

In the fall of 1969 Bob Devaney was in danger of similarly belonging to the past. He had come to Nebraska in 1962 and finished no worse than 9–2 in his first five seasons. By the late 1960s, however, his teams had fallen from the standard that he had helped set, going 6–4 in both the 1967 and 1968 seasons and failing to reach a postseason bowl game.[24] Making matters worse, the Huskers finished the 1968 season by taking a 47–0 thrashing at the hands of their archrival, the Oklahoma Sooners, on national television. At this point, some of the donors and alumni had begun grumbling that it might be time for a coaching change. Some donors in Omaha went so far as to start a petition calling for Devaney's removal.[25] Faced with this reality, Devaney knew that changes had to be made, thus providing the impetus for what later became known, thanks to Epley, as "Husker Power."

In reality, Nebraska had begun experimenting a bit with resistance training before Epley joined the athletic department staff. Weight training had been part of the physical education curriculum at Nebraska since the late 1950s, and the courses were so popular that they were often filled beyond their capacity.[26] Following the 1968 football season, Cletus Fischer, then an assistant offensive line coach, had seen some high school football teams undergoing a station-based, circuit-type conditioning program on a recruiting trip to Texas. He suggested to Devaney that a similar program be implemented at Nebraska.[27] Athletic trainer George Sullivan and assistant track coach Dean Brittenham were tasked with developing the program.[28] So Nebraska's first winter conditioning program was modeled on the circuit-based workouts seen in Texas and consisted of eight drills/stations, at which exercises were performed for five minutes each. Because of the high number of repetitions performed at each station, no significant strength gains were made by the team from this program.

On August 15, 1969, however, Epley began implementing a more modern program with the Nebraska team in the newly outfitted weight room.[29] After some initial testing, the Cornhuskers followed a dramatically different kind of weight-training program than the circuit work that they had been doing the previous winter. Epley's program, which the men did during the football season, was an amalgamation of bodybuilding, powerlifting, and Olympic lifting. As a competitive powerlifter and Olympic lifter himself until 1972, Boyd knew that the heavy training style of powerlifters, utilizing squats, bench presses, and deadlifts, would maximize the players' strength. The quick, explosive Olympic lifts required more athleticism and helped to produce power.

The turnaround for the Huskers was immediate. During the 1969 season, they posted a 9–2 record that included a 44–14 thumping of Oklahoma and a 45–6 trouncing of Georgia in the Sun Bowl.[30] Following the 1969 season,

Boyd took over control of the winter conditioning program as well. As the Huskers continued to dominate on the football field during the 1970 and 1971 seasons, both of which ended in national championships, Epley grew in stature and power at Nebraska. When Devaney stepped down as head football coach following the 1972 season, he became the athletic director and turned over coaching duties to Tom Osborne, his hand-picked successor. Osborne made sure that he did not lose Epley.

THE EVOLUTION OF HUSKER POWER

Osborne's ascent to head coach ushered in a new era for Husker football, as Osborne took a different approach to the game than Devaney had. According to Epley, Devaney's preparation for games varied little with respect to the opponent; he simply said, "This is how we're going to line up, and we're going to run right here."[31] Under Devaney, the Huskers did what they were going to do and dared the opponent to stop them. Osborne, in contrast, was a meticulous planner. He has been called "relentless in his pursuit of information" and "as resourceful as they come." Each week he created a game plan tailored to the upcoming opponent and required all of the Nebraska quarterbacks to pass a written exam on that plan. To Osborne, the process of preparing to play the game was crucial: his emphasis on preparation was part of the secret of his great success.[32] The process of preparing to play is where strength and conditioning come in. Epley gives a great deal of credit to Osborne saying that the strength program "was really his idea . . . he's the one who recognized the need [for the program]."[33]

For his part, Epley was no less meticulous than Osborne, and every bit the student of his craft that Osborne was. He also credits Devaney's ultimatum with shaping his approach to the profession. Devaney made him realize that the program would need to produce measurable results and do so quickly.[34] To that end, Epley knew he had to devise and employ tests that could objectively demonstrate an improvement in the players' performance. Devaney's biggest fear was that heavy strength training would cause his players to become slower. To prove that this was not the case, Epley initially tested players every two weeks on the forty-yard dash. To do these tests in the beginning, however, he had to borrow stopwatches from the physical education department. While he was there, he began making friends with some of the physical education faculty, to whom he could then turn for advice. One bit of advice that revolutionized athletic testing came from the department's chairman, Dr. Carl Weir, who suggested that he include a test that he referred to as the "jump reach" or vertical jump test as a way to measure athletic power.

Looking back on some of the early aspects of the program, Epley seemed almost embarrassed when he was interviewed. The testing of the forty-yard dash at such regular intervals was "crazy," in Epley's own words, but he was beginning to realize that his program was always a work in progress and that as the developer he would probably always be tinkering. While he tinkered, of course, the Nebraska players got stronger and stronger. In the beginning, Epley says, "I was testing everything I could, because I didn't know any better, trying to find something that could help us win."[35]

The first significant change that Epley made was dropping one of the stations that emphasized aerobic conditioning by having the players run continuously for five minutes.[36] Epley understood the concept of specificity and realized that a football game will never require a player to run constantly for that length of time, obviating the need for players to practice doing so. While he may not have categorized it as energy-systems training, he began to tailor his program to sport-specific needs early on. Another early change was in the testing format. Regular testing of the forty-yard dash was dropped because Epley recognized that two-week intervals were insufficient to allow performance improvements and because of the risk of hamstring injuries. Owing to his willingness to tailor the program to the demands of the sport, testing of the forty-yard dash was largely replaced by testing of a ten-yard sprint. Again, Epley reasoned that the new test was a better fit for the sport. Rarely will players ever get the opportunity to get up to full speed, as is evaluated in the forty-yard dash. They *will* be asked to be explosive for a few yards on every play, however, so evaluating how quick their first few steps are is probably more relevant to enhancing their football performance. Records are still kept and the "forty" is still tested at Nebraska, although now the rationale for running forty-yard sprints is that it remains the measuring stick used by talent evaluators for the National Football League.

Epley was lucky in his choice of assistant strength coach Mike Arthur, who was hired by Epley in 1977 and, like Boyd, was serious about the scientific aspects of training. One of Arthur's early contributions was a computer program called "Strength Disk," which allowed Epley and his assistants to create individualized workouts with benchmarks for each athlete, taking account of their performance during the most recent testing session.[37] While they both realized that individualized training was the best approach, Epley and his staff were seriously hampered by the large number of players who came out for the team. It was not unusual for them to have more than two hundred athletes trying out for the team, most of whom were Nebraska boys with little strength-training background. While the talent pool was wide, it was not always as deep as in more densely populated states like California and Texas, so player development became a top priority for Epley and the program. Epley quickly realized that he could not really train more than 200 players who wanted to try to be part of the Nebraska team. He needed a way to determine which athletes were likely to benefit the most from training and which ones were already naturally talented. With the help of assistant coach Mike Arthur and football fan and criminal justice professor Chris Eskridge, Epley developed the "Performance Index," a system of ranking athletes. It used what they termed a "power curve" to rank each athlete's performance at a series of specific tasks based on body weight and to measure performance improvements following a set period of training. Athletes with high scores on the initial tests who still improved would be given more weighted points than athletes with low initial scores who improved by the same value. In this way, the performance-adjusted index was used to quantify who the mediocre, good, and possibly great athletes were within the larger group. Epley and his assistants then focused their efforts on developing the most highly ranked athletes.[38]

In his classic book *From Ritual to Record* (1978), sport historian Allen Guttmann describes what he considers to be the seven characteristics of modern sport: secularism, equality, bureaucratization, specialization, rationalization, quantification, and obsession with records. Although Guttmann's model is generally thought of in reference to sport itself rather than the process of training for sport, the strength and conditioning program at Nebraska during the Epley years underwent exactly the kind of conceptual shift described by Guttmann. Guttmann's fourth characteristic of a modern sport, for example, is an increase in specialization. In his book he specifically cites football as an example of a sport with a high degree of specialization, with twenty-two different positions, not including "special teams." He goes on to point out that such specialization also results in an "intricate system of supportive personnel."[39] Most teams, even at the high school level, have coaches who specialize in coaching one or two positions. Furthermore, the teams have a sports-medicine staff to keep the players healthy, a sports-marketing staff to promote the game, and a variety of people involved in making the whole thing run (referees, equipment managers, ticket-takers, ushers, and so forth). So specialization within the sport leads to specialization of those involved in preparation for the game. By hiring Epley, Bob Devaney took an important step in accelerating this process. On its face, it appears that Epley as the strength coach is just one more specialist on the payroll. After all, conditioning duties had largely been handled previously by the athletic trainer or coaches with an interest in that area. Epley may thus seem just a more specialized version of those individuals.

Closer examination, however, reveals that the hiring of Epley represented an important step in the evolution of the collegiate athlete. Prior to the introduction of the "winter program," Nebraska football players would show up in the fall for preseason camp and "play their way into shape."[40] Once the season was over, they were free until spring football, during which time they became football players again for several weeks before becoming free once more during the summer until fall camp started. In this system, when players were not playing football, they could, if they desired, focus all of their energy on being students. During football season and spring ball, the players were de facto vocational students according to Burton Clark and Martin Trow's classification of student subcultures.[41] Vocational students are those who are "working anywhere from twenty to forty hours a week . . . to many of these hard-driven students, ideas and scholarship are . . . a luxury and distraction." This "vocation" became more time-consuming with the introduction of Epley's new year-round conditioning program, and Nebraska football players never stopped being football players. They now had a year-round vocation: football. Former Nebraska player George Mills said as much in his 2004 book, commenting that "the addition of strength coach Boyd Epley to the staff legitimized weight lifting; it had the effect of giving the players another job."[42]

According to Guttmann, "the crucial factor in professionalization is not money but time—how much of a person's life is dedicated to the achievement of athletic excellence? In other words, to what degree does a person specialize in such excellence?"[43] As such, the addition of a conditioning program was an important step in the evolution away from the notion of "student-athletes" toward collegiate "athletes."

The heavy focus on player development allowed Nebraska to develop what Epley refers to as an "assembly line" of great players. Development of athletic talent was integral to the success of the Husker program, and the expectation of year-round effort became established as part of the recruitment process. Armen Keteyian remarked in his book *Big Red Confidential* that "without question, no football team in this country—college or pro—takes more pride in its strength and conditioning program than the University of Nebraska. One look at the weight room and its attendant motto printed proudly on a sign—'Where the Best Athletes Come to Get Better'—tells you that."[44]

During their recruitment, players sat through a presentation by Epley, which took place atop the altar-like "records platform," a central feature of the West Stadium weight room. Epley would emphasize what coming to Nebraska could do for them in terms of their development as athletes. Due to Osborne and Epley's player-development philosophy, freshmen and sophomores rarely played, particularly at nonskill positions.[45] In contrast, if the players had elected to go to other schools, they might have had the chance to jump right into the mix for playing time. Part of Epley's recruiting task was convincing players that spending the time in training would be more beneficial for their athletic careers over the long term: "We would look at the recruit and ask, 'How much do you weigh? How much do you want to weigh?' [Then we'd tell them] you might as well go somewhere [like Nebraska] where they know how to help you do that. Here are some examples of athletes at your position that we've helped."[46]

The records platform also had a large video screen above it that played footage of Nebraska football greats throughout the presentation, allowing prospective players to see the results of the program being sold to them with unmistakable clarity. They could see Neil Smith, who would go on to be selected six times for the NFL's Pro Bowl, and how he gained fifty pounds in as many weeks and became the fastest defensive lineman in Nebraska history. They could see Dave Rimington, the only back-to-back winner of the Outland Trophy (given to college football's best interior lineman), using 900 pounds or more on the hip sled. Offensive and defensive linemen, in particular, were sold on the notion of what the strength program could do for them. If they chose to play at Nebraska, they were told up front that there was a "no missed-workout" policy. So ingrained was this philosophy, Epley said with pride, that at one point they "went 15,000 workouts without an offensive lineman missing a workout." Of his role in the recruiting process, he said, "By the end of the demonstration, parents and recruits were pretty well convinced that Nebraska was focused on helping athletes improve their performance. Not all schools were. A lot of schools they just recruit you and then they didn't even have a strength program. They recruit you and you either played well or they'd get someone else and you were done."[47]

The Husker Power program was actually what sold Dave Rimington on playing at Nebraska. Heavily recruited out of high school, the Nebraska native chose to stay in state for his collegiate career because of the strength program. "I was really hooked on the weights by my senior year and I knew Nebraska had a great tradition and a big weight room. The choice was easy."[48]

While a large portion of the emphasis was placed on player development due to the personal philosophies of both Epley and Osborne, some of this emphasis was a result of necessity. With a large supply of athletes willing to work but a relatively small pool of really talented athletes, Nebraska's success depended on extracting the best from the talent they had. Additionally, as Epley pointed out, in Nebraska they did not have mountains like Colorado or beautiful beaches like Miami. As a result, recruiting efforts pitched what

Nebraska *did have*: a weight room and a man who knew how to employ it to build bigger and better athletes.[49]

Guttmann wrote in *Ritual to Record* that if you "combine the impulse to quantification with the desire to win, to excel, to be the best . . . the result is the concept of a record."[50] In order to motivate players and show progress, Epley established a school record board in the spring of 1970.[51] Located prominently in the weight room, the record board tallied best lifts in events such as the bench press, squat, hang clean, vertical jump, and forty-yard dash and served as a prominent reminder of what could be achieved with dedication to the Husker Power program. Carrying specialization even further, Epley made sure that records were established for each sport as well as for the entire athletic program. In addition to the overall records, the Performance Index was used to rank records with respect to the size of each athlete by using an elaborate scoring system. They even posted the best overall Performance Index score, a composite of athletes' scores on all of the tests factored against their body size. What started as a simple board used to track a handful of best lifts quickly evolved into an elaborate ranking system, which now necessitates statistical software. As the historian John Hoberman noted, our love of records and "quantified sports performances" is part of "a mania for measurement that continues unabated to this day."[52]

Under Epley's direction, the preparation methods for all varsity sports at Nebraska began assuming more and more of Guttmann's characteristics of modernity. Keeping track of records allowed athletes to compete against not only their current teammates but the school's all-time greats. Using the scaled scores of the Performance Index even allowed athletes to compare themselves to athletes in other sports, regardless of size and gender. Guttmann's principle of rationalization, a prescription of rules with a "logical relationship between means and ends . . . in order to this, we have to do that," ideally fits the process of physical training. Guttmann suggests that "training implies a rationalization of the whole enterprise, a willingness to experiment, a constant testing of results achieved."[53]

In the case of football, the overarching goal is obviously to get the football into the opponents' end zone in accordance with a specified set of rules, but some of the particulars of that process are left up to the players and coaches. Tom Osborne preferred to get the ball into the end zone through the brute force of a Power-I option attack. Barry Switzer, one-time coach of the Oklahoma Sooners, said of Nebraska's rushing attack: "Everyone knows what Nebraska is going to do! The trick is stopping it! You don't win with schemes or playbooks, you win with players. . . . Other people run the Nebraska offense, but they run the ball on first down and it's second-and-eight. When

Nebraska runs it, it's second-and-two. They run it again, and it's first-and-ten."[54] The prescribed rules of the game allow players to throw the ball over their opponents. The Huskers, however, preferred to run over and through them. The strength program, with its emphasis on explosiveness and sheer strength, is an emblem of rationalization. The original record board included the bench press and did not include the ten-yard dash. Testing of the bench press was dropped because Epley felt that it did not evaluate football talent.[55] The ten-yard dash was added because a short, explosive burst of speed did. The strength program was a component of rationalization in that it allowed the Huskers to move the ball into the opponents' end zone more effectively, using a ground attack that conformed to the prescribed rules of the sport.

In giving credit to Osborne for starting the program, Epley is quick to point out that it would not have been as successful as it eventually became if not for Osborne's football philosophy. Had Osborne sought to spread the field and build a speedy passing attack, big, powerful linemen and backs would not have been as necessary. Owing to Osborne's preference for a grinding running game, the strength program became an essential part of Nebraska football.

Another aspect of modernity is the creation of bureaucratic entities to support and administer sports. Epley's first contribution to this characteristic of modern sport was the formation of the Husker Power Club. This club, started by Epley in 1984, served as a booster club specifically for the strength and conditioning program. Membership dues to the club were used to update the facilities and purchase new strength equipment used by Husker athletes. Membership categories ranged from a $50 annual donation up to $5,000, with benefits commensurate with the amount donated. The lowest level allowed the donors to receive a quarterly newsletter that kept them up to date on the training progress of Nebraska athletes. A donation of $5,000 or more earned donors a personal invitation to view training sessions and the opportunity to "become a Husker Strength and Conditioning Coach for a day."[56] The prestige of the program that Epley built was so great that many fans paid just to pretend they had his job for a day. According to Epley, the club had raised more than 2 million dollars in support of the strength and conditioning program at Nebraska by 2010.[57] Thanks in part to the Husker Power Club, Nebraska athletes now train in the palatial Osborne Athletic Complex, whose weight room includes twenty-eight multiracks and twenty-three lifting platforms—a far cry from the handful of racks and benches on Epley's initial list in 1969.[58]

Nebraska fans enthusiastically supported the weight program because the work ethic promoted by the Husker Power weight program fit well with their perceptions of the values embodied by their state. As documented by Roger Aden, many Nebraskans believe that they have been instilled with a unique work ethic, which results from a combination of the often inhospitable climate and hard agricultural work.[59] Aden points to the state's founding by homesteaders in the early 1860s, who were awarded 160 acres if they were willing to live on and improve the land for five years, as evidence of the lineage of hard work embraced by Nebraskans. A team that was able to dominate others through gritty, hard, physical work on the field and in the weight room was a team that many Nebraskans felt embodied the ethos of the state. This perception is also personified in the school's mascot, the Cornhusker, who performs tedious and difficult but necessary work.

THE NATIONAL STRENGTH AND CONDITIONING ASSOCIATION

Epley's second contribution to the evolution of sporting bureaucracy was to have a much more far-reaching impact. In September 1977, before the Huskers kicked off a home game against the Alabama Crimson Tide, he was introduced to the commissioner of the Southeastern Conference (SEC), Boyd McWhirter.[60] The commissioner inquired about the exact nature of Epley's position at Nebraska and then asked if Alabama had anyone in a similar position. Surprised that a conference commissioner could be unaware of the existence of professional strength coaches, Epley decided that some kind of unification and professionalization of the field was in order to ensure the success of his fledgling profession. Consequently, he sent a letter to schools around the country to establish a national directory of strength coaches in 1978.[61] He got back 377 letters and compiled the results into a ninety-page directory titled *The National Directory of Strength Coaches*.

Following the publication of the directory, a few coaches began discussing the idea of a formal organization for the profession. After discussing the idea with a handful of his colleagues over a series of months, Epley offered to host the first annual meeting of the National Strength Coaches' Association on July 29, 1978. More than seventy-five men made the trip to Lincoln. Although most of them were not then called strength coaches, they oversaw what strength training was then being done at their schools. At that meeting Epley was unanimously elected president and executive director of the new organization. A mission statement was written noting that the NSCA proposed to "unify its members and facilitate a professional exchange of ideas in the area of strength development as it relates to the improvement of athletic performance and fitness."[62]

Epley and these early pioneers knew that legitimization of the strength coaching profession rested upon their ability to prove that training really did improve the performance of athletes. Like many other professional associations, they used a scientific approach to the sharing of ideas by establishing a national conference each year, establishing a series of regional clinics organized by the six new regional directors, and in December 1978 began publishing an organizational newsletter.[63] The first newsletter was sent to over 8,000 coaches, YMCA directors, and other "interested people" across the country, promising that "each issue will be packed with the latest information on strength and conditioning for football, basketball, baseball, track and field, swimming, wrestling, gymnastics, women's sports, and more. We'll investigate and present the latest theories and research in the strength and conditioning field and present it in a fashion that is easily understood . . . you'll have the important information necessary to ensure that your athletes are trained at their best."[64] This first issue satisfied both of the established needs of the emerging organization: it increased awareness of strength coaches through the wide dissemination of the newsletter and furthered the exchange of best practices in the field.

Epley's impact on collegiate athletics was now being felt on a national scale. By the end of the 1970s nearly every major university in America had at least one person listed as a "strength coach," and the National Strength Coaches' Association was quickly growing in size and stature. Epley was very influential because many of these new strength professionals had worked with him as assistant strength coaches and graduate assistants. In fact, more than sixty-four of Epley's former assistants went on to direct strength-coaching activities for a variety of universities and professional teams. As they moved into their new positions, they continued to use the methods that they had learned from Epley. He also actively disseminated information about the Husker Power system. He authored multiple books on strength and conditioning as well as an entire series on training for a variety of sports (football, swimming, wrestling, baseball, and so forth) and along the way also helped market "the Nebraska way."[65]

The nascent strength coaches' organization grew quickly; attendance at the second annual convention in 1979 approached three hundred, up from seventy-six the year before. The increased membership brought diverse interests, while the first four issues of the NSCA Newsletter had focused largely on strength programs for football. Members clamored for information about other sports, nutrition, and physiology. The feedback led to the enlargement and splitting of NSCA publications into two formats in 1979: the NSCA Bulletin and the NSCA Newsletter. The Bulletin was intended to convey organizational information, while the Newsletter would carry articles related to strength training. The *Newsletter* expanded rapidly and by the fifth bimonthly issue had transitioned to the *NSCA Journal*. A free sample of the *Journal* was sent out to 17,000 coaches, scientists, and other potentially interested parties in 1980, to generate interest in the organization. Many of those recipients were interested: by May 1980 the organization had grown to include more than 2,600 members. While the influx of members strengthened the financial base of the organization, it diluted the proportion of members who were actual strength coaches. In order to reflect this changing demographic, the organization's name was changed from the National Strength Coaches' Association to the National Strength and Conditioning Association in May 1981.

The name change of the organization coincided with a change in the NSCA's mission. Along with generating recognition for the nascent profession, the association and its publications were initially intended to serve as forums to exchange ideas about strength and conditioning. Shortly after the group's founding, however, the focus shifted from discussing research to producing research. Just as establishing the NSCA cemented Boyd Epley's legacy in the pantheon of strength coaches, the NSCA's commitment to strength-related research would prove to be its enduring legacy.

CHAPTER 6

•

BRIDGING THE GAP

The National Strength and Conditioning Association
and Its Impact

n April 1982 the *National Strength and Conditioning Association Journal* (*NSCAJ*) published the first in a series of highly unusual articles for a professional journal, titled "An Introduction to Research: Reading and Understanding." It informed readers that the series was intended to "help our membership gain insight into the reading and understanding of research papers."[1] Written by Wyoming doctoral student William J. (Bill) Kraemer, the article suggested that coaches have at least one "library research day" each month during which they find and read articles relevant to program design for their athletes. In the next issue Kraemer published "Research: Reading and Understanding: The Starter Steps." In that piece and in the four that followed it, the NSCA taught a minicourse in scientific research methods.[2] The series' authors—Kraemer, Gary Dudley, Steve Fleck, Josie Sifft, and Al Starck—described how to read a literature review, how to select subjects for a scientific study, and what constituted an adequate sample. They explained what the results section of a scientific report should contain and how the discussion section at the end should describe a study's findings, discuss its applicability, and raise questions for future research. In addition, the articles taught readers the basic differences between validity and reliability, described how to develop a hypothesis, and discussed sampling methods.[3] To say that the articles were unusual for a professional journal is inadequate; they may well be unprecedented. Scientific journals typically assume that their readers have the ability to understand the methodological and statistical data of the studies that they contain. In the early 1980s, however, the readership of the *NSCAJ* differed significantly from the readership of other academic journals. For the most part, the early readers of NSCA publications were not scientists but practitioners. They were the first generation of modern strength coaches, and nearly all of them shared the desire to

132

take the emerging practice of strength training for sport and make it into a reputable and scientifically based profession.

When the National Strength Coaches' Association held its first meeting in 1978, the majority of the seventy-six individuals that accepted Nebraska strength coach Boyd Epley's invitation and traveled to Lincoln had no specialized training in the scientific underpinnings of strength training. While most of these early members were college educated, many had been selected to serve as strength coaches (1) because they had been working as an athletic trainer or assistant coach and a higher-ranking coach tapped them to take on additional lifting responsibilities, (2) because they had used weights to prepare themselves for either football or the field events, or (3) because they were competitive powerlifters or weightlifters.[4] NCAA shot-put champion Dana LeDuc of the University of Texas at Austin (UT), for example, who graduated with a basic physical education degree that contained no specialized coursework in strength and conditioning, was typical of these early coaches.[5] When hired as UT's first full-time strength coach in 1977, LeDuc was well aware that his ability to demonstrate proper technique for power cleans and snatches and the fact that he both looked and was physically powerful were the main qualifications considered by UT administrators when he was chosen to strengthen the Longhorns.[6] To be clear, this is not to suggest that LeDuc or any of the other late 1970s strength coaches had not tried to avail themselves of scientific research before the formation of the NSCA. However, in the 1970s the dearth of scientific knowledge about strength and sport in the United States meant that even those who desired greater knowledge had few places to gain that information until the NSCA began publishing its professional journals.

Due to a paucity of research, the *National Strength and Conditioning Association Journal*, begun in 1979, struggled to find scientific content in the beginning. Edited by Ken Kontor, who had been hired by Epley to help run the new organization, the *Journal* in the early issues almost exclusively contained short descriptive articles about training modalities for different athletic constituencies.[7] The sixth issue of the first volume, for example, contained an article on the "All-American Strength Team," a report titled "Steeler Strength the Powersafe Way," a piece by coach Carl Miller on Olympic lifting techniques, a short article on neck injury rehabilitation, an article describing the University of Miami's baseball strength program, a report on Vitamin B-15, an article on static stretching, and, at the very back, a piece called "Nutrition and Women in Sports," which contained a few citations of other academic articles on nutrition. Filling out the journal's slim forty-one pages was a "Research Report" by Eric Bannister (PhD) of Simon Fraser

University in Canada, dealing with muscle physiology, aging, and training state. More review essay than scientific study, Bannister's work was nonetheless the only article in the *Journal* containing any research-based analysis of strength.[8]

In *Foundations of Clinical Research* (2009), Leslie Portney and Mary Watkins explain that what people consider to be reliable knowledge emerges from a hierarchically arranged series of sources that begins with tradition and folk wisdom and then transfers first to figures of authority, then to knowledge gained through trial and error, then to logical reasoning, and, at the very top, to the reliability of the scientific method.[9] Early strength coaches like Epley and LeDuc no doubt began their introduction to the field of strength and conditioning by learning from others who were already lifters and by reading popular magazines like *Strength & Health, Muscle Power, Iron Man, Mr. America*, and *All American Athlete*.[10] Even exercise physiologist Bill Kraemer, who began his professional life as a strength, football, and wrestling coach, cited Joe Weider's *All American Athlete* as being "inspirational" to him as a young athlete in the 1960s and instrumental in exposing him to ideas about strength training for sport performance.[11] Similarly, Epley explained in a 1997 interview that he was like many young athletes of his generation who were largely "guessing the most effective way to train" when he began his career and acknowledged that he was keenly aware that very little information related to strength for sport had been created through actual research studies.[12] In the earliest years of the NSCA, then, nearly all members typically operated in the bottom half of the Portney and Watkins pyramid. They used information handed down to them by their coaches, routines from machine and barbell manufacturers, routines published in popular magazine articles, and personal experience based on experimentation with themselves and their teams. Epley learned some of what he knew about creating muscular hypertrophy from bodybuilder Pat Neve, who became his training partner for a time.[13] Dana LeDuc trained as a varsity track athlete under the guidance of UT athletic trainer Charlie Craven but then gravitated to an off-campus gym in downtown Austin, where he learned even more about strength development from local powerlifters and bodybuilders.[14]

Epley, LeDuc, and most other strength coaches in this era, however, were hungry for scientific information. As track athletes Epley and LeDuc were conscious that Russia, East Germany, and many other European nations were rapidly surpassing America in the Olympic Games and that advanced strength-training programs were a major factor in their Cold War dominance. Although it has been assumed by many that anabolic steroid use primarily accounted for the rise of Communist sport teams in the 1960s and 1970s, an equal—and perhaps even greater—cause was that Eastern Bloc nations were so far ahead of the United States in the scientific study of strength. According to sport historian James Riordan, by the time of the NSCA's second meeting (at which the professional journal was founded) the Soviet Union already had approximately four thousand people working in the area of sport research.[15] Moreover, researchers in fields related to sport physiology and training technique were incentivized with bonuses and gold medals for high-quality work. An early result of the Soviet drive to apply scientific study to sport training was periodization theory, which was used by the Soviet Union in preparing teams for the 1960 Olympics and by the East Germans as they prepared for the Mexico City Games in 1968. Most American coaches had not even heard of periodization until a decade later when the NSCA was formed and began discussing it in the *Journal* and at conferences.

Just how scientifically far behind the Eastern Bloc America was at this time is eloquently captured in *The National Directory of Strength Coaches*, the paperback address book and resource guide that Epley put together prior to the first NSCA meeting in 1978. In addition to cataloging collegiate and professional strength coaches and describing the equipment they used with their athletes, Epley included a section on books and material resources available for strength coaches. In the "Journals and Articles" section, he listed a mere nineteen periodicals. Eight of these could be regarded as professional publications (although not strength-related) and included titles such as the *NCAA News*, *Athletic Administration*, and *Scholastic Coach*. The other eleven titles were all nonprofessional "muscle magazines," such as *Strength & Health*, *Muscle Builder/Power*, *Iron Man*, *Body Forum*, and even a short-lived bodybuilding magazine called *Looking Good*. Notably absent from the list were any scientific journals from the field of physiology, any European sport science or physiology publications, and, surprisingly, *Research Quarterly*, the academic journal of the American Alliance for Physical Education, Recreation and Dance, which had on a few occasions published scholarly articles about strength prior to 1978.[16] *Research Quarterly's* absence from Epley's list demonstrates the primitive state of scientific knowledge in America at this time, as does his failure to mention Michael Yessis's *Soviet Sports Review*, which began in 1966 in an attempt to introduce Eastern Bloc training methods and scientific reports to the United States.[17]

Epley's *Directory* contained an additional section on books, which listed the few research-based monographs then available from authors such as Peter Karpovich, Jack Leighton, Benjamin Massey, Pat O'Shea, Thomas DeLorme, and others.[18] Again, however, the list also contained a number of nonacademic trade publications like Arnold Schwarzenegger's autobiographical *Education of a Bodybuilder* and several how-to books on basic bodybuilding like the one by hypnotist/trainer Lou Ravelle.[19]

The need for a stronger scientific foundation for the NSCA became particularly evident in May 1979 during the group's second meeting at Northwestern University in Evanston, Illinois. In the lead-up to the conference, Epley and Ken Kontor, then editor of both the *Newsletter* and the *Journal* and the NSCA's assistant or executive director from 1978 to 1992, had contacted Allan J. Ryan, editor of *Physician and Sportsmedicine* and one of the most distinguished members of the American College of Sports Medicine. The pair sought Ryan's help in arranging speakers who could talk authoritatively about exercise physiology as it related to strength for the conference. The resulting program read like a *Who's Who* of physiology and sports medicine for that era, with PhD holders Jack Wilmore, David Costill, Richard Nelson, Steven Wolf, Reggie Egerton, Alexander Lind, and Eric Bannister speaking alongside several notable physicians, including Ryan himself. Kontor was accurate when he wrote before the conference that "great care was taken in finding speakers who would make the convention an educational experience."[20]

Unfortunately, much of the information was beyond the reach of the practitioner-based audience. Kontor noted in the next issue of the *Newsletter* that "the presentations provided by the physicians might have sent the average strength coach to his physiology textbook to reacquaint himself with such concepts as fiber splitting, myofibril and sarcomere functions to name a few." While he characterized the presentations as "stimulating," Kontor also expressed concern that the strength coaches were out of their depth dealing with such detailed physiological discussions. As a result, as Kontor explained in an editorial, "every effort must be made to form a bridge of communication between these authorities and the strength coach."[21] As it happened, a man who would do a great deal to spearhead just such an effort was about to join the organization.

A former varsity football player at La Crosse State University (now the University of Wisconsin–La Crosse), Bill Kraemer began his association with the NSCA in 1978 when he was listed in Boyd Epley's original *Directory of Strength Coaches*. At the time, Kraemer had recently completed a master's degree in exercise physiology at the University of Wyoming and was working as an assistant professor and a football, wrestling, and strength and conditioning coach at Carroll College (now University) in Waukesha, Wisconsin. Working both as an academic and as a coach, Kraemer typically found his summers filled with camp obligations. In 1980 Kraemer decided to refocus on an academic career, return to the University of Wyoming to pursue his doctorate in physiology and biochemistry. The decision ended his summer-camp obligations and allowed him to attend his first NSCA conference, held that year in Dallas, Texas. Kraemer likened the 1980 NSCA meeting to football-coaching conferences that he had attended. At those conferences coaches mostly listened to give talks others in their profession about drills and strategy, networked for jobs, and socialized. The initial NSCA conferences, he explained, had a very similar feel, which made him worry about the organization's future.[22] "If we didn't have research," he explained in an interview, "then we'd become just another coaching organization."[23]

Committing himself to the idea that the NSCA had value and needed a stronger scientific footing in the late 1970s, Kraemer began calling the small circle of researchers interested in strength training as a research subject in order to gauge their interest in joining the organization.[24] He started with a call to his friend and former football teammate from his undergraduate days at La Crosse, Steve Fleck. Having completed his PhD in exercise physiology at the Ohio State University (OSU) in 1978, Fleck was the first exercise physiologist hired by the U.S. Olympic Training Center in Colorado Springs, Colorado. Fleck, in turn, recruited one of his OSU colleagues, Gary Dudley, while Kraemer contacted Mike Stone, who, with his PhD in exercise science from Florida State, was then working as an assistant professor at Auburn University. With Stone at Auburn was John Garhammer, a biomechanist, who had done his dissertation on power production in Olympic weightlifters at UCLA. Through such networking, the NSCA quickly began to gain scientists with varied research interests and academic specializations as new members.

Kraemer was not the only person in the NSCA who wanted to put the profession on a more scientific footing, of course. In the second issue of the *NSCA Newsletter* released in February 1979, for example, University of New Hampshire strength coach George Elder lambasted a book that he had just received from the organization: *Strength Training for Football: The Penn State Way* by Daniel Riley. "I in no way paid for this unsolicited and poorly written unscientific book," wrote the impassioned Elder, adding, "if this field is to advance, we had better redirect its efforts." To that end, Elder called for more "unbiased" studies and urged the organization to use its funds to sponsor research in order to lead the profession out of "the dark ages."[25]

Elder's desire for more research was shared by others in the group, and at the 1979 business meeting the members voted to establish a Research Committee as a way to help the association move away from simply sharing strength programs based on anecdotal wisdom and move toward creating and disseminating research-based information.[26] This was a departure from the organization's original mission statement, which suggested that the organization existed to "unify its members and facilitate a professional exchange of ideas in the area of strength development as it relates to the improvement of athletic performance and fitness."[27] Karen Knortz, head athletic trainer for women at the University of Nebraska, was the first chair of the committee. According to Dan Wathen, who was an athletic trainer at Youngstown State University when he was asked to join the group, the other members were Tim Garl, an athletic trainer at the University of Mississippi and later at Indiana University, doctoral student Bill Kraemer, and Garry Benford, the physical director of the downtown YMCA in Columbus, Ohio.[28]

Journal editor Ken Kontor shared the view that for the field and the association to grow and prosper it must move beyond simply being a platform for the "exchange [of] ideas" and become a professional body that "bridged the gap" between practitioners and researchers. A graduate of the University of Nebraska with a bachelor's in journalism and experience in both powerlifting and weightlifting, Kontor presciently argued that bringing these groups closer together "through the blending of research and application" would mean that "a better conditioned, improved athlete will emerge."[29]

Once formed, the NSCA Research Committee's original mandate was to "conduct and report on research in strength training" and "contribute to the new research section" of the *NSCAJ*.[30] Karen Knortz served as the first chairperson.[31] The committee's first contribution to the *Journal* was a column called "The Kinesiology Corner," published in April 1980, that included detailed discussions of the muscles used in common strength-training movements.[32] In August "Abstracts from the World of Strength and Conditioning" began appearing as well. Committee members combed the pages of journals like *Medicine & Science in Sports & Exercise*, *Physician and Sports Medicine*, *Journal of Sports Medicine*, and *Research Quarterly* and wrote short summaries of the research studies that they felt might be relevant for strength coaches. The abstracts also introduced readers to more advanced topics like muscle fiber type and muscular power, trainability, and motor unit activation.[33] In October 1981 "The Exercise Physiology Corner" made its first appearance.[34] In an editor's note introducing the new column, Kontor explained that an understanding of exercise physiology was indispensable for a strength and conditioning coach and that the physiology series was being added to the *Journal* to help inform coaches about the basics of adaptations to various exercise stimuli.

In addition to the need to educate nonscientists, the NSCA and its Research Committee also faced other challenges. For example, many individuals were unsure about the propriety of strength training for women.

When author Jan Todd was interviewed by Auburn women's athletic director Johanna Davenport in 1980 for a strength-coaching position with her women's teams, Davenport told Todd that she did not want her women athletes lifting weights during their menstrual periods, a position shared by many other coaches and administrators in this era. An even bigger challenge, however, was to end the general public's confusion about the value and safety of strength training.[35] Although many schools had begun to incorporate strength training for their athletes by the late 1970s, numerous coaches, administrators, and physicians still held tightly to older beliefs about the dangers of muscle-binding. When Kraemer took over as chair of the Research Committee in 1981, he understood that part of his task (and that of the *NSCAJ*) would be to battle such mythology.[36]

Over the next several years Kraemer and Kontor encouraged authors to tackle these topics in their articles and to discuss safety as well. "Weights Don't Hurt Knees" (published in 1980) was part of this campaign, as was Paul Hoolahan's article on the value of weight training for basketball players published later that year, along with a few articles on training women's teams.[37] Over time the visible evidence of highly successful weight-trained athletes like Billy Cannon and Jimmy Taylor and the success of Epley's Nebraska football teams, combined with the scientifically backed recommendations expressed in the *NSCA Journal*, began to change public opinion.

MACHINES VERSUS FREE WEIGHTS: EARLY RESEARCH EFFORTS

As committee members and the NSCA learned, however, the Research Committee also needed to tackle another obstacle if the association was going to make the full shift to a nonpartisan scientific association: how best to maintain scientific objectivity amid a growing number of corporate sponsors. In order to launch the NSCA, Epley had needed financial support. In this regard, Arthur Jones—inventor and tireless promoter of his Nautilus machines—contacted Epley in the spring of 1978 and urged him not to hold a meeting for strength coaches. As Epley tells the story, Jones was afraid that the formation of a group like the NSCA would diminish him as an "authority" on strength training and also make possible an open dialogue on the value of machine training.[38] However, after visiting Jones at his home in Deland, Florida, Epley convinced him to become a sponsor for the new group, so Nautilus had full-page ads on the strategically important inside front and inside back covers of *The National Directory of Strength Coaches* in 1978. The front cover ad claimed that Jones's machines were "the ultimate equipment for athletes." The back cover ad was all text and stated: "Through medical research, our goal is to dissolve the fallacies which exist in the realm of sports medicine. Our endeavor is to present the facts of this little understood area to the public, refined by the light of scientific research." The ad continued by noting, "We are concerned with the torrent of false claims against which the public has little defense. As a result, our desire is to build the structure that is legitimate sports medicine."[39]

Jones no doubt hoped that by becoming closely linked with the NSCA he could shape and control the field in this nascent era of the organization. Clearly, Jones and the other early advertisers in the NSCA publications (like York Barbell, Universal Gym, Hydra Gym, Paramount Health Equipment, and Mini Gym) must have felt that things were headed in the right direction when an editorial by Ken Kontor in the *NSCA Journal* praised the companies for their loyalty to the association and suggested that they had used research on muscle function to develop tools that allowed the achievement of "maximum results." Kontor went so far as to urge readers to "take the time to contact each of the companies within the pages of this *Journal*" and "ask them about the equipment they sell." He suggested that companies would inform coaches of the utility of their products, describe their strengths and weaknesses, and explain how training needs would be met. Kontor even told his readers that they needed to understand that speaking with equipment companies was "part of your job."[40] In retrospect, Kontor's admonitions crossed the line of objectivity.

Company "pitch men" have always been a source of information about strength training, but the Nautilus claims began to trouble NSCA members because of Jones's insistence that his Nautilus method was based on scientific research studies. Space does not permit a full discussion of the debate that raged within the pages of the *NSCA Journal* over the next several years regarding the topic of "free-weights vs. machines" or a full exploration of the intricacies of Nautilus's self-funded "Colorado Experiment," in which bodybuilder Casey Viator and Jones himself were the sole subjects in a "study" that allowed Nautilus to claim that by training only on Nautilus machines, and with only one set per exercise, Viator had gained sixty-three pounds of muscle in only four weeks.[41] However, it was becoming increasingly clear to the Research Committee and the NSCA that they needed to preserve their academic objectivity and remove conflicts of interest even if that meant testing the claims of advertisers who were closely affiliated with the association.

In 1980 Dan Wathen reported his research on the efficacy of the Mini-Gym Leaper.[42] Wathen, a founding member of the NSCA and an athletic trainer at Youngstown State University, compared the Mini-Gym Leaper—an isokinetic machine that mimicked the squat—to standard barbell squats in terms of its ability to increase vertical jumping in football players. Mini Gym was also an important NSCA sponsor and had a two-page ad in the *Directory* containing written endorsements by Al Roy and NSCA founder Boyd Epley. Mini Gym machines were among the most common devices reported as being used by strength coaches in the 1978 *Directory*. Oklahoma State, for example, reported that its athletic weight room had twelve such machines. The Cleveland Browns' weight room had eight. Based on some early research demonstrating the superiority of isokinetic over isotonic training for increasing muscular power, Mini Gym Corporation took the position that its equipment would produce larger performance gains than traditional training.[43] In Wathen's study, however, users of the Mini-Gym Leaper did not improve their jumping ability at the end of an eight-week training program, while the barbell-trained group did. Although this was a simple study by modern standards, Wathen's research would be cited repeatedly in articles about another NSCA sponsor, Nautilus.

The controversy over Nautilus was brought to the fore in NSCA publications by George Elder. The New Hampshire strength coach, who had called for more research on strength training in the second issue of what was to become the *NSCAJ*, questioned the utility of machine training in the third issue. In an article titled "Machines: A Viable Method for Training Athletes?" Elder described his view of the "machine age" that had come to sport training.[44] Relying on anecdotal evidence from his own training and observations of his athletes, he asserted that machines were inferior to barbells because the training lacked specificity; machines did not engage stabilizing muscles to the same extent as did free weights; did not allow the same speed of movement; and did not require the same degree of balance. Worse, according to Elder, he and his athletes lost strength after training on machines, though it should be noted that the strength loss was evaluated by using barbell maximal lifts.

The next issue of the *NSCAJ* contained a response from Nautilus. The company invited readers to join in the "search for truth and war on ignorance in the field of sports medicine." Sticking to arguments made for the machines in numerous previous publications, the statement maintained that the barbell was limited by gravity, so that trainees became disproportionately strong only in the mid-range of movement. The special Nautilus cam overcame this limitation by changing resistance throughout the range to accommodate changing moment arms and a muscle's specific length-tension curves. Elder had reached some erroneous conclusions, Nautilus said, in confusing the skill required by weight-training movements with the strength developed by their machines. Although the company maintained that its goal was to promote a program based on scientific research, the statement included no citations.[45]

Michael Yessis, a biomechanics professor at California State University–Fullerton, took exception to the Nautilus discussion of strength in a "Viewpoint" editorial.[46] His critique was countered by New York University physical education professor Michael Wolf, who defended Nautilus.[47] Yessis and Wolf continued their duel through two more "Viewpoint" columns. Wolf's second response was accompanied by a full-length article from Nautilus in the same issue.[48] The four back-and-forth articles, Elder's piece, and the two articles attributed to Nautilus repeatedly mentioned research but provided no specific citations.

This changed when Mike Stone and John Garhammer published "Viewpoint: Some Thoughts on Strength and Power." The article cited their own research, including an article by Stone in *Athletic Training* that compared Nautilus training to free weights in the production of strength and power as well as Garhammer's dissertation on power output in Olympic weightlifters.[49] Like Wolf, the two authors disagreed with some of Yessis's discussion of the relationship between strength and power, but they agreed with Yessis that free weights "can produce greater gains in power and strength than Nautilus and other machines."[50] This was followed by a two-part article beginning in the next issue of the *NSCAJ*. The first part, authored by Garhammer, pointed out that proponents of machines had a financial interest in their success, that the constant velocity of Nautilus machines was unlike sporting movements, which include uneven acceleration and countermovements, and that those with competitive experience tended to be barbell advocates. "In many cases the 'machine influence' has hurt progress in strength training in the United States," Garhammer continued, asserting that "if this continues our athletes will be at a major disadvantage in international competition since foreign athletes from the world sport powers use the best means to train rather than the easiest or most novel way."[51]

In the following issue of the *NSCAJ*, Mike Stone refuted the Nautilus claims nearly point by point, citing research for each contention. Stone said that movement specificity was important, the fastest motor units *were* recruited at high velocities, higher volume was superior in producing hypertrophy, and barbell training was far less expensive than the machines. Regarding injuries, no study had compared Nautilus machines to barbell training, so there was no evidence for the claim that Nautilus was safer because it was not ballistic. Until that time only two studies had compared barbell training to machines—Wathen's Mini Gym study and Stone's own study that demonstrated greater improvements in strength and power in a barbell-trained group than in a Nautilus-trained group. "We have presented arguments backed by research and by empirical observation, as to why free weight training better meets the requirement of training," Stone said, adding: "clearly, free weights have numerous advantages over machines."[52]

In addition to refuting the claims made by equipment companies, Michael Stone and John Garhammer also worked together to test the effectiveness of periodized training. Their experimental evidence was supplemented by numerous articles by Michael Yessis. For his part, Yessis had been publishing English translations of articles from Soviet sport science journals since the mid-1960s in his periodical, *Soviet Sports Review*. It had a limited circulation, however, and many of the ideas that Yessis relayed in the publication failed to gain widespread attention among American coaches until the 1980s. With the advent of the *NSCA Journal*, Yessis was able to expose a larger audience of sport and strength coaches to the training programs employed by the Soviets. In a series of articles titled "Trends in Soviet Strength and Conditioning," Yessis described the multiyear periodization model utilized by Russian sport scientists, including how they might train an American football team.[53] Running concurrently with Yessis's series was a similar collection of explanatory articles on periodization by Jimmy Pedemonte, a track and conditioning coach at Genoa University in Italy, including the methodology's history and how to implement it.[54]

In addition to the explanatory articles by Yessis and Pedemonte, the work of Stone, Garhammer, and others demonstrated for members of the fledgling group of strength coaches that periodized training was effective. In a 1981 article, for example, the researchers compared a nonperiodized program consisting of three sets of six repetitions, with weight increased as needed, to a periodized program that decreased in volume as intensity increased over the course of six weeks. At the end of the experiment, the periodization group had increased lean mass, lower body strength, and power significantly more than the nonperiodized group.[55] While this work was not published in the *NSCAJ*, it was discussed the following year in the *Journal* in articles outlining periodized programs.[56]

The articles discussing the mechanics of periodized training programs were complicated. They typically included a series of tables and charts with intersecting lines depicting variables like intensity, volume, and specificity. A strength coach of the early 1980s could easily have been overwhelmed. As Nicholas Bourne has pointed out, this likely worked in the NSCA's favor in generating new members.[57] If strength coaches—who had probably earned their position due more to their own physical prowess than to an intricate understanding of training methodology—hoped to understand the new "scientific" training, they would need the guidance of experts. They would have to join the NSCA to help them interpret and master these new training methodologies.

BEYOND AN ORGANIZATION FOR STRENGTH COACHES

Expanding the size of its membership was one of the NSCA's earliest goals. From the outset the organization's executives sought to recruit members from beyond the ranks of strength coaches. Membership dues collected from several thousand members, they understood, were much more likely to keep the group afloat than dues from only a few hundred collegiate strength coaches.[58] As a result, the NSCA's leadership began recruiting as many members as possible.

As previously mentioned, the group's first meeting in 1978 drew a small but respectable seventy-six attendees. Thanks in part to the attention garnered by the publication of the *NSCA Newsletter*, attendance at the 1979 convention increased to nearly three hundred. By 1980 membership had increased fourfold to more than 1,200. It increased by the same proportion in the next two years, with membership in 1982 topping 5,000.[59] As Thomas Baechle, NSCA president from 1983 to 1985, pointed out, the dramatic increase in membership was not an accident.[60] With the initiation of official publications, the NSCA also began several "Free Look" campaigns in which the *Newsletter* and *Journal* were sent to a variety of "interested parties" that included high school and college coaches, exercise scientists, YMCA directors, health club personnel, and others. The first issue of the *Newsletter* went out to 8,000 such individuals in early 1979. When it transitioned to the *NSCAJ* in the fall of that year, another 17,000 issues were sent out to a similar pool.[61]

By the time Baechle assumed the presidency in 1983 as the first successor to Epley, the group had grown to more than six thousand members.[62] That same year a survey was conducted to get a better understanding of just who these members were. Nearly eight hundred members responded to the three-page survey. Their answers showed a membership that was young, with more than one-third of members having worked in the field for less than three years. It was a diverse group in terms of employment: just over half of the members worked in collegiate settings, another third worked in health clubs or sports medicine facilities, and the majority of the remaining members were high school coaches. Nearly half the members held at least a master's degree.[63] When asked where the NSCA should devote its efforts, the clear favorite was education, which opened a conversation within the NSCA for a new kind of journal.

By 1982 the NSCA was officially working to "bridge the gap" between its diverse membership of scientists and strength and conditioning practitioners. Editor Ken Kontor used the phrase in an editorial urging researchers to make the relevance of their research more apparent, while chiding strength coaches that they must "make a sincere effort to understand the language of research." Kontor explained that the *Journal's* mission was to "bring these groups closer together by offering research, research applications, and programs and techniques currently used in the field." He affirmed again that both creating and applying research were essential to enhancing athletic performance.[64] In the fall of that year the *NSCAJ* began one of its most important educational series. The front cover (volume 4, number 5) carried not a photograph but a beautifully rendered anatomical drawing showing the muscles used during the bench press. The article, written and illustrated by Bruce Algra, took readers through the mechanics of the lift, demonstrating precisely which muscles were involved at various stages of the movement, and covered "bad" as well as "good" technique issues.[65] Algra's cover art and article had a huge impact—as did the many that followed it.

Coaches cut the article out of the journal and put it on their bulletin boards; weight training and biomechanics instructors photocopied it for their course packets. The next issue of the journal featured another Algra-drawn cover showing a male basketball player preparing to make a two-handed dunk. This time the cover drawing and other illustrations inside the *Journal* linked to an article written by Kraemer and members of the strength-training staff at the University of Wyoming entitled "Improved Rebounding Performance through Strength Training." The feature discussed the biomechanics of the movement, which exercises were most useful for strengthening particular muscles, and, of course, included a how-to training program.[66] It was science and practice all in one. For more than a decade every issue of the *NSCAJ* carried similar articles and cover illustrations breaking down the individual elements of sport while teaching coaches the basics and interplay of anatomy, biomechanics, and programming. Called the "Sport Performance Series," it remains one of the *NSCAJ's* most important contributions to the quest to make strength coaching a science-based profession.

In addition to the "Sport Performance Series," another important feature in the *NSCAJ*, the "Roundtable" articles, began in 1982. Through the series, Ken Kontor explained, the *Journal* sought to provide "a forum for the professional exchange of applied strength and conditioning theory." Readers were asked to send requests for future topics.[67] The articles consisted of questions sent to individuals with expertise on particular subjects. The answers from each panelist were then compiled alongside each other to give the article the feel of listening to a conversation between individuals at a conference. The first Roundtable article, which included strength coaches from UCLA, Pennsylvania State University, the University of Florida, and several others, discussed the mechanics of off-season conditioning for college football.[68] The second article discussed training for basketball, while the third dealt with the role of strength and conditioning in the prevention of injuries.[69]

By the second Roundtable, Thomas Baechle, holder of an EdD and dually employed in the departments of physical education and athletics, had joined the panel. By the third, scientists Mike Stone and Pat O'Shea had been called upon for their expertise. Three more academics, including Yessis, joined a discussion on speed development in the fifth Roundtable.[70] By the seventh article the series had changed from the "Coaches' Roundtable" to simply "Roundtable."[71] The eighth article, titled "Determining Factors of Strength—Part One," included twelve contributors, of whom six held doctorates. Moreover, several panelists, for the first time, included citations in their responses. As with the trajectory of the NSCA as a whole, the Roundtable articles moved from anecdotal information provided by coaches toward evidence-based work that included academics. As a result, they contained a mixture of science and practice that both exposed the membership to research and showed how it could be used. The format was a mainstay in the *NSCAJ* in the 1980s and continued to appear periodically in its current version, the *Strength and Conditioning Journal* (*SCJ*), through 2010.

THE PUSH FOR CERTIFICATION

As the research committee was beginning to come into its own in the early 1980s, Tom Baechle was spearheading an effort to create a certification program. He published the results of a survey regarding attitudes about establishing a program to verify a minimum level of competence for strength coaches. Of the 186 responses received, 86 percent believed that a certification program was needed, 89 percent thought that the profession required at least a bachelor's degree, and 62 percent thought that the degree should be in an area related to physical education, physiology, or kinesiology.[72]

In a 1981 editorial Ken Kontor asserted that certification was the next logical step for the organization. Certification was crucial to demonstrating that strength coaches were highly qualified professionals, he explained. By instituting a credential and thus boosting the perception of expertise, strength and conditioning professionals could move beyond their current domains in athletics and into the corporate world, expand their presence in health clubs, and even be recognized as capable of training the armed forces. According to Kontor, health club managers were finding it difficult to differentiate between qualified and unqualified trainers. Managers of both blue-collar and white-collar workers were increasingly coming to appreciate the increased productivity of healthy workers.[73] Baechle echoed Kontor's sentiment in his first few months as NSCA president, saying that a certification program would be vital in establishing credibility for the profession.[74]

By 1984 the certification program was officially underway, with the first test to become a "Certified Strength and Conditioning Specialist (CSCS)" set for June 1985 at the organization's national convention in Dallas, Texas.[75] Content for the exam included a breadth of topics ranging from physiology to program design, nutrition, psychology, administration, ergogenic aids, and more. The purpose of the examination, according to Baechle, was not to determine who the most qualified strength coaches were; rather, the exam was designed to "assure a minimum level of competence among all practitioners."[76]

By the time the first exam was offered, NSCA membership had grown to include more than nine thousand members in all fifty states and thirty-two countries.[77] Additionally, concrete evidence of the impact that strength and conditioning coaches had made on athletes in the prior decade had recently been published in the *NSCAJ*. A survey of the size and strength of football players in 1974 and 1984 showed that the average Division I offensive lineman of the 1980s was more than twenty pounds heavier, was bench pressing over sixty pounds more, was squatting nearly one hundred pounds more, and had dropped two-tenths of a second from his forty-yard dash time compared to his counterparts a decade earlier.[78]

At the 1985 NSCA convention in Dallas, 168 prospective CSCS candidates took the exam, with 126 passing. While Baechle, Kontor, and many others saw the certification as an important step forward in achieving legitimacy for the profession, many strength coaches considered it a waste of time. According to Boyd Epley, many who had been coaching for years "expected to be grandfathered into certification."[79] Epley himself did not become certified until six years after the initial test was offered: when he did, news of his CSCS status was trumpeted in the *NSCA Bulletin*.[80] Getting Epley, who had been working as a strength coach for more than twenty years at that point, on board was an important message for those pushing certification. If the founder of the organization took the time to get his credential, how could other coaches think that they were too qualified? In spite of Epley's public declaration that "the CSCS credential should be a minimum for all strength coaches" the sentiment remained among many that while Epley was certified, so too was "John Doe down at the health club," which diminished certification in the eyes of many older strength coaches.[81] The resistance to certification highlighted a growing schism in the organization between the group's initial core of collegiate strength coaches and its growing constituency of personal trainers, athletic trainers, and others.

Baechle took to the *Journal* to defend the CSCS in 1986.[82] He reminded members that the program was created in response to the overwhelming sentiment in the 1980 membership survey that certification was desirable. Financial gain for the NSCA was not the driving force behind the creation of the certification program, Baechle assured members: instead it was ensuring respect and credibility for strength and conditioning professionals. In spite of the criticisms, both membership and the number of credentialed professionals continued to increase. By 1988 the organization's membership had topped twelve thousand. Only three years after the initiation of the CSCS exam there were nearly a thousand "Certified Strength and Conditioning Specialists."[83]

It should be noted that the NSCA's push for certification was part of a broader movement to get everyone working in fitness to earn some sort of credential. The early 1980s were marked by a huge "fitness boom," with fitness-related products constituting a nearly $1 billion industry by 1984.[84] Historian Shelly McKenzie has called the 1980s "the fitness decade."[85] Preceded by the joggers and runners of the 1970s, exercisers flocked to gyms in the 1980s. In the decade after the formation of the NSCA in 1978 the number of private fitness facilities increased from three thousand to fifteen thousand.[86] Between the early 1970s and 1988 the number of Americans with gym memberships increased from 1.7 million to more than 10 million.[87] By the late 1970s some commentators were remarking on the "new coed character" of the fitness boom, and industry insiders in the mid-1980s estimated that nearly two-thirds of participants in the fitness movement were women. Many of those women took up aerobic dance as a form of exercise, with almost 23 million people reporting that they participated in "aerobics."[88] With mass participation, however, came injuries. One survey found that nearly half of the participants in aerobics classes and more than three-quarters of instructors reported suffering injuries related to exercise.[89] Media reports lamented "health club victims," stricken by injuries as a result of unqualified instructors. Fewer than one in twenty instructors held a degree in a related field or a credential from a nationally recognized association, like the American College of Sports Medicine or the International Dance-Exercise Association (IDEA).[90]

Leading physicians including Allan J. Ryan and Hans Kraus also questioned instructor preparation. Ryan, then in the midst of his thirteen-year editorship of *Physician and Sportsmedicine*, asserted that aerobics was the leading cause of fitness-related injuries. Kraus, who has been called the "originator of sports medicine in the United States," lamented that most classes were led "by people who don't know what they are talking about."[91] As a result, professional certification programs grew exponentially in the early 1980s. A 1985 article in *Physician and Sportsmedicine* discussed the NSCA's new certification program. Ken Kontor asserted to the non-NSCA readers of the journal that the credential was created to ensure quality and demonstrate that individuals know how to coach safely.[92]

A SECOND JOURNAL

Growth and diversification of membership spurred a call for additional publications, beyond the *Journal* and *Bulletin*. Bill Kraemer had been working to make a second journal a reality since 1982.[93] Although still a doctoral student at the time, Kraemer began serving as the "Scientific Editorial Supervisor" for the *NSCAJ* in October 1982.[94] Following the annual meeting of the American College of Sports Medicine (ACSM) in Minneapolis in 1982, Kraemer discussed the creation of a scientific research journal with Kontor, Baechle, and Fleck. After the meeting, Kraemer went to work in attempting to sway some of the more recognized scientists in the field to lend their names to the proposed publication. His initial recruiting efforts in 1980 had been aimed at getting young scientists, like Fleck and Stone, to join the NSCA. In order to establish a second journal, Kraemer sought out the most recognized names in the field. Though this recruiting effort began in 1982, it was not until 1985, the year after Kraemer finished his PhD, that he was officially tapped to head a task force to develop the new journal.[95]

Two of the most pivotal members of the task force were Jack Wilmore and David Costill. Wilmore, who passed away in 2014, was then a full professor in the Department of Kinesiology and Health Education at the University of Texas at Austin. He served as the president of the ACSM from 1977 to 1979 and as the editor in chief of the association's *Exercise and Sport Science Reviews* from 1972 to 1975. He was also an associate editor for *Research Quarterly* during the same span. Wilmore had served as an associate editor of the *NSCAJ* since October 1982 and also agreed to serve in the same capacity for the new journal.[96] As a man who has been called "one of the most influential exercise physiologists in the world," his affiliation was crucial in lending credibility to the new journal.[97] Costill, another past president of

ACSM, who would be later described by the *New York Times* as "a legend in the field" and as one of the first to "apply scientific methods to the study of exercise and training," also agreed to lend his considerable academic stature to the task force.[98]

In one of his "President's Message" articles in 1983, Tom Baechle thanked contributors to the *Journal* and said that the organization was indebted to them, particularly Kraemer, who had "made an unbelievable commitment to promoting the scientific areas of the *Journal*." "It is my hope that very soon we will be recognized as *the* voice of strength and conditioning in the United States."[99] At the 1985 NSCA National Convention in Dallas the group came closer to that goal, as the NSCA Board of Directors voted to pursue the establishment of a research-only journal.[100]

The rationale for the additional publication lay in the size of the organization. With so many members, coaches were clamoring for practical programs for a wider variety of sports, while academics were pushing for more space to publish. One option would be simply to make the existing journal larger. "This would be a disservice to our research-oriented membership," Kontor argued, "because academic circles require works to be published in totally peer-reviewed journals."[101] To serve this group better, the best option was an additional research journal. To stay consistent with the mission of bridging the gap between practitioner and coach, however, it was decided that the new journal would require a "practical application" section in each article. The goal was to encourage researchers to think about the utility of their work, rather than churning out articles on esoteric topics not useful on some level for coaches.

In the same issue with Kontor's editorial Kraemer lauded the growing professionalization and complexity of the field. "Just as the physician or scientist of the 1800s did not have to deal with genetic structure and function, the strength and conditioning specialist did not have to attend to scientific principles and understanding in the late 70s and early 80s," he wrote. However, he warned, as the field of strength coaching becomes more scientific, "the possibility exists that the individuals who are interested only in the empirical development of their athletes and not the scientific basis of strength and conditioning may not be selected in the evolution of this profession."[102] The organization's shift toward scientists was exemplified by the *Journal*'s editorial board, which boasted fifty-three associate editors at the end of 1985, forty-eight of whom held doctorates. This was up from six associate editors listed in the *Journal*'s first volume in 1979, only three of whom held doctorates.

In an open letter to the membership in 1985, Kraemer defended the idea of the new scientific journal, after acknowledging that the profession of strength and conditioning would always involve some degree of "art." However, he explained that the use of "solid, high-quality applied science" to help practitioners make sound programming decisions was essential to the growth of the profession. Furthermore, the new peer-reviewed journal would provide strength researchers with a mechanism through which they could publish their research and thereby advance their careers.[103]

THE FIRST POSITION PAPERS

Along with pushing for a research journal in the mid-1980s, some members of the NSCA began exploring the scientific literature to generate the organization's first two "Position Statement" articles. The first of these was a "Position Statement on the Use and Abuse of Anabolic Steroids," published in the April 1985 issue of the *NSCAJ*. The one-page summary of the organization's stance on anabolic steroids came out just one year after the ACSM released its own position statement and First Lady Nancy Reagan began her "Just Say No" antidrug campaign.[104] The statement also came out amid a torrent of criticism and concern about drug use. *Sports Illustrated*, the most important sports magazine in America in this era, published a special report on "the steroid explosion" in May 1985 that described anabolic steroid use as "a spreading wildfire that is touching athletes at every level of sport."[105]

Leaders of the NSCA felt compelled to create the position statement in order to respond to criticism about the organization's soft stance on use of the drugs.[106] One of the primary causes of that criticism was that some strength coaches, hoping to show that their teams made improvement, not only encouraged players to use anabolic drugs but at times also helped their athletes acquire them. In the same month that the NSCA's Position Statement was published, Vanderbilt University strength coach E. J. "Doc" Kreis was indicted for his role in illegally distributing anabolic steroids to Commodore athletes as well as athletes at Clemson and Colgate universities.[107] Kreis eventually pleaded guilty and was placed on probation, along with Clemson strength coach Sam Colson.[108]

Despite the negative publicity and the NSCA's desire to take a firm stand against drug use, both Bill Kraemer and Mike Stone found themselves—as scientists—unable to find objective scientific evidence regarding either positive benefits from the use of anabolic steroids or potentially deleterious health effects.[109] No one had done the studies. The final version of the Position Statement confirmed their view. The document concluded that the NSCA was united with other sporting bodies "in condemning the use of anabolic-androgenic steroids by athletes." To reach that position, how-ever, the document appealed to "ethical principles" and the "regulations of competition" rather than to any inherent danger. Anabolic steroids posed a threat to health, though the magnitude of that threat was "undefined." The article went on to point to "limitations and deficiencies" in understanding the positive and negative effects of the drugs, stating that the NSCA would support research to learn more about both.[110]

Six months later, in October 1985, the *NSCAJ* reprinted the original one-page position statement, which was accompanied by a literature review, authored by army physiologist James Wright and Mike Stone. The authors pointed out that methodological issues, lack of controls, and difficulty con-cealing which was the treatment group made it difficult to draw definitive conclusions about the effects of the drugs. In trained athletes, they noted, the majority of studies appeared to support the conclusion that administration of the drugs was more effective at increasing muscular size and strength than training alone. Not to provide too rosy an assessment, the second half of the article discussed physiological changes from the use of anabolic steroids, ranging from liver damage to a variety of cancers, cardiovascular disease, mood disturbances, sexual dysfunction, and more. "Just as the ultimate ana-bolic potential of these drugs is unknown, so, frighteningly are the potential, and especially long-term hazards," the authors concluded.[111]

In spite of the organization's official condemnation of anabolic steroids, it was unable to escape the "spreading wildfire," as *Sports Illustrated* character-ized the drugs. The NCAA voted in 1986 to institute random drug testing for a host of drugs, including anabolic steroids, and during the 1986 football bowl season several universities got burned.[112] The University of Oklahoma lost its All-American linebacker Brian Bosworth, along with two reserve linemen, for the Orange Bowl. The University of Arkansas lost an outside linebacker for the same game, and the University of Southern California was without two-time All-American lineman Jeff Bregel for the Citrus Bowl.[113] Another flare-up occurred in early 1988 when Pat Jacobs, an assistant strength coach who worked with the football and men's basketball teams at the University of Miami (Florida) pleaded guilty to trafficking in anabolic steroids.[114] In response, the NSCA used the "Code of Ethics" that had been published along with the position statement as grounds to suspend Jacobs for a minimum of five years.[115] Within two years the anabolic wildfire engulfed the NSCA.

In October 1988 *Sports Illustrated* featured an article on steroids co-au-thored by former University of South Carolina (USC) football player Tommy Chaikin.[116] It began with a two-page spread depicting him with a gun under his chin, poised to end his life due to severe anxiety and a feeling that he was "going crazy," symptoms that Chaikin attributed to his abuse of anabolic steroids. Among other allegations in the article, Chaikin claimed that South Carolina's strength coach and then NSCA president, Keith Kephart, knew that players were using the drugs. According to Chaikin, when several players began experiencing severe side effects, rather than advising them to quit using the drugs Kephart advised only that they cut back on their dosage.[117] The *Sports Illustrated* article spurred a federal investigation into Chaikin's claims, including his assertion that fifty out of one hundred players on the Clemson team were using steroids in 1986. Kephart, who in addition to being the NSCA's president had been awarded its "Strength Coach of the Year" honor in 1981, was indicted following that investigation, along with three other coaches on the USC staff.[118] Kephart ultimately pleaded guilty to one count of purchasing and importing anabolic steroids without a prescription and was sentenced to three months in a halfway house and three years of probation.[119] The Kephart affair would cast a shadow over the NSCA and the strength-coaching profession for many years to come.

After Jacobs pleaded guilty to distributing anabolic steroids to Miami athletes in 1988, the *NSCAJ* took on the steroid problem more directly, publishing an article describing "a realistic approach" for strength coaches to deal with anabolic steroids. Written by Mike Clark, then a strength coach at the University of Oregon, the article outlined the balance that a strength coach must strike in acknowledging that the drugs work but avoiding scare tactics that might harm the coach's credibility.[120] In the same issue physician Mauro Di Pasquale discussed the mechanics of testing for anabolic steroids via urinalysis.[121] Youngstown State University athletic trainer Dan Wathen advised coaches how to stop anabolic steroid abuse, highlighting the "often unpredictable side-effects" and the fact that steroids would not improve actual sport skills. He included excerpts of his own university's policies.[122] Ken Mannie took a tone more reminiscent of the hyperbolic chord struck by many *Sports Illustrated* articles. Steroids in America's high schools were "the new drug crisis," according to Mannie. High school students, in his experience, were aware of the minor side effects of steroid use like acne, bloating, and aggression but not of their possibly "devastating effects" on a user's long-term health. Coaches were obligated to educate students on all possible effects, lest the students get "street info" on the drugs, which was "as inaccurate as some of the nonsense our kids hear about the 'safe use' of cocaine and crack."[123]

The characterization of anabolic steroid use in high schools as a crisis was particularly interesting in light of an article that appeared in the *Journal of the American Medical Association* in the same year. Citing public perception that anabolic steroid use had "grown to epidemic proportions," researchers surveyed more than three thousand high school senior males and found that just over 6 percent reported past or current use.[124] The result was consistent with the perceptions of high school strength coaches surveyed by the NSCA in 1989, 98 percent of whom believed that less than 10 percent of the male students at their high school used anabolic steroids.[125] Despite the low estimates of actual use, 86 percent of high school strength coaches said they had discussed the drugs with students, likely due to their prevalence in the media. While less than half of coaches hosted formal education sessions on anabolic steroids, more than three-quarters said they would be interested in developing such a program if resources were available.

To that end, the NSCA formed a "Performance Enhancing Substance Abuse Committee" in the spring of 1989.[126] Along with updating the four-year-old Position Stand, one of the group's key action items was to "create a rationale against the use of anabolic substances."[127] Rather than just condemning the use of those substances as in 1985, the association was committing itself to working actively to prevent their use. The committee ultimately produced a fact sheet about anabolic steroids and a fifteen-page packet to help coaches, parents, and school officials combat drugs in sport.[128] The steroid education packet contained information on how to develop and implement school policies, counseling of athletes, sample letters to parents and school administrators, and an athlete pledge form.[129]

Along with information about how to educate adolescent athletes, the NSCA sought to produce an evidence-based document on how to train those athletes. Four months after publication of the original Position Statement on anabolic steroids in 1985, the NSCA's "Position Paper on Prepubescent Strength Training," was published.[130] It followed on the heels of a position statement by the American Academy of Pediatrics (AAP) that discussed weight training and weightlifting in youths and adolescents.[131] The AAP position separated weight training, which involved machines and pulleys but "no free weights," from weightlifting, which included the competitive lifts performed by both Olympic lifters and powerlifters. Weight training, the pediatricians assured parents, would not lead to muscle-boundness and would enhance athletic performance. Weightlifting, however, could result in growth plate fractures. Injuries of the low back, knee, and shoulder were also "common" in individuals who performed these lifts.[132] Because the NSCA had fought so hard against the "machine age" in the years leading up to the AAP's position statement, it would have to take a stand of its own to reassure parents who had a new reason to be skeptical about weights.[133]

Contrary to the AAP's position, the NSCA, while mentioning a paucity of evidence, asserted that preadolescents *could* improve overall strength with weight training.[134] Moreover, the authors of the NSCA paper, including Tom Baechle and Michael Yessis, pointed to athletes from Eastern Bloc countries to demonstrate the effectiveness of strength training in youth athletes. The injuries associated with lifting weights, they said, were not the result of the strength training itself but of improper form and programming. Not surprisingly, the NSCA authors also stressed the importance of proper coaching. In closing, the position paper stated unequivocally that weight training even for prepubescent subjects was both "safe and efficacious" if properly implemented and supervised.[135]

A common theme in both of the first two Position Papers was the scarcity of research to support a definitive conclusion. In February 1987 the NSCA took a step toward alleviating this shortage with the creation of a research journal dedicated to strength and conditioning. When the NSCA's second journal debuted, Bill Kraemer, who had spearheaded the effort, was listed as the senior editor. The *Journal of Applied Sport Science Research* (*JASSR*) was initially published as a pull-out in the first issue of that year's *NSCAJ*. Consisting of four studies and containing a mere nineteen pages, the original issue was slight but significant. One of its most important features was the list of fifty-nine associate editors, fifty-seven of whom held doctorates. The editors represented some of the most well-respected research institutions in the country and the US Olympic Training Center in Colorado Springs. As Kraemer later recalled, "some of those guys helped out just by giving name recognition to the *Journal* in the early days, so that people would want to put articles in a thing that wasn't even on any service yet."[136] While it would take time for the new journal to be indexed in PubMed and other search engines, submissions to the journal grew quickly. By the second issue of volume three, it began to be printed as a stand-alone journal.

Kraemer was elected to serve a two-year term as president of the NSCA beginning in 1989 and held firm to the importance of "bridging the gap" between scientists and practitioners, saying that it "has been and will continue to be the greatest challenge in our profession."[137] To make the incorporation of research more relevant to strength coaches, Kraemer used the example of a medical doctor. "Just as we ask a physician to make judgment calls based on scientific and medical literature," he asserted, "the strength and conditioning specialist has to do the same in the field of strength and conditioning."[138] As he had in previous editorial pieces, Kraemer then went on to admonish those who did not intend to commit themselves to continued learning by citing an aphorism from his father: "in life, one only progresses or regresses; there is no standing still."[139]

Indeed there was no standing still for the organization as a whole, as membership continued to increase and new members were increasingly employed in fields other than coaching athletes. In an editorial in late 1991 Ken Kontor observed that membership hovered around 14,000 members.[140] He estimated that only 350 to 400 of them were employed as head or assistant strength coaches at NCAA Division I institutions, with another 100 working in professional sports. The group initially founded by strength coaches at major universities had now grown so large that actual strength coaches constituted just over 3 percent of its membership. As a result, Kontor and other authors in the *Journal* stressed the importance of meeting the needs of professionals in a variety of settings.

One step in this direction was taken in early 1989 with the founding of the National Strength and Conditioning Foundation.[141] This group was created to focus on the needs of NSCA members who were employed in fitness settings, including health clubs and corporate wellness. A separate organization was necessary, according to Kontor, in order to "deliver the conditioning message to the general population without diluting the mission of the NSCA."[142] Shortly after the group was officially formed, the foundation itself began to branch out beyond the traditional fitness industry, with the development of a conditioning program for law-enforcement officers.[143] Establishment of the foundation also marked the launch of a new publication in 1990 aimed at personal trainers, called *Conditioning Instructor*.[144] This small publication was joined by three others that same year, including *Conditioning for Volleyball*, *Conditioning for Women's Basketball*, and *Conditioning for Cycling*. In introducing the new periodicals, Kontor made the case that they were crucial for the continued growth and financial health of the NSCA, saying that they had the potential to introduce as many as 10,000 more people to the field of strength and conditioning.[145]

INCREASING GENDER DIVERSITY AND THE WOMEN'S COMMITTEE

While the employment settings for NSCA members were diversifying, one area where diversity lagged was in the number of women involved in the organization. In the first issue of what was to become the *NSCAJ*, an appeal to prospective members pledged that the publication would not only include articles on conditioning for football, basketball, baseball but also focus on conditioning for women's sports.[146] The goal of appealing to women made a great deal of sense in the late 1970s, as the number of women playing interscholastic and intercollegiate sports had increased dramatically during that decade. The number of girls competing in interscholastic sports rose from 294,000 across almost 15,000 schools in 1971 to 1.8 million athletes at almost 76,000 schools by 1979.[147] Female collegiate athletes more than doubled from 30,000 to 74,200 between 1972 and 1982.[148]

In addition to traditional high school and collegiate sports, women were also gaining a foothold in strength sports previously reserved only for men. The first competitive powerlifting competition for women in the United States was organized in 1977, with the first national championships in Olympic weightlifting taking place four years later in 1981. It is worth noting that the first women's world championship in weightlifting did not take place until 1987 and that it was not included on the Olympic program until 2000.[149] The first women's championship in competitive bodybuilding was held in 1980 and was won by Rachel McLish, with Laura Combs being crowned the first Ms. America in the same year.[150] Unfortunately for proponents of strength training, it was the image of female bodybuilders that became indelibly etched onto the minds of the American public when it came to the effects of strength training for women.[151]

In light of women's increasing presence in fitness centers, gymnasiums, and athletic fields, it was only good business sense for the NSCA to attempt to cater to them. In spite of the pledge in the first issue that the *NSCA Journal* would focus on conditioning for women's sports, relatively few articles that discussed weight training for female athletes actually appeared in its pages through the early 1990s. According to the *Journal'* index, the first thirteen volumes of the publication included 114 articles on training for football, 88 articles on exercise techniques, 76 articles on high school sports, 73 articles on exercise methods, and only 37 dedicated specifically to women's issues or women's sports.[152]

A survey of individuals holding the CSCS credential in 1985 included 140 respondents, though only 4 of these were women.[153] The lack of women in the organization at the time did not escape the notice of NSCA leaders, who commissioned a special Women's Committee in the fall of 1986.[154] With the passage of Title IX almost fifteen years earlier and the subsequent expansion of women's athletic programs, strength training for women had become a subject of interest for athletes, coaches, and parents.[155] The official charge of the women's committee was to draft a position paper on strength training for female athletes, and its first task was to search the literature and determine whether any differences were required in methodology or program design because of gender.[156]

The committee consisted of six members, only one of whom, Meg Ritchie (Stone), was employed full-time as a strength and conditioning coach. At the time Ritchie was the head strength and conditioning coach at the University of Arizona. Like Epley and LeDuc, the most important credential that Ritchie possessed for her job at Arizona was not her CSCS credential, her master's degree in exercise physiology, or the fact that she was a two-time Olympian in the shot put and discus and the NCAA champion in both events. Rather, like many early strength coaches, she earned the position because of her performance in the weight room.[157] Football players had reportedly seen Ritchie squat more than 500 pounds and clean more than 300 pounds during her workouts to prepare for her field events and, not surprisingly, came to her seeking advice for increasing their own strength. At the time, the Wildcat football team trained primarily with Nautilus equipment and used hip sleds in lieu of squatting. Seeing Ritchie's tremendous strength inspired a handful of players to ask the head football coach, Larry Smith, if she could head up their program. So with Smith's blessing Ritchie became the first female head strength and conditioning coach (overseeing both male and female athletes) in an NCAA Division I athletic program.[158]

Ritchie was joined on the Women's Committee by Denise Gaiter, holder of a master's degree from the University of Texas at Austin, who was then working as an exercise physiologist at an Arizona fitness resort; Jean Barrett Holloway, who taught continuing education classes in strength training at the University of California–Los Angeles; Lori Gilstrap, a graduate student and part-time strength and conditioning coach at Georgia Tech University; Lynne Stoessel, a graduate student in exercise physiology at Auburn University; and Jan Todd, coordinator of weight training for the Department of Kinesiology at the University of Texas at Austin and a world and national record holder in powerlifting.[159]

Shortly before the Women's Committee's three-year anniversary in 1989, the *NSCAJ* published the first half of its work, "Strength Training for Female Athletes: A Position Paper: Part I."[160] The second installment followed in the next issue. Members of the committee reviewed more than two hundred studies and combined the findings with their own experience to conclude that "males and females should train for strength in the same basic way, employing similar methodologies, programs, and types of exercises."[161]

Following this publication, the work was lauded by then president Bill Kraemer, who went on to task the committee with working on methods to get more women involved in the field of strength and conditioning and creating more professional opportunities for women.[162] As a result of the position paper, the scientific stigma against women engaging in strength training began to weaken. Kraemer went so far as to say that "the myth is long since dead that strength training is for men only."[163]

While Kraemer believed that the scientific stigma had diminished, the social stigma remained, as evidenced by an article published two years after the women's position paper appeared. Interested in the status of women within the field of strength and conditioning, authors Jan Todd, Dorothy Lovett, and Terry Todd conducted two surveys. The first was a survey of those who belonged to the NSCA in 1990; 817 men and 196 women responded. Only 3 of the women held the primary title of strength and conditioning coordinator or strength coach. A more detailed survey was then mailed to 300 strength coaches at NCAA Division I institutions in the fall of 1989, which showed that 99 percent of head strength coaches were male. In the schools that had a separate strength coach for female athletes, only 2 were women, compared to 17 men. Only 16 percent of female strength coaches had any responsibility for working with male athletes. These disparities led the authors to conclude that, while strength training for female athletes was generally accepted, "there appears to be considerable resistance to the hiring of women to oversee training programs of female athletes and almost total resistance to the hiring of women as strength and conditioning coaches for male athletes."[164]

The *Journal* made some attempt to offset the bias against female strength coaches by featuring them more prominently.[165] Nonetheless, in a 1993 Roundtable feature the female strength coaches who participated in the article described a persistent lack of respect, ranging from limited assignments to coaches and players not heeding their advice to weight-room visitors asking female strength coaches to locate the male strength coach for them.[166] In a separate interview the same year, Jean Barrett Holloway, a former chair of the Women's Committee, lamented that the notion that "one should look like what they teach" limited both the number of opportunities and the ceiling for women seeking positions as strength and conditioning coaches.[167]

AT A CROSSROADS

By the early 1990s male strength coaches were also starting to feel a lack of respect, as least insofar as their standing within the NSCA was concerned. In 1992 Bruno Pauletto, who had assumed the presidency after Kraemer, described the organization as standing at "a crossroads," in part because the organization had failed to meet the needs of collegiate strength and conditioning coaches.[168] Later in the same year *Journal* editor Ken Kontor described an incident at the NSCA National Conference in which a speaker had made a disparaging statement about powerlifters that led to one audience member, an elite powerlifter, storming out of the room.[169] By the end of the year the association's founding father, Boyd Epley, had called for a refocusing of the organization. Strength coaches "are the hub of the organization and we must be careful not to forget them along the way," Epley said, warning that "the organization must never fail to serve the people who identify most closely with it."[170] The following year marked the NSCA's fifteenth anniversary. In celebration, and because of concerns about leaving behind the association's bedrock of strength coaches, Pauletto announced both a restructuring of the organization and an overhaul of the *Journal*.[171]

The NSCA national office was reorganized in response to dire financial straits announced at the 1992 annual convention.[172] Recognition of the association's financial condition came about after William Kraemer's push to create an evaluation tool to justify raises for national office staff. Implemented at the start of Pauletto's presidency, the executive director's evaluation tool revealed what appeared to be shortcomings in the administrative abilities of staff, particularly with regard to budget and membership reporting. The discrepancies led to an outside audit that revealed a nearly $23,000 budget shortfall for 1991, with the proposed 1992–1993 budget calling for a $96,000 deficit. Moreover, while the association sent out more than 13,000 issues of the *Journal* every other month, auditors were able to find only 11,000 members.[173]

In order to move the NSCA back into the black, the number of staff at the national office was reduced, cost controls were implemented, and several programs were discontinued. Ken Kontor resigned his role as executive director.[174] His replacement, Maelu Fleck, would play a critical role in turning the organization around. Unlike earlier administrators in the NSCA, Fleck had a business degree and had spent most of her career working for health insurance giant Blue Cross Blue Shield. At the NSCA she implemented a more corporate-style organizational model and hired other individuals with similar training. Both Bill Kraemer and the official NSCA history credit her efforts in returning the group to financial viability.[175] In order to do that, state associations and "LiftAmerica," a program that used lifting events as fundraisers, were both found to be too costly and were suspended.[176] To save printing costs and enhance the quality and visibility of the publication, the *JASSR* was outsourced to the publisher Human Kinetics beginning in 1993.[177] Its name also changed to the current title, *Journal of Strength and Conditioning Research (JSCR)*. Beginning in 1994, *JSCR* would be joined at Human Kinetics by the *NSCAJ*, which was also retitled as *Strength and Conditioning: The Professional Journal of the National Strength and Conditioning Association*.[178]

In the interim, the new-look *NSCAJ* featured reprints of classic articles and a promise from Pauletto that the *Journal* would return to "practical 'nuts and bolts' information on strength and conditioning."[179] This shift toward more "practical" articles on program design and exercises was a nod to the organization's base of practitioners who felt increasingly disenfranchised by the ever-growing organization. To assuage some of their concerns, a new committee was commissioned: the College Strength and Conditioning Coaches Committee. The group's initial chair, Boyd Epley, said that its task was to resolve the issue that "some strength coaches are unhappy with the NSCA."[180]

Despite efforts to reengage the association's original constituency, growth remained a leading priority. One of the fastest-growing membership categories in the early 1990s was personal trainers. As part of the reorganization, the National Strength and Conditioning Foundation was merged back into the larger NSCA and the group's publication *Conditioning Instructor* was retitled *Personal Trainer*.[181] By the end of 1993 almost 35 percent of NSCA members listed their primary job title as "personal trainer," easily eclipsing the number who were primarily strength coaches.[182] As a result of the demographic shift, the organization moved to institute its second credential: the NSCA Certified Personal Trainer (NSCA-CPT) in 1993.[183]

Teachers and professors also constituted a large portion of the NSCA's membership, with nearly 20 percent of members claiming "educator" as their primary job responsibility.[184] The ever-expanding list of job titles that applied to NSCA members, ranging from professor to personal trainer, chiropractor, dietitian, physician, athletic trainer, physical therapist, and many more, led incoming NSCA president Mike Stone to observe that the group's diversity might be a strength but could also lead to weakening the organization.[185]

In spite of Stone's trepidation about the NSCA's big tent, throughout the late 1990s the group continued to add approximately a thousand new members each year. Those members continued to be primarily educators, whose single largest job setting was in high schools.[186] Stone, one of the first physiologists to join the NSCA, was succeeded as president by Donald Chu in 1996. As a credentialed physical therapist, athletic trainer, and CSCS, Chu represented the group's professional diversity and called for continued expansion, setting a goal of 20,000 members by the year 2000 as he was leaving office in 1998.[187] Chu was succeeded by Dan Wathen, one of the earliest NSCA members and an athletic trainer by trade. Shortly after Wathen took the helm in 1998, the group stood at 17,000 members. To ensure that all of the myriad professions had a voice in the organization, Wathen announced the creation of "special interest groups" for coaches in specific sports, personal trainers, sports medicine professionals, and more. Collegiate strength and conditioning coaches had their own special interest group. "I counter the notion that the NSCA is not what it once was originally intended to be with the idea that it is what it once was and so much more," Wathen defensively asserted. He added: "We have a big table and set it for all that are interested in strength and conditioning."[188]

Many collegiate strength coaches disagreed. What they viewed as relegation to a role as one special interest group among many was too much. The table was no longer set for them at the NSCA as far as they were concerned. Led by Chuck Stiggins, strength coach at Brigham Young University, they broke off to form their own specialized organization in 2000: the Collegiate Strength and Conditioning Coaches Association (CSCCa).[189] The turn of the twenty-first century ultimately marked the end of the NSCA's hegemony in the world of strength and conditioning. Along with a new organization for strength coaches, the profession would be shaped by an emphasis on "functional" training and the rising CrossFit movement. The NSCA had battled the untested claims of marketers of strength-training machines and advocated strongly for highly specialized year-round training programs as embodied in the model of periodization. Training for sport in the twenty-first century has become in many ways a pushback against the NSCA's efforts.

CONCLUSION

Sport historian Scott McQuilkin observed in 1995 that "if there had been no other accomplishment by the NSCA, the development of a knowledgeable journal for strength and conditioning professionals made the NSCA venture worthwhile."[190] At that time the *JSCR* had only recently undergone its name change and started to gather more widespread attention. Twenty years later, the NSCA and the *JSCR* are much more than merely "worthwhile": they have transformed the world of strength and conditioning. The *NSCAJ*, now *SCJ*, still contains articles of a practical and applied nature. Each includes citations of relevant literature. The focus is typically on methods to utilize that literature in an actual conditioning program. *JSCR* articles still have a "practical applications" section, but the focus is on experimental research. The two publications work synergistically. Authors of the experimental research in *JSCR* close by discussing the relevance of their work to the practitioner, and *SCJ* articles distill that information into detailed discussions of the application of that information.

The field of strength and conditioning is now backed by volumes of research, much of it published in the *JSCR*, which has swelled from sixteen articles in its first volume to more than four hundred in its most recent one.

What a sea change from the 1970s, when the pioneers in the field of strength and conditioning worked largely from anecdotal evidence and relied on muscle magazines and the quasi-scientific assertions of nonobjective pitch men for strength-training equipment companies. By fostering and publishing experimental research, the NSCA was able to demonstrate which training techniques actually improved performance and which "commonsense" approaches did not bear fruit. As the mythologies started to fall under the onslaught of scientific investigation, the profession and strength training both gained new respectability. Moreover, the professionals who applied that evidence gained stature at their home institutions with the implementation of the CSCS, which ensured that those who passed had acquired a basic level of knowledge about the effects of strength and conditioning programs and their implementation. Through the combination of research and certification, a group of individuals who taught athletes how to lift weights became a full-fledged profession.

CHAPTER 7

•

STRENGTH COACHING IN THE TWENTY-FIRST CENTURY

New Paradigms and New Associations

I n the January/February 2000 issue of the *NSCA Bulletin* Dan Wathen, NSCA president, addressed the more than 18,000 members of the organization.[1] For almost a decade before his article NSCA officials and members, including Boyd Epley, had warned that the association no longer met the needs of strength and conditioning coaches.[2] Wathen acknowledged this in his message and went on to discuss a committee tasked with looking into the working conditions of college strength coaches. Wathen explained that the committee—which he led—was recommending that strength coaches be taken off sports coaching staffs and be recognized as sports medicine personnel. The group believed that by changing the strength coach's line of supervision from a sports coach to the athletic director the strength coach would have greater job security. "I am tired of seeing friends lose their jobs because the football team didn't win enough games," Wathen explained.[3] Wathen supported this new orientation for strength coaches by stressing the important role that strength coaches played in injury prevention. As a certified athletic trainer, Wathen's support for this suggestion is understandable. However, what he could not have foreseen was how collegiate strength coaches would feel about such a change in status.

Wathen's article and the committee's suggestion to reclassify strength coaches as sports medicine staff struck many college strength coaches as beyond tone-deaf. Chuck Stiggins, then the strength and conditioning coach at Brigham Young University, was particularly incensed by the suggestion and penned a letter to the *Bulletin*'s editor.[4] In the letter Stiggins expressed respect for the various constituencies within the NSCA and then went on to observe that the organization had been headed almost exclusively by those constituencies, rather than by a practicing strength coach, for nearly a decade. In his view, those who were credentialed as an athletic trainer or physical therapist had their own professional organizations. The NSCA, he believed, should be run by a practicing strength coach because they were the impetus for the organization's formation in the first place.

Stiggins was simply giving voice to a sentiment held by many NSCA-affiliated strength coaches: the NSCA no longer felt like "their" organization. After writing his letter to the *Bulletin*, Stiggins, much as Boyd Epley had done several decades earlier, sent a letter to strength coaches across the country that he titled "Some Thoughts and Concerns for the Collegiate Strength and Conditioning Coach."[5] The letter proposed creating a new organization dedicated solely to the interests of collegiate strength and conditioning coaches. Heartened by the responses, Stiggins organized an exploratory meeting in May 2000 in Las Vegas that was attended by twenty-three full-time strength and conditioning coaches from across the country. To the surprise of many, one of those who made the trip was NSCA founder Boyd Epley.[6] Epley, then in his thirty-first year as head strength coach at the University of Nebraska, originally intended to try to talk the alienated strength coaches out of forming their own organization.[7] An additional organization, he felt, would damage the profession and dilute the credibility that the NSCA had spent more than two decades building. While at the conference, however, Epley began to see things differently as he talked with those attending. He came to believe that the unique needs of collegiate strength coaches were no longer being met by the NSCA. When the coaches took a formal vote to begin a new organization, on May 20, 2000, Epley voted along with all the other coaches in attendance, to create the Collegiate Strength and Conditioning Coaches' Association (CSCCa).[8] In a move that surprised many, Epley further agreed to become a member of the new group's board of directors.[9]

The CSCCa's goals were in many ways a repudiation of what the NSCA had become. The first goal was to "reclaim [our] identity as professionals," something that the members felt had been lost in the NSCA's big tent.[10] Furthermore, the new organization strongly discouraged individuals from fulfilling multiple professional roles. Dual responsibilities as a strength coach *and* athletic trainer or strength coach *and* educator were eschewed, because the lack of strong affiliation with only one profession was the impetus for the creation of the group in the first place.[11]

In an echo of the NSCA's original mission statement, the CSCCa also committed itself to the professional development of its members through the sharing of experience. One key aspect of the NSCA's philosophy did not change in the new organization, however, as the CSCCa explicitly stated that it was committed to "bridging the gap" between researchers and practitioners.[12] Thanks in part to the efforts of the NSCA to generate research related to strength and conditioning, the CSCCa was not compelled to actively promote research. With the removal of the stigma on strength training research and massive expansion of studies related to it since the 1980s, the new group would instead rely on more experienced strength coaches to relay the relevance of current research to other members.[13]

Like the NSCA, the CSCCa also created a certification program for strength coaches. One of the key criticisms of the NSCA's original CSCS credential had been that it was only necessary to pass a test in order to be certified. There was no internship component as required in other fields, such as athletic training, and no requirement to demonstrate an ability actually to teach strength training technique to anyone. In the words of Rob Oviatt, then strength coach at Washington State University, "if a taxi driver wants to buy the study materials and send in his 300 dollars, takes the test and passes it, he's a certified strength coach." To rectify that perceived shortcoming, the CSCCa's new credential, the Strength and Conditioning Coach Certified (SCCC), required an 1,000-hour internship that had to be completed under a coach who was certified by the organization.[14]

In many ways the internship requirement made sense, as there was a lot more for the strength coach to learn in 2000 than there had been when the CSCS credential was created in 1985. According to one study, the average NCAA Division I strength coach of the early 2000s worked more than seventy hours per week during the season, sixty out of season, handled many disciplinary matters for the team, was responsible for budgeting and purchasing supplies and equipment, played a role in recruiting, served as a liaison to professional scouts, and often had to keep up with the demands of multiple teams—at an average salary of about $47,000.[15] In addition to a grueling work schedule, strength coaches in the early twenty-first century faced the daunting task of keeping up with the findings of several thousand journal articles related to exercise that were published annually, as opposed to a few hundred shortly after the NSCA's founding.[16] To minimize the crush of information, the NSCA's *Strength and Conditioning Journal* (*SCJ*) stood out as the primary source of knowledge about the field of strength and conditioning. In a 2003 survey of NCAA Division I strength coaches, 94 percent claimed to read the publication.[17] The next most common sources of information were peers, professional clinics, the NSCA's text *Essentials of Strength Training and Conditioning*, and the trade magazine *Training and Conditioning* (*T and C*).[18] According to their website, *T and C*'s subscribers include athletic trainers, strength and conditioning coaches, sports nutrition professionals, and fitness directors who work with professional, college, high school, and top amateur athletes.[19] Because of their eclectic clientele, the magazine, although highly professional in its presentation, often contains articles on popular training theories that have not yet undergone rigorous scientific study. Such was the case in the 1990s when *T and C* began discussing "functional training" in its pages—a sharp departure from the periodized training routines popularized by the NSCA during the prior decade. Functional training has come to dominate the discourse about strength training in the early twenty-first century and began as a response to the popularity of machine training.

Weight machines like the lat pulldown and the leg press began to proliferate in the years after World War II when commercial gyms sought to appeal to a wider variety of clientele, including women and more casual fitness enthusiasts.[20] In the 1980s machines began to dominate all forms of training and some health clubs and gyms, like the popular Nautilus chain, had no barbells available at all.[21] The development led some strength coaches to lament the "machine age." Many continued to advocate barbell and dumbbell training because of their utility in engaging stabilizing muscles and resistance movements that were similar to those performed in sport, like running and jumping.

The fields of rehabilitation and sports medicine also began to push back against the rise of the machines. By the late twentieth century exercises like the knee extension, used so extensively by DeLorme and others in the post–World War II years, had become part of the standard rehabilitation protocol. According to physical therapist and athletic trainer Gary Gray, who would be tremendously influential in shaping the "functional training" movement, this approach made no sense.[22] Exercising one joint in isolation was not how the body operated in real life, as during walking or running, where multiple joints operated simultaneously and the resultant movement was dependent upon the interaction of those joints. Using terminology coined by Arthur Steindler in a 1955 text, Gray discussed closed chain exercises as those in which the distal joint was fixed to an immovable or substantial resistance.[23] An example might include squatting, where the foot is fixed to the ground, as opposed to a knee extension, where it is not. Closed chain exercises were often referred to synonymously as "functional" exercises because the intent was to mimic movements performed during normal daily or sporting activities.[24]

Closed-kinetic chain and "functional" exercise became standard for rehabilitation protocols during the 1990s.[25] As Donald Chu, physical therapist and NSCA president from 1996 to 1998 observed, "if you're going to be effective, exercise has to simulate real life."[26] Along with sports medicine practitioners, strength coaches increasingly agreed with that observation.[27] In addition to the seemingly commonsense appeal of training movements similar to those performed in competition, bodybuilding had gained an unsavory reputation due to its association with anabolic steroids.[28] Furthermore, without Arnold Schwarzenegger on the dais, the sport no longer had a charismatic star to burnish its image. As the reputation of competitive bodybuilding waned, so too did the single-joint movements that characterized its training.

Throughout the 1990s both the *Strength and Conditioning Journal* and *Training and Conditioning* featured articles on functional training.[29] In both publications Robert Panariello, physical therapist, athletic trainer, and strength coach for St. John's University, emphasized the importance of performing exercises that involved the legs, even if the exercise was ostensibly being performed for the upper body.[30] As an example, he cited the push press, a variant of the Olympic clean and jerk, as being preferable to a standing military press because it engaged the lower body to a greater extent.

Vern Gambetta, director of strength and conditioning for Major League Baseball's Chicago White Sox and president of his own training firm, wrote voluminously in *T and C* throughout the decade, also arguing for the implementation of functional training programs. "The concept of strength cannot be defined as simply the number of pounds lifted or number of repetitions completed," Gambetta said, adding that "strength is better thought of in terms of functional strength i.e. the strength that can be applied to performance."[31]

This view was not entirely new, as physical therapist John Jesse, whom Gambetta cited, had asked nearly fifteen years earlier: "Who can bench press the most? Who can squat the greatest weight? Who cares? What good is that on the football field or track?"[32] As early as 1957 some research had indicated that strength gains developed through one method of training may not necessarily translate to other tasks.[33] Hence training, like sporting movements, should be largely performed standing, occur in multiple planes, and involve multiple joints simultaneously, according to Gambetta and other functional training proponents.[34]

As these ideas about functional training gained currency Greg Glassman, a personal trainer in Santa Cruz, California, developed his own twist.[35] With a background in gymnastics, Glassman put clients through intense workouts at gyms that involved circuits of jumping on boxes, sprinting, pull-ups, climbing poles, lifting weights overhead, and then dropping them. The routines did little to endear him to gym administrators, leading Glassman to open his own facility in 1995.[36] To the new facility, which he had begun calling "CrossFit," Glassman brought a cadre of loyal clients and a host of officers from the Santa Cruz sheriff's department who had asked him to train them.

Among the hallmarks of Glassman's regimens were high-intensity, "functional" movements, and randomness.[37] The workouts lacked a clearly defined training cycle, which is central to periodization training. That was also part of CrossFit's appeal. Further, Glassman's clients did not have to plan their own workout—they just showed up and did the "WOD" (Workout of the Day) designed by Glassman. As an example, one of the early CrossFit workouts, dubbed "Fran," entailed going back and forth between an exercise called a thruster and pull-ups. Performed back-to-back and timed, the workout calls for twenty-one repetitions of each, followed by fifteen repetitions, and then nine. According to CrossFit lore, Glassman created the workout in his garage as a teenager. The intensity both caused him to vomit and inspired him to create more workouts like it in the future.[38] As with "Fran," many of those WODs also bore human names.

CrossFit found early adherents among police officers, firefighters, and military personnel who had to be prepared, in Glassman's words, for "the unknown and the unknowable."[39] As an example of the varied metabolic, strength, and endurance demands imposed by CrossFit, a 2017 trio of WODs consisted of maximal back squats for five sets of one repetition the first day, followed by a workout on a rowing ergometer for ten all-out rounds the next day, and a combination of weighted 800-meter runs, pull-ups, burpee box jumps, and 185 pound cleans for as many as fourteen rounds the next day.[40]

The relative randomness in exercise selection also proved attractive to many who valued variety and who saw it as a pushback against specialization in training programs. "Our specialty is not specializing," Glassman has said.[41] With the advent of the strength and conditioning coach, athletes became increasingly specialized. As more was learned about the effects of strength training and athletes who trained with weights were more successful, younger athletes began to use training programs increasingly specific to the sport in which they participated. The NSCA sanctioned strength training for prepubescent and adolescent athletes in 1985 and has continued to publish articles discussing it since that time.[42] Two years later Grant Hill, then a doctoral student at the University of Iowa, performed some of the first research into the trend of youth sport specialization.[43] Using a survey of high school athletic directors in the Midwest, Hill reported that nearly three-quarters of the administrators perceived an increase in sport specialization in the prior decade. Sport specialization was defined as participation in only a single sport with year-round participation. In a follow-up article Hill and Jeffrey Simons referred to such specialization as "a growing national trend."[44] As noted by sport historian Maureen Smith, emphasis on only one sport to the exclusion of others began as early as the 1950s in individual sports; in the 1980s, however, that trend spread into team sports.[45] The trend toward single-sport participation in the 1980s coincided with athletic programs that became more commercialized and national in scope during the same era.[46] As high school programs began to more closely resemble their collegiate counterparts and strength coaches came to be increasingly seen as integral to collegiate athletes, some strength coaches began to work with younger athletes who hoped to one day develop into collegiate athletes. By 1999 the NSCA's *Strength and Conditioning Journal* included a regular feature for coaches who trained high school athletes.[47] The following year Vern Gambetta explained in *T and C* how to structure a year-round training program properly for an adolescent athlete.[48] For those athletes who came of age during the burgeoning era of hyperspecialization in one sport, CrossFit's program of random "functional exercises" was particularly appealing.[49]

In addition to pushing back against specialization, CrossFit pushed back against established professional organizations like the NSCA and the American College of Sports Medicine (ACSM). The company's website asserts that Glassman "was the first person in history to define fitness in a meaningful, measurable way," which denies definitions of fitness previously crafted by organizations like the ACSM.[50] Several authors, including one of CrossFit's primary public relations specialists, Russell Berger, have been sharply critical of the ACSM's recommendations and its "Exercise Is Medicine" outreach program.[51] The real issue, of course, is market share.

"Exercise Is Medicine" (EIM) is a collaboration between the ACSM and the American Medical Association (AMA).[52] The program was founded in 2007 with the goal of encouraging physicians to include physical activity as a piece of their overall assessment of a patient. If the patient is insufficiently active, physicians are urged to "prescribe" more physical activity. To assist with those prescriptions the EIM program includes resources on programs and professionals who are credentialed and recognized by EIM.[53] To CrossFit advocates, the program appears to be a form of collusion between two organizations within the medical establishment that can squeeze out newcomers—like CrossFit. Proponents of EIM argue that their recommendations are based on decades of scientific and epidemiological studies, while the efficacy of CrossFit programs has only recently begun to be scientifically examined.

The issue of scientific backing for CrossFit-type programs came to the fore in 2014 when the CrossFit organization filed a lawsuit against the NSCA. The subject of the suit was an article published in the *Journal of Strength and Conditioning Research* in November 2013. Though the findings were largely favorable, with CrossFit training shown both to increase aerobic capacity and to decrease body fat in both men and women, the article's discussion singled out the "unique concern" of overuse injury associated with the high-intensity style of training. According to the authors, 16 percent of the study's participants failed to complete the program, which "may call into question the risk-benefit ratio for such extreme training programs."[54] The findings in *JSCR* received widespread attention when they were discussed in an article in *Outside* magazine the same month, titled "Is CrossFit Killing Us?" In that article author Grant Davis pointed to the high dropout rate due to injury as a "troubling statistic" and included the observation of a chiropractor that CrossFit was good for business due to the high rates of injury.[55]

In response, "the CrossFit community went berserk" according to a follow-up article in *Outside* magazine.[56] In hindsight, it appears that they had good reason. The *JSCR* issued an erratum sheet on the article in October 2015, which said that the originally cited injury rate had been based on information provided by the club owner, which he denied.[57] Follow-up interviews with the subjects who dropped out revealed that only two of the dropouts, not nine, had withdrawn from the study due to injury. To make matters worse for the NSCA, a California federal judge found in a preliminary ruling in September 2016 that, based on communication between the *JSCR* editors and the study authors, "a reasonable fact finder could conclude that the NSCA pressured the authors to include data disparaging CrossFit's exercise regimen." Furthermore, the judge continued, the available evidence could reasonably support the finding that the NSCA knowingly published false data in order to protect its position in the fitness market.[58]

As with the ACSM, the real battle between CrossFit and the NSCA was about the allotment of the fitness pie. In their complaint against the NSCA the attorneys for CrossFit said as much, observing that all three organizations derive a substantial proportion of their income from fitness certifications and alleging that the NSCA was using its publications in an attempt to delegitimize CrossFit's certification process.[59] According to its website, CrossFit "is committed to results-based education and training" that includes two entry-level certificate courses and two advanced credentials achieved via examination—the Certified CrossFit Level 3 Trainer and the Certified CrossFit Level 4 Coach.[60] While we were unable to find a hard number on how many individuals hold at least one of these certifications from CrossFit, it is certainly in the high thousands. Including the examination fee, becoming an entry-level CrossFit certified trainer costs $1,000, while becoming a Certified Strength and Conditioning Specialist through the NSCA costs $475 and testing for the ACSM personal trainer certification costs $349.[61] With recertification fees ranging from $45 to $500 due every two to five years, certification has surely become big business.[62] In 2015 approximately

40,000 people carried one of the NSCA certifications.[63] Including exercise physiologists, more than 31,000 people carry a credential from the ACSM.[64]

In addition to challenging the authority of established fitness organizations, CrossFit has also reshaped strength training by generating interest among women; by one estimate, 50 percent of members across all CrossFit affiliates are women.[65] Author and CrossFit enthusiast J. C. Herz has asserted that a CrossFit "box" (gym) "is one of the few settings where it's admirable, sexy even, for a woman to unequivocally and aggressively compete for score, for time, physically, against other women or against men."[66] The lack of mirrors in CrossFit affiliates, an emphasis on competition over aesthetics, the co-ed classes, and an environment where classmate-competitors cheer each other on through a grueling circuit of exercises seem to have attracted many adherents among women.[67]

Not only have more women, especially young women, taken up strength training in the last twenty years, whether through regimens like CrossFit or as part of training for sports, but more women have also decided to become professional strength coaches. While still underrepresented in the field, women filled nearly one-third of the strength-coaching positions at NCAA Division I institutions in late 2016.[68] Further, in a 2013 study, Division I women strength coaches reported high satisfaction in their jobs.[69] Problems remain, however, as the 2016 study revealed: 28 percent of female strength coaches felt that their opportunities for professional advancement were limited by their gender; 26 percent complained of a lack of respect from athletes, coaches, and administrators; and 19 percent said that they were not allowed to work with male teams due to their gender.[70] In a study examining the attitudes of athletes in the NCAA's highest division, researchers found that female athletes did not care whether the person directing their training was male or female, while male athletes preferred to work with a male strength coach, regardless of the qualifications that a female coach might possess.[71]

Some research suggests that male and female athletes at the high school level are treated differently with respect to strength-training protocols. A 2012 survey of high school baseball, softball, basketball, and soccer coaches found a marked difference in the volume of training done by male and female athletes. In the sample, 50 percent of strength coaches working with male athletes required their athletes to lift, yet only 9 percent of coaches of female athletes made strength training a required part of their program. Coaches of male athletes were also more likely to hold an advanced degree in a field related to physical education. Another noteworthy finding in this study was the quantifiably different modes of exercise were used in training males and females. Training for female athletes often included what were called "female preferred" modalities like yoga, bodyweight exercise, Pilates, and low-intensity, high-repetition training routines. In response to an open-ended question on the survey related to this, a coach of both male and female athletes opined that "girls are not challenged to work as hard as the boys, perhaps because of the perception that girls are to be 'dainty' and 'not sweat too hard.'"[72]

In some ways, the incorporation of significant bodyweight training into the programs of female athletes is not surprising and mirrors trends in strength training as a whole. Since 2007 the American College of Sports Medicine's *Health and Fitness Journal* has featured a survey to predict fitness trends for the following year.[73] To get a feel for what is popular and what is likely to be popular in the fitness industry, editors of the *Journal* distribute thousands of electronic surveys to fitness professionals across the globe annually. In addition to listing exercise methods like "Yoga" and "High-Intensity Interval Training," the ballot also includes topics like "Group Training," "Wearable Technologies," and "Educated, Certified and Experienced Fitness Professionals," making it a problematic predictor of what exercise system is truly most favored.[74] However, as a way to measure when fitness trends emerge and ascend in popularity, the annual ranking is highly useful. In the first survey for 2007, "functional fitness" ranked fourth as a fitness trend, with traditional strength training coming in sixth.[75] The two were differentiated by functional training's emphasis on balance and coordination to improve activities of daily living, while more traditional strength training tended to incorporate machines as well as free weights and focus on muscular strength, endurance, and hypertrophy.

In 2013 bodyweight training made its first appearance on the list, coming in third, just behind traditional strength training. An offshoot of the functional training movement and popularized by "suspension training systems" like TRX, the author identified bodyweight training as "a trend to watch as more people get 'back to basics.'"[76] Bodyweight training overtook the top spot as the most popular fitness in 2015 trend but fell to fourth place in 2018.[77] Traditional strength training has been among the top six trends in fitness since the first survey, peaking at second and sitting at fifth in 2018.[78] In the discussion of the popularity of strength training in the original survey, the author referred to it as "one of the longer-lasting trends in all of the fitness markets," which included commercial, corporate, clinical, and community fitness programs. "Thanks to the scientists who study strength training," he said, "fitness professionals now incorporate strength training programs even for patients with diagnosed heart disease and for those patients recovering from heart surgery."[79] The number one trend for 2018, by the way, was High-Intensity Interval Training (HIIT), which was also number one in 2014. HIIT training typically involves short bursts of high-intensity exercise followed by a brief period of rest or recovery; a total workout may take as little as thirty minutes or less. However, since CrossFit does not appear as an option in the list of training methods in the 2018 survey, it is certainly possible that some people chose HIIT because it sounded like the closest thing to CrossFit workouts.[80]

CONCLUSION

In the late nineteenth and early twentieth centuries the prevailing theory among physicians, physical educators, and scientists was that high-intensity strength training was likely to be deleterious to both health and performance. In spite of this, the evangelizing of barbell and publishing magnates like Alan Calvert, Bob Hoffman, and Joe Weider convinced many to take up strength training to improve their athletic performance, their appearance, and their health. As barbell-trained athletes took the field in greater numbers against untrained counterparts, the holes in the prevailing theory became evident. In Thomas Kuhn's terminology, the athletes were anomalies: inconsistencies in the dominant paradigm.[81] The "barbell men" became the subjects of researchers in the middle decades of the twentieth century as well as becoming researchers themselves. As investigators began to subject the effects of strength training to the scientific method, it became increasingly clear that strength training not only did not hamper athletic performance but in fact improved it.

With scientific validation and the anecdotal evidence of bigger, faster, and stronger athletes being more successful on the field, the prevailing paradigm about strength training shifted. Coaches began hiring specialists to incorporate strength training for their athletes, and scientists began to devote their careers to the study of the effects of that training. By the 1980s the focus had fully shifted from whether to strength train to how to do it most effectively. In 1990 the American College of Sports Medicine recommended weight training for everyone as a component of a comprehensive fitness program.[82] The recommendation marked the completion of the revolution in strength training: the dominant paradigm now is that strength training is beneficial for athletic performance and overall health.

In spite of widespread agreement on the utility of strength training, the field of strength and conditioning itself has become increasingly fractured in the twenty-first century. As the field expanded, many other organizations joined the NSCA and the CSCCa in certifying strength coaches. The

National Academy of Sports Medicine offers "Performance Enhancement Specialist (PES)" certification. The National Council on Strength and Fitness provides "Certified Strength Coach" certification. The International Sport Sciences Association offers "Strength and Conditioning Certification." It is even possible to become a "Certified Functional Strength Coach," the only listed prerequisite for which is being a "CNP (Certified Nice Person)."[83]

As that prerequisite suggests, the qualifications required for individuals to hold some sort of certification vary dramatically. Some, like the CSCCa's SCCC, require an undergraduate degree, an internship, passing a written certification exam, and a practical test of the applicant's ability to perform and teach a variety of exercises. Others, like the Certified Functional Strength Coach or the certification sold by the National Council on Strength and Fitness, require only passing the exam and paying appropriate fees in order to be credentialed. The expansion of certifications that allow individuals with dubious preparation to be strength coaches garnered national attention in January 2017 when three football players from the University of Oregon were hospitalized following a particularly strenuous workout.[84]

In that case, Oregon strength coach Irele Oderinde put players who had recently returned from winter break through a continuous series of body-weight exercises that included push-ups and up-downs for an hour.[85] After the workout several players complained of significant muscle soreness and discolored urine. Upon further testing several of them had elevated blood levels of creatine kinase, an enzyme used as a proxy for damage to skeletal and cardiac muscle; three required hospitalization. One of those hospitalized was diagnosed with rhabdomyolysis, a condition in which profuse damage to skeletal muscle causes its contents to leak into the bloodstream, which can damage the kidneys and even lead to total kidney failure.[86] In the ensuing media firestorm it was noted that Oderinde's only certification was through the United States Track and Field and Cross Country Coaches' Association (USTFCCCA), whose certification process requires completion of a twenty-one-hour course, passing eighteen online quizzes, and creation of a training program for a hypothetical athlete. Candidates who are able to demonstrate concurrent certification in cardiopulmonary resuscitation (CPR), automated external defibrillation (AED), and first aid and possess an undergraduate degree are awarded "Advanced Endorsement."[87]

Despite the debatable rigor of an online certification that does not necessarily require college preparation, Oderinde's certification met the basic requirements of the NCAA. Bylaw 11 of the NCAA's Division I athletic personnel employment rule, adopted in April 2014, stipulates only that coaches possess a credential from a "nationally accredited strength and conditioning certification program."[88] Universities are left to interpret for themselves what constitutes a nationally accredited certification program. Notably, not only are the level of preparation and certification ambiguous but certification itself was not even required until 2014.

According to Boyd Epley, the hiring of a collegiate strength coach does not necessarily proceed through the normal human resource channels at most universities. If a head football coach wants particular individuals, they are hired "qualified or not." The lack of preparation has enabled what University of Oklahoma athletic trainer Scott Anderson has called college football's "dirty little secret": that off-season workouts are far more likely to result in fatalities than actual football activities.[89] Between 2000 and 2012 twenty-one NCAA football players died as a result of conditioning workouts.[90] According to Anderson, while the game itself is relatively safe, "we're killing kids in preparation for the game."[91]

The level of qualification of the coach is not, of course, the only reason that players are much more likely to die during conditioning than during an actual football game. Another reason is the role of strength coaches. According to former University of Tennessee football coach Butch Jones, players spend more than 86 percent of their organized football time with the strength and conditioning coaches.[92] The strength coaches have much more contact with the players than the actual football coaches do, so strength coaches become proxies for the head coach.[93] They are charged not only with physically preparing the players for the game but also with preparing them mentally. Often this means instilling a certain level of "toughness" in an environment where quitting is not an option, even at the cost of personal injury. The workout that put the Oregon players in the hospital was meant to instill mental toughness more than to train any of the movements that would actually be required in a football game.

Chris Doyle, currently the highest-paid college football strength coach, oversaw a workout similar to the one at Oregon.[94] As the head strength coach for the Iowa Hawkeyes Doyle had football players, who were also returning from winter break, perform 100 front squats for time using 50 percent of their one-repetition maximum, followed by a series of weighted sled pushes.[95] As a result of the workout, thirteen players were hospitalized with rhabdomyolysis.[96] Doyle is an educated, experienced, and decorated strength coach. He holds the Master Strength and Conditioning Coach certification from the CSCCa, was once named the Big Ten Strength Coach of the Year by the NSCA, and currently serves on the CSCCa's Board of Directors.[97]

Similarly, at the University of Nebraska, in January 2018 two football players were hospitalized for rhabdomyolysis within a week of returning to campus from winter break.[98] The workouts were supervised by Zach Duval, who trained under Boyd Epley as both a student and an assistant strength coach with the Huskers for eight years. Like Doyle, Duval is an experienced strength coach who has earned the Master Strength and Conditioning Coach distinction from the CSCCa.[99] He returned to Nebraska in late 2017 with former Husker quarterback and newly appointed head coach Scott Frost. The workouts were some of the first supervised by Duval and his staff upon their return to Lincoln.[100]

That fact is likely significant in that some of the most prominent college coaches in recent years have garnered notoriety for hitting the ground running with grueling workouts for their new teams. Urban Meyer, one of the most successful coaches in college football and recently the head football coach at Ohio State University, introduced himself to his new team when he started at the University of Utah in 2003 by locking the weight-room doors and setting out trash cans for players to vomit.[101] At Florida in 2005 he made players carry boulders and chains up the steps of the football stadium.[102] All of this, in the words of sports writer Wright Thompson, was aimed at "purging the weak" and "forcing the unworthy to quit."[103]

Harkening back to the methods of Darrell Royal and "Bear" Bryant, contemporary college coaches introduce themselves to their teams with punishing workouts to weed out anyone who might not want to convert to the philosophies of the new regime. The strength coach becomes the task master who must conduct the initial winnowing process. This appears to be part of what happened at Oregon and may have played a role at Nebraska. For their part, Nebraska coaches expressed surprise at the injuries that resulted from the workout. Frost told local newspaper reporters that the workouts had been modified after initial testing, that the session in question had even been cut from a planned forty minutes down to thirty-two, and that the athletic training staff had been on hand. "My impression of [rhabdomyolysis] before was that the people that had players that got to that point were probably doing some crazy military-style workout or up-downs until they puked or running until they dropped," said an astonished Frost. He added: "We lifted weights, it was a weight workout."[104]

More than thirty years ago Bill Kraemer wrote in open letter to NSCA members that the profession of strength and conditioning would never be a purely scientific one: practitioners would have to regularly make "clinical" decisions about programming based on a combination of experience and scientific research.[105] Despite headline-grabbing incidents like the ones at Oregon, Iowa, and Nebraska, it appears that, on balance, strength coaches have been doing just that. A 2016 survey of NCAA strength coaches found that they employed a wide variety of training methods and implements. While the use of barbells, dumbbells, and variants on the Olympic lifts represented the majority of programming by those coaches, many also incorporated "odd-shaped objects" used in competitive strongman events as well as cardio-based activities, kettlebells, resistance bands, and more.[106] This is consistent with the findings of a 2003 survey indicating that coaches used a wide variety of implements as well as a wide variety of training philosophies, ranging from periodized training to training to failure, following Eastern European intensity schemes, plyometrics, and more.[107]

This combination of the "art" and "science" of strength coaching has yielded tangible results on the field. As an example, American football was one of the earliest sports to embrace strength coaching, as evidenced by the hiring of Al Roy and Boyd Epley. A recent examination of the height, weight, and body composition of collegiate and professional football players between 1942 and 2011 found that player weight increased significantly during that span.[108] While that finding is not particularly surprising given that the weight of Americans as a whole has increased over that same era, it is noteworthy that professional football linemen increased weight yet had improved body composition.[109] Professional offensive and defensive linemen, on the whole, are larger but not necessarily fatter, meaning that additional muscle mass accounts for most of the gain. Another study (referenced in chapter 6) demonstrated that between 1974 and 1984 collegiate players got larger, stronger, and faster over the course of the decade.[110] In that study, offensive linemen saw a twenty-pound increase in average weight and a nearly 4 percent decrease in their forty-yard dash time. The mean weight for collegiate defensive linemen increased nearly thirty-six pounds, with a concomitant decrease of 3 percent in their forty-yard dash time.

A more recent work compared collegiate football players between 1987 and 2000 and found that offensive linemen had increased their average weight by nearly 9 percent while increasing their vertical jump more than 3 percent. Defensive linemen increased their weight by 6 percent while increasing their vertical jump by 9 percent and raising their squat max by nearly 7 percent. The wide receivers in the 2000 cohort were also faster, more powerful, stronger, and leaner than their colleagues from the 1980s. The authors concluded that players in college football's highest division "in general have become bigger, stronger, faster, and more powerful." Another analysis of professional football players singled out "jumbo linemen" as the biggest change between players in the 2010s and 1980s. "The cluster of players who are at least 6'3" and 300 pounds is one of the most popular body types," author Tony Manfred noted: "that player did not exist in 1980."[111]

All of this is not to deny that other factors are at play. Anabolic steroids, human growth hormone, creatine, and a host of other legal and illegal performance-enhancing substances have obviously played a role. It should be noted, however, that anabolic steroids have been around since the late 1950s and that athletes have both been lifting and using for decades. In spite of this, player size, strength, and speed have not plateaued. Selection bias is also likely at play. Anthony Anzell and colleagues noted that rule changes barring linemen from going out for passes or blocking below the waist have created a demand for larger linemen.[112] David Epstein has pointed to a "big bang of body types" that accompanied sport specialization. Since the mid-twentieth century athletes have become more specialized, which has led to a sorting along anthropometric lines. According to Epstein, "as performance requirements become stricter, only the athletes with the necessary physical structure consistently make the grade at an elite level." As it pertains to the NFL, Epstein contends that an additional centimeter of height or six and a half pounds can mean as much as an additional $45,000 to an NFL player's earnings.[113]

While pharmacological aids, rule changes, and selection have no doubt played a role in creating bigger, stronger, and faster players, specialized strength training has likely made a more significant impact. As mentioned earlier, the phenomenon of single-sport specialization in children and adolescents was first noted in the late 1980s. At that time the NSCA and other groups began discussing specialized strength-training programs for children. The children who grew up in the late 1980s and 1990s were more likely to be specialized athletes who weight trained for their sport and became the bigger, stronger, faster, and leaner players noted in the cohort studied in 2000. The first cohort from 1987 would have had some exposure to strength training, although the fact that the NSCA and the formalized profession of strength coaching were less than ten years old makes this impact hard to evaluate. The 1987 cohort would also have had access to anabolic steroids—perhaps even more access than the later cohort, given that anabolic steroids became a Schedule III drug in 1990.[114]

It appears that the primary explanation for the differences observed in those two cohorts is the combination of specialization and strength training. It is reasonable to conclude that the magnitude of observed differences in size, strength, and power would also have been less had it not been for knowledgeable professionals who knew how to structure and implement strength and conditioning programs. The advent of the professional strength coach thus appears to be the most important sport innovation of the twentieth century.

IN MEMORIAM: DR. TERRY TODD (1938–2018)

*Pioneering Powerlifter, Writer, Sport Promoter, and Historian
Who Changed the Cultural Paradigm for Strength*

"Don't Weaken." Pencils adorned with the phrase are found in small holders throughout the H. J. Lutcher Stark Center for Physical Culture and Sports at The University of Texas at Austin (UT). The phrase is actually shorthand for a favorite saying of Dr. Terry Todd, one of the Center's directors, the fuller version of which is "it's a good life if you don't weaken." Indeed, the Stark Center itself is a physical representation of Dr. Todd's commitment to that axiom. What began in the late 1950s as his relatively small collection of magazines and books related to strength training and physical culture, evolved into a library unlike any other in the world by 2009. Along with his wife, Dr. Jan Todd, Terry Todd established the Stark Center as a library and research center dedicated to the history of strength and physical culture. Occupying more than 27,500 square feet in the north endzone of UT's football stadium, and home to more than 30,000 volumes, the Stark Center is the largest facility of its kind, regularly visited by scholars from around the world (18).

Dr. Terry Todd passed away on July 7, 2018 due to complications from a heart attack (15). As he was, the Stark Center is larger than life and full of amazing stories about strength. While it is tempting to point to such a unique mecca of muscle as Dr. Todd's legacy, indeed he called it his most significant accomplishment, that would sell him far short. His full impact is found among the hundreds he coached, the thousands he taught, and the untold numbers who read his books, magazine, and journal articles, and watched his films. Dr. Todd was a physical and figurative giant in the world of strength, and his will be an enduring legacy in the world of physical culture.

This article originally appeared in the *Journal of Strength and Conditioning Research* 23.11 (November 2018): 2995–3003. It is reproduced here verbatim.

EARLY YEARS

Terry Todd was born in Beaumont, Texas on January 1, 1938 to B. C. Todd and Ima Williams Todd. Eight years later, in 1946, the family moved to Austin where Terry attended public schools and participated in a wide variety of athletic contests. As a boy, he was a standout in youth baseball, a three-time winner of the city-wide Cheerio-Top Yo-Yo competition, and winner of several city table tennis championships in high school (15). When not on the diamond or yo-yoing, Terry could often be found lying on the couch of his paternal grandparents, reading from a host of novels housed on shelves in their living room. In particular, Terry enjoyed the works of Edgar Rice Burroughs, whose famous characters included Tarzan and the adventurer of Mars, John Carter. More than the primary protagonists, however, Terry was taken by the stories' supporting casts that included immense and physically strong aliens, dogs, elephants and gorillas. The stories provided an early spark for what would become a lifelong fascination with strength. So engrossed was Terry in the stories that his grandparents joked that the only way they could tell if he "had passed out or on," was when he either blinked or turned a page (51).

In addition to works of fiction, Terry was inspired by the more tangible strength of his maternal grandfather, whom Terry would accompany on hunting trips. Sitting in a river bottom pecan grove, quietly waiting for their quarry, "Papa" leaned over and picked up a hard-shell pecan. Gesturing to Terry, he placed it between his thumb and index finger and cracked the shell. "Very few men can do that," he informed a wide-eyed Terry with a smile, "and no boys" (49,52). Even at the height of his strength almost a decade-and-a-half later, and with four inches and nearly 100 pounds on Papa, Terry recalled that he was never able to perform the feat his grandfather had with such ease.

On the tennis court, however, Terry did perform with relative ease. His father taught him the game on the public courts of South Austin's parks and, by high school, Terry was a standout. He lettered in tennis at Travis High School and earned a scholarship offer to play tennis at UT. In the summer of 1956, before he enrolled at the university, Terry took up weight training, not to improve his tennis game, but instead to increase the size of his left arm. Due to his years of tennis training, Terry joked that he looked like a crawfish whose claw had been broken off and only half grown back (11). To bring his undersized left arm back in line with his dominant right, he began a program of curls, presses, and other barbell exercises. When he began school that fall, Terry tipped the scales at 195 pounds. His coach, Wilmer Allison, noticed his increased size with disapproval. Allison, like many coaches of his day, believed that weight training would result in a muscle-bound athlete who was slow and inflexible due to the added bulk. As a result of this misplaced concern, Allison gruffly informed Todd that he would have to abandon his weight training (54).

From experience, however, Todd knew better. Though he had added 30 pounds by his freshman year, he was quicker than before he took up barbells and played better tennis. So, despite his coach's admonishment, Todd continued lifting. Fortuitously, he met Roy "Mac" McLean, an instructor and former wrestling and cross-country coach who oversaw the physical training classes at UT (43). In addition, McLean had a significant collection of physical culture magazines and books, which Todd read in the afternoons in his study. It was in that study that Todd says his love of strength truly blossomed as he read stories of legendary strongmen and contemporary weightlifters in the pages of *Strength & Health*, *Iron Man*, and *Muscle Power* (53). As he became increasingly enamored of weight training, Todd registered for competitions though, to avoid detection by Allison, always under an assumed name. His favorites were "Paul Hepburn" and "Doug Anderson" transpositions of Paul Anderson and Doug Hepburn the top two super-heavyweight lifters of the day (54).

By his junior year Todd's physique was far from the skinny, lanky build of a typical tennis player, and his coach issued an ultimatum: give up the weights or give up tennis (27). Having already lettered, Todd forfeited his scholarship to concentrate on lifting. By the time he quit the tennis team, Todd tipped the scales at a muscular 240 pounds, making him larger than any man on the football team except one, who weighed 245 (54). By 1961, he had grown to more than 270 pounds when he was summoned by not-yet legendary Texas football coach Darrell Royal for an "off the record" meeting. Royal had seen Todd play tennis and was aware of his athleticism as well as his strength training habits through talks with some of the football players. What Royal wanted to know, was whether the type of training Todd performed could help his players improve, coming off of a disappointing 1960 season (54).

Versed in the testimonials of athletes in the pages of muscle magazines, as well as his own training experience, Todd argued that heavy weight training would be a wise addition to the football program. As evidence, he pointed to shot putter Parry O'Brien, Red Sox outfielder Jackie Jensen, Chicago Bears offensive lineman Stan Jones, and Houston Oilers running back Billy Cannon, who had won the Heisman trophy two years prior at Louisiana State University. All were "barbell men," featured in *Strength & Health*, and Todd noted that he could even jump higher weighing 270 than he could before he started training and weighed 195 (54). While Royal was eager to implement heavy weight training with his Longhorn team, he was hesitant to anger the team's long-time athletic trainer, Frank Medina, who adamantly believed that heavy training would decrease the quickness of football players. Based on an early 1950s film about the training employed by Northwestern University during their most successful seasons, which promoted light weights and high repetitions, Medina asserted, "a pair of 20 or 25 pound dumbbells is enough for anybody, no matter how big or strong he is" (43). Such was Medina's political influence that it would be several more seasons before Royal was able to implement heavy training for the Longhorns, and when he did, Todd himself chronicled the program in the pages of *Strength & Health* (28).

Late in the spring of 1961, Todd completed his Bachelor of Arts degree in English at UT, though he stayed in Austin to begin working on his Doctor of Philosophy (PhD) degree in the interdisciplinary "History and Philosophy of Education" program. In addition to his studies and serving as a teaching assistant in physical training, Todd progressed in his own lifting career. Weighing just short of 300 pounds, the "ponderous" Terry Todd captured his first major title in 1963, winning the Amateur Athletic Union (AAU) junior national weightlifting championship (10). The same meet also featured a physique competition following the weightlifting, as well as an emerging type of strength contest: powerlifting. With particularly large biceps and forearms, Todd had some difficulty catching the "clean" when performing the "clean and jerk" Olympic lift and knew that his ability to succeed in the sport would be constrained. As a result, he transitioned to the new sport of powerlifting, winning the first men's national championships in the event in 1964. He followed by winning the first Senior Nationals in 1965. As a powerlifter, Todd held 15 records at one time or another and was the first man to squat 700 pounds, as well as the first to total 1600, 1700, 1800, and 1900 pounds. His best official lifts included a 720-pound squat, 515-pound bench press, and 742-pound deadlift (16).

While working on his doctorate, Todd moved to York, Pennsylvania in the fall of 1964 to take over as managing editor for *Strength & Health* magazine. Along with his editorial duties and writing for the magazine, he was tasked with coordinating research projects for the Bob Hoffman Foundation. His most important impact at the magazine, however, was helping to define the new sport of powerlifting in its formative years. In addition to writing about powerlifting in both *Strength & Health* and *Muscular Development*, the massive 340-pound Todd himself was often the subject of articles and photos and featured lifting massive weights. The articles captured the imagination of many and inspired readers to take up the emerging sport (4). With championships in both powerlifting and Olympic weightlifting, a 1966 *Muscular Development* article noted that Todd had the highest combined total of any lifter, making him the best of the "Supermen of the Iron Game" (4).

EARLY ACADEMIC CAREER

Also in 1966, Todd completed his PhD. His dissertation, titled, "The History of Resistance Exercise and Its Role in United States Education" was a landmark in the field as one of the first academic treatments on the history of resistance training (29). Beginning with the ancient Egyptians and continuing through the mid-twentieth century, the manuscript explored the history of resistance exercise, numerous training methods, famous strongmen, the interaction between strength training and athletics, and the use of resistance training in physical education. After its completion, Todd accepted a position in the College of Education at Auburn University. The new position marked the end of his tenure as a magazine editor and the end of his competitive powerlifting career. Though he continued to lift for the rest of his life, by the time he was preparing to enter this new phase of his career, Todd decided that he had "fulfilled [his] curiosity about becoming big and strong" and devoted himself to his academic work (9).

While ultimately known for his contributions to the world of strength sports and their history, Todd's focus in his earliest academic positions was the improvement of American schools. After three years at Auburn, Todd accepted a position at Mercer University in Macon, Georgia. There he served as an Associate Professor of Education, Physical Education and Sociology. Despite having slimmed down to 250-pounds since his competitive days, Todd stood out on campus not only for his exceptional size, but also for his commitment to activist causes and civil rights, playing a leading role in founding the university's African American Studies program in 1969. He also ran a series of summer seminars on educational reform, convincing luminary educational theorists John Holt, James Herndon, and Edgar Friedenberg, considered by some to be the most important public intellectuals on school reform of the era, to come and speak (15). Decades later, Mercer students still recalled the first time they formally met Todd in a freshman seminar. The title of the talk was "The Educational Value of Hucking Around," a consideration of Twain's *Adventures of Huckleberry Finn* and adolescent development. At a small Baptist college in that era, the title proved both risqué and unforgettable.

At Mercer, Terry Todd met Jan Suffolk. As one of the many students sitting in the seminar, Jan knew of Todd, but it was at an end-of-season intramural softball party three years later that she truly made an impression on him. Todd played host for the party and as the athletes sat and chatted atop stacks of logs he had recently cut following an unseasonal ice storm, the talk turned to contests of strength; specifically, to caber tossing (30). Most of the party-goers were unfamiliar with this mainstay of the Scottish Highland Games in which an athlete stands a log upright, walks a few steps and then tosses the log end-over-end for distance, but they were eager to pit themselves against one of the logs. After a reasonably heavy specimen was pulled from the stack, faculty and students alike tried their hand at giving it flight. Notably, however, all of the participants were male. After a member of the philosophy faculty failed repeatedly to flip the log, Jan—then a junior working on a double major in philosophy and English—stepped forward to attempt the feat. She made short work of the timber, flipping it on her first try. "As near as I can tell," Todd would later write, "that was the day I began to love her" (30).

In spite of his official retirement from competitive lifting and his academic work which was, at best, tangentially related, Terry still felt called to be involved with the "iron game." After a brief interlude in the late 1960s, he began once again to write articles on powerlifting in 1971 for *Muscular Development* and *Iron Man* magazines (16). In those pages, Todd wrote instructional articles but, more importantly, he covered major powerlifting contests. Moonlighting as a sportswriter, Todd's articles were different from typical meet recaps; his told a story. Drawing on his own experience as a champion lifter, Todd crafted dramas through his retelling of the meet's events and included personal vignettes of many of the lifters involved. "When he shows up to an event," legendary powerlifter Larry Pacifico wrote, "that event becomes more important because lifters know that what they do with him watching will live on through his accurate, honest words" (16). Such was Todd's presence, that Pacifico claimed it inspired lifters to heft more pounds than they thought possible just because they wanted to see how he would write about them.

One lifter about whom he would write voluminously was Jan after their marriage in 1973. After they began dating, Jan started to accompany Terry to the weight room, partly out of curiosity, as lifting weights was Terry's form of recreation, and she was interested to learn more. Initially, she lifted light weights for high repetitions, attempting to correct her posture and fearful of adding bulk. During winter break that year, Jan accompanied Terry back to Austin to visit with his family for Christmas. While they were there, they dropped by one of his old haunts, the Texas Athletic Club, where Jan watched as a petite woman who weighed no more than 125-pounds deadlift

225-pounds. The woman was a competitive powerlifter; Jan struck up a conversation with her and, before she left, had pulled 225 herself (27). On the way home, she quizzed Terry about weight training and he was only too eager to share.

He told Jan of Katie Sandwina, the legendary strongwoman who performed in circuses at the turn of the twentieth century. Sandwina's signature feats included carrying a 600-pound cannon on her back, bending iron, and juggling her much smaller husband—as if she was doing the manual of arms with a rifle. Once at home, Terry showed Jan stories in muscle magazines and old books about other early women strength performers. They also came across a page in the *Guinness Book of World Records* that listed the heaviest deadlift ever performed by a woman, a lift made by Mlle Jane de Vesley of France in 1926, at 392-pounds. Though the record had stood for nearly half a century, Jan stared at the page momentarily before pronouncing excitedly, "I think I can beat that" (27, 30). With that declaration, Terry Todd, lifting champion, academic, and writer, took on a new role he would continue to perform for the rest of his life: coach.

When they returned to Georgia, they crafted a plan to get Jan to her goal. After sixteen months of training with Terry at a gym in downtown Macon, the two traveled to Chattanooga, Tennessee for Jan's first powerlifting meet in May of 1975. After a heavy warm-up for her first attempt, Jan broke de Vesley's record with her second, pulling 394.5-pounds and re-writing the *Guinness Book* (30). As they were preparing for the meet, Terry had been offered a new academic post as an Associate Professor of Educational Sociology at Dalhousie University in Halifax, Nova Scotia, Canada. In the fall of 1975, they packed their belongings and moved to Canada where they soon purchased a 185-acre farm near New Germany, Nova Scotia. While Terry pursued his university career and Jan taught high school English, they also worked their land with draft horses, lived in a house with only wood stoves for heat, and raised most of what they ate on their own land (17). Terry continued his writing in a chicken house that he converted into a makeshift office (24). At a desk below a suspended bag of seed, stored safely from hungry rodents, Terry wrote his first two books: *Fitness for Athletes*, and the influential *Inside Powerlifting* (30,55). The latter of the two was the first book written about the nascent strength sport. In that work, his masterful storytelling is in full evidence as he detailed the history of the competition, described the events, detailed training routines, and profiled nine elite lifters, including Jan.

In addition to his academic duties at Dalhousie and his writing Terry, along with Jan, coached lifters at both Dalhousie University and in New

Germany, Nova Scotia, where the Todds and their high school team trained in the back of Jan's classroom. During that time they also helped organize the first national women's powerlifting meet in the United States in 1977 (63). Along with the collegiate and interscholastic lifters, Terry continued to coach Jan and helped organize her training. At a meet in Newfoundland, in June 1977, Jan totaled a then world-record 1,041 pounds in the three competitive powerlifts (17, 30). Not only was it a world record but shattered the previous mark by nearly 100-pounds. The accomplishment led to a feature article in *Sports Illustrated* (*SI*) in which Jan was dubbed the strongest woman in the world (17). Following the article, the couple was invited to New York City for a series of television appearances, and a visit to the *SI* offices. After chatting with the magazine's editors, Terry was asked to write an article on arm wrestling champion Al Turner (31). More assignments followed and Terry wrote voluminously for the magazine in the late 1970s and early 1980s.

Among those articles was a profile of powerlifter Lamar Gant, a lifter in the 123 and 132-pound weight classes with the rare distinctions of having won more than 9 world titles and deadlifting of more than 5 times his own bodyweight (40). In addition to covering Gant in *Muscular Development* and *Sports Illustrated*, Todd coached Gant after he and Jan moved back to Auburn University in 1979. After four years in Canada, the Todds were drawn back to the United States by the prospect of starting the National Strength Research Center at Auburn. Along with exercise scientists Mike Stone, John Garhammer and Tom McLaughlin, Todd organized research and coached athletes. Those athletes ranged from elite powerlifters like Gant and Bill Kazmaier to intercollegiate lifters, Auburn varsity female athletes, and more. With his growing reputation as an expert on strength, and his melodic baritone voice that once prompted an attendee at an academic conference to declare that she would gladly listen to him read the phone book, Todd was regularly invited to serve as a color commentator for NBC, CBS and other networks when powerlifting appeared on TV (2,8). He was also involved with the early broadcasts of the "World's Strongest Man" contest and, in the early 1980s, worked as CBS television's "Consultant on Strength Sports," organizing "The Strongest Man in Football Contest," for the network between 1980 and 1982 (19).

GONE TO TEXAS (LATE ACADEMIC CAREER)

After four years at Auburn, Terry took a position at his alma mater, The University of Texas, in 1983. Because he was heavily involved with *Sports Illustrated* and CBS at the time, Todd joined the faculty as a lecturer, in order to have the academic freedom to pursue his career as a broadcaster and journalist. By then, the Todds had also amassed more than 380 boxes of books and magazines related to the field of physical culture and strength training and had begun to dream of establishing a special library. Terry continued to write for *SI*, profiling powerlifters Larry Pacifico and Lamar Gant; writing about pro football players and their training habits, including Herschel Walker, Bob Young, and Dave Rimington; and covering the Bulgarian Olympic weightlifting champion whom he would dub the "vest-pocket Hercules"— Naim Suleimanov (32,35,36,39). But it was his writing about wrestler Andre Roussimoff, better known as "Andre the Giant," that became one of his most talked-about pieces, even running later as a re-print in *Readers Digest* magazine (33,34). One of his most influential articles, however, was not a profile but a discussion of the growing prevalence of anabolic steroids in elite sports (37). Todd outlined the emerging "steroid predicament," examining the history of the drugs, their use in a variety of sports, their effects, and the lengths to which athletes are willing to go to win. The article was met with applause from readers in the following issues of *SI* and came to be considered one of the most important on doping in the 1980s (5).

Todd also brought his discussion of anabolic steroids into academic circles, calling them "the Gremlins of Sport," and detailing their development and proliferation in the *Journal of Sport History* (42). He co-authored two more books in the mid-1980s, both related to training methods (27,61). The first detailed the training techniques of Herschel Walker while the second was based on research he helped perform while at Auburn. Co-authored with Jan, *Lift Your Way to Youthful Fitness* was based on studies done with sedentary, middle-aged men and women. In light of the success of the training interventions, readers were instructed about the importance of maintaining strength to stave off age-related declines. In addition to writing about the utility of weight training for adults, he wrote about weight training for athletes in the *NSCA Journal* (renamed *Strength and Conditioning Journal*).

Having experienced first-hand the prejudice and fears about weight training for athletes in the mid-twentieth century, Todd made sure strength coaches were aware of the field's evolution in one of his seminal articles, "The myth of the muscle-bound lifter" (41). In addition to fearing weights more generally, some coaches were specifically reticent about the squat exercise, fearing, based on research dating back to the 1960s, that it was harmful for an athlete's knee ligaments. In another widely read piece, Todd provided historical context for the idea, discussing the original research and helping to give strength coaches background on that "myth" as well, should they encounter a coach apprehensive having their athletes squat (38). Through that work, he and Jan came to the realization that there was a need for an outlet on the history of physical culture (56). Until the mid-1980s, magazines like *Strength & Health* and *Iron Man* had included historical features, but the former folded in 1986 and the latter had phased them out. Academic journals, like those of the NSCA and the *Journal of Sport History*, would publish work on the history of physical culture, but it was relatively atypical. Seeking to create an academic journal dedicated to the history of physical culture, Terry and Jan assembled and editorial board and began publishing *Iron Game History: The Journal of Physical Culture* in 1990. With that, they added "editor" to their long list of responsibilities, one which continues to this day as *Iron Game History* nears 30 years of publication.

As he had at Auburn, Todd coached the powerlifting team along with Jan, continuing in that role for ten years and leading the Longhorn team to multiple national championships (63). In the middle of that run at the Texas high school state powerlifting championships, the Todds met a young man of unparalleled strength (25). At eighteen, Mark Henry was a three-time state champion in powerlifting who could squat and deadlift over 800, while bench pressing more than 500. Terry thought, given Henry's flexibility, that he would make an equally outstanding Olympic weightlifter and convinced him to move to Austin to train and attend college. Within two years, Henry was a two-time Olympian, competing at both the Barcelona Games in 1992 and Atlanta Games in 1996. Five years later, in 2001, Terry was asked by Arnold Schwarzenegger and Jim Lorimer to create a professional strongman contest for the "Arnold Classic" (52).

At the initial contest in 2002, Todd invited athletes from powerlifting, weightlifting, and the sport of strongman in the hope of truly identifying the world's strongest man. He also chose events that used genuinely heavy weights moved over short distances to more accurately measure strength—and not muscular endurance. Mark Henry claimed the first "Arnold Strongman Classic" title, and over the next 17 years as the sport of strongman grew internationally, The Arnold Strongman Classic was recognized as the most important contest in the sport of strongman. Moreover, Todd's influence on the sport was hailed as being transformative (3). Todd took particular pride in the fact that each year after the Arnold Classic was over, the giant athletes are taken to Dr. Bill Kraemer's lab at Ohio State University for medical examinations, blood work, body composition analysis, and other diagnostic tests that help these unique athletes monitor their health.

As Jan entered graduate school and began working on a PhD specializing in sport history, she and Terry became frequent collaborators on academic articles covering all aspects of the history of strength and conditioning. To that end, they authored a series of articles for the *Journal of Strength and Conditioning Research (JSCR)* on the scientific pioneers who studied the phenomenon of human strength. In that series, the Todds profiled physiologists Peter Karpovich, Richard Berger, Herbert deVries, and Pat O'Shea (57,58,59,60). Then, in an article selected as a Dudley Memorial Paper in *JSCR*, the Todds and co-author Jason Shurley explored the contributions of physician Thomas DeLorme, who provided medical validation for intense strength training (26). The trio also covered the important role of the NSCA in generating and disseminating research related to strength training and athletic performance, and have written a book on the history of the strength coaching profession in America that will be released in 2019 (21,22). In *Iron Game History*, Terry wrote voluminously about the history of strength training for athletes, strongmen, weightlifters, bodybuilders and other legends of days past, publishing more than 66 articles in that journal (43,44,45,46,47,48,49).

In 2009, Terry and Jan Todd moved their now much larger collection (more than 3000 boxes of magazines and books related to physical culture and sport, thousands of photographs and a large assortment of antique barbells, dumbbells, and various other exercise implements) into a more fitting location in the newly-constructed north endzone of the UT football stadium (50). Since then, Terry has served as a co-director, along with Jan, of the H. J. Lutcher Stark Center for Physical Culture and Sports. Designated one of only three Olympic Studies Centers in the United States, the facility is truly world-class and one of which Terry was duly proud.

CONCLUSION

"Properly done," Terry wrote, "weights can work magic. I know." Through his work, so do we. At final tally, he authored or co-authored more than 500 articles in popular magazines and academic journals, and 7 books (7,22,27,30,55,61,62). He was inducted into numerous halls of fame, including the International Sports Hall of Fame, and the halls of both men's and women's powerlifting (15). He received the National Strength and Conditioning Association's highest honor—the Al Roy Award—in 2017; was honored as a "Legend" by the Collegiate Strength and Conditioning Coaches Association in 2009, and, in 2013, received the Honor Award of the North American Society for Sport History for his contributions to that academic field (1,12,15). He was a champion of two different strength sports, setting 15 records along the way. He was a coach of some of the most elite lifters in the world, as well as many who just wanted to learn how to get a little bit stronger. He created and directed strongman contests, was a commentator on national television broadcasts, wrote reams of popular press and academic articles, and also taught undergraduate kinesiology and introductory weight training courses for decades. Through years of collecting, acquiring, and fundraising, he and Jan turned an assortment of books and magazines on physical culture into an archive like no other.

The reason he was truly a legend and a pioneer, however, is that he made strength approachable. Terry told the story of strength training's evolution from a curiosity in the early twentieth century to a pillar of health, fitness and sport programs in the twenty-first. He explored Americans' simultaneous fascination with strength and their hesitation to take up the implements that produced it. Through his intelligence and welcoming personality, he led by example in bringing weight training out of the dark ages. He was able to demonstrate through his own experience that weights did not hurt athletic performance and he told others at every opportunity. Through his wit and charisma, he disabused many of the notion that weight trainers were unintelligent eccentrics. Through his writing and broadcasting, he brought his awe of strength into living rooms across the country. He had a deep admiration for physical power and a respect for those who possessed it, which enabled him to show the human side of strength in a way few others could. That wonder made it more palatable and interesting for a lay audience who would not otherwise be engaged by the strength aspect of sports. Even academics were swayed, as he helped bring research on strength training into academic respectability by providing historical context.

True to the aphorism, Terry did not weaken and was still hard at work this summer. He had already begun preparation for the 2019 Arnold Strongman Classic. In addition, he recently added "producer" to his lengthy curriculum vitae, serving in that capacity for a series of documentaries sponsored by the equipment manufacturer, Rogue Fitness. Those films include *Levantadores*, about stone lifting in Spain, *Stoneland*, covering strength traditions in Scotland, and *Fullsterkur*, a forthcoming film discussing the strength traditions of Iceland, as well as profiles of Eugen Sandow and Louis Uni (6,13,14,20,23). His final book, *Strength Coaching in America: A History of the Innovation That Transformed Sport*, of which he is a co-author along with Jason Shurley and Jan Todd, is due out in 2019 (22). As a long-time friend observed when they learned of his passing, "It may seem that our world is a bit weaker today but actually we are all immeasurably and eternally stronger for having known him" (15).

REFERENCES

1. Alvin Roy Award for Career Achievement--2017. National Strength Cond Assoc. Available at https://www.cscca.org/about/awards/legendsaward/2009/todd. Accessed August 8, 2018.

2. Berryman, JW. *Remarks delivered at Terry Todd memorial service.* Austin, TX. July 28, 2018.

3. Crawford W. *Remarks delivered at Terry Todd memorial service. Austin, TX.* July 28, 2018.

4. Fair, JD. *Muscletown USA.* University Park, PA: Penn State University Press, 1999, 214-216.

5. Flood, G, ed. 19th hole: Readers take over. *Sports Illustrated*, August 14, 1983, 70.

6. Fullsterkur. *Rogue Fitness.* Available at https://www.roguefitness.com/theindex/video/fullsterkur-trailer-a-documentary-film. Accessed August 8, 2018.

7. Holowchak, MA, and Todd, TC, eds. *Philosophical Reflections on Strength.* Lewiston, NY: Edwin Mellen Press, 2010.

8. Howlett, PG. Letter from the publisher. *Sports Illustrated*, November 17, 1980, 4.

9. Hutson, M. Former weight lifters Terry and Jan Todd call Austin their home. *Daily Texan*, November 30, 2012.

10. Junior nationals report. *Strength Health*, October 1963, 10-11.

11. Kubina, B. Carrying the load. *Daily Texan*, March 24, 2014.

12. Legends in the field--2009: Terry Todd. *Coll Strength Cond Coach Assoc.* Available at https://www.cscca.org/about/awards/legendsaward/2009/todd. Accessed August 8, 2018.

13. Levantadores: The Basque strongman. *Rogue Fitness.* Available at https://www.roguefitness.com/theindex/video/levantadores-the-basque-strongman-a-documentary-film. Accessed August 8, 2018.

14. Louis "Apollon" Uni--Rogue Legends Series. *Rogue Fitness.* Available at https://www.roguefitness.com/theindex/video/the-rogue-legends-series-chapter-2-louis-apollon-uni-8k. Accessed August 8, 2018.

15. Obituary: Terry Todd, Ph.D. *Austin American Statesman*, July 10, 2018. Available at https://www.legacy.com/obituaries/statesman/obituary.aspx?n=terry-todd&pid=189508071. Accessed August 8, 2018.

16. Pacifico, L. Introduction. In *Inside Powerlifting*. Chicago, IL: Contemporary Books, 1978, v–xii.

17. Pileggi, S. The pleasure of being the world's strongest woman. *Sports Illustrated*, November 14, 1977, 60-71.

18. Pollack, B. H. J. Lutcher Stark Center for Physical Culture and Sports. *Handbook of Texas Online.* Available at https://tshaonline.org/handbook/online/articles/lch03. Accessed August 8, 2018.

19. Rogers, T. Men of steel. *New York Times*, June 28, 1982, C2.

20. Sandow--Rogue Legends Series. *Rogue Fitness.* Available at https://www.roguefitness.com/sandow. Accessed August 8, 2018.

21. Shurley, JP, Todd, JS, and Todd, TC. The science of strength: Reflections on the National Strength and Conditioning Association and the emergence of research-based strength and conditioning. *J Strength Cond Res* 31 (2017): 517-530.

22. Shurley, JP, Todd, JS, and Todd, TC. *Strength Coaching in America*. Austin, TX: University of Texas Press, 2019.

23. Stoneland. *Rogue Fitness*. Available at https://www.roguefitness.com/stoneland. Accessed August 8, 2018.

24. Sutton, KF. Letter from the publisher. *Sports Illustrated*, October 9, 1978, 6.

25. Sweeten-Shultz, L. Muscle mettle: Olympian Mark Henry goes Raw for WWE. *Times Record (Wichita Falls, TX)*, February 26, 2010.

26. Todd, JS, Shurley, JP, and Todd, TC. Thomas L. DeLorme and the science of progressive resistance exercise. *J Strength Cond Res* 26 (2012): 2913-2923.

27. Todd, JS, and Todd, TC. *Lift Your Way to Youthful Fitness*. Boston, MA: Little, Brown, and Co., 1985.

28. Todd, TC. Progressive resistance for football at the University of Texas. *Strength Health*, September 1964, 18-19.

29. Todd, TC. The history of resistance exercise and its role in United States education. PhD diss., University of Texas at Austin, 1966.

30. Todd, TC. *Inside Powerlifting*. Chicago, IL: Contemporary Books, 1978.

31. Todd, TC. Arming himself for the fray. *Sports Illustrated*, October 8, 1978, 56-64.

32. Todd, TC. Still going strong. *Sports Illustrated*, November 17, 1980, 47-67.

33. Todd, TC. To the giant among us. *Sports Illustrated*, December 21, 1981, 76-92.

34. Todd, TC. A giant among us. *Reader's Digest*, May 1982, 114-118.

35. Todd, TC. My body's like an army. *Sports Illustrated*, October 3, 1982, 94-108.

36. Todd, TC. A man of heft who's also deft. *Sports Illustrated*, November 8, 1982, 40-45.

37. Todd, TC. The steroid predicament. *Sports Illustrated*, July 31, 1983, 62-78.

38. Todd, TC. Karl Klein and the squat. *Strength Cond J* 6 (1984): 26-31.

39. Todd, TC. Behold Bulgaria's vest-pocket Hercules. *Sports Illustrated*, June 11, 1984, 32-46.

40. Todd, TC. He bends but he doesn't break. *Sports Illustrated*, October 22, 1984, 46-62.

41. Todd, TC. The myth of the muscle-bound lifter. *Strength Cond J* 7 (1985): 37-41.

42. Todd, TC. Anabolic steroids: The gremlins of sport. *J Sport Hist* 14 (1987): 87-107.

43. Todd, TC. The history of strength training for athletes at the University of Texas. *Iron Game History* 2 (1993): 6-13.

44. Todd, TC. Remembering Bob Hoffman. *Iron Game History* 3 (1993): 18-23.

45. Todd, TC. Paul Anderson: 1932-1994. *Iron Game History* 3 (1994): 1-3.

46. Todd, TC. The expansion of resistance training in US higher education through the mid-1960s. *Iron Game History* 3 (1994): 11-16.

47. Todd, TC. The PGA Tour's traveling gym--how it began. *Iron Game History* 3 (1994): 14-19.

48. Todd, TC. John Grimek--The man. *Iron Game History* 5 (1999): 1-5.

49. Todd, TC. The quest for the quarter master. *Iron Game History* 9 (2005): 21-31.

50. Todd, TC. Announcing the H. J. Lutcher Stark Center for Physical Culture and Sports. *Iron Game History* 9 (2007): 1-6.

51. Todd, TC. Books. *Blog: Don't Weaken*, October 2, 2009. Available at https://www.starkcenter.org/2009/10/. Accessed August 8, 2018.

52. Todd, TC. Philosophical and practical considerations for a strongman contest. In *Philosophical Reflections on Strength*. Lewiston, NY: Edwin Mellen, 2010, 49-88.

53. Todd, TC. Helping hands. *Blog: Don't Weaken*, May 12, 2010. Available at https://www.starkcenter.org/2010/05/. Accessed August 8, 2018.

54. Todd, TC. Memories of Coach Darrell K. Royal. *Iron Game History* 12 (2013): 1-6.

55. Todd, TC, and Hoover, D. *Fitness for Athletes*. Chicago, IL: Contemporary Books, 1978.

56. Todd, TC, and Todd, JS. Editorial--a statement of purpose. *Iron Game History* 1 (1990): 1.

57. Todd, TC, and Todd, JS. Pioneers of strength research: The legacy of Dr. Richard A. Berger. *J Strength Cond Res* 15 (2001): 275-278.

58. Todd, TC, and Todd, JS. Dr. Patrick O'Shea: A man for all seasons. *J Strength Cond Res* 15 (2001): 401-404.

59. Todd, TC and Todd, JS. Herbert A. deVries: 60 years of exercise and science. *J Strength Cond Res* 16 (2002): 5-8.

60. Todd, TC, and Todd, JS. Peter V. Karpovich: Transforming the strength paradigm. *J Strength Cond Res* 17 (2003): 213-220.

61. Walker, H, and Todd, TC. *Herschel Walker's Basic Training*. New York, NY: Doubleday, 1985.

62. Walker, H, and Todd, TC. *Herschel Walker's Basic Training*, revised edition. New York, NY: Doubleday, 1989.

63. Women's Hall of Fame--2004: Terry Todd. *USA Powerlifting*. Available at http://www.usapowerlifting.com/womens-hall-of-fame/terry-todd/. Accessed August 8, 2018.

NOTES

INTRODUCTION

1. Steve Berkowitz, "Everything's Bigger in Texas: Longhorns, Aggies, Top List of Revenues for NCAA Division I Public Schools," *USA Today*, June 28, 2018: https://www.usatoday.com/story/sports/college/2018/06/28 /texas-texas-am-top-list-ncaa-revenue-2017/742363002/.

2. In 2011 the University of Texas signed a deal with the sports network ESPN (Entertainment and Sports Programming Network) to broadcast Longhorn sports twenty-four hours per day on Texas's very own "Longhorn Network." ESPN agreed to pay the university a total of $300 million over twenty years for those rights. More recently, in the summer of 2016, the Big Ten Conference signed deals with ESPN, Fox Sports, and CBS (Columbia Broadcasting System) for the rights to broadcast their sporting events. ESPN agreed to pay the conference $190 million annually for six years, while Fox Sports anted up $240 million per year, and CBS will pay $10 million per year for basketball-only rights. The total package between the Big Ten and broadcasters is worth $2.64 billion. John Ourand and Michael Smith, "UT to Unveil 20-Year, $300M Deal with ESPN for Longhorn Network," *Sports Business Daily*, January 19, 2011: https://www. sportsbusinessdaily.com /Daily/Morning-Buzz/2011/01/19/Texas-ESPN.aspx; John Ourand, "ESPN Stays in the Game," *Sports Business Daily*, June 20, 2016: https://www .sportsbusinessdaily.com/Journal/Issues/2016/06/20/Media/ESPN-Big-Ten .aspx.

3. Emily Caron, "Highest-Paid NCAA Football Coaches: Nick Saban, Urban Meyer . . . and Lovie Smith?" *Sports Illustrated*, October 3, 2018: https://www.si.com/ college-football/2018/10/03/nick-saban-urban-meyer-jim -harbaugh-jimbo-fisher-highest-paid-football-coaches-2018.

4. Ibid.; "2016 NCAA Salaries: NCAAF Coaches," *USA Today* (n.d.): https://www .sports.usatoday.com/ncaa/salaries/ (accessed October 21, 2017).

5. "2016 NCAA Salaries: NCAAF Coaches."

6. Caron, "Highest-Paid NCAA Football Coaches"; Nicholas Piotrowicz, "Ohio State to Pay Assistant Coaches More Than $1M," *Toledo Blade*, February 14, 2018: https://www.toledoblade.com/sports/college/2018/02/14 /Ohio-State-to-pay-Schiano-Day-more-than-1M/stories/20180214166.

7. Scott Keepfer, "Clemson Opens New Football Center, Just in Time for Signing

Day," *Greenville News*, January 31, 2017: https://www
.greenvilleonline.com/story/sports/college/clemson/2017/01/31
/clemson-opens-new-football-center-just-time-signing-day/97274716/.

8. Craig Garcia, "The Hatfield-Dowlin Complex in Perspective," *Daily Emerald*
    (Eugene, OR), August 12, 2013.

9. Daniel Uthman, "Stunning Amenities in Oregon's New Football Facility," *USA
    Today*, August 1, 2013: https://www.usatoday.com/story/sports
    /ncaaf/2013/08/01/outrageously-unique-amenities-in-oregons-new-football
    -facility-hatfield-dowlin-complex/2606223/.

10. Greg Bishop, "Oregon Embraces 'University of Nike' Image," *New York Times*,
    August 2, 2013.

11. Luke Kerr-Dineen, "Texas Players Lose Their Minds after Seeing Their Amazing
    New Locker Room for the First Time," *USA Today*, August 3, 2017:
    https://ftw.usatoday.com/2017/08/university-of-texas-football-longhorns
    -locker-room-pictures-video.

12. Ibid. A major national supplier of strength training equipment to colleges and
    universities (Power Systems, Inc.) lists the price of lifting stations between
    $2,000 and $4,500. Power Systems, Inc., "Lifting Stations, Racks, and
    Platforms," at https://www.power-systems.com/s-39-lifting-stations-racks-and-
    platforms.aspx (no longer available; accessed May 30, 2012).

13. Andrew Gribble, "Scott Cochran 'Humbled Every Day' by Alabama's $9 million,
    'Jaw Dropping' Weight Room," February 27, 2013: https://www.al.com
    /alabamafootball/index.ssf/2013/02/scott_cochran_weight_room.html.

14. Bruce Feldman, "Heavy Lifting's Best Starts with Horns," June 23, 2010:
    http://insider.espn.go.com/ncf/blog?name=feldman_bruce&id=5318369;
    David Mitchell, "Strength and Conditioning Center: KU Offers Sneak Peak,"
    February 19, 2003: http://www2.kusports.com/news/2003/feb/19
    /strength_and_conditioning/.

15. The University of Kansas has the same system, created by a company called
    EliteForm, as do Oklahoma University, Marquette University, and others.
    "Facilities: Anderson Strength Center," KUAthletics.com (n.d.): https://
    www.kuathletics.com/sports/2013/6/27/facilities-anderson-strength-center
    .aspx?id=193 (accessed November 4, 2017).

16. Steve Berkowitz, "Iowa Strength Coach Chris Doyle, Already Highest Paid, Gets a
    Raise to $725,000," *USA Today*, July 10, 2018: https://www.usatoday.com
    /story/sports/ncaaf/bigten/2018/07/24/iowa-strength-coach-chris-doyle-gets
    -raise-725-000/829562002/; see also "2017 NCAA Salaries: NCAAF Strength
    Coaches," *USA Today* (n.d.): https://www.sports.usatoday.com/ncaa/salaries
    /football/strength (accessed May 23, 2018).

17. "Database: State of Iowa Employee Salaries," *Des Moines Register*, January 8,
    2018: http://db.desmoinesregister.com/state-salaries-for-iowa.

18. Berkowitz, "Iowa Strength Coach."

19. Rich Kaipust, "Ex-Husker Strength Coach Boyd Epley Will Receive Lifetime
    Achievement Award," *Omaha World Herald*, May 29, 2014: https://www.
    omaha.com/huskers/ex-husker-strength-coach-boyd-epley-will-receive-lifetime-
    achievement/article_57d0c9d0-79cd-5451-b45d-76492a41e921.html.

20. Rick Suttle, "How Much Do Strength and Conditioning Coaches Make on
    Average?" *Houston Chronicle* (n.d.): https://work.chron.com/much-strength
    -conditioning-coaches-make-average-19363.html; "Strength and Conditioning

Coach Salary" ZipRecruiter.com, (n.d.): https://www.ziprecruiter.com/s /strength-and-conditioning-coach-salary ; "Average Salary for Certification: Certified Strength and Conditioning Specialist," PayScale.com (n.d.): https:// www.payscale.com/research/US/Certification=Certified_Strength_and_ Conditioning_Specialist_(CSCS)/Salary (all accessed May 23, 2018).

21. Outsized salaries have even made their way to the high school ranks, though the numbers are not quite as staggering. In May 2018 teachers in Eastern Hancock, Indiana, protested when a newly hired strength coach was offered a total compensation package of nearly $60,000, more than the compensation of nearly two-thirds of the districts' teachers. Evan Myers, "Eastern Hancock Teachers Speak Out against New Hire," *Greenfield (IN) Daily Reporter*, May 17, 2018: http://www.greenfieldreporter.com/2018/05/18 /eastern_hancock_teachers_speak_out_against_new_hire/.

22. Pat Forde, "Strength Coaches Doing Heavy Lifting," ESPN.com, June 24, 2010: http://www.espn.com/college-football/columns/ story?columnist=forde_pat&id=5310210.

23. Jim Catalano, "Building Strength," *Athletic Management*, June/July 2003: http://www.momentummedia.com/articles/am/am1504/strength.htm.

24. The first intercollegiate athletic contest was a dual rowing meet between Harvard and Yale Universities in 1852. Just three years later, controversy emerged when Yale protested Harvard's decision to bring back a graduate student to serve as coxswain at the 1855 race. By 1889 there were allegations that Harvard and Princeton were enrolling athletes in professional programs in order to keep them eligible to compete beyond their undergraduate years. Ronald Smith, *Sports & Freedom: The Rise of Big-Time College Athletics*.

25. N. Travis Triplett, Chat Williams, Patrick McHenry, and Michael Doscher, "Strength and Conditioning Professional Standards and Guidelines."

26. Steven J. Fleck and William J. Kraemer, *Designing Resistance Training Programs*, 3.

27. Vladimir M. Zatsiorsky, *Science and Practice of Strength Training*, 25.

28. John Hoberman, *Mortal Engines: The Science of Performance and the Dehumanization of Sport*; John Hoberman, *Testosterone Dreams: Rejuvenation, Aphrodisia, Doping*; Daniel Rosen, *Dope: A History of Performance Enhancement in Sports from the Nineteenth Century to Today*; Thomas Hunt, *Drug Games: The International Olympic Committee and the Politics of Doping, 1960–2008*; Matt Chaney, *Spiral of Denial: Muscle Doping in American Football*; Shaun Assael, *Steroid Nation: Juiced Home Run Totals, Anti-Aging Miracles, and a Hercules in Every High School*.

29. Jan Todd, "Size Matters: Muscle, Drugs and Sport," 20 (emphasis added).

30. See, for example, Jan Todd and Terry Todd, "Legacy of Iron: A History of the Men, Women, and Implements That Created the 'Iron Game'"; Terry Todd, "Steroids: An Historical Perspective," 1–3; Jan Todd, "The Mystery of Minerva"; Terry Todd, "A Pioneer of Physical Training: C. H. McCloy"; Jan Todd, "The Legacy of Pudgy Stockton"; Jan Todd, "From Milo to Milo: A History of Barbells, Dumbbells, and Indian Clubs"; Jan Todd, "'Chaos Can Have Gentle Beginnings': The Early History of the Quest for Drug Testing in American Powerlifting: 1964–1984."

31. John Fair, "George Jowett, Ottley Coulter, David Willoughby, and the Organization of American Weightlifting 1911–1924"; John Fair, "Father Figure or

Phony?: George Jowett, the ACWLA and the Milo Barbell Company 1924–1927";
John Fair, "From Philadelphia to York: George Jowett, Mark Berry, Bob Hoffman
and the Rebirth of American Weightlifting, 1927–1936"; John Fair, "'That Man's
Just Too Strong for Words to Describe': The Weightlifting Exploits of John C.
Grimek"; John Fair, "Searching for the Real Paul Anderson"; John Fair, "Mr.
America: Idealism or Racism: Color Consciousness and the AAU Mr. America
Contests, 1939–1982"; John Fair, "Katie Sandwina: 'Hercules Can Be a Lady'";
John Fair, "Jimmy Payne: The Forgotten Mr. America"; John Fair, *Mr. America:
The Tragic History of a Bodybuilding Icon.*

32. Kimberly Beckwith, "Building Strength: Alan Calvert, the Milo Bar-Bell
Company, and the Modernization of American Weight Training"; Kimberly
Beckwith, "Thomas Jefferson 'Stout' Jackson: Texas Strongman"; Kimberly
Beckwith and Jan Todd, "Requiem for a Strongman: Reassessing the Career
of Professor Louis Atilla"; Kimberly Beckwith, "Weight-Lifting 'as a Sport, as a
Means of Body Building, and as a Profession': Alan Calvert's *The Truth about
Weight-Lifting*"; Kimberly Beckwith and Jan Todd, "George Hackenschmidt vs.
Frank Gotch: Media Representations and the World Wrestling Title of 1908";
Kimberly Beckwith and Jan Todd, "*Strength*, America's First Muscle Magazine:
1914–1935."

33. David Chapman, *Sandow the Magnificent: Eugen Sandow and the Beginnings of
Bodybuilding*; David Webster, *The Iron Game: An Illustrated History of Weight-
Lifting*; David Webster, "Giovanni Belzoni: Strongman Archaeologist"; David
Webster, "Oscar Heidenstam"; David Webster, "Monte Saldo"; David Webster "A
Chronology of Significant Events in the Life of Eugen Sandow"; David Webster,
"William Pagel: Circus Strongman"; David Webster, "The Flemish Hercules."

34. Randy Roach, *Muscle, Smoke, and Mirrors, Volume One*; Randy Roach, *Muscle,
Smoke, and Mirrors, Volume Two.*

35. Chapman, *Sandow the Magnificent*; Kenneth R. Dutton, *The Perfectible Body:
The Western Ideal of Male Physical Development*; John F. Kasson, *Houdini,
Tarzan, and the Perfect Man: The White Male Body and the Challenge of
Modernity in America.*

36. Jan Todd, *Physical Culture and the Body Beautiful: Purposive Exercise in
the Lives of American Women, 1800–1870*; Jan Todd, "Bernarr Macfadden:
Reformer of the Feminine Form"; Jan Todd, "The Classical Idea and Its Impact
on the Search for Suitable Exercise: 1774–1830"; Jan Todd, "'As Men Do Walk
a Mile, Women Should Talk an Hour . . . Tis Their Exercise,' and Other Pre-
Enlightenment Thought on Women and Purposive Exercise"; Patricia Vertinsky,
*The Eternally Wounded Woman: Women, Doctors, and Exercise in the Late
Nineteenth Century*; Roberta Park, J. A. Mangan, and Patricia Vertinsky, *Gender,
Sport, and Science: Selected Writings of Roberta J. Park.*

37. Harvey Green, *Fit for America: Health, Fitness, Sport and American Society*;
Shelly McKenzie, *Getting Physical: The Rise of Fitness Culture in America.*

38. Jonathan Black, *Making the American Body: The Remarkable Saga of the Men
and Women Whose Feats, Feuds, and Passions Shaped Fitness History.*

39. Daniel Kunitz, *Lift: Fitness Culture, from Naked Greeks and Acrobats to
Jazzercise and Ninja Warriors.*

40. Scott McQuilkin, "'The World's Source for Strength and Conditioning
Information': A History of the National Strength and Conditioning Association,
1978–1993." This was also published in book form as Scott McQuilkin and

Ronald Smith, *A History of the National Strength and Conditioning Association, 1978–2000.*

41. John Fair, *Muscletown USA: Bob Hoffman and the Manly Culture of York Barbell.*

42. Mark Kodya, "An Exploration of the History of Weightlifting as a Reflection of the Major Socio-Political Events and Trends of the 20th Century."

43. William Kutzer, "The History of Olympic Weightlifting in the United States."

44. Nicholas Bourne, "Fast Science: A History of Training Theory and Methods for Elite Runners through 1975."

45. Jan Todd, "The Origins of Weight Training for Female Athletes in North America"; Todd, *Physical Culture and the Body Beautiful*; Jason Shurley, Jan Todd, and Terry Todd, "The Science of Strength: Reflections on the NSCA and the Emergence of Research-Based Strength and Conditioning"; Jan Todd, Jason Shurley, and Terry Todd, "Science from Strength: Thomas L. DeLorme and the Medical Acceptance of Progressive Resistance Exercise"; Terry Todd and Jan Todd, "The Science of Reps: The Strength Training Contributions of Dr. Richard A. Berger"; Jan Todd and Terry Todd, "The Conversion of Dr. Peter Karpovich"; Terry Todd and Jan Todd, "Pioneers of Strength Research: Herbert A. deVries: 60 Years of Exercise and Science"; Terry Todd and Jan Todd, "Pioneers of Strength Research: John Patrick O'Shea: A Man for All Seasons."

46. Terry Todd, "The History of Resistance Exercise and Its Role in United States Education"; Terry Todd, "The Myth of the Muscle-Bound Lifter"; Terry Todd, "Al Roy: Mythbreaker"; Terry Todd, "Al Roy: The First Modern Strength Coach"; Terry Todd, "The History of Strength Training for Athletes at the University of Texas"; Terry Todd, "The Expansion of Resistance Training in U.S. Higher Education through the Mid-1960s."

47. "In Memoriam: Dr. Terry Todd (1938–2018) Pioneering Powerlifter, Writer, Sport Promoter and Historian Who Changed the Cultural Paradigm for Strength."

48. "Auburn University Women's Strength Coach," *Opelika-Auburn News*, June 30, 1980.

CHAPTER 1: BEFORE BARBELLS

1. The German physiologist Emil du Bois-Reymond also speculated that the massive muscularity of the Farnese Hercules would render a person with those proportions unable to walk. John Hoberman, *Mortal Engines: The Science of Performance and the Dehumanization of Sport*, 47–49.

2. Arthur Saxon, *The Development of Physical Power*, 18.

3. The Quest for Victory: A History of Weight Training for Sports was an online exhibit hosted by the H. J. Lutcher Stark Center for Physical Culture and Sports from 2010 to 2017. While the online exhibit has been removed, the original sources for the exhibit are housed at the Stark Center and available on request. Nigel Crowther, "Weightlifting in Antiquity: Achievement and Training"; "Ancient Greece," The Quest for Victory: A History of Weight Training for Sports, H. J. Lutcher Stark Center for Physical Culture and Sports.

4. David Henry James Larmour, *Stage and Stadium*, 56–58; Crowther, "Weightlifting in Antiquity."

5. Stephen G. Miller, *Ancient Greek Athletics*, 63–68; Jan Todd and Terry Todd,

"Legacy of Iron: A History of the Men, Women and Implements That Created the 'Iron Game'"; Jan Todd, "From Milo to Milo: A History of Barbells, Dumbbells, and Indian Clubs," 4.

6. Todd, "From Milo to Milo."
7. Jack W. Berryman, "Ancient and Early Influences," in Charles M. Tipton, ed., *Exercise Physiology: People and Ideas*, 6.
8. Philostratus, "Gymnasticus," 471–491; Jason Konig, *Athletics and Literature in the Roman Empire*, 328–329; Berryman, "Ancient and Early Influences," 8.
9. Berryman, "Ancient and Early Influences," 8.
10. Todd, "From Milo to Milo," 4–5; Todd and Todd, "Legacy of Iron," 185.
11. Todd, "From Milo to Milo," 4.
12. Juvenal, *Satires*, trans by G. G. Ramsey (1918), Satire 6: http://www.tertullian .org/fathers/juvenal_satires_06.htm; The Quest for Victory: A History of Weight Training for Sports.
13. Ibid., 186; Shirl James Hoffman, *Good Game: Christianity and the Culture of Sports*, 45–50.
14. Todd, "From Milo to Milo," 4–5 (quotation); "1531 & 1544: Renaissance Authors Elyot and Camerarius Suggest Weight Training," The Quest for Victory: A History of Weight Training for Sports; Terry Todd, "The History of Resistance Exercise and its Role in United States Education," 34–35.
15. Todd, "From Milo to Milo," 5–6.
16. Michel de Montaigne, "Of Drunkenness," *Essays*, no. 8 (1580): http://www .gutenberg.org/files/3600/3600-h/3600-h.htm#link2HCH0059; "1580: Michel de Montaigne Describes Weight Training for Sport," The Quest for Victory: A History of Weight Training for Sports.
17. Jurgen Giessing and Jan Todd, "The Origins of German Bodybuilding: 1790– 1970," *Iron Game History* 9, no. 2 (December 2005): 8–11; Jan Todd, *Physical Culture and the Body Beautiful: Purposive Exercise in the Lives of American Women 1800-1870*, 33–37; "1809: Father Ludwig Jahn and the Birth of German Gymnastics," The Quest for Victory: A History of Weight Training for Sports.
18. Friedrich Ludwig Jahn and Ernst Eiselen, *Die Deutsche Turnkunst zur Einrichtung der Turnplatze Dargesteldt von Friedrich Ludwig Jahn und Ernst*; Erich Geldbach Marburg-Cappel, "The Beginning of German Gymnastics in America," 238.
19. Jan Todd, "Physical Culture and the Body Beautiful: An Examination of the Role of Purposive Exercise in the Lives of American Women, 1800–1870," 115–118.
20. Todd discusses many of these early exercise routines in *Physical Culture and the Body Beautiful*.
21. Charles Beck, *A Treatise on Gymnastics, Taken Chiefly from the German of F. L. Jahn*, 123–124.
22. "Benjamin Franklin to His Son," letter dated August 19, 1772, in Albert Henry Smyth, *The Writings of Benjamin Franklin*, vol. 5 (New York: MacMillan, 1905), 411–412.
23. James West Davidson, *Nation of Nations: A Narrative History of the American Republic*, 321–343.
24. Quoted in Elliott Gorn and Warren Goldstein, *A Brief History of American Sports*, 81.
25. Ibid., 98.
26. Jack W. Berryman, "Exercise and Medical Tradition from Hippocrates through

Antebellum America: A Review Essay," in *Sport and Exercise Science: Essays in the History of Sports Medicine*, 35–47; James C. Whorton, *Crusaders for Fitness: The History of American Health Reformers*, 270–271.

27. Roberta Park, "Physiology and Anatomy Are Destiny?!: Brains, Bodies and Exercise in Nineteenth Century American Thought," 47–48; Roberta Park, "Muscles, Symmetry, and Action: 'Do You Measure Up?'—Defining Masculinity in Britain and America from the 1860s to the Early 1900s," 1617; Rob Beamish and Ian Ritchie, "From Fixed Capacities to Performance-Enhancement: The Paradigm Shift in the Science of 'Training' and the Use of Performance-Enhancing Substances," 414–416; Anson Rabinbach, *The Human Motor: Energy, Fatigue, and the Origins of Modernity*, 52–68.

28. Randolph Faires, "Physical Education," 173. To justify this assertion, Faires discussed the limited quantity of blood and believed that directing it toward one area of the body deprived other areas, causing them to "suffer." This theory had been discussed twelve years earlier by another University of Pennsylvania physician and professor of nervous diseases, Dr. Horatio Wood. Park, "Physiology and Anatomy," 42.

29. Harvey Green, *Fit for America: Health, Fitness, Sport, and American Society*, 137–138 (quotations); Park, "Physiology and Anatomy," 40.

30. Park, "Physiology and Anatomy," 42.

31. Victor Vaughan, "Hygiene and Public Health," 778.

32. The notion of conservation of energy was also used as justification to prevent women from pursuing serious academic or athletic endeavors. Menstruation was said to pose such a strain on women's energy reserves that either intellectual or physical exertion could be disastrous. With menstruation consuming so much of their energy, women would clearly be unable to devote as much effort as men to academics or athletics. Park, "Physiology and Anatomy," 36–37.

33. Thomas Wentworth Higginson, "Gymnastics," 289.

34. "William Wood Dead: Had Trained Many Athletes," *New York Times*, September 22, 1900. Wood's obituary states that his first gym was named "Wood's and Attington's Gym." This is undoubtedly a misprint. No information on Attington has been found by the authors, although there are numerous references to Ottignon. "Bodily Exercise the Best Medicine: Ottignon and Montgomery's Gymnasium," *American Phrenological Journal*, 25 (September 1857): 71; H. Wilson, compiler, *Trow's New York City Directory for the Year Ending May 1, 1859* (New York: John F. Trow's Publisher, 1859), 620.

35. "William Wood Dead: Had Trained Many Athletes."

36. "1854: Hubert Ottignon and William Curtis," The Quest for Victory: A History of Weight Training for Sports.

37. Louis Moore, "Black Sparring Masters, Gymnasium Owners, and the White Body, 1825–1886," 466–469.

38. Photograph by George Kendall Warren in *Harvard Class of 1865 Photographic Year Book. Harvard College Photographs* (Cambridge, MA: Harvard University, 1865), 71.

39. Jan Todd, "'Strength Is Health': George Barker Windship and the First American Weight Training Boom"; Joan Paul, "The Health Reformers: George Barker Windship and Boston's Strength Seekers."

40. "Charles F. Ottignon's Sparring Academy, 58 West 30th St, New York" (circa 1845), original at the City Museum of New York: http://collections.mcny

.org/Collection/Charles-F.-Ottignon's-Sparring-Academy,-58-West-30th-St,
-New-York.-2F3XC5N5DC_B.html.

41. "New York City: Gymnastics: The Advantages of Physical Training," *New York Times*, October 15, 1852. See also "New York City: Meeting of the Gymnasts," *New York Times*, April 15, 1853.

42. "Young America: Mr. Montgomery in His Exercises with the Dumb Bells," *New York Clipper*, May 17, 1856.

43. "Miscellany: Strong Men," *New York Daily Reformer* (Waterton, NY), August 8, 1865. Montgomery moved to Albany in either 1859 or 1860. He worked as a postal clerk there, managed the Albany gymnasium, and drifted away from public exhibitions. *Albany Directory for the Year 1860*. (Albany, NY: George Adams, 19860).

44. Higginson, "Gymnastics," 289. Higginson is wrong about Montgomery's first name. See "Young America: Mr. Montgomery in His Exercises."

45. Higginson, "Gymnastics," 289.

46. Todd, "Strength Is Health," 3.

47. Ibid.

48. Historian Harvey Green has described the event that led to Windship's taking up weight training, in which he was teased by a bully, as "a scenario that would become a classic in the marketing of bodybuilding." The scenario was immortalized in the twentieth-century advertising campaign of "Charles Atlas" (Angelo Siciliano). Green, *Fit for America*, 199.

49. George Barker Windship, "Autobiographical Sketches of a Strength Seeker."

50. David Webster, *The Iron Game: An Illustrated History of Weight-Lifting*, 27; Todd, "Strength Is Health," 8.

51. Webster, *The Iron Game*, 70; Todd, "Strength Is Health."

52. Todd, "Strength Is Health," 6-7.

53. Ed James, *Practical Training for Running, Walking, Rowing, Wrestling, Boxing, Jumping, and All Kinds of Athletic Feats*, 70.

54. Melvin Adelman, "The First Modern Sport in America: Harness Racing in New York City, 1825-1870," in David K. Wiggins, ed., *Sport in America: From Wicked Amusement to National Obsession*, 96.

55. Gorn and Goldstein, *A Brief History of American Sports*, 79.

56. Stephen Hardy, "Adopted by All the Leading Clubs: Sporting Goods and the Shaping of Leisure," in Wiggins, *Sport in America*, 133-150 (quotation on 146).

57. Curtis has been called "the Father of American Amateur Athletics." "The Life of an Athlete: William B. Curtis, The Father of American Amateur Athletics," *New York Times*, July 8, 1900; Lowell M. Seida, *William Buckingham "Father Bill" Curtis: Father of American Amateur Athletics*, 33-39, 42-43; Richard G. Wettan and Joe D. Willis, "William Buckingham Curtis: The Founding Father of American Amateur Athletics, 1837-1900"; Kimberly Beckwith, "Building Strength: Alan Calvert, the Milo Bar-Bell Company, and the Modernization of American Weight Training," 62-64; Gorn and Goldstein, *A Brief History of American Sports*, 113.

58. "1870s: A Weight Training for Athletics Explosion," The Quest for Victory: A History of Weight Training for Sports.

59. "1866: Sim D. Kehoe Advocates a Heavier Approach to Indian Club Training," The Quest for Victory: A History of Weight Training for Sports.

60. "1870s: A Weight Training for Athletics Explosion."

61. Whorton, *Crusaders for Fitness*, 271 (quotation); David Chapman, *Sandow the Magnificent: Eugen Sandow and the Beginnings of Bodybuilding*, 3.

62. Quoted in Clifford Putney, *Muscular Christianity: Manhood and Sports in Protestant America, 1880-1920*, 30-31. G. Stanley Hall worked extensively on child development between 1884 and 1920. According to Hall, "too few realize[d] what physical vigor is in man or woman and how dangerously near weakness often is to wickedness" (31).

63. Carl Degler, *In Search of Human Nature: The Decline and Revival of Darwinism in American Social Thought*, 20-25.

64. The fear of "race suicide" was a key aspect of the anxiety about physical fitness in the latter decades of the nineteenth century. As immigrants came increasingly from southern and eastern Europe, some fretted that white Anglo-Saxon Protestants were being outbred by "beaten men from beaten races; representing the worst failures in the struggle for existence" (Francis A. Walker, "Restriction of Immigration," *Atlantic Monthly* [June 1896]). Physical culturists like Eugen Sandow and Bernarr Macfadden encouraged physical culture to "raise the average standard of the race as a whole" and, in the case of Macfadden, offered financial incentives for physically fit men and women to wed and have children. John F. Kasson, *Houdini, Tarzan, and the Perfect Man: The White Male Body and the Challenge of Modernity in America*, 10; Chapman, *Sandow the Magnificent*, 108-109; Mark Adams, *Mr. America: How Muscular Millionaire Bernarr Macfadden Transformed the Nation through Sex, Salad, and the Ultimate Starvation Diet*, 127.

65. Benjamin Rader, *American Sports: From the Age of Folk Games to Televised Sports*, 123-126 (quotation).

66. Putney, *Muscular Christianity*, 63.

67. "1870s: A Weight Training for Athletics Explosion," The Quest for Victory: A History of Weight Training for Sports.

68. Putney, *Muscular Christianity*, 67.

69. Lewis G. Janes, *Health-Exercise: The Rationale and Practice of the Lifting-Cure or Health Lift*, 44 (quotation); "1876: The Death of George Barker Windship and the Emergence of the Anti-Weightlifting Position," The Quest for Victory: A History of Weight Training for Sports.

70. "1876: The Death of George Barker Windship"; Benjamin Lee, "The Health Lift: Is it Rational, Scientific, or Safe?"

71. Todd, *Physical Culture and the Body Beautiful*, 218.

72. Ibid. (quotation); Whorton, *Crusaders for Fitness*, 275-277.

73. Todd, *Physical Culture and the Body Beautiful*, 222.

74. Dio Lewis, *The New Gymnastics*, 62 (quotation); Terry Todd and John Hoberman, "Yearning for Muscular Power," 22-23; Terry Todd, "The Myth of the Muscle-Bound Lifter."

75. Jim Murray and Peter Karpovich, *Weight Training in Athletics*, 44.

76. James Whorton has referred to Sargent as the "Newton of his field." Whorton, *Crusaders for Fitness*, 283.

77. Dudley Allen Sargent, *Dudley Allen Sargent: An Autobiography*, 33, 82 (quotations); Russell Trall, *The Illustrated Family Gymnasium*, 58.

78. The students, Sargent claimed, viewed the apparatus as "a form of torture." Ibid., 92.

79. Ibid., 101.

80. In his 1904 book *Health, Strength, & Power*, Sargent pointed out that "it is very seldom at the present day that one's life depends upon the speed with which he can run, or the distance he can jump, though his ability to swim might be the means of self-preservation. It is a question, therefore, how far boys should be encouraged to attain a high degree of excellence in these various sports" (46). Carolyn De la Pena, "Dudley Allen Sargent: Health Machines and the Energized Male Body."

81. Sargent, *Dudley Allen Sargent: Autobiography*, 142–145. See also Bruce Bennett, "Dudley A. Sargent: A Man for All Seasons."

82. Dudley Allen Sargent, *Anthropometric Apparatus with Directions for Measuring and Testing the Principal Physical Characteristics of the Human Body*, 13–14; William McArdle, Frank Katch, and Victor Katch, *Exercise Physiology: Energy, Nutrition, and Human Performance*, xl–xlv.

83. Doug Bryant, "William Blaikie and Physical Fitness in Late Nineteenth Century America"; Whorton, *Crusaders for Fitness*, 284.

84. De la Pena, "Dudley Allen Sargent," 6.

85. Sargent warned that "overdevelopment of any one part, organ, or function throws the remaining organism out of gear, and constitutes a greater or less tendency to disease." Sargent, *Health, Strength & Power*, 16.

86. De la Pena, "Dudley Allen Sargent," 14; Jack W. Berryman, *Out of Many, One: A History of the American College of Sports Medicine*, 4.

87. De la Pena, "Dudley Allen Sargent," 14.

88. Though McKenzie was not an advocate of heavy strength training, it is important to note that he was a strong advocate of both exercise and athletics. R. Tait McKenzie, *Exercise in Education and Medicine* (1924), 22 (quotation); "Muscles, Symmetry and Action," 1616; Whorton, "'Athlete's Heart,'" 113.

89. Ferdinand LaGrange, *Physiology of Bodily Exercise*, 242; Herbert Conn and Caroline Holt, *Physiology and Health*, 215–216.

90. Quoted in Todd, "The Myth of the Muscle-Bound Lifter," 38. For example, the famed French-Canadian strongman Louis Cyr, measured five feet, ten and a half inches and 315 pounds in his prime in the late 1800s. Webster, *The Iron Game*, 36–38.

91. McArdle, Katch, and Katch, *Exercise Physiology*, 521.

92. Benjamin H. Massey, *The Kinesiology of Weightlifting*, 18.

93. For example, in their 1921 text *Physiology and Health*, Conn and Holt continued to warn that "the man who gives his body too much severe exercise is a little more foolish than the one who takes none at all" (215), contending that the overexerciser would die early from the strain on the heart. In 1936 weight-training advocate and magazine publisher Bob Hoffman asked readers, "Have you been led to believe that exercise or athletics may injure your heart?" If so, he advised them, "you have been misinformed": "Your Heart and Exercise," 12.

94. Percy Dawson, *The Physiology of Physical Education for Physical Educators and Their Pupils*, 489.

95. The maneuver was described by Italian physician Antonio Maria Valsalva in 1704. Alterations in cardiovascular function as a result of the maneuver were first described by German physiologist Edward Weber in 1851. Luiz Fernando Junqueira Jr., "Teaching Cardiac Autonomic Function Dynamics Employing the Valsalva (Valsalva-Weber) Maneuver."

96. Dawson, *The Physiology of Physical Education*, 489.

97. McKenzie, *Exercise in Education and Medicine*, 52.

98. Bicycle face was "characterized by a strained facial expression, a result of continually trying to maintain balance while pedaling hard." Other maladies that resulted from strenuous bicycle riding included "bicycle throat" from breathing dusty air and "bicyclist's heart," the same type of condition that affected a variety of other athletes. Green, *Fit for America*, 232.

99. A. M. Kerr, "Safeguarding the Heart in High School," 16.

100. Michael Murphy, *Athletic Training*, 149.

101. Whorton, "'Athlete's Heart,'" 119.

102. Physician Ferdinand LaGrange attributed dilation of the heart to chronic overwork. He discussed hypertrophy as a positive effect of exercise, resulting in a heart that was "thicker, [and] heavier, with stronger walls." Dilation occurred when there was "excessive exercise," which "induces wearing and degeneration of the fibres, lessening the resisting power of the organism and, while producing dilation of the cavities of the heart, at the same time leads to a thinning of their walls and to diminished strength of their fibres." LaGrange, *Physiology of Bodily Exercise*, 158–159.

103. It is not surprising that the physician would be "seized with air hunger" while mountain climbing, given the decreased partial pressure of oxygen and saturation rate of hemoglobin. Felix Deutsch and Emil Kauf, *Heart and Athletics: Clinical Researches upon the Influence of Athletics upon the Heart*, 23.

104. Ibid., 172–174.

105. Ibid., 80–81. Bacchus is the Roman iteration of the Greek god Dionysus, god of wine and intoxication.

106. George Gillesby, "The Physiologists Speak on Weight-Lifting," 16.

107. Beckwith, "Building Strength," 46.

108. Chapman, *Sandow the Magnificent*, 35 (quotation); Kasson, *Houdini, Tarzan, and the Perfect Man*, 28, 7.

109. Chapman, *Sandow the Magnificent*, 9–11.

110. "1893: European Strongman Louis Derlacher Becomes Gentleman Jim Corbett's Strength Coach," The Quest for Victory: A History of Weight Training for Sports. For additional information about Atilla's career, see Kim Beckwith and Jan Todd, "Requiem for a Strongman: Reassessing the Career of Professor Louis Atilla."

111. Kasson, *Houdini, Tarzan, and the Perfect Man*, 68–69.

112. Beckwith, "Building Strength," 46, 23.

113. Robert Ernst, *Weakness Is a Crime: The Life of Bernarr Macfadden*, 4 (quotations); Clifford Waugh, "Bernarr Macfadden: The Muscular Prophet," 7.

114. Adams, *Mr. America*, 11 (quotation); Ernst, *Weakness Is a Crime*, 7.

115. Adams, *Mr. America*, 16–17 (quotation), 21.

116. Waugh, "Bernarr Macfadden," 15.

117. Adams, *Mr. America*, 35.

118. Waugh, "Bernarr Macfadden," 23 (quotation), 25.

119. Chapman, *Sandow the Magnificent*, 129.

120. Ibid., 189; Adams, *Mr. America*, 51–52.

121. Jan Todd, "Bernarr Macfadden: Reformer of the Female Form."

122. Adams, *Mr. America*, 55–56.

123. "1898: Bernarr Macfadden Founds Physical Culture Magazine," The Quest for Victory: A History of Weight Training for Sports.

124. Chapman, *Sandow the Magnificent*, 90.

125. Waugh, "Bernarr Macfadden," 45.

126. Ibid. (quotation); Beckwith, "Building Strength," 116–117.

127. Earl C. Gregory, "Exercise Your Swimming Muscles," 52 (quotation); "1898: Bernarr Macfadden Founds Physical Culture Magazine," The Quest for Victory: A History of Weight Training for Sports.

128. Ruth's trainer was an accomplished athlete himself, having been an amateur boxing champion as well as professional boxer and multievent track athlete. "1898: Bernarr Macfadden Founds Physical Culture Magazine," The Quest for Victory: A History of Weight Training for Sports; Art McGovern and Edwin Goewey, "Babe Ruth Brought Back by Physical Culture."

129. "Babe Ruth Statistics," ESPN.com (n.d.): http://espn.go.com/mlb/player/stats /_/id/27035/babe-ruth (accessed January 27, 2013).

130. Kimberly Beckwith and Jan Todd, "*Strength*: America's First Muscle Magazine, 1914–1935"; Beckwith, "Building Strength," 15–44, 69–95.

131. Beckwith, "Building Strength," 35, 94.

132. "1902: Alan Calvert Founds the Milo Barbell Company," The Quest for Victory: A History of Weight Training for Sports.

133. Beckwith and Todd, "*Strength*," 14; Beckwith, "Building Strength," 77–78, 107–111.

134. Quoted in Beckwith and Todd, "*Strength*," 18–19.

135. A 1922 feature by David Wayne discussed the training routine of professional track athlete R. P. Williams. Williams credited Calvert with convincing him that weight training would not cause muscle-binding and credited weight training as playing a key role in his performance. Similarly, in 1923 Harry Glick asserted that weights enhanced speed and coordination and concluded that "if the weights had made me slow or clumsy, I would have quit them a long time ago." David Wayne, "The Greatest of Them All"; Harry Glick, "Does Lifting Make You Muscle Bound?"; Beckwith and Todd, "*Strength*," 20; Alan Calvert, "What Does 'Muscle-Bound' Mean?," 2–5.

136. Todd and Todd, "Legacy of Iron," 192–193.

137. These tricks are discussed at length in Beckwith, "Building Strength," 179–190.

138. John Fair, "George Jowett, Ottley Coulter, David Willoughby, and the Organization of American Weightlifting, 1911–1924," 3.

139. Ibid., 3–15; John Fair, "Father-Figure or Phony?: George Jowett, the ACWLA and the Milo Barbell Company, 1924–1927"; John Fair, "From Philadelphia to York: George Jowett, Mark Berry, Bob Hoffman, and the Rebirth of American Weightlifting, 1927–1936."

140. Beckwith, "Building Strength," 98.

141. Austin Flint, *On the Source of Muscular Power: Arguments and Conclusions Drawn from Observations upon the Human Subject, under Conditions of Rest and Muscular Exercise*, 15 (quotation), 23. Discussing his own training, Flint said, "At the age of forty years and weighing one hundred and eighty-three and three-quarter pounds without clothing, I myself accomplished the feat of raising with one hand above my head and standing erect with the arm straight under a dumb-bell weighing one hundred and eighty and one-half pounds" (23).

142. Dorothy Needham, *Machina Carnis: The Biochemistry of Muscular Contraction in Its Historical Development*, 127; Steven Vogel, *Prime Mover: A Natural History of Muscle*, 38.

143. A. F. Huxley and R. Niedergerke, "Structural Changes in Muscle during

Contraction: Interference Microscopy of Living Muscle Fibres"; H. Huxley and J. Hanson, "Changes in the Cross-Striations of Muscle during Contraction and Stretch and Their Structural Interpretation."

144. Beamish and Richie, "From Fixed Capacities to Performance-Enhancement," 415–416.

145. Norman Bingham, *The Book of Athletics and Out-of-Door Sports*, 29, 58–59.

146. Ronald A. Smith, *Sports & Freedom*, 34–35.

147. Murphy, *Athletic Training*, 30–51.

148. Frederick Winslow Taylor, *The Principles of Scientific Management*; De la Pena, "Dudley Allen Sargent," 13; Beamish and Richie, "From Fixed Capacities to Performance Enhancement," 417.

149. Andrea Johnson, "Human Performance: An Ethnographic and Historical Account of Exercise Physiology," 76 (quotation), 87. The Fatigue Lab "formed the cornerstone for research in modern laboratories of exercise physiology." McArdle, Katch, and Katch, *Exercise Physiology*, xlv. See also Steven M. Horvath and Elizabeth Horvath, *The Harvard Fatigue Laboratory: Its History and Contributions*; Carleton B. Chapman, "The Long Reach of Harvard's Fatigue Laboratory, 1926–1947."

150. Alan J. McComas, "The Neuromuscular System," 73 (first quotation); Tudor Hale, "History of Developments in Sport and Exercise Physiology: A. V. Hill, Maximal Oxygen Uptake, and Oxygen Debt," 368 (second quotation).

151. Needham, *Machina Carnis*, 127; Vogel, *Prime Mover*, 41.

152. Vogel, *Prime Mover*, 41.

153. Ibid.; McComas, "The Neuromuscular System," 72–73.

154. McComas, "The Neuromuscular System," 72–73.

155. Needham, *Machina Carnis*, 77–78.

156. McComas, "The Neuromuscular System," 73.

157. A. Szent-Györgyi, "Discussion," *Studies from the Institute of Medical Chemistry, University of Szeged* 1 (1943): 67–71, cited in Vogel, *Prime Mover*, 44; A. F. Huxley, "Review Lecture: Muscular Contraction."

158. Charles Sherrington, "Some Functional Problems Attaching to Convergence"; McComas, "The Neuromuscular System," 43–45.

159. McComas, "The Neuromuscular System," 46; Derek Denny-Brown, "The Histological Features of Striped Muscle in Relation to Its Functional Activity."

160. George A. Brooks and L. Bruce Gladden, "The Metabolic Systems: Anaerobic Metabolism (Glycolytic and Phosphagen)," 337 (quotation); McComas, "The Neuromuscular System," 39–80. For a contemporaneous discussion of the revolution in muscle physiology, see Arthur Steinhaus, "Physiology at the Service of Physical Education: The Theory of Muscular Contraction Is Being Renovated."

161. Arthur Steinhaus, "Chronic Effects of Exercise," 106–107; Arthur Steinhaus, "Physiology at the Service of Physical Education: Chemical Changes in Muscle Due to Training."

162. Arthur Steinhaus, "Physiology at the Service of Physical Education."

163. Arthur Steinhaus, "Physiology at the Service of Physical Education: Muscle Hypertrophy"; Steinhaus, "Chronic Effects of Exercise," 137–138; Beamish and Richie, "From Fixed Capacities to Performance Enhancement," 416.

164. E. H. Starling and M. B. Visscher, "The Regulation of the Energy Output of the Heart."

165. Francis A. Bainbridge, Arlie V. Bock, and David. B. Dill, *The Physiology of Muscular Exercise*, 76, 86.
166. Adrian G. Gould and Joseph A. Dye, *Exercise and Its Physiology*, 308.
167. Arthur Steinhaus, "Physiology at the Service of Physical Education: The Heart Size—Effects of Training," 42.
168. Bainbridge, Bock, and Dill, *The Physiology of Muscular Exercise*, 183, 241.
169. Ibid., 220–235.
170. Gould and Dye, *Exercise and Its Physiology*, 179, 377–380.
171. Arthur Steinhaus, "Physiology at the Service of Physical Education: Muscle Hypertrophy," 36–37.
172. John Capretta, "The Condition Called Muscle-Bound," 43, 54.
173. Murray and Karpovich, *Weight Training in Athletics*, 37.
174. Capretta, "The Condition Called Muscle-Bound."
175. Thomas S. Kuhn, *The Structure of Scientific Revolutions*.

CHAPTER 2: BUILDING THE BARBELL ATHLETE

1.   Arthur Steinhaus, "Why Exercise?," 5–6; Berryman, *Out of Many, One: A History of the American College of Sports Medicine*, 7.
2.   Quoted in George Gillesby, "The Physiologists Speak on Weight-Lifting," 16.
3.   Kimberly Beckwith, "Building Strength: Alan Calvert, the Milo Bar-Bell Company, and the Modernization of American Weight Training," 292–294.
4.   John Fair, "Father-Figure or Phony?: George Jowett, The ACWLA and the Milo Barbell Company, 1924–1927," 13 (quotation); Beckwith "Building Strength."
5.   Fair, "Father-Figure or Phony?"; Alan Calvert, *An Article on Natural Strength Versus "Made" Strength, Preceded by an Explanation of Why I Abandoned the Field of Heavy Exercise*; Alan Calvert, *Confidential Information on Lifting and Lifters*.
6.   Fair, "Father-Figure or Phony?," 18.
7.   Ibid., 17–20. Though the number of the meets held across the country increased in 1926, the ACWLA national meet in November of that year had to be canceled due to insufficient entries.
8.   John Fair, "From Philadelphia to York: George Jowett, Mark Berry, Bob Hoffman, and the Rebirth of American Weightlifting, 1927–1936," 4–6.
9.   Mark Dyreson, *Making the American Team: Sport, Culture, and the Olympic Experience*, 2–3.
10. Eliot Gorn and Warren Goldstein, *A Brief History of American Sports*, 169, 178.
11. David Chapman, *Sandow the Magnificent: Eugen Sandow and the Beginnings of Bodybuilding*, 125.
12. Ibid.
13. Gorn and Goldstein, *A Brief History*, 180–181.
14. James West Davidson, *Nation of Nations: A Narrative History of the American Republic*, 693, 702.
15. Ronald A. Smith, "Far More Than Commercialism: Stadium Building from Harvard's Innovations to Stanford's 'Dirt Bowl.'"
16. Murray Sperber, *Onward to Victory: The Crises That Shaped College Sports*, xx.
17. As noted by Eliot Gorn and sports writer Robert Lipsyte, the "Golden Age of Sport" or "Era of Heroes" could just as easily be known at the "Golden Age of

Sports Promoters." Quoted in ibid., xx; Gorn and Goldstein, *A Brief History*, 192–193.

18. Fair, "From Philadelphia to York."

19. Bob Hoffman, "How to Improve at Your Chosen Sport," 6.

20. For example, in a 1931 lecture on training athletes for the shot put, discus, and javelin at New York City's Stuyvesant High School, physical educator H. J. Colbath stated that "form was nine-tenths of success in the weight events and urged extensive practice for the development of form among athletes competing in them." No mention of weight training or other methods was made. "Favors Sugar Diet," *New York Times*, January 11, 1931.

21. Hoffman, "How to Improve at Your Chosen Sport," 6; Alan Calvert, *The Truth about Weight Lifting*, 7.

22. Bob Hoffman, "Editorial," *Strength & Health* (December 1932): 1.

23. In some of Sandow's earliest writings he portrayed himself as a "healthy and well-formed" but average child. In later writings he had become "exceedingly delicate" as a boy. This led historian John F. Kasson to remark that "the more he retold the story, the more his health as a youth declined": *Houdini, Tarzan, and the Perfect Man: The White Male Body and the Challenge of Modernity in America*, 30; Chapman, *Sandow the Magnificent*, 4–5.

24. John Fair, *Muscletown USA: Bob Hoffman and the Manly Culture of York Barbell*, 12; Bob Hoffman, "'Tis Never Too Late to Start," 11, 26.

25. Bob Hoffman, "The Story of the World Famous York Barbell Club," 15 (quotation); Bob Hoffman, *Weight Lifting*, 71.

26. Hoffman, *Weight Lifting*; Bob Hoffman, "Reaching Your Physical Goal," 8; Bob Hoffman, "Editorial," *World Health Ecology News*, 5, Bob Hoffman, *Bob Hoffman's Simplified System of Barbell Training*, 1.

27. Hoffman later claimed to have won the race. Herman Weiskopf, "A Corner on American Muscle," *Sports Illustrated*, April 9, 1962; Fair, *Muscletown USA*, 14; Hoffman, "The Story of the World Famous York Barbell Club," 15 (quotation).

28. Hoffman, "The Story of the World Famous York Barbell Club," 15.

29. Regarding Hoffman's views on youth training, see Booker O'Brien and John Fair, "'As the Twig Is Bent': Bob Hoffman and Youth Training in the Pre-Steroid Era."

30. Hoffman says that these manual resistance exercises were part of a mail-order course that his father had purchased. The course was called the "Swoboda" system, though Hoffman points out that it was "not the great Viennese lifter who held the world's record in the continental jerk, but another who had adopted that famous name." Hoffman, "The Story of the World Famous York Barbell Club," 15.

31. Hoffman, *Weight Lifting*, 71.

32. Hoffman claimed that he only weighed 140 pounds when he first reached his stature at six feet, three inches around the age of fifteen. Before he signed up to join the war effort in 1917, he weighed 167 pounds; upon returning home at the age of twenty-one, he weighed 180 pounds, still at six feet, three inches in height. Ibid., 70; Hoffman, "The Story of the World Famous York Barbell Club," 15 (quotation).

33. Bob Hoffman, "Should We Prepare for War?," 29; Fair, *Muscletown USA*, 16.

34. Bob Hoffman, *I Remember the Last War*, 53.

35. Hoffman, "Should We Prepare for War?," 29 (quotation); Bob Hoffman, "Especially for *Strength and Health's* Boys" (December 1934), 20 (quotation), 48.

36. Fair, *Muscletown USA*, 18–19.

37. Hoffman, "*Strength & Health*'s Boys" (December 1934), 48.

38. Hoffman, "Should We Prepare for War?," 43; Hoffman, *I Remember the Last War*, 54 (quotations)–55.

39. Hoffman, "The Story of the World Famous York Barbell Club," 36.

40. Fair, *Muscletown USA*, 21.

41. Hoffman, "The Story of the World Famous York Barbell Club," 36, 37 (quotations)–38.

42. John Fair, "From Philadelphia to York: George Jowett, Mark Berry, Bob Hoffman and the Rebirth of American Weightlifting, 1927–1936."

43. Hoffman, *I Remember the Last War*, 53; Hoffman, "Should We Prepare for War?," 43.

44. Bob Hoffman, "Why You Should Be Strong," 5.

45. "Few of us would aspire and perspire, persist to develop muscles just to look at," Hoffman claimed in a 1949 editorial. Instead, in Hoffman's opinion, most people lifted weights because of the "unusual endurance, ability to do things . . . improved feelings, super health, resistance to disease, [and] the expectancy of a long and useful life which is obtained through weight training": "Editorial—What Good Are Muscles?," 3, 5, 7.

46. Joe Weider, Ben Weider, and Mike Steere, *Brothers of Iron: How the Weider Brothers Created the Fitness Movement and Built a Business Empire*, 2–5. Joe's actual date of birth is unknown. He says, "Ma had a rough idea" that it was November 29, either 1920 or 1922. Various forms, he claims, have one date or the other. He typically gives 1922 as his year of birth so that he can claim he started his magazine empire at the age of seventeen. Given that Ben's date of birth is known to be February 1, 1923, and the two were three years apart in school, it is more likely that he was born in 1920. Randy Roach, *Muscle, Smoke, and Mirrors—Volume I*, 145.

47. Weider, Weider, and Steere, *Brothers of Iron*, 14 (quotation)–19.

48. Ibid.; John Foster, "How It All Began."

49. Weider, Weider, and Steere, *Brothers of Iron*, 28.

50. Joe Weider, "Editorial," 21–22.

51. Ibid., 4. As an example, a 1942 *Your Physique* article delineates the differences between the two types of training. Weightlifting was "a means of attaining the utmost strength and being able to display it," while "bar-bell exercise" was "recognized by more and more people who have no intentions of becoming weight-lifters, but who realize that they can overcome certain physical deficiencies and become more shapely by spending a few hours a week with bar-bell exercises." Harvey Hill, "Is Heavy Exercise Necessary?," 6–7.

52. Roach, *Muscle, Smoke, and Mirrors*, 247.

53. Ibid., 24; Weider, Weider, and Steere, *Brothers of Iron*, 24 (quotation).

54. The same month that Weider began publishing *Your Physique*, a magazine inspired by his transformational experience with weights, Hoffman's *Strength & Health* included an article that asked, "How many thousands of readers of this magazine have made their start in physical training because they found they were 'picked on' by their bigger and stronger, more capably physical playmates?" Bob Hoffman, "Are the Germans Superior?," 10 (quotation)–11, 37–39.

55. George Barker Windship, "Autobiographical Sketches of a Strength Seeker."

56. Chapman, *Sandow the Magnificent*, 4; William H. Taft, "Bernarr Macfadden."

57. Sammy R. Danna, "Charles Atlas," 50.

58. Sammy R. Danna, "The 97 Pound Weakling . . . Who Became the 'World's Most Perfectly Developed Man.'"

59. Jacqueline Reich, "'The World's Most Perfectly Developed Man': Charles Atlas, Physical Culture, and the Inscription of American Masculinity," 449 (quotations). Sociologist Alan Klein noted that "Joe Weider personifies the Charles Atlas ad scenario": *Little Big Men: Bodybuilding Subculture and Gender Construction*, 86.

60. Michael Kimmel, "Consuming Manhood: The Feminization of American Manhood and the Recreation of the Male Body, 1832–1920."

61. Kenneth R. Dutton, *The Perfectible Body: The Western Ideal of Male Physical Development*, 189. Psychologists Harrison Pope, Katharine Phillips, and Roberto Olivardia have gone a step further and pathologized this quest for the exaggerated male physique as "The Adonis Complex." They note that physical size and strength is one of the few ways in which a contemporary man can accomplish something that women cannot. As a result, according to them, the goal of hypermuscularity is in part the consequence of "threatened masculinity" and a way to carve out a uniquely male identity: Harrison Pope, Katharine Phillips, and Roberto Olivardia, *The Adonis Complex: The Secret Crisis of Male Body Obsession*, 22–24.

62. Michael Kimmel, *Manhood in America: A Cultural History*, 9.

63. Thomas Johansson, "What's Behind the Mask? Bodybuilding and Masculinity."

64. Dutton, *The Perfectible Body*, 236–239.

65. "Hoffman, "Editorial—What Good Are Muscles?," 3 (quotation); Dutton, *The Perfectible Body*, 179–180; Brian Baily and James Gillett, "Bodybuilding and Health Work: A Life Course Perspective"; Tara Magdalinski, *Sport, Technology, and the Body: The Nature of Performance*, 65.

66. See, for example, Joe Weider, "Editorial—Bring Out Your Reserve Power!," 3. In the editorial Weider assured readers that, whatever their affliction, it could be overcome by a strong will and exercise. Similarly, some of the earliest issues of Hoffman's *Strength & Health* featured multiple articles by Alan Carse titled "Survival of the Fittest," in which the author asserted: "All of life is a fight. . . . The man who, through heredity, training or mode of living learns to excel physically is the man who succeeds most." Alan Carse, "Survival of the Fittest," 18; Alan Carse, "A Tale of Survival of the Fittest." Also see Barton Horvath, "What Can Weight Training Do for Me Besides Build Big Muscles?"; Joe Weider, "You Can Be Strong and Muscular!"; Charles Smith, "Jack Delinger—From Rheumatic Fever to the World's Perfect Man"; Joe Weider, "Alex Aronis Makes Good."

67. Frederick Tilney, "Getting Acquainted with Your Editor-in-Chief Joseph E. Weider," 8–9.

68. Weider, Weider, and Steere, *Brothers of Iron*, 48.

69. Horatio Alger, *Ragged Dick; or, Street Life in New York with the Boot Blacks*.

70. Hoffman generally tended to claim that he was average or normal before strength training but had achieved exceptional strength and health from weight training. For example, in *Weight Lifting* he said, "I revere my mother more with each passing year, as my appreciation grows for the physical normalcy with which she endowed me" (3); Mark Kodya, "An Exploration of the History of Weightlifting as

a Reflection of the Major Socio-Political Events and Trends of the 20th Century," 42; Fair, *Muscletown USA*, 43–46.

71. Hoffman recounted a story to this effect from his own childhood. He claimed to have contracted typhoid fever from contaminated drinking water. In his retelling, a doctor had declared him dead, but "when [the doctor] found there was still a spark of life in me, he said that I would never amount to anything, even if I lived, for my heart and other organs were too badly damaged." Hoffman, like the other strongmen, had proven a doctor wrong and rebuilt himself through physical training. Fair, *Muscletown USA*, 13.
72. Hoffman, *Weight Lifting*, 92.
73. Miller claimed to have started training around the age of ten, which (based on other dates in the article) puts the creation of his homemade weight set around 1919. Weider claimed to have started training at the age of thirteen. Given his birth date of 1920, his train-axle weight workout would have occurred around 1933. Joe Miller, "Joe Miller's Rise to Fame," 8–9. For additional examples of men who overcame debility through weight training, see Phil Gundelfinger, "Once a Cripple Now a Lifter!"; Joe Raymond, "All That I Am, I Owe to Barbell Training"; Roger Eells, "I Was Given Three Months to Live."
74. Harry Good, unlike his highly successful brothers, Bill and Walter, did not compete in amateur weightlifting contests because of his articles in *Strength & Health* and his founding of the Good Barbell Company. Harry Good, "Are Strong Men Born or Made?," 29.
75. Walter Laberge, "Little Known Facts concerning the Heart," 12, 5.
76. Harry Good, "Facts to Disprove Time Worn Opinions," 41.
77. Siegmund Klein, "Why We Need Exercise," 6, 50.
78. Bob Hoffman, "Your Heart and Exercise," 38.
79. A. M. Gibson, "Does Exercise Harm the Heart?," 37, 57; A. M. Gibson, "Is Weightlifting Dangerous?"
80. Arthur Dandurand, "I Am Young at Sixty-Two," 5, 18, 22.
81. Mark Berry, "Physical Training Problems Simplified," 4. For additional examples of refutation of the existence of athlete's heart, see W. A. Pullum, "Are Weightlifters Slow?"; Martin Franklin, "Arthur Saxon's Views on Weightlifting"; A. T. Petro, "The Effect of Barbell Exercise on the Heart"; Bob Hoffman, "What Can We Believe?"
82. Harry Good, "Barbells and Their Use versus Public Opinion," 9, 18.
83. Bob Hoffman, "Improving Athletic Ability through Barbell Training," 19; Pullum, "Are Weightlifters Slow?"
84. Alan Carse, "Muscle Bound Frank," 19 (quotation); Alan Carse, "The Old Athlete Tells a Secret." Hoffman also made this charge: Bob Hoffman, "Editorial" (March 1934), 19.
85. Bob Hoffman, "How Many Repetitions?"; Bob Hoffman, *Secrets of Strength and Development*, 28–29.
86. See, for example, John Paul Endres, "The Effect of Weight Training Exercise upon the Speed of Muscular Movement"; Edward K. Capen, "The Effect of Systematic Weight Training on Power, Strength, and Endurance," 83; Edward F. Chui, "The Effect of Systematic Weight Training on Athletic Power," 188; William Zorbas and Peter Karpovich, "The Effect of Weight Lifting upon the Speed of Muscular Contractions," 145.
87. For an additional example of Hoffman and other writers describing the effects

of weight training on Hoffman's performance, see Bob Hoffman, "Improving Athletic Ability through Barbell Training"; John Terpak, "You Can Improve Your Athletic Ability"; Tony Sansone, "A Miracle of Barbells."

88. Bob Hoffman, "How to Become an Athletic Star," 9. Also see Steve Stanko, "Strength Most Important in Football Success"; W. J. McClanahan, "Strength Most Important in Football Success," 20, 34.

89. Bob Hoffman, "Your Training Problems," 9.

90. Hoffman, "How to Improve at Your Chosen Sport," 6.

91. Hoffman, "Improving Athletic Ability through Bar Bell Training," 19, 40. Hoffman also issued challenges to athletes to compete against the York lifters in an "all around contest" to determine which athletes had the greatest "physical ability." Dick Zimmerman, "Best Weightlifters Are Best Athletes"; Bob Hoffman, "Editorial—Weightlifters Are Successful in Other Sports."

92. Hoffman, "How to Improve at Your Chosen Sport"; Bob Hoffman, "There Should Be a Law against It," 36 (quotation); see also Harry Good, "Gordon Venables: Weight Lifting Champion and Athlete Extraordinary."

93. Bob Hoffman, "Are You a Fighter?"

94. Jules Bacon, "What Can You Do?" (September 1941), 19.

95. Ibid.

96. Hoffman, "How to Become an Athletic Star," 8–9.

97. Jules Bacon, "What Can You Do?" (October 1941).

98. For examples of the athletic Alger tale, see Stanko, "Strength Most Important in Football Success"; Nate Hanson, "A Strength and Health Boy Grows Up"; Jim Murray, "Do You Think You Are Too Small for Football?"; Bob Hoffman, "You Can Be a Better Athlete."

99. Frank Schofro, "How I Got That Way"; Frank Schofro, "How I Got That Way—Part II." It is worth noting that Schofro was able to win the championship primarily because John Davis, who was undefeated in the same weight class from 1938 to 1952, was overseas serving in World War II. Davis had beaten Schofro's total of 850 pounds in his first national championship six years earlier—when he was seventeen. Bob Hoffman, "1938 National Championships—Can We Beat the Germans?"; Bob Hoffman, "1938 World's Weightlifting Championships at Vienna"; William Kutzer, "The History of Olympic Weightlifting in the United States," 85–148.

100. Stanko, "Strength Most Important in Football Success," 20–21, 43 (quotation).

101. McClanahan, "Strength Most Important in Football Success," 34.

102. Bernard H. Lange, "The Proven Way," 19.

103. D. A. Downing, "Barbell Training in the Service."

104. Tony Terlazzo, "Barbell Men in the Service" (August 1943).

105. Tony Terlazzo, "Barbell Men in the Service" (June 1944).

106. Jan Todd, "The Halcyon Days of Muscle Beach: An Origin Story," in *Sport in Los Angeles*, 244.

107. During the war, Hoffman had great difficulty securing a sufficient amount of iron to continue to manufacture barbells at a high rate. As a result, some sets were made with concrete plates when iron ran short. For additional details on the manufacture of barbells during the war years, see Fair, *Muscletown USA*, 71–104; Dick Bachtell, "Weight Training in the Service"; Bob Hoffman, "Physical Training in the Service."

108. Fair, *Muscletown USA*, 95.

109. Rosetta Hoffman, "Physical Training Builds Health, Strength and Beauty for the Ladies."

110. Jan Todd, "The Origins of Weight Training for Female Athletes in North America," 5.

111. Dana Hamilton, "Are Girl Athletes Masculine?" *Strength* 11 (November 1926): 31–33, 80–82; Charles MacMahon, "Cash In on Trained Muscles," *Strength* 12 (June 1927), 25 (quotations); Gertrude Artelt, "Is Strength Masculine and Weakness Feminine?"

112. Todd, "The Origins of Weight Training for Female Athletes," 5–7.

113. Photo caption, *Strength & Health* (September 1940), 23.

114. Jan Todd, "The Legacy of Pudgy Stockton."

115. Pudgy Stockton, "Barbelles"(May 1946); Pudgy Stockton "Barbelles" (May 1950); Pudgy Stockton, "Barbelles" (October 1950).

116. Pullum, "Are Weight-Lifters Slow?," 75.

117. Wilf Diamond, "The Story of Jack Johnson"; Charles B. Roth, "Toughest Man on Earth"; S. Muzumdar, "The Great Gama"; Edmond Desbonnet, "Yousouf: The Terrible Turk."

118. Franklin, "Arthur Saxon's Views," 20, 42.

119. Joe Weider, "Sports and Lifting," 8–9.

120. George Weaver, "What's Wrong with Strength?," 9, 31–32 (quotations).

121. Barton R. Horvath, "Weight Training Helped Make Him a Champion."

122. Len Elliott and Barbara Kelly, *Who's Who in Golf*, 180; see also Terry Todd, "The PGA Tour's Travelling Gym: How It Began," 17–18.

123. Earle Liederman, "Barbells and a Golf Champion!" An article on swimmer and film star Johnny Weissmuller in *Your Physique* in March 1948 discusses his use of weights for keeping fit for his films. However, at the time he was already retired as an athlete. George Lowther, "How Johnny Weissmuller Keeps Fit."

124. Horvath, "Weight Training Helped Make Him a Champion," 38.

125. Stranahan was also featured in Joseph Weider, "Weight Training Made Frank Stranahan a Champion."

126. Jules Bacon, "What Can You Do?"; Hoffman, "Editorial—Weightlifters Are Successful in Other Sports," 3–4. Stranahan was featured later in Leo Stern, "How Frank Stranahan Trains for Golf."

127. Horvath, "Weight Training Helped Make Him a Champion."

128. Liederman, "Barbells and a Golf Champion!," 49.

129. John Davis, "Irving Mondschein—U.S. Decathlon Champion."

130. Bob Hoffman, "Weightlifting Builds Better Athletes."

131. Jim Murray, "Canadian Barbelle Glamazon Seeks Olympic Games Victory"; George Bruce, "Parry O'Brien—Shotput Champion"; William Goellner, "Aggie Weight Star Credits Barbells for Improvement"; Harry Paschall, "Kansas' Bill Nieder."

132. Jim Murray, "British Empire Speedster Uses Weight Training"; Harry Paschall, "Can Shelton Break the 7-Foot Barrier?"; Harry Paschall, "The Don Bragg Story."

133. Cover, *Strength & Health* (July 1952). See also "Bob Richards Interview Part Two," *Vaulter Magazine*, November 8, 2013: http://www.vaultermagazine.com/bob-richards-interview-part-two-vaulter-magazine-2013-video.

134. Paul Donelan, "Baseball Star Says Weight Training Helps," 11 (quotation); Owen Lake, "Sox Sluggers' Secret of Success"; Roy Terrell, "All-Star Who Can Do

without Glory," *Sports Illustrated*, June 23, 1958. Though the *Sports Illustrated* article did not mention Jensen's weight training specifically, it did strongly suggest that his muscularity and power brought about much of his success: "If there is any secret involved in his performance this year, Jackie doesn't know what it is. 'I think it's just experience,' he says. 'A hitter should continue to improve up into his middle 30s, just as long as he stays in good physical condition.' Then he unbuttons a size 44 uniform shirt from around a size 17 neck, and as he walks to the shower the muscles ripple across the broad back and shoulders and in the powerful legs. There is marked unconcern in the Red Sox dressing room over Jackie Jensen's physical condition."

135. Hali Helfgott, "Al Wiggins, College Swimmer," *Sports Illustrated*, January 14, 2002; Torseten Ove, "Obituary: Albert M. Wiggins Jr." *Pittsburgh Post-Gazette*, July 3, 2012.

136. Pete George, "The World's Greatest Swimmer." In a 1953 article Hoffman cited the following athletes as having "reached stardom" due to weight training: Dick Cleveland (Ohio State swimmer, 100 meters world record holder) Bob Richards (Olympic pole vault champion), Mal Whitfield (Olympic 800 meters champion), Henry Wittenberg (National Amateur Athletic Union wrestling champ and 1948 and 1952 Olympian), Walter Barnes (All-American football lineman at Louisiana State University and professional football player), Frank Stranahan (golfer), and Bob Feller (Major League baseball pitcher for the Cleveland Indians). Bob Hoffman, "You Can Be a Better Athlete," 52.

137. Hoffman, "Weightlifting Builds Better Athletes," 30. The 1946 *York Barbell and Dumbbell System* included two courses that provided a total-body program of barbell and dumbbell exercises. By 1951 Hoffman had published an *Advanced Methods of Weight Training* booklet that included twenty-four separate courses, including one for football. Interestingly, the football program consists exclusively of lower body exercises and omits variations of the Olympic lifts. Bob Hoffman, *York Barbell and Dumbbell System*; Bob Hoffman, *York Advanced Methods of Weight Training*, 44–45.

138. Jim Murray, "Summer Training for Football—With Barbells"; Murray, "Too Small for Football?" 10–11, Goellner, "Aggie Weight Star," 36–37.

139. Bill Williams, "Barbells Build Winning Football Team," 39; Harry Paschall, "Barbells and Basketball."

140. In the July 1950 issue of *Your Physique* Weider outlined ten predictions for the future of bodybuilding, fitness, and health in the United States in succeeding decades. Among his predictions was that "bodybuilding will become a stepping stone to every other sport and physical activity." The statement encapsulated the way he viewed the hierarchy of sport—bodybuilding as the base, with all other activities as adjuncts. Joe Weider, "Editorial—I Predict," 5.

141. Dan Lurie, "Heavy Exercise and Sports."

142. Bob Leigh, "Barbells: A Springboard to Sports."

143. Hoffman, "You Can Be a Better Athlete," 11. Depictions of Weider and bodybuilders in *Strength & Health* included "Abysmal Q. Multiflex," a cartoonish character whose unnatural muscles served only to impress women. In contrast, cartoonist Harry Paschall presented Bosco, an old-time strongman whose square musculature appeared to be carved from stone. Bosco's physique accompanied his tremendous strength, which was occasionally used to abuse the representation of

the Weider men. In response to Hoffman's criticism and Paschall's cartoons, the Weider writers stressed the usefulness of muscles built through bodybuilding-style training. They insisted that the training would improve conditioning in preparation for sport. Weider specifically challenged Paschall in a 1955 *Muscle Builder* article that advocated the use of some bodybuilding movements to improve strength. Harry Paschall, "Bosco"; Jack LaLanne, "Do You Want Strength Plus Endurance?" 37; I. J. MacQueen, "Recent Advances in the Technique of Progressive Resistance Exercise" (1955).

144. Tudor Bompa and Gregory Haff, *Periodization: Theory and Methodology of Training*, 140.

145. Mel Siff, *Supertraining: A Scientific Teaching Method for Strength, Endurance, and Weight Training*, 33–34.

146. "Barbells on Campus," The Quest for Victory: A History of Weight Training for Sports, H. J. Lutcher Stark Center for Physical Culture and Sports.

147. See, for example, James P. Tuppeny, "Barbells on Campus: Weight Training for Track and Field Men at Villanova"; Wesley Ruff, "Barbells on Campus: Stanford University"; Roy McLean and Karl Klein, "Barbells on Campus: The University of Texas"; William Hottinger, "Barbells on Campus: The University of Illinois.

148. Weider's earlier *Mr. America* had ceased publication in 1953. Jan Todd, Joe Roark, and Terry Todd, "A Briefly Annotated Bibliography of English Language Serial Publications in the Field of Physical Culture," 31.

149. Charles Sipes, "How I Use Weider Power Methods to Build Championship Football Teams"; E. M. Orlick and Joe Weider, "Barbells and Baseball"; Joe Weider, "Barbells and Swimming"; Ed Theriault, "Barbells and Running"; Joe Weider, "Barbells and Football"; Joe Weider, "Barbells and Shot-Putting"; Joe Weider, "Barbells and Basketball"; Joe Weider, "Barbells and Boxing"; Joe Weider, "Barbells and Bowling"; Joe Weider, "Barbells and Wrestling"; Ben Weider, "Barbells and the Decathlon"; Jim Murray, "Weight Training for the Shot Put."

150. Thomas R. Baechele and Roger W. Earle, eds., *Essentials of Strength Training and Conditioning*, 379–380.

151. "Energy systems" refers to whether adenosine triphosphate (ATP), the molecule that actually "fuels" muscle contraction, is produced with or without oxygen. Specific training can increase the enzymes and substrates as well as facilitate structural changes that make the body more efficient at producing energy aerobically or anaerobically. For specific information, see William McArdle, Frank Katch, and Victor Katch, *Exercise Physiology: Energy, Nutrition, and Human Performance*, 134–169.

152. Jim Murray and Peter Karpovich, *Weight Training in Athletics*, 114–153.

153. Orlick and Weider, "Barbells and Baseball"; Joe Weider, "Barbells and Swimming"; Theriault, "Barbells and Running"; Weider, "Barbells and Football"; Weider, "Barbells and Shot-Putting"; Weider "Barbells and Basketball"; Weider, "Barbells and Boxing"; Weider, "Barbells and Wrestling"; Weider, "Barbells and the Decathlon"; Murray, "Weight Training for the Shot Put."

154. Weider, "Barbells and Bowling."

155. Theriault, "Barbells and Running."

156. E. M. Orlick to Ben Weider, July 19, 1963, E. M. Orlick Papers, Collection of Reuben Weaver, Annandale, Virginia.

157. Ben Weider to E. M. Orlick, July 26, 1963. E. M. Orlick Papers, Collection of Reuben Weaver, Annandale, Virginia.

158. In keeping with his tradition of not always changing volume and issue numbers when titles changed, the first issue is designated volume 6, number 4, a continuation of the *Mr. America* numbering system.

159. More than twenty articles appear in *All American Athlete* 6:4 (November 1963), including E. M. Orlick, "Athletic Diets—Fads or Facts," 5-7; The Editors, "Mr. America Salutes Frank Budd," 1-15; Elvan George and Ralph Evans, "Weight Training for Football," 23-28; Murray Warmuth, "Conditioning Football Players," 28-32; Jim Murray, "Added Resistance for Overload," 38-42; Weider Research Clinic, "What's New on the Medical/Sports Front," 7-9; and Weider Research Clinic, "Monthly Report on Nutrition/Sports," 51-53.

160. The articles were taken from a 1961 book: Tom Ecker, ed., *Championship Track and Field by 12 Great Coaches*. *All American Athlete* 6:4 (December 1963) included Oliver Jackson, "The Sprint," 38-39; Jim "Jumbo" Elliott, "The Quarter-Mile," 40-41, 100; Brutus Hamilton, "The Distance Races," 42-43, 101; Larry Snyder, "The Hurdles," 44-45, 101; Ed Flanagan, "The High Jump," 46-47; 102; and Gordon Fisher, "The Broad Jump," 48-49, 104.

161. Armand Tanny, "The Man on the Surfboard"; Ronald James, "Olympic Paddlers Swing to Scientific Weight Training."

162. Siff, *Supertraining*, 265-271.

163. George Jowett, "Speedy Muscles."

164. George Jowett, "How You Can Build Super Speed in Your Muscles," 29. Specifically, he called for using 50 percent of a person's one-repetition maximum (1RM), which is the greatest amount of weight an individual can lift one time, for sets of three to four repetitions. This is quite similar to contemporary programs, which often call for 20-40 percent 1RM and the same repetition range.

165. Ben Weider, "Helpful Hints for Athletes." It is highly likely that Ben did not write this article, as he told E. M. Orlick on July 26, 1963: "Do not forget to insert my name to at least one article in each edition of the *All American Athlete*." Ben Weider to E. M. Orlick, July 26, 1963, E. M. Orlick Papers, Collection of Reuben Weaver, Annandale, Virginia.

166. A note in March 1964 explains that original editions of the magazine are being published in German, French, Spanish, and Italian, and that it is also being "reprinted in: Russian, Chinese, Bulgarian, Hungarian, Polish and Yugoslavian." "For the Athlete in Action," 98.

167. E. M. Orlick, "Let's Answer the Communist Sports Challenge." Irving Jaffee, "We Deserve to Lose the Olympics"; Elliot Denman, "Russia Wins the Olympics."

168. E. M. Orlick, "Introducing a New Scientific Strength Building Service," 5, 54 (quotation); Orlick, "Let's Answer the Communist Sports Challenge."

169. Orlick, "Introducing a New Scientific Strength Building Service," 54.

170. "Why You Should Advertise in *All American Athlete*," 114. Because *All American Athlete* split off from *Mr. America*, this 81,000 figure probably represents that publication's circulation. In a "Publisher's Sworn Statement" dated June 14, 1963, Weider reported a circulation of 82,300 for "All American Athlete—Mr. America." E. M. Orlick Papers, Collection of Reuben Weaver, Annandale, Virginia. Weider claimed in January 1965 that *All American Athlete* had only 23,000 subscribers. Joe Weider to Elliott (no last name), January 5, 1965, E. M. Orlick Papers, Collection of Reuben Weaver, Annandale, Virginia.

171. Ronald Orlick to Joe Weider, undated, E. M. Orlick Papers, Collection of Reuben

Weaver, Annandale, Virginia. This letter is not signed, but Reuben Weaver believes that it came from Ron Orlick.

172. Joe Weider to "Elliott" (no last name) January 5, 1965. E. M. Orlick Papers, Collection of Reuben Weaver, Annandale, Virginia.

173. Jim Murray, interview with Jan Todd, August 11, 2012.

174. After the April 1965 issue of *All American Athlete*, the magazine essentially disappeared until July 1967, when the title of *Mr. America* added the subhead *All American Athlete* once again. In August 1968 it appears again as a stand-alone magazine numbered vol. 10, no. 1, followed by vol. 10, no. 2 (November 1968); vol. 10, no. 3 (March 1969); vol. 10, no. 4 (July 1969); and vol. 10, no. 5 (October 1969).

175. Jim Murray, interview with Jan Todd.

176. "Obituary: Walter Marcyan, 94; Bodybuilder Sold Fitness Equipment, Owned Gyms," *Los Angeles Times*, September 22, 2007.

177. *Physical Power* articles by Jim Murray: "Weight Training and Football, "Taking a Look at Isometric Exercise," "Pre-Season Football Training," "Weight Training for Wrestlers."

178. Stan Burnham, "Football Conditioning at the University of Texas"; Terry Todd, "Progressive Resistance for Football at the University of Texas."

179. See *Physical Power* articles by Stan Burnham: "Strength for Fitness and Competition," "Better Rebounding through Weight Training," "The Value of Combined Isometric and Isotonic Exercise," "A Conditioning Program for Football Players."

180. For examples of a variety of sports featured, see Bud Hanson, "In-Season Basketball Conditioning"; John P. Jesse, "Weight Training for Middle-Distance Runners"; Howard Benioff, "Track and Field Special Feature: The Story of Bob Humphreys"; Richard Gilberg, "How High School Football Champions Train"; Gene Mozee, "Weight Training for Baseball: How Jim Winn Became a Pro through the Use of Weights"; John Nelson, "Summer Football Training"; Gene Mozee, "L. Jay Silvester"; Howard Benioff, "The Mike Connelly Story."

CHAPTER 3: THE SCIENCE CONNECTION

1. Interview with Fraysher Ferguson by Terry Todd, July 2002. For a more complete discussion of the opposition to weight training espoused by Springfield College in the early twentieth century and the role Ferguson played in changing that, see Jan Todd and Terry Todd, "The Conversion of Dr. Peter Karpovich," 4 (quotations).

2. *Men of Muscle* (RKO Radio Pictures, circa 1935–1940): https//cdm16122. contentdm.oclc.org/digital/collection/p15370coll2/id/20981/rec/10.

3. Harvey Allen, "Weight Lifting in the Association," 48–49.

4. Howard Wilson, "Uplifting Weight-Lifting," 86–87.

5. C. F. Benninghoff, "Weight Lifting," 96.

6. "Bob Hoffman Exhibits His Troupe at Weekly Forum," *Springfield (MA) Student* (April 10, 1940), in Todd and Todd, "The Conversion of Dr. Peter Karpovich," 4.

7. Ted Krause, "Trends in 'Y' Weight Lifting," 94.

8. James H. McCurdy and Leonard A. Larson, *The Physiology of Exercise: A Text-Book for Students of Physical Education*, 39–40, 97.

9. Quoted in Todd and Todd, "The Conversion of Dr. Peter Karpovich," 7.

10. Portions of this section of the chapter also appeared in Jan Todd, Jason Shurley, and Terry Todd, "Thomas L. DeLorme and the Science of Progressive Resistance Exercise."

11. In June 1940 General George C. Marshall, then the army chief of staff, told a congressional panel, "For the first time in our history we are actually trying to prepare for war before becoming involved." "America on Guard—Mobilizing Our Might," *New York Times*, June 9, 1940.

12. Bob Hoffman, "Should We Prepare for War?," 43.

13. Robert Edwards, "Physical Fitness through Weight-Lifting," 606–607 (quotations), 635.

14. Wilbur McCandless, "Body-Building and Weightlifting," 64–65 (quotations), 75–76.

15. Sanders Marble, *Rehabilitating the Wounded: A Historical Perspective on Army Policy*, 35, 56; E. E. Vogel, M. S. Lawrence, and P. R. Strobel, "Professional Service of Physical Therapists in World War II" (1968): https://history.amedd.army.mil
/corps/medical_spec/chapterviii.html

16. In a 1947 article University of Minnesota professor Ralph A. Piper noted, "Many doctors have traditionally prescribed bed rest indiscriminately as a conservative treatment for practically all medical disorders": "Values of Early Ambulation and Exercise in Surgical and Medical Treatment," 297. On prolonged bed rest, see also Alfred Fleishman, "Exercise to Recovery"; on the previous exercise protocols, see Dorothy G. Hoag, "Physical Therapy in Orthopedics with Special Reference to Heavy Resistance, Low Repetition Exercise Program," 291; Thomas L. DeLorme, "Restoration of Muscle Power by Heavy Resistance Exercises," 645.

17. Hoag, "Physical Therapy in Orthopedics," 291.

18. R. Tait McKenzie, *Exercise in Education and Medicine* (1924), 368–369.

19. R. Tait McKenzie, *Exercise in Education and Medicine* (1917), 321–322.

20. Frank Butler Granger, *Physical Therapeutic Technic*, 244.

21. Ernest Nicoll, "Principles of Exercise Therapy," 749.

22. For a discussion of this type of program, see C. H. McCloy, "Physical Reconditioning in the Army Service Forces." The rapid progression to games skips several steps that have been incorporated into contemporary rehabilitation programs. By performing basic strengthening exercises and emphasizing muscular endurance, the patients still would not have gained enough strength to stabilize the damaged joint. Moreover, they would not have regained joint position sense or the ability to perform basic athletic tasks like changes of direction. As a result, patients with unstable joints, who lacked position sense, were rapidly put into the unpredictable environment of team games, making reinjury somewhat likely. For examples of the contemporary rehabilitation plan of care, see Craig R. Denegar, Ethan Saliba, and Susan Saliba, *Therapeutic Modalities for Musculoskeletal Injuries*, 6–11; William E. Prentice, *Rehabilitation Technique for Sports Medicine and Athletic Training*, 4–17, 340–363.

23. E. H. Anderson, "Heavy Resistance, Low Repetition Exercises in the Restoration of Function in the Knee Joint," 397.

24. Eleanor P. DeLorme, telephone interview with Terry Todd, July 6, 2010, Thomas DeLorme Collection, H. J. Lutcher Stark Center for Physical Culture and Sports, University of Texas at Austin.

25. Jack Finkelstein, "Bama's Hercules Displays Weight-Lifting Abilities," *Crimson*

White, undated clipping, Thomas DeLorme Collection, H. J. Lutcher Stark Center for Physical Culture and Sports, University of Texas at Austin.

26. Ibid.; Owen Lake, "Pioneer of Physical Medicine: Dr. Thomas DeLorme."
27. Todd, Shurley, and Todd, "Thomas L. DeLorme," 2913.
28. Thaddeus Kawalek, telephone interview by Terry Todd, December 5, 2003, Thomas DeLorme Collection, H. J. Lutcher Stark Center for Physical Culture and Sports, University of Texas at Austin.
29. Thomas L. DeLorme and Arthur L. Watkins, *Progressive Resistance Exercise: Technic and Medical Application*, 1, 2 (quotation)–3.
30. DeLorme, "Restoration of Muscle Power by Heavy Resistance Exercises," 667.
31. Thomas L. DeLorme, "Heavy Resistance Exercises," 608.
32. Anderson, "Heavy Resistance, Low Repetition Exercises," 397.
33. Sarah J. Houtz, Annie M. Parrish, and F. A. Hellebrandt, "The Influence of Heavy Resistance Exercises on Strength."
34. Todd, Shurley, and Todd, "Thomas L. DeLorme," 2916–2917; Marcia T. Keith, "Emphasis on Exercise as a Therapeutic Agent in a Naval Physical Therapy Department."
35. John R. Hall, "Citation for Legion of Merit," December 4, 1945; "Captain Thomas L. DeLorme Receives Legion of Merit," *Pulse*, undated clipping, Thomas DeLorme Collection, H. J. Lutcher Stark Center for Physical Culture and Sports, University of Texas at Austin.
36. J. S. Barr, W. A. Eilliston, H. Musnick, Thomas DeLorme, J. Hanelin, and A. A. Thibodeau, "Fracture of the Carpal Navicular (Scaphoid) Bone: An End-Results Study in Military Personnel"; Thomas L. DeLorme, R. S. Shaw, and W. G. Austen, "Musculoskeletal Functions in the Amputated Perfused Human Being Limb"; Thomas L. DeLorme, R. S. Shaw, and W. G. Austen, "A Method of Studying 'Normal' Function in the Amputated Human Limb Using Perfusion"; Thomas L. DeLorme, "Treatment of Congenital Absence of the Radius by Transepiphyseal Fixation."
37. The article included a discussion of "counterbalancing" in which the injured limb, if unable to move through the full range of motion, was assisted with weighted pulleys. Just enough weight was provided to allow completion of the full range of motion. The assisting weight was progressively decreased, so that the muscle was overloaded despite the assistance. Thomas L. DeLorme and Arthur L. Watkins, "Technics of Progressive Resistance Exercise."
38. Thomas L. DeLorme, R. S. Schwab, and Arthur L. Watkins, "The Response of the Quadriceps Femoris to Progressive-Resistance Exercise in Polio Patients."
39. J. Roswell Gallagher and Thomas L. DeLorme, "The Use of the Technique of Progressive Resistance Exercise in Adolescence."
40. Jack W. Berryman, *Out of Many, One: A History of the American College of Sports Medicine*, 6, 33.
41. In the May 1936 issue of the *Journal of Health and Physical Education* McCloy authored an article titled "How about Some Muscle?" in which he criticized the move of physical education away from activity and toward a more encompassing field that included psychology, hygiene, character education, and more. He did not specifically advocate heavy strength training, though he did argue that a lack of muscle was a detriment to a person's quality of life. As Eleanor B. English has shown, McCloy's philosophy was met with criticism from fellow physical

educators, who argued that he appeared to be more interested in "education of the physical" rather than "education through the physical." C. H. McCloy, "How about Some Muscle?"; Eleanor B. English, "The Enigma of Charles H. McCloy."

42. C. H. McCloy, "A Half Century in Physical Education"; Eleanor B. English, "Charles H. McCloy: The Research Professor of Physical Education."

43. English, "Charles H. McCloy," 16.

44. Ibid.

45. C. H. McCloy, "Weight Training for Athletes?"

46. C. H. McCloy, "Endurance," 10.

47. C. H. McCloy, "Adequate Overload," 69.

48. Edward F. Chui, "The Effect of Systematic Weight Training on Athletic Power."

49. Edward K. Capen, "The Effect of Systematic Weight Training on Power, Strength, and Endurance."

50. Bernard Ross Walters, "The Relative Effectiveness of High and Low Repetitions in Weight Training Exercises on Strength and Endurance of the Arms."

51. Clayton G. Henry, "Comparison of the Effectiveness of Two Methods of Exercise for the Development of Muscular Strength."

52. Everett W. Faulkner, "A Comparison of the Effectiveness of Two Methods of Exercise for the Development of Muscular Strength."

53. William F. Teufel, "A Comparison of the Effectiveness of Two Methods of Exercise for the Development of Muscular Strength."

54. The training manual depicted men lifting weights, while the women's strength-training program involved only bodyweight exercises. Arthur Steinhaus, Alma Hawkins, Charles Giauque, and Edward Thomas, *How to Keep Fit and Like It: A Manual for Civilians and a Plan for a Community Approach to Physical Fitness*, 6, 28 (quotation)–29.

55. Thune also studied the personality of weightlifters to determine why some men might gravitate toward the activity. He described the weightlifters as shy, lacking confidence, and with clear desires to be strong and dominant. John B. Thune, "Defense of Weight Training," 58 (quotation); John B. Thune, "Personality of Weightlifters."

56. D. E. Strain, "Body Building with Weights."

57. J. L. Rudd, "Medical Aspects of Weight Lifting—Its Use in Rehabilitation," 53–54.

58. J. L. Rudd, "Weight Lifting—Healthful—Harmful?"

59. Joseph Wolffe and Grover Mueller, "The Heart of the Athlete," 4 (quotations); Joseph Wolffe and Victor A. Diglio, "The Heart in the Athlete: A Study of the Effects of Vigorous Physical Activity on the Heart."

60. John Fair, "Bob Hoffman, the York Barbell Company, and the Golden Age of American Weightlifting, 1945–1960."

61. Bob Hoffman, "If You Want to Beat the Russians"; Arthur Daley, "The Musclemen," *New York Times*, May 15, 1958.

62. Bob Hoffman, "Results of the World Championships," 49.

63. Daley, "Musclemen," 38. It should be mentioned that the Russians likely sought the trophy out of fear for their own safety as well as embarrassment. According to Nikolai Romanov, chair of the Soviet Sports Committee in the late 1940s, participation in international competition required a personal guarantee of victory to Joseph Stalin before athletes were permitted to leave the country.

Romanov was removed from his position in 1948, following an unexpected loss by the Soviet speed-skating team. David Goldblatt, *The Games: A Global History of the Olympics*, 211–212; James Riordan, "The Rise and Fall of Soviet Olympic Champions."

64. Hoffman, "If You Want to Beat the Russians," 16–18.
65. In 1948 the Central Committee of the Communist Party began the "mobilization of vast resources in a nationwide search for sporting talent and the systematic development of athletes necessary to attain world sporting domination." Nicholas Bourne, "Fast Science: A History of Training Theory and Methods for Elite Runners through 1975," 363; see also Allen Guttmann, "The Cold War and the Olympics"; "Muscle Pop through Iron Curtain," *Life*, July 28, 1952, 15–19; James Riordan, *Soviet Sport: Background to the Olympics*, 45–46.
66. Allen Guttmann, *Women's Sports: A History*, 173.
67. Quoted in Douglas A. Noverr and Lawrence E. Ziewacz, *The Games They Played: Sports in American History, 1865–1980*, 223.
68. The physician is referred to as Dr. Matveyev and is mentioned talking to the primary author, Antoni Ekart, with no first name is given. This is not Leo Pavlovic Matveyev, the "Father of Periodization." Antoni Ekart, Egerton Sykes, and E. S. Virpsha, *Vanished without a Trace: The Story of Seven Years in Soviet Russia* (London: Max Parrish, 1954), 207, quoted in Riordan, *Sport in Soviet Society: Development of Sport and Physical Education in Russia and the USSR*, 167.
69. Riordan cited the Russian newspaper *Pravda* of October 22, 1945: "To stimulate greater sports proficiency, the Council of People's Commissars of the USSR has permitted the All-Union Committee on Physical Culture and Sports Affairs to award monetary prizes for outstanding sports results. An award ranging from 15,000 to 25,000 rubles will be given for setting an All-Union record that betters the world record, and from 5,000 to 15,000 rubles will be given for setting an All-Union record; 1,000 to 3,000 (in the form of valuable gifts) for setting an All-Union junior record. Those who come first, second, or third in USSR championships will be awarded prizes to value from 2,000 to 5,000 rubles": *Sport in Soviet Society*, 162.
70. The October 1945 decree announcing cash awards for top performances also announced that eighty new sport schools would be established to train talented young athletes. Riordan, *Sport in Soviet Society*, 162.
71. Ibid., 163.
72. Bourne, "Fast Science," 361.
73. Riordan, *Sport in Soviet Society*, 170–171.
74. Bourne, "Fast Science," 361.
75. Dale A. Lewis, "Collegiate Tennis Conditioning."
76. Evelyn Loewendahl, "Muscle Development in Athletic Training."
77. Edward Capen, "The Effect of Systematic Weight Training on Power, Strength, and Endurance."
78. Edward F. Chui, "The Effect of Systematic Weight Training on Athletic Power" (October 1950).
79. Thomas L. DeLorme, F. E. West, and W. J. Shriber, "The Influence of Progressive Resistance Exercise on Knee Function following Femoral Fractures," 924 (quotation); George Wackenhut, "The Cardiovascular System—What You Should

Know about It." A 1954 study would show that a season of training required by intercollegiate middle-distance running, boxing, wrestling, baseball, and water polo resulted in improved cardiovascular function. Franklin M. Henry, "Influence of Athletic Training on the Resting Cardiovascular System."

80. David Halberstam, *The Fifties*, 62–77.

81. Shelly McKenzie, "Mass Movements: A Cultural History of Physical Fitness and Exercise, 1953–1989," 69.

82. Hans Kraus and Ruth P. Hirschland, "Muscular Fitness and Health," 18.

83. McKenzie, "Mass Movements," 29–40.

84. Williams S. Zorbas and Peter V. Karpovich, "The Effect of Weight Lifting upon the Speed of Muscular Contractions." For additional information on the life and contributions of Peter Karpovich, see Todd and Todd, "The Conversion of Dr. Peter Karpovich"; Jim Murray, "Weightlifting's Non-Lifting Patron Saint."

85. Quoted in Todd and Todd, "The Conversion of Dr. Peter Karpovich," 4.

86. Ibid.; Jim Murray, "Weightlifting's Non-Lifting Patron Saint."

87. Zorbas and Karpovich, "The Effect of Weight Lifting," 148.

88. Peter V. Karpovich, "Incidence of Injuries in Weight Lifting," 71–72.

89. DeLorme and Watkins, *Progressive Resistance Exercise*, xi.

90. Laurence E. Morehouse and John M. Cooper, *Kinesiology*, 213–216.

91. The study was Wilkin's 1951 master's thesis, "The Effect of Weight Training on Speed of Movement," at the University of California–Berkeley. Bruce M. Wilkin, "The Effect of Weight Training on Speed of Movement" (October 1952).

92. Thomas L. DeLorme, B. G. Ferris, and J. R. Gallagher, "The Effect of Progressive Resistance Exercise on Muscle Contraction Time," 86 (quotation); DeLorme, West, and Shriber, "The Influence of Progressive Resistance Exercise."

93. This article built upon the master's theses of Hairabedian and Donaldson. John W. Masley, Ara Hairabedian, and Donald Donaldson, "Weight Training in Relation to Strength, Speed, and Coordination"; Ara Hairabedian, "Weight Training in Relation to Strength and Speed of Movement"; Donald Donaldson, "Weight Training in Relation to Strength and Muscular Coordination."

94. Philip Rasch, "Relationship of Arm Strength, Weight, and Length to Speed of Arm Movement."

95. Richard L. Garth, "A Study of the Effect of Weight Training on the Jumping Ability of Basketball Players"; C. H. McCloy, "Weight Training Routine Used by State University of Iowa Basketball Team in the Training Season Preceding the Competitive Schedule in 1954"; McCloy, "Weight Training for Athletes?"; "Iowa Basketball Yearly Record," *2011–2012 University of Iowa Men's Basketball Media Guide* (2011–2012), 196: http://grfx.cstv.com/photos/schools/iowa/sports/m -baskbl/auto_pdf/2011-12/misc_non_event/mediaguide-12.pdf.

96. Frank A. Buckiewicz, "An Experimental Study of the Effects of Weight Training on Fine Motor Skills."

97. I. J. MacQueen, "Recent Advances in the Technique of Progressive Resistance Exercise," 1197 (quotation).

98. James E. Counsilman, "Does Weight Training Belong in the Program?," 17–18, 20.

99. Edward K. Capen, "Study of Four Programs of Heavy Resistance Exercises for Muscular Strength."

100. The weight-trained group did show a reduction in one of the seven flexibility

measures (shoulder extension), but the authors still concluded that weight
training did not adversely affect "overall" range of motion. Benjamin H. Massey
and Norman L. Chaudet, "Effects of Systematic, Heavy Resistive Exercise on
Range of Joint Movement in Young Male Adults."

101. Paul Hunsicker and George Greey, "Studies in Human Strength."

102. Ivan Kusinitz and Clifford E. Keeney, "Effects of Progressive Weight Training on
Health and Physical Fitness of Adolescent Boys."

103. Sidney Calvin, "Effects of Progressive Resistance Exercises on the Motor
Coordination of Boys," 387 (quotations).

104. Hugh L. Thompson and G. Alan Stull, "Effects of Various Training Programs on
Speed of Swimming."

105. Stratton F. Caldwell, "Weight Training," 17–18.

106. Rembert Garris, "The Rise of Weightlifting in the YMCA," 77–78.

107. F. A. Schmidt, "Opinions on Heart Exercise and Acute Heart Dilation," 13
(quotation).

108. Jim Murray and Peter Karpovich, *Weight Training in Athletics*, 48. See also Jan
Todd and Terry Todd, "Peter V. Karpovich: Transforming the Strength Paradigm."

109. Murray and Karpovich, *Weight Training in Athletics*, 114.

110. Benjamin H. Massey, Harold W. Freeman, Frank R. Manson, and Janet A.
Wessel, *The Kinesiology of Weight Lifting*, 9.

111. Ibid., 132–133. Their eight principles are as follows. Exercise is only one phase
of the conditioning program. Physical condition is specific to a sport. Muscles
may differ in kinds of condition. The conditioning program must be based
on an analysis of the sport. General overall physical fitness is basic to athletic
performance. The off-season conditioning program is just as important as the on-
season program. Overload is essential to all development. Boredom and laziness
are the chief obstacles to "getting into shape."

112. Peter V. Karpovich, *Physiology of Muscular Exercise*, 22, 30, 75, 152–154.

113. Andrea Johnson, "Human Performance: An Ethnographic and Historical
Account of Exercise Physiology," 54.

114. Walter Kroll, "Putting Science into Coaching: A Dilemma," 13.

115. Philip Rasch, "In Praise of Weight Training," 12–13 (quotations).

116. Lake, "Pioneer of Physical Medicine."

117. George Eiferman, "Weight Training—The Key to Greater Athletic Ability," 32.

118. C. H. McCloy, "Weight Training for Athletes?"; McCloy's work was also
highlighted in the Weider publications. See Jim Murray, "How Weight Training
Makes Basketball Giants"; Jim Murray, "Scientific Studies and High Quality
Publications Attest to the Value of Weight Training Exercise." For additional
information about McCloy, see Terry Todd, "A Pioneer of Physical Training: C. H.
McCloy." Hoffman also mentioned Karpovich and McCloy in a 1955 editorial:
"Editorial—Barbells Build Better Athletes."

119. Bourne, "Fast Science," 364; Riordan, *Soviet Sport*, 146–147.

120. In the 1956 Summer Games the Soviets amassed 98 total medals: 37 golds, 29
silvers, and 32 bronze. The United States won 74 medals and second place overall
with 32 golds, 25 silver, and 17 bronze. In 1960 the gap widened to a total medal
count of 103 for the Soviets (43 gold, 29 silver, and 31 bronze) to 71 medals for
the United States (34 gold, 21 silver, and 16 bronze). Donald Mrozek, "The Cult
and Ritual of Toughness in Cold War America," 263; "Map of Olympic Medals,"

New York Times, August 4, 2008. David Maraniss, *Rome 1960: The Olympics That Changed the World*, 426 (quotation); Riordan, *Soviet Sport*, 147.

121. Maraniss, *Rome 1960*, 100, 10.

122. It is worth noting that Johnson lifted weights as part of his preparation for the games. Following an automobile accident in 1959, his track coach at the University of California at Los Angeles, Craig Dixon, recommended that he use weights to speed his recovery. The weights "substantially" improved his performance in the shot put, discus, and javelin throw. For his part, Vlasov easily won gold, out-totaling James Bradford and Norbert Schemansky of the United States by fifty-five and eighty-two pounds, respectively. Ibid., 36–37, 106 (quotation), 108; "Rome 1960—Weightlifting" Olympic.org (n.d.): https://www .olympic.org/content/results-and-medalists/gamesandsportsummary/?sport =31728&games=1960%2f1&event=121594 (accessed February 7, 2013).

123. Jeffrey Montez de Oca, "The 'Muscle Gap': Physical Education and U.S. Fears of a Depleted Masculinity, 1954–1963."

124. John F. Kennedy, "The Soft American," *Sports Illustrated*, December 26, 1960.

125. Maraniss, *Rome 1960*, 383–386; David W. Zang, *Sports Wars: Athletes in the Age of Aquarius*, 74.

126. Robert F. Kennedy, "A Bold Proposal for American Sport," *Sports Illustrated*, July 27, 1964. For additional discussion of the utility of Olympic sports in promoting American interests abroad, see Toby C. Rider, *Cold War Games: Propaganda, the Olympics, and U.S. Foreign Policy*.

127. The Harvard Fatigue Laboratory has been called the "cornerstone of exercise physiology in the U.S." because it fostered collaboration between scientists with diverse backgrounds who were interested in the study of the effects of a variety of stressors on human physiology. The lab helped solidify exercise physiology as a separate discipline. Over the course of its twenty years of operation, the lab published "at least 352 research papers, numerous monographs, and a book." When the lab closed, scientists interested in exercise physiology spread to universities across the country and established a host of new laboratories. As noted by Andrea Johnson, "almost all exercise physiologists inevitably trace their lineage to the Fatigue Laboratory in only one or two academic generations": "Human Performance," 78; William McArdle, Frank Katch, and Victor Katch, *Exercise Physiology: Nutrition, Energy, and Human Performance*, l–lii. See also Steven M. Horvath and Elizabeth Horvath, *The Harvard Fatigue Laboratory: Its History and Contributions*; Carleton B. Chapman, "The Long Reach of the Harvard Fatigue Laboratory, 1926–1947."

128. Quoted in Johnson, "Human Performance," 112–113.

129. Ibid., 113–114.

130. David H. Clarke, "Correlation between Strength/Mass Ratio and the Speed of Arm Movement"; David H. Clarke and Franklin M. Henry, "Neuromuscular Specificity and Increased Speed from Strength Development"; Leon E. Smith and Jim D. Whitley, "Relation between Muscular Force of a Limb, under Different Starting Conditions, and Speed of Movement"; Leon E. Smith, "Influence of Strength Training on Pre-Tensed and Free-Arm Speed."

131. Smith, "Influence of Strength Training on Pre-Tensed and Free-Arm Speed"; Richard C. Nelson and Richard A. Fahrney, "Relationship between Strength and Speed of Elbow Flexion"; John A. Colgate, "Arm Strength Relative to Arm Speed";

Jim D. Whitley and Leon E. Smith, "Influence of Three Different Training Programs on Strength and Speed of Limb Movement"; Edward F. Chui, "Effect of Isometric and Dynamic Weight-Training Exercises upon Strength and Speed of Movement."

132. Jim D. Whitley and Leon E. Smith, "Influence of Three Different Training Programs on Strength and Speed of Limb Movement," 141.

133. Terry Todd and Jan Todd, "Pioneers of Strength Research: The Legacy of Dr. Richard A. Berger," 275.

134. Ibid., 275–278.

135. See the articles by Richard A. Berger based on this research: "Effect of Varied Weight Training Programs on Strength," "Optimum Repetitions for the Development of Strength," "Comparative Effects of Three Weight Training Programs," "Comparison of the Effect of Various Weight Training Loads on Strength."

136. Richard A. Berger and Billy Hardage, "Effect of Maximum Loads for Each of Ten Repetitions on Strength Improvement."

137. Richard A. Berger, "Effect of Static and Dynamic Training on Vertical Jumping Ability."

138. Richard A. Berger, "Comparison of Weight Lifting Ability between Lifters"; Richard A. Berger, "Effects of Isometric Training"; Richard A. Berger and Joe M. Henderson, "Relationship of Power to Static and Dynamic Strength." A similar study in the same issue examined the interplay between increased strength and muscular power. Though strength was related to power, its author concluded that gains in strength were not related to gains in power. Lawrence E. McClements, "Power Relative to Strength of Leg and Thigh Muscles."

139. Patrick O'Shea, "Effects of Selected Weight Training Programs on the Development of Strength and Muscle Hypertrophy." See also Terry Todd and Jan Todd, "Dr. Patrick O'Shea: A Man for All Seasons."

140. Vermon S. Barney and Blauer L. Bangerter, "Comparison of Three Programs of Heavy Resistance Exercise," 146.

141. J. D. Dennison, M. L. Howell, and W. R. Morford, "Effect of Isometric and Isotonic Exercise Programs on Muscular Endurance." There was quite a bit of research into isometric training in the early 1960s after three York lifters dramatically improved their performance, purportedly because of an isometric program. In reality their increased performance was due to the addition of the first anabolic steroid as part of their training regimen. Terry Todd, "A History of the Use of Anabolic Steroids in Sport."

142. Maxwell L. Howell, Ray Kimoto, and W. R. Morford, "Effect of Isometric and Isotonic Exercise Programs upon Muscular Endurance."

143. Jerry R. Ball, George O. Rich, and Earl L. Wallis, "Effect of Isometric Training on Vertical Jump Ability."

144. Lynn W. McCraw and Stan Burnham, "Resistive Exercises in the Development of Muscular Strength and Endurance."

145. Robert L. Campbell, "Effects of Supplemental Weight Training on the Physical Fitness of Athletic Squads," 348.

146. Clayne R. Jensen, "Effect of Five Training Combinations of Swimming and Weight Training on Swimming the Front Crawl."

147. George B. Dintiman, "Effects of Various Training Programs on Running Speed."

148. John F. Alexander, Clare J. Drake, Peter J. Reichenbach, and James B. Haddow,

"Effect of Strength Development on Speed of Shooting of Varsity Ice Hockey Players."

149. While both overload groups improved velocity, it is important to note that their improvement was not significantly greater than that of the traditionally trained group. Donald E. Brose and Dale E. Hanson, "Effects of Overload Training on Velocity and Accuracy of Throwing."

150. Gordon W. Schultz, "Effect of Direct Practice, Repetitive Sprinting, and Weight Training on Selected Motor Performance Tests."

151. Jimmy Pedemonte, "Foundations of Training Periodization Part One: Historical Outline"; Mel Siff, *Supertraining: A Scientific Method for Strength, Endurance, and Weight Training*, 311–312; Vladimir B. Issurin, "Periodization Training from Ancient Precursors to Structured Block Models."

152. Siff, *Supertraining*, 311.

153. Pedemonte, "Foundations of Training Periodization Part One," 65.

154. Bourne, "Fast Science," 377.

155. Ibid., 381–383; Jimmy Pedemonte, "Foundations of Training Periodization Part Two: The Objective of Periodization," 27.

156. Bourne, "Fast Science," 385.

157. The Soviets and Americans competed head-to-head at both Summer and Winter Olympic Games in 1952 through 1976 and 1988. The Soviets won both Summer Games and Winter Games in 1956–1964, 1972, 1976, and 1988. Riordan, "The Rise and Fall of Soviet Olympic Champions," 32–33.

158. Riordan, *Sport in Soviet Society*, 376.

159. Guttman, *Women's Sports*, 190–191.

160. Welch Suggs, *A Place on the Team: The Triumph and Tragedy of Title IX*, 48–49.

161. Jennifer Hargreaves, *Sporting Females: Critical Issues in the History and Sociology of Women's Sports*, 216.

162. Susan K. Cahn, *Coming on Strong: Gender and Sexuality in Twentieth-Century Women's Sport*, 164–181 (quotation), 182–184. Cahn contends that female athletes of this era had to take an "apologetic stance" for their athletic skill and went out of their way to display overt aspects of femininity, including through dress, hobbies, or discussion of male love interests. Rob Beamish and Ian Ritchie, "Totalitarian Regimes and Cold War Sport: Steroid 'Ubermenschen' and 'Ball-Bearing Females,'" 19–20.

163. Theodor Hettinger, *Physiology of Strength*, 12, 42.

164. Harry McLaughlin, "Barbells Aid Olympic Swimming Aspirants."

165. John Piscapo, "Strength."

166. John P. Jesse, "A New Look at Strength Development in Track and Field Athletes," 74.

167. E. M. Orlick, "Editorial—Let's Close the Scientific Sports Gap!," 5.

168. Campbell, "Effects of Supplemental Weight Training," 343–348.

169. Bourne, "Fast Science," 348, 387–393.

CHAPTER 4: PIONEERS OF POWER

1.   Matt Bristol, "Born of Controversy: The G.I. Bill of Rights."

2.   Raymond Van Cleef, "Barbells on Campus: Weight Training at San Jose State."

3.   Gordon C. Smith, "Barbells on Campus: Weightlifting at Michigan State U.," 36.

4. Neither the undergraduate student nor the "director of physical education" was named in the article. N. M. Jorgensen, "The Development of Weight Training at East Carolina College," 6.

5. Bill Curry ran groups of fifty soldiers at a time using barbells made from pipe and paint cans when he was the physical training instructor at Fort McClellan in Alabama during World War II. Al Thomas, "Where Are They Now? Bill Curry and the Gospel of Physical Fitness," 18.

6. For example, physical educator Richard Berger was introduced to weight training by a friend who had also served in the marines. Exercise physiologist Patrick O'Shea started training at the YMCA after encountering Junior National Champion lifter Al Kornke in high school. Many of the members of the University of Maryland's barbell club had begun lifting in high school. Terry Todd and Jan Todd, "Pioneers of Strength Research: The Legacy of Dr. Richard A. Berger," 275; Terry Todd and Jan Todd, "Dr. Patrick O'Shea: A Man for All Seasons," 401; Larry Walsh, "Barbells on Campus: The University of Maryland," 20.

7. George W. Ritchey, "Barbells on Campus: L.S.U.," 59.

8. Louise E. Alley, "Barbells on Campus: State University of Iowa," 25, 52.

9. Donald Mrozek, "The Cult and Ritual of Toughness in Cold War America," 259–260.

10. Quoted in Kurt E. Kempner, *College Football and American Culture in the Cold War Era*, 22.

11. As an example, Mrozek pointed to a 1964 *Life* magazine portrayal of swimming training at the University of Indiana that emphasized the "agony" and "training by torture" aspects of the program. "Pain was portrayed not as an accident of training," asserted Mrozek, "but at its very core." Mrozek, "The Cult and Ritual of Toughness," 263–264.

12. Jim Dent, *The Junction Boys: How Ten Days in Hell with Bear Bryant Forged a Championship Team*; Michael Oriard, *Bowled Over: Big-Time College Football from the Sixties to the BCS Era*, 37–39.

13. Oriard, *Bowled Over*, 111. It should be noted that one reason coaches used such tactics was to open up scholarships. After schools were permitted to give a limited number of scholarships based on athletic ability, coaches like Royal used harsh drills and conditioning to coerce less-skilled players into quitting. Gary Shaw, *Meat on the Hoof: The Hidden World of Texas Football*, 122–134.

14. As noted by Michael Oriard, "No Golden Age of fleet and brawny dean's-list scholars ever reigned in college football. Numerous gridiron heroes since the 1920s have undoubtedly been football players who enrolled in classes rather than students who played football, but until 1956 the colleges and universities belonging to the NCAA could claim otherwise" (*Bowled Over*, 129). See also Randy Roberts and James S. Olson, *Winning Is the Only Thing: Sports in American since 1945*, 73–94; Murray Sperber, *Onward to Victory: The Crises That Shaped College Sports*, 285–357; John Sayle Watterson, *College Football: History, Spectacle, Controversy*, 158–176, 201–240; Michael Oriard, *King Football: Sport and Spectacle in the Golden Age of Radio and Newsreels, Movies and Magazines, the Weekly and Daily Press*, 101–125.

15. John Underwood, "The Desperate Coach," *Sports Illustrated*, August 25, 1969, 74.

16. Roy J. McLean and Karl K. Klein, "Barbells on Campus: The University of Texas";

Bob Hoffman, "Barbell Training in the Service," 43; Terry Todd, "The History of Strength Training for Athletes at the University of Texas."

17. Each section enrolled twenty-five to thirty men. By the time of McLean's retirement in 1967, the number of sections was up to twenty-two. As a result, McLean "taught tens of thousands of Longhorn men to lift weights." Jan Todd, Terry Todd, Matt Bowers, Peter Ullmann, Dominic Morais, Fozzy Whitaker, Ryan Munson and Jenna Galloway. "Roy McLean," *Longhorn Power: An Online Exhibition on Strength Training for UT Sports* (2012): https://www.archives .starkcenter.org/omeka/exhibits/show/longhornpower/mclean; Todd, "The History of Strength Training for Athletes," 8.

18. Todd, "The History of Strength Training for Athletes," 8.

19. In McLean's thirteen seasons as cross-country coach, his athletes captured thirteen conference titles. He also coached some outstanding wrestlers, including Ralph Hammond, who placed fourth in the 174-pound class in the 1928 Olympic Games and lettered in football at Texas. Todd, "History of Strength Training for Athletes," 6–8.

20. Paul Gill, "The Strength of His Convictions: Strongman Priest Bernard Lange Forged His Boys into Men of Iron," *Notre Dame News* (Spring 1987): http://www .frlangesgym.com/pages/?page_id=147. Bernard H. Lange was also a regular contributor for *Strength* magazine in the early 1920s. See, for example, "How to Use the Gymnasium" (February 1922); "How to Use the Gymnasium" (March 1922); "How to Use the Gymnasium" (April 1922); "Football as a Bodybuilder" (October 1922); "Football as a Bodybuilder" (December 1922); "The Neck and How to Develop It" (May 1923); "Build up Your Back" (October 1923).

21. Gill, "The Strength of His Convictions"; Jim Sheridan, "Notre Dame Football Strongman Father Lange, the Crown Jewel of Irish Legends," *Bleacher Report*, February 27, 2011: https://bleacherreport.com/articles/620911-notre-dame -strongman-father-langethe-crown-jewel-of-irish-legends.

22. Sheridan, "Notre Dame Football Strongman Father Lange"; Gill, "The Strength of His Convictions."

23. Gill, "The Strength of His Convictions."

24. Lange received the first PhD awarded by the college. While at Saint Edward's, Lange built a replica of Notre Dame's famed grotto in front of the university's main building. "Campus Beautification Continues under Direction of Father Lange," *Saint Edward's Echo*, January 28, 1931: http://www.frlangesgym .com/pages/?page_id=294; "Father Lange Continues Campus Beautification," *Saint Edward's Echo*, February, 10, 1932: http://www.frlangesgym.com /pages/?page_id=296; "Father B.H.B Lange Receives First Ph.D. from University," *Saint Edward's Echo*, June 10, 1931: http://www.frlangesgym.com /pages/?page_id=286; Lange, "How to Use the Gymnasium" (March 1922).

25. George Otott, "Barbells on Campus: Notre Dame"; Gill, "The Strength of His Convictions"; Dan Broderick, "If Father Lange Would Only Talk," *Notre Dame Scholastic* (n.d.): http://www.frlangesgym.com/pages/?page_id=268 (accessed November 14, 2016).

26. Kent Durso, "Letters to the Editor: Father Lange's Legacy."

27. Otott, "Barbells on Campus: Notre Dame."

28. Kent Durso, a former student who trained with Lange, said that Lange corresponded with Steve Stanko and John Grimek at York and that the two

periodically sent brand-new York sets for the gym at no charge. Durso, "Letters to the Editor: Father Lange's Legacy."

29. The preceding season Parseghian had recommended that safety Mike Burgener seek out Lange's assistance. Burgener had been exposed to weight training while in high school, but his father, who had played football at Millikin University, forbade him from lifting because it would make him "muscle-bound." When Burgener met Father Lange, he weighed 165 pounds. Within a year of training with Lange he had added 17 pounds to his frame, decreased his forty-yard dash time by a tenth of a second, and become a crucial member of the Fighting Irish secondary. Mike Burgener interview, March 3, 2015: https://www.youtube.com /watch?v=G6svvjQGQqA; Sheridan, "Notre Dame Football Strongman Father Lange."

30. Parseghian said that he and the other Notre Dame coaches were "deeply indebted to [Father Lange] for his aid to our program." Otott, "Barbells on Campus: Notre Dame"; R. J. Mahoney, "Barbells on Campus: Notre Dame"; Gill, "The Strength of His Convictions"; "Year by Year Records" *2018 Notre Dame Football Media Guide* (2018), 189–190: https://und.com/documents/2018/8/27/Full_Guide.pdf.

31. Gene Mozee, "The Mighty Trojans: How they Use Weights in Training"; University of Southern California Athletics, "Tommy Trojan" (2018): https://usctrojans.com /sports/2018/7/25/usc-history-traditions-tommy-trojan-statue.aspx; San Diego Hall of Champions, "Russ Saunders" (n.d.): http://sandiegosportsassociation.com /hall-of-fame/russ-saunders/ (accessed October 10, 2012).

32. Gene Mozee, "University of Southern California: National Football Champions."

33. During the 1942 season Penn State went 6–1–1, defeating the University of Pennsylvania and University of Pittsburgh to claim the top spot in the state. The record was not a dramatic improvement over the previous seasons, when Penn State had gone 7–2, 6–1–1, and 5–1–2. Alan Carse, "Barbell Training in Universities"; Pennsylvania State University Athletics, "Year-By-Year Record," *2018 Penn State Football Yearbook* (2018), 288–289: https://issuu.com /gopsusports/docs/2018_penn_state_football_yearbook.

34. H. T. Meaders, "Iron Men of Georgia."

35. See, for example, Jim Scott, "Who Are America's Weight Trained Athletes?"; Bob Hoffman, "Editorial—Barbells Build Better Athletes," 63; James P. Tuppeny, "Barbells on Campus: Weight Training for Track and Field Men at Villanova."

36. Wesley Ruff, "Barbells on Campus: Stanford University"; David Shaw and Mitchell Landsberg, "L.A. Icon Otis Chandler Dies at 78," *Los Angeles Times*, February 27, 2006; Scott, "Who Are America's Weight Trained Athletes?"

37. Gordon C. Smith, "Barbells on Campus: Weightlifting at Michigan State U."; Patrick O'Shea and G. I. Strahl, "Barbells on Campus: Michigan State."

38. Louisiana Sports Hall of Fame, "Jimmy Taylor" (n.d.): https://www.lasportshall .com/inductees/football/jimmy-taylor/?back=inductee (accessed October 11, 2012).

39. "Year by Year Results," *Louisiana State University Football Media Guide* (2011), 157: https://www.lsusports.net/ViewArticle .dbml?DB_OEM_ID=5200&ATCLID=205181481.

40. Terry Todd, "Al Roy: The First Modern Strength Coach," 14; Terry Todd, "Al Roy: Mythbreaker."

41. Bob Hoffman, "Barbells Build Winning Football Team"; Ace Higgins, "Football's Weightlifting All-American: Billy Cannon."

42. Jimmy Taylor would go on to be drafted in the second round in the 1958 National Football League (NFL) draft by the Green Bay Packers. He joined former Notre Dame running back and Heisman Trophy winner Paul Hornung in the backfield and was a key component of the Packers' famed running attack of that era. When he retired after the 1967 season, Taylor had amassed 8,207 rushing yards in the "Green and Gold" and was the all-time leader in rushing yards for the franchise. Between 1960 and 1964 Taylor had five straight seasons in which he rushed for more than 1,000 yards. Taylor's career in Green Bay also included four NFL championships in 1961, 1962, 1965, and 1966. In 1976 Taylor was inducted into the NFL Hall of Fame. Todd, "Al Roy: Mythbreaker," 15 (quotations); "Hall of Famers: Jimmy Taylor" (n.d.): https://www.packers.com/history/hof/jim-taylor (accessed November 15, 2016).

43. Quoted in Todd, "Al Roy: Mythbreaker," 15.

44. Higgins, "Football's Weightlifting All-American," 35.

45. "All Americans," *Louisiana State University Football Media Guide* (Baton Rouge: Louisiana State University Athletics, 2011), 164.

46. Ritchey, "Barbells on Campus: LSU."

47. Matt Chaney, *Spiral of Denial: Muscle Doping in American Football*, 46–47; Alvin Roy, "The Strength Program of the San Diego Chargers."

48. Todd, "Al Roy: The First Modern Strength Coach." Roy worked for the Chargers through the 1967 season. The team reached the AFL title game every year he was in San Diego. In 1968 he joined the Kansas City Chiefs and oversaw the strength program that helped them achieve their only Super Bowl victory to date in 1970. Roy became the first strength coach for the Dallas Cowboys in 1973. Bob Ward and Mac Engel, *Building the Perfect Star. Changing the Trajectory of Sports and the People in Them*, 66–67.

49. Scott, "Who Are America's Weight Trained Athletes?," 30; "Year-by-Year Records," *2017 Washington Football Media Guide* (2017), 185–186: https://gohuskies.com/documents/2017/7/24/2017_FB_Guide.pdf.

50. Joe Kolb, "Weight Training for Football: The Fort Lauderdale Story," 42.

51. Joe Uhls, "Football + F.I.C. = Stronger Football Players."

52. In the three seasons preceding the introduction of the weight program, the SEMO basketball team had gone 5–13, 11–9, and 11–9. In the three seasons after the introduction of strength training, the team went 13–9, 25–3, and 18–7. "Year by Year Records," *Southeast Missouri State University Men's Basketball Guide* (2012), 102: https://gosoutheast.com/documents/2012/10/19/201213MBKGu ide.pdf?id=1024 ; Uhls, "Weight Training for Basketball: SEMO State Hoopsters Use Weights in and out of Cage Season."

53. Founded in 1948, Stonehill enrolled just 600 students in 1961. Joseph Faul, "Barbells on Campus: Stonehill College."

54. Jack R. Leighton, "Barbells on Campus: Eastern Washington College of Education."

55. Sidney Glauser, "Barbells on Campus: Temple University."

56. According to David Maraniss, Villanova's track program was "renowned" and widely respected in the late 1950s and early 1960s: *Rome 1960: The Olympics That Changed the World*, 178; Tuppeny, "Barbells on Campus"; Norm Harvey, "Barbells on Campus: Villanova University."

57. David Baillie, "Barbells on Campus: Springfield College."

58. Joseph Goldenberg, "Barbells on Campus: New York University."

59. William Hottinger, "Barbells on Campus: University of Illinois."

60. John Neumann, "Barbells on Campus: The University of California," 40–41.

61. Ibid.; John Neumann, "Weight Training for Football Players."

62. "History of Cal Football, Year-by-Year," *University of California Football Media Guide (2007)*, 153: http://www.cstv.com/auto_pdf/p_hotos/s_chools/cal/sports/m-footbl/auto_pdf/pdf-07FB151to190-072007.

63. Eugene G. Hooks, "The Prediction of Baseball Ability through an Analysis of Selected Measures of Structure and Strength."

64. Eugene G. Hooks, "Barbells on Campus: Wake Forest University," 50 (quotations); "All-Time Results," *Wake Forest University 2018 Football Media Guide* (2018) 129–136: https://godeacs.com/documents/2018/8/18//123_136_Results.pdf?id=8925.

65. Terry Todd, "Progressive Resistance for Football at the University of Texas"; University of Texas Football Official Website, "All-Time Results" (2013): https://texassports.com/sports/2013/7/21/FB_0721134841.aspx.

66. Terry Todd, "The History of Strength Training for Athletes at the University of Texas," 9.

67. Todd, "The History of Strength Training for Athletes at the University of Texas," 9; Todd, "Progressive Resistance," 56; Donald Mrozek, "The Cult and Ritual of Toughness in Cold War America," 259–260; Stan Burnham, "Football Conditioning at the University of Texas."

68. University of Texas Football Official Website, "All-Time Results."

69. Joe Fournier, "Naval Academy Turns to Weightlifting," 17.

70. Frank Swetz, "Barbells on Campus: Marist College."

71. John Grimek, "Barbells on Campus: Mt. Saint Mary's."

72. Joseph Figliolino, "Barbells on Campus: Bloomsburg State College," 62.

73. Roy Judy, "Barbells on Campus: Gordon Military College."

74. Stan Plagenhoef, "Barbells on Campus: Wesleyan College of Connecticut."

75. Dub Manis, "The Weight Trained Track Team of Abilene Christian College"; George Colfer, "Barbells on Campus: Ithaca College."

76. Jack Weingarten, "Barbells on Campus: Franklin and Marshall College"; Ken Wyle, "Barbells on Campus: Kendall College."

77. Cynthia Wyatt (as told to Tommy Kono), "Cindy Wyatt Wants to Be a Champion."

78. "Cindy Wyatt," Greater Buffalo (NY) Sports Hall of Fame (May 15, 2016): https://www.buffalosportshallfame.com/member/cindy-wyatt.

79. Interview with Cindy Wyatt Reinhoudt by Jan Todd, May 18, 1988. See also Marshall Smith, "How Reds 'Mobilized' to Win Olympic 'War,'" *Life*, July 28, 1952, 16–17.

80. Bob Lee and Jerri Lee, "Weight Training for a Mountain Marathon."

81. Zenta Thomas, "Britain's Weight-Trained Lady Jumper."; Dan Levin, "What Makes Audrey Pedal? Tiga Muk!" *Sports Illustrated*, November 24, 1969; "Bunny from B.C." *Time*, January 20, 1967, 37.

82. Patrick O'Shea, "Barbells on Campus: Oregon State University," 29.

83. For example, the University of Texas's key conference rival, Texas A&M University, adopted weight training for football the year after Texas did. Spec Gammon, "The Texas A&M Weight Program for Football."

84. The swimming, track, and football teams at Oregon State trained with weights year-round by the late 1960s, as did the football team at Westminster College

in Salt Lake City, Utah. O'Shea, "Barbells on Campus"; Patrick O'Shea, "Oregon State University's Weight Trained Track Stars"; Ronald Nay, "In-Season Weight Training for Football."

85. David W. Zang, *Sports Wars: Athletes in the Age of Aquarius*, xv.

86. Athletic protests in the late 1960s affected the prominent universities of Maryland, Washington, Wyoming, Indiana, and Oregon State. Small colleges, such as Carnegie Tech, Adelbert College, and Providence College, also saw player and team rebellions. For additional information, see Oriard, *Bowled Over*, 15–56; Underwood, "The Desperate Coach."

CHAPTER 5: AN EMERGING PROFESSION

1. Terry Todd, "Al Roy: The First Modern Strength Coach," 14.

2. Ken Leistner and Sandy McLeod, "Alvin Roy: Fitness for Football," 51.

3. Terry Todd, "Al Roy: Mythbreaker," 12.

4. Boyd Epley, "NSCA Timeline," BoydEpley.com (n.d.): http://boydepley.com /NSCATimeline.pdf (accessed February 8, 2010).

5. Boyd Epley, videotaped interview by Terry Todd, Las Vegas, Nevada, June 2009, on deposit at the H. J. Lutcher Stark Center for Physical Culture and Sports at the University of Texas at Austin.

6. Boyd Epley, telephone interview with Jason Shurley, February 24, 2010.

7. Epley, interview with Terry Todd.

8. George R. Mills, *A View from the Bench: The Story of an Ordinary Player on a Big-Time Football Team*, 72.

9. Epley, interview with Terry Todd.

10. Pat Neve, "Biography," Official Pat Neve Website (n.d.): patneve.com/bio/index .php (no longer available; accessed May 14, 2010).

11. Epley, interview with Jason Shurley.

12. Ibid.

13. According to one of Epley's books, *The Path to Athletic Power*, the original equipment list included two squat racks and bars, lifting plates and racks to hold them, one bench and bar, a light pulley system for shoulder work, dumbbells in pairs from 5 to 100 lbs, a preacher curl bench and weights, two work benches, and two incline benches.

14. Boyd Epley, *The Path to Athletic Power: The Model Conditioning Program for Championship Performance*, 27.

15. Epley, interview with Terry Todd. According to *The Path to Athletic Power*, the list of additional equipment included fixed barbells, EZ curl bars, a neck machine, a lat-pulldown machine, and a low lat-pull.

16. Ibid.

17. Epley did not mention being aware of the work of Peter Karpovich, Thomas DeLorme, or any other scientists who did pioneering research on the effects of strength training prior to his meeting. In an e-mail to Jan Todd (August 5, 2012), however, he did mention having been exposed to the magazines of Bob Hoffman, Joe Weider, and Parry Rader and even remarked that he had a picture of bodybuilder Sergio Oliva on his fridge in the late 1960s. As a result, he was almost certainly familiar with the boosterism and logical appeals of the magazines and their promotion of strength training for sport.

18. Epley, interview with Terry Todd.

19. Ibid.

20. Devaney played at Alma College in Alma, Michigan, lettering for three years and graduating in 1939 with a bachelor of science degree in social science. Frank Litsky. "Bob DeVaney, 82, Nebraska Coach, Dies." *New York Times*, May 10, 1997.

21. For example, he told Richard Berger, then a football player for the Spartans, "I don't want to hear about you doing any of that lifting. It's bad for you. I want you to get a summer job doing heavy construction work. That's what you need, not those weights." Terry Todd and Jan Todd, "Pioneers of Strength Research: The Legacy of Richard A. Berger," 275. While he voiced his support for weight training in a 1959 *Strength & Health* article, it is important to note that the article mentions other athletes training with weights but does not mention strength training for football players. Gordon C. Smith, "Barbells on Campus: Weightlifting at Michigan State U."

22. Between 1947 and 1954 Munn's teams went 54–9–2, at one point winning twenty-eight consecutive games. The Spartans also won the 1952 national championship and the 1954 Rose Bowl under Munn. Michigan State University Archives and Historical Collections, "Clarence L. Munn: An Inventory of His Papers" (East Lansing: MSU Archives, n.d.): http://archives.msu.edu/findaid/ua17-75.html (accessed October 15, 2012); "Obituary: Duffy Daugherty, Ex-Coach," *New York Times*, September 26, 1987.

23. Harry Paschall, "Weight Training for Athletics: Football," 44.

24. "Nebraska through the Years" (n.d.): http://huskers.com//pdf5/638597.pdf (accessed May 4, 2010).

25. Epley, interview by Jason Shurley.

26. Peary Rader, "Weight Training at University of Nebraska for Student Body."

27. Fischer had a good rapport with Devaney, having been one of the few coaches retained from the previous Nebraska coaching regime, largely to assist with recruiting. Devaney and Fischer had traversed the state in a car with no heat or radio and shared hotel rooms on the road in the early 1960s. Litsky, "Bob DeVaney." It is probable that he witnessed athletes using a Universal machine and a circuit program similar to that employed as one aspect of the Texas Longhorns offseason program, begun in 1963. For specifics of the circuit program, see Stan Burnham, "Football Conditioning at the University of Texas."

28. Boyd Epley, "Husker Power Timeline—The Schulte Fieldhouse Years" (n.d.): http://boydepley.com/SchulteFieldHouse.pdf (accessed February 8, 2010).

29. University of Nebraska Athletics, "Strength and Conditioning Timeline" (n.d.): http://huskers.com/ViewArticle.dbml?SPSID=183&SPID=41&DB_OEM_ID=100&ATCLID=8568 (accessed June 29, 2010).

30. University of Nebraska Athletics, "Year by Year Results" (n.d.): http://huskers.com//pdf5/638605.pdf (accessed May 4, 2010).

31. Epley, interview with Jason Shurley.

32. Armen Keteyian, *Big Red Confidential: Inside Nebraska Football*, 65 (quotations), 181, 38.

33. Epley, interview with Jason Shurley.

34. Epley, interview with Terry Todd.

35. Epley, interview with Jason Shurley.

36. For a detailed discussion of the early 1970s winter program at Nebraska, see Mills, *A View from the Bench*, 63–75.

37. Epley, "Husker Power Timeline—The Schulte Fieldhouse Years."
38. Epley, interview with Jason Shurley.
39. Allen Guttmann, *From Ritual to Record: The Nature of Modern Sports*, 16, 38 (quotations).
40. Epley, interview with Jason Shurley.
41. Murray Sperber, *Beer and Circus: How Big-Time College Sports Is Crippling Undergraduate Education*, 7–9.
42. Sperber, *Beer and Circus*, 7 (quotations); Mills, *A View from the Bench*, 192.
43. Guttmann, *From Ritual to Record*, 39.
44. Keteyian, *Big Red Confidential*, 170.
45. Ibid., 46.
46. Epley, interview with Jason Shurley.
47. Ibid.
48. Terry Todd, "A Man of Heft Who's Also Deft," 44.
49. Ibid.
50. Guttmann, *Ritual to Record*, 51.
51. Epley, "Husker Power Timeline—The Schulte Fieldhouse Years."
52. John Hoberman, *Mortal Engines: The Science of Performance and the Dehumanization of Sport*, 5.
53. Guttmann, *Ritual to Record*, 40, 43.
54. Quoted in Keteyian, *Big Red Confidential*, 57.
55. Epley, interview with Terry Todd.
56. The Husker Power Club ceased operations after 2010. When this research was initiated, the club was still functioning and all information was gathered in early 2010. Husker Power Club, "Welcome" (n.d.): huskerpowerclub.com /hpc_welcome.htm (no longer available; accessed May 17, 2010).
57. Boyd Epley, "Husker Power Timeline—The West Stadium Years," BoydEpley.com (n.d.): http://boydepley.com/WestStadium.pdf (accessed February 8, 2010).
58. Mike Arthur, director of Strength and Conditioning at the University of Nebraska, e-mail to Jan Todd, July 12, 2010.
59. Roger C. Aden, *Huskerville: A Story of Nebraska Football, Fans, and the Power of Place*, 76–92.
60. Scott McQuilkin, "'The World's Source for Strength and Conditioning Information': A History of the National Strength and Conditioning Association, 1978–1993," 8.
61. Boyd Epley, "NSCA Timeline," The Quest for Victory: A History of Weight Training for Sports, H. J. Lutcher Stark Center for Physical Culture and Sports.
62. Ken Kontor, "Editorial," 2 (quotation); Boyd Epley, *The National Directory of Strength Coaches*.
63. Boyd Epley, "NSCA Timeline," The Quest for Victory: A History of Weight Training for Sports, H. J. Lutcher Stark Center for Physical Culture and Sports.
64. Boyd Epley, "Join the NSCA!," 1.
65. Boyd Epley's books include *The Strength of Nebraska, Cardiovascular Fitness . . . The Nebraska Way, Body Composition Assessment: How to Gain or Lose Bodyweight, Husker Power for '83–'84, Interval Sprints for Football . . . The Nebraska Way, Motivate Your Athletes . . . The Nebraska Way, Multi-Purpose Machine Exercises . . . The Nebraska Way, Neck Exercises . . . The Nebraska Way, Strength Training for Basketball . . . The Nebraska Way, Strength Training for*

Baseball and Softball . . . The Nebraska Way, Strength Training for Football . . . The Nebraska Way, Strength Training for Golf . . . The Nebraska Way, Strength Training for Racquet Sports . . . The Nebraska Way, Strength Training for Swimming . . . The Nebraska Way, Strength Training for Track & Field . . . The Nebraska Way, Strength Training for Wrestling . . . The Nebraska Way, Stretching . . . The Nebraska Way, Survivor Circuit Training . . . The Nebraska Way, Test Your Athletes . . . The Nebraska Way, When, How and Why to Begin Lifting Weights . . . The Nebraska Way, Dynamic Strength Training for Athletes, Boyd Epley Workout for Football, Husker Power: Committed to Improving Performance, and (with Tom Wilson), *Weight Training Instruction Manual.*

CHAPTER 6: BRIDGING THE GAP

1. William J. Kraemer, "An Introduction to Research: Reading and Understanding," 11.
2. William J. Kraemer, "Research: Reading and Understanding: The Starter Steps," 49.
3. Josie Sifft and William J. Kraemer, "Research: Reading and Understanding: Introduction, Review of Literature, Methods," 24–25; Gary A. Dudley and Steven J. Fleck, "Research: Reading and Understanding: The Results Section: Major Concepts and Compounds," 22; Al Starck and Steven J. Fleck, "Research: Reading and Understanding: The Discussion Section," 40–41; Josie Sifft, "Research: Reading and Understanding: Utilizing Descriptive Statistics in Sport Performance," 26–28; Josie Sifft, "Reading and Understanding Research: Guidelines for Selecting a Sample," 26–27.
4. "The First Five Years: Results and Analysis of the 1982–83 Member Survey"; William J. Kraemer, "President's Message: Time to Train," 74–75.
5. "Coach Dana LeDuc," FZN Junior Panther Football Association (n.d.), https://everysport.net/jrpantherfootball/Teams/T3Training.aspx (accessed July 14, 2015).
6. Dan Riley, who began his strength coaching career at the United State Military Academy in 1974 before moving on to Pennsylvania State University and the NFL's Washington Redskins, commented that administrators and coaches of that era "assumed that if you knew how to lift, you knew how to coach lifting." Riley went on to comment that "in the 70s if you were a weightlifter, you could probably misspell dumbbell on the application and still get a job as a strength coach." "Dana LeDuc—Biography," Longhorn Power Timeline, Starkcenter.org (n.d.), https://archives.starkcenter.org/omeka/exhibits/show/longhornpower/dana-leduc-bio (accessed February 5, 2019); Tim Layden, "Power Play," *Sports Illustrated*, July 27, 1998, 60–65.
7. "May 1979: National Strength and Conditioning Association History," NSCA Timeline, The Quest for Victory: A History of Weight Training for Sports, H. J. Lutcher Stark Center for Physical Culture and Sports.
8. The issue's articles included Ken Kontor, "Meet America's Strongest: A Final Look at the National Strength Coaches' Association All-American Strength Team"; Lou Riecke, "Steeler Strength the Powersafe Way"; Carl Miller, "Rotary Action of the Legs and Hips Common to Many Sports"; Larry Crouch, "Neck Injuries—Prevention to Aid Rehabilitation, Part II"; Ray Ganong, "University

of Miami Baseball Strength and Conditioning"; "Nutrition Report: Vitamin B-15"; Bob Anderson, "Conditioning Report: Static Stretching for Athletes"; Joan Werblow, Alice Hennemen, and Hazel Fox, "Women's Report: Nutrition for Women in Sports"; E. W. Bannister, "Research Report: Strength Gains from Muscle Training: Preparation for Competition."

9. Leslie G. Portney and Mary P. Watkins, *Foundations of Clinical Research: Applications to Practice.*

10. Jason Shurley and Jan Todd, "Joe Weider, All-American Athlete, and the Promotion of Strength Training for Sport, 1940–1969"; Jason Shurley, "Strength for Sport: The Development of the Professional Strength and Conditioning Coach," 216.

11. Quoted in Shurley and Todd, "Joe Weider."

12. "Member Spotlight: Boyd Epley, CSCS," 4.

13. Jason Shurley and Jan Todd, "'The Strength of Nebraska': Boyd Epley, Husker Power, and the Formation of the Strength Coaching Profession."

14. "Charlie Craven: Weight Training," Longhorn Power Timeline, Starkcenter.org (n.d.), https://archives.starkcenter.org/omeka/exhibits/show/longhornpower /weights (accessed November 15, 2016).

15. James Riordan, *Soviet Sport: Background to the Olympics.*

16. Richard Berger, "Effect of Varied Weight Training Programs on Strength"; Richard Berger, "Comparison of the Effect of Various Weight Training Loads on Strength"; Edward K. Capen, "The Effect of Systematic Weight Training on Power, Strength, and Endurance"; Patrick O'Shea, "Effects of Selected Weight Training Programs on the Development of Strength and Muscle Hypertrophy"; Edward F. Chui, "The Effect of Systematic Weight Training on Athletic Power"; Jim D. Whitley and Leon E. Smith, "Influence of Three Different Training Programs on Strength and Speed of Limb Movement"; William S. Zorbas and Peter V. Karpovich, "The Effect of Weight Lifting upon the Speed of Muscular Contractions."

17. Nicholas Bourne, "Fast Science: A History of Training Theory and Methods for Elite Runners through 1975."

18. Peter V. Karpovich, *Physiology of Muscular Exercise*; Jack R. Leighton, *Progressive Weight Training*; Benjamin H. Massey, *The Kinesiology of Weightlifting*; Patrick O'Shea, *Scientific Principles and Methods of Strength and Fitness*; American Association for Health, Physical Education, and Recreation, *Weight Training in Sports and Physical Education*, ed. Frank Sills, Laurence Morehouse, and Thomas DeLorme.

19. Lou Ravelle, *Bodybuilding for Everyone.*

20. Ken Kontor, "Nine Months of Progress . . . Nine Months of History," 1.

21. Ken Kontor, "Convention II—300 Strong," 1.

22. Epley, *The National Directory for Strength Coaches*; William Kraemer, telephone interview with Jason Shurley, May 21, 2015.

23. Quoted in Scott A. McQuilkin "'The World's Source for Strength and Conditioning Information': A History of the National Strength and Conditioning Association, 1978–1993," 34.

24. Kraemer, telephone interview with Shurley.

25. George Elder, "Letters to the Editor," 15.

26. Kontor, "Convention II."

27. "The National Strength and Conditioning Association Timeline," The Quest for Victory: A History of Weight Training for Sports, H. J. Lutcher Stark Center for Physical Culture and Sports.

28. Dan Wathen, personal communication with Jan Todd, 2010. Our efforts to locate an official list of committee members were not successful.

29. "Ken Kontor: Assistant Executive Director and Editor," 9; Ken Kontor, "Editorial"; Ken Kontor, "Editorial: The NSCA Story," 2; Ken Kontor, "Editorial: Bridging the Gap," 11 (quotations); "The NSCA 15-Year Chronology."

30. Kontor, "Convention II," 1.

31. Wathen, personal communication with Jan Todd, 2010.

32. Karen Knortz, "Kinesiology Corner: The Upright Row," 40.

33. W. S. Barnes, "The Relationship of Motor Unit Activation to Isokinetic Muscular Contraction at Different Contractile Velocities"; Edward F. Coyle, David L. Costill, and G. R. Lesmes, "Leg Extension Power and Muscle Fiber Composition"; P. A. Eisenman, "The Influence of Initial Strength Levels on Responses in Vertical Jump Training"; M. T. Sanders, "A Comparison of Two Methods of Training on the Development of Muscular Strength and Endurance."

34. Steven J. Fleck, "Exercise Physiology Corner: Determination of Body Fat Via Skinfold Measurements."

35. Terry Todd, "The Myth of the Muscle-Bound Lifter."

36. William Kraemer, "Kinesiology Corner: Wrist Curls."

37. Concerns about the safety of the squat for the knees would persist long after the myth of muscle-binding had been dispelled. In 1991, to alleviate anxiety about the exercise, the NSCA published a "Position Paper," asserting in its first bullet point that squats were "not only safe, but may be a significant deterrent to knee injuries." T. Jeff Chandler and Michael Stone, "NSCA Position Paper: The Squat Exercise in Athletic Conditioning: A Position Statement and Review of Literature"; Paul Hoolahan, "Strength and Conditioning for Basketball: The University of North Carolina Program—Why Strength Training?"; "Weights Don't Hurt Knees"; Ken Kontor, "Editorial: Myths Persist."

38. "The National Strength and Conditioning Association Timeline."

39. "Nautilus Advertisement," in The National Directory of Strength Coaches, front and back covers.

40. Ken Kontor, "Editorial: Equipment Companies," 4.

41. Arthur Jones, "The Colorado Experiment."

42. Dan Wathen, "A Comparison of the Effects of Isotonic and Isokinetic Exercises, Modalities, and Programs on Vertical Jump in College Football Players."

43. "The Football Coaches' Choice . . . Mini-Gym," in Epley, The National Directory of Strength Coaches, 66–66a.

44. George Elder, "Viewpoint: Machines: A Viable Method for Training Athletes?," 24, 28.

45. "Viewpoint: Nautilus—A Statement of Purpose," 21–23.

46. Michael Yessis, "Viewpoint: A Response to Nautilus."

47. Michael Wolf, "Viewpoint: A Response to the Yessis Critique of Nautilus."

48. Michael Yessis, "A Response to the Reaction of Dr. Wolf to the Yessis Critique of Nautilus"; Michael Wolf, "The Nautilus Controversy: Continued Response to a Continuing Critique"; "Strength Training Modes: Nautilus: The Concept of Variable Resistance."

49. Mike Stone, Robert L. Johnson, and David R. Carter, "A Short Term Comparison

of Two Different Methods of Resistance Training on Leg Strength and Power";
John Garhammer, "Evaluation of Human Power Capacity through Olympic
Weightlifting Analyses."

50. Stone and Garhammer, "Viewpoint," 24.

51. John Garhammer, "Strength Training Modes: Free Weight Equipment for the
Development of Athletic Strength and Power—Part I," 24–26.

52. Mike Stone, "Strength Training Modes: Free Weights—Part II: Considerations
in Gaining a Strength–Power Training Effect (Machines vs. Free Weights),"
22–24. One of Nautilus's key claims was that the uniquely shaped cam on the
machines varied resistance throughout the range of motion, keeping muscle
tension maximized in spite of changes in muscle length and joint angle. Many
contemporary machines have similarly shaped cams for the same reason. In spite
of these claims, it has been found that the relationship between the machine
arm angle and the amount of torque that it provides is highly variable across
manufacturers, including Nautilus machines, and markedly different from the
muscle's actual capacity across the range of motion. Everett Harman, "Resistive
Torque Analysis of Five Nautilus Exercise Machines"; Jonathan Folland and
Beth Morris, "Variable-Cam Resistance Training Machines: Do They Match the
Angle-Torque Relationship in Humans?"

53. See these works by Michael Yessis: "The Athlete Defined: A Soviet System of
Rank," "Trends in Soviet Strength and Conditioning: The Role of Specificity
in Strength Training for Track, Gymnastics, and Other Sports," "Trends
in Soviet Strength and Conditioning: The Soviet Sports Training System:
The Yearly Cycle," "If the Soviets Had Football," "Trends in Soviet Strength
and Conditioning: From Macro to Meso to Microcycles," "Trends in Soviet
Strength and Conditioning: The Role of All-Around General Preparation in
the Multiyear and Yearly Training Programs," "Trends in Soviet Strength and
Conditioning: The Competitive Period in the Multiyear and Yearly Training
Programs," "Trends in Soviet Strength and Conditioning: The Transitional
(Post-Competitive) Period."

54. See these articles by Jimmy Pedemonte: "Training of General, Specific, and Special
Strength: A Key to Improved Performances in Sport," "Updated Acquisitions
about Training Periodization: Part One," "Updated Acquisitions about Training
Periodization: Training the Young and Intermediate Athlete," "Training Notes:
The Preparation of Soviet Throwers for the Moscow Olympics," "Foundations
of Training Periodization Part I: Historical Outline," "Historical Perspectives:
Foundations of Training Periodization Part Two: The Objective of Periodization."

55. Mike Stone, Harold O'Bryant, and John Garhammer, "A Hypothetical Model for
Strength Training."

56. Mike Stone, Harold O'Bryant, John Garhammer, Jim McMillan, and Ralph
Rozenek, "A Theoretical Model of Strength Training"; Tim Stowers, Jim
McMillan, Dwight Scala, Voris Davis, Dennis Wilson, and Mike Stone, "The
Short-Term Effects of Three Different Strength-Power Training Methods."

57. Bourne, "Fast Science," 395–396.

58. Thomas Baechle commented in a 1993 interview: "We could not maintain a
$1 million organization on so few strength coaches." McQuilkin, "'The World's
Source,'" 15.

59. Ken Kontor, "Editorial: Strength Coach Certification—The Next Step"; Kontor,
"Editorial: Myths Persist."

60. Thomas Baechle, "President's Message: The *NSCA Journal* and Certification: Tools for a Stronger Association."
61. McQuilkin, "'The World's Source for Strength and Conditioning Information,'" 15–16.
62. Baechle, "President's Message: The *NSCA Journal*."
63. Baechle commented in 1984 that the majority of the members were still coaches involved with football but that the group also included "researchers, athletic trainers, physicians working with sports medicine, health center directors, and coaches in many other sports." "Results and Analysis of 1982–1983 Membership Survey," 54; Thomas Baechle, "President's Message: Opportunities for Greater Participation: Dual Responsibility," 50 (quotation).
64. Kontor, "Editorial: Bridging the Gap," 11.
65. Bruce Algra, "An In-Depth Analysis of the Bench Press."
66. Tom Richardson, Pete Schmotzer, Jim Brandenburg, and William Kraemer, "Sports Performance Series: Improved Rebounding Performance through Strength Training."
67. "Coaches' Roundtable: Winter Conditioning: Off-Season Training for Football," 15 (quotation); "Coaches' Roundtable: Off-Season Strength and Conditioning for Basketball."
68. "Coaches' Roundtable: Winter Conditioning."
69. "Coaches' Roundtable: Off-Season Strength and Conditioning"; "Coaches' Roundtable: Prevention of Athletic Injuries through Strength Training and Conditioning."
70. "Coaches' Roundtable: Speed Development."
71. "Coaches' Roundtable: Power Clean."
72. Tom Baechle, "An Analysis of Attitudes Concerning the Topic of Establishing Certification Standards for Strength Coaches: A National Survey."
73. Kontor, "Editorial: Strength Coach Certification."
74. Baechle, "President's Message: The *NSCA Journal*," 52.
75. Thomas Baechle, "President's Message: Certification Update."
76. Thomas Baechle, "President's Message: Certified Strength and Conditioning Specialists Underway for 1985," 54.
77. Thomas Baechle, "President's Message: 9000 and Climbing."
78. John R. Olson and Gary R. Hunter, "A Comparison of 1974 and 1984 Player Sizes, and Maximal Strength and Speed Efforts for Division I NCAA Universities," 27. The average offensive lineman of 1974 weighed 239.55 pounds, bench pressed 296.66, squatted 381.38, and ran a 5.27 40-yard dash. The average offensive lineman of 1984 weighed 260.67 pounds, bench pressed 357.55, squatted 477.96, and ran a 5.08 forty-yard dash. Across all positions players added an average of 10 pounds of bodyweight, added 52 pounds to their bench press, 82 pounds to their squat, and 35 pounds to their power clean, and shaved 0.16 seconds off of their forty-yard dash.
79. McQuilkin, "'The World's Source,'" 70.
80. "Member Update."
81. The quotation about John Doe is attributed to Bill Allerheiligen, NSCA president from 2003 to 2006. McQuilkin, "'The World's Source,'" 71.
82. Thomas Baechle, "Certified Strength and Conditioning Specialists Program: Certification—Now and in the Future."

83. Ken Kontor, "Editorial: NSCA Five Year Plan: 1983-'88 and 1989-'94."

84. Jack McCallum, "Everybody's Doin' It."

85. Shelly McKenzie, *Getting Physical: The Rise of Fitness Culture in America*, 164.

86. Ibid., 168; Marc Stern, "The Fitness Movement and the Fitness Center Industry, 1960-2000," *Business and Economic History Online* 6 (2008): 11.

87. Ibid.; McKenzie, *Getting Physical*, 164.

88. Stern, "The Fitness Movement," 8, 83.

89. Jeff Copeland, "Are Health Clubs Risky?" *Newsweek*, February, 1986, 62, cited in McKenzie, *Getting Physical*, 176.

90. Karen Peterson, "Exercise at Your Own Risk," *Washington Post*, April 17, 1983, A1, cited in McKenzie, *Getting Physical*, 176.

91. McCallum, "Everbody's Doin' It," 83-84 (quotations); "Dr. Hans Kraus, 90, Originator of Sports Medicine in U.S., Dies," *New York Times*, March 7, 1996.

92. Heyward L. Nash, "Instructor Certification: Making Fitness Programs Safer?," 154-155.

93. Kraemer, interview with Shurley.

94. Ibid.; Kraemer, "Kinesiology Corner: Wrist Curls"; "Associate Editors," 3.

95. Kraemer, interview with Shurley; Ken Kontor, "Editorial: The Second Journal."

96. "Associate Editors—Gary Dudley and Jack Wilmore," 3.

97. "Jack Willmore, Hall of Honor—2008 Inductee," Department of Kinesiology and Health Education at the University of Texas at Austin (2015): https://education .utexas.edu/departments/kinesiology-health-education/about/hall-honor /past-inductees/jack-h-wilmore.

98. "Development Task Force"; Gina Kolata, "Scientist at Work: David Costill; A Career Spent in Study of Training and Exercise, Lap by Grueling Lap," *New York Times*, October 30, 2001 (quotations).

99. Baechle, "President's Message: The *NSCA Journal*," 52.

100. Kontor, "Editorial: The Second Journal," 14.

101. Ibid.

102. William J. Kraemer, "An Open Letter to the NSCA Membership," 42A.

103. William J. Kraemer, "The Second Journal: *Applied Sport Science Journal* Addition," 41-42.

104. Vern D. Seefeldt and Martha Ewing, "Youth Sports in America: An Overview"; Timeline: America's War on Drugs," NPR (April 2, 2007): http://www.npr.org /templates/ story/story.php?storyId=9252490.

105. William Oscar Johnson, "Steroids: A Problem of Huge Dimensions," 40. *Sports Illustrated* ran a host of articles on the use of anabolic steroids in sport during the 1980s and early 1990s. For more on the role that the magazine played in shaping public opinion and public policy toward the drugs, see Bryan E. Denham, "*Sports Illustrated*, the 'War on Drugs,' and the Anabolic Steroid Control Act of 1990"; and Terry Todd, "The Steroid Predicament."

106. Mcquilkin, "'The World's Source,'" 80.

107. "Three Men Indicted for Illegally Dispensing Steroids to College Athletes," *Los Angeles Times*, April 20, 1985.

108. "Kreis Sentenced," New York Times, November 28, 1985; Bill Lohmann, "Two Former Clemson University Coaches Caught Distributing Steroids," United Press International, March 12, 1985: https://www.upi.com/Archives/1985/03/12 /Two-former-Clemson-University-coaches-caught-distributing-steroids

-and/5922479451600/; Tony Barnhart, "Ex-S. Carolina Strength Coach Says He Knew about Steroid Use," *Chicago Tribune*, October 21, 1988.

109. Kraemer commented in a 1993 interview with McQuilkin that "most of the information that was gathered to get steroids to be made a trafficked drug was done from the emotionalism of sport and had little to do with the immediate impact of actual known side effects." Mike Stone echoed Kraemer's sentiments in a separate interview, saying that "the scientific literature doesn't always agree with what you read in the newspaper." McQuilkin, "'The World's Source,'" 79, 85–86.

110. "Position Statement: Use and Abuse of Anabolic Steroids," 27.

111. James E. Wright and Michael H. Stone, "NSCA Statement on Anabolic Drug Use: Literature Review," 45–59 (quotation on 54).

112. Johnson, "Steroids: A Problem of Huge Dimensions," 40 (quotation); Gordon S. White Jr., "NCAA Votes for Drug Testing," *New York Times*, January 15, 1986.

113. The other Oklahoma players who tested positive were offensive lineman Gary Bennett and defensive tackle David Shoemaker. David Dudley, an outside linebacker for the University of Arkansas, also tested positive. "Sooners' Bosworth Fails Steroids Test, Is Out of Bowl," *Los Angeles Times*, December 26, 1986.

114. Hilmer Anderson, "University of Miami Assistant Strength Coach Pat Jacobs Pleaded Guilty," *United Press International*, March 15, 1988: https://www .upi.com/Archives/1988/03/15/University-of-Miami-assistant-strength-coach -Pat-Jacobs-pleaded/4922574405200/; Jim Schachter, "Steroid Ring Broken; Ex-Olympian Held," *Los Angeles Times*, May 22, 1987.

115. "Official Document: Code of Ethics for the National Strength and Conditioning Association"; Boyd Epley, *The Path to Athletic Power: The Model Conditioning Program for Championship Performance*, 18.

116. Tommy Chaikin and Rick Telander, "The Nightmare of Steroids."

117. Kephart was NSCA president from June 1985 to July 1987. Chaikin alleges the steroid use ran from 1984 to 1987. Boyd Epley, "NSCA Timeline," The Quest for Victory: A History of Weight Training for Sports, H. J. Lutcher Stark Center for Physical Culture and Sports.

118. The other coaches indicted were defensive coordinator Thomas Gadd, defensive line coach James Washburn, and tight ends coach Thomas Kurucz. "Four Ex-Football Aides Indicted in South Carolina Steroid Case," *New York Times*, April 20, 1989.

119. "Coaches Plead Guilty to Steroid Charges," *United Press International*, June 2, 1989: https://www.upi.com/Archives/1989/06/02/Coaches-plead-guilty-to -steroid-charges/6719612763200/; "Sentences in Steroid Case," *New York Times*, August 11, 1989; Ron Heitzinger, "Getting Serious about Steroids," *Athletic Business*, September 1987, https://www.athleticbusiness.com/drugs-alcohol /getting-serious-about-steroids.html.

120. Mike Clark, "A Realistic Approach for Strength and Conditioning Coaches to Deal with Steroids."

121. Mauro G. Di Pasquale, "Anabolic Steroid Detection."

122. Dan Wathen, "Stopping Anabolic Steroid Abuse on a Zero Dollar Budget."

123. Ken Mannie, "Anabolic-Androgenic Steroids in the High School: The New Drug Crisis," 64–65.

124. William E. Buckley, Charles E. Yesalis, Karl E. Friedl, William A. Anderson,

Andrea L. Streit, James E. Wright, "Estimated Prevalence of Anabolic Steroid Use among Male High School Seniors."

125. "Perceptions of High School Strength Coaches Regarding Steroid Use: A Pilot Study."

126. Ibid., 70.

127. The updated position stand was published in 1993: J. E. Wright and Michael H. Stone, "Position Statement: Literature Review: Anabolic-Androgenic Steroid Use by Athletes."

128. "Steroid Education: What the Coach, Athlete, and Parent Need to Know about Anabolic Drugs: A Fact Sheet."

129. A copy of the packet can be found at http://kdhs.sesdweb.net/UserFiles/Servers /Server_143104/File/Departments/Athletics/Coach%20and%20Game/ Intro%20to%20Strength/Steriod_Awareness.pdf (accessed January 31, 2019).

130. "Official Document: The National Strength and Conditioning Association: Position Paper on Prepubescent Strength Training."

131. American Academy of Pediatrics Committee on Sports Medicine, "Weight Training and Weightlifting: Information for the Pediatrician."

132. One of the potential shoulder injuries was "a symptom complex termed 'weight lifter's shoulder.'" Ibid., 161.

133. Other articles in the early 1980s also cast doubt on the safety of weight training for adolescents. See, for example, Thomas A. Brady, Bernard R. Cahill, and Leslie M. Bodnar, "Weight-Training Related Injuries in the High School Athlete"; Eugene W. Brown and Richard G. Kimball, "Medical History Associated with Adolescent Powerlifting."

134. According to the AAP statement, "Prepubertal boys do not significantly improve strength or increase muscle mass in a weight training program because of insufficient circulating androgens." For the same reason, the paper also said: "Females after menarche may develop strength but do not significantly increase their muscle mass during weight training at any age unless they take anabolic steroids, a practice not recommended for youths or adults in sports." American Academy of Pediatrics Committee on Sports Medicine, "Weight Training and Weightlifting," 160.

135. "Official Document: The National Strength and Conditioning Association: Position Paper on Prepubescent Strength Training," 29.

136. Kraemer, interview with Shurley.

137. William J. Kraemer, "President's Message: Represent Your Profession"; William J. Kraemer, "President's Message: Bridging the Gap: Examining the Concept," 75 (quotation)–77.

138. William J. Kraemer, "President's Message: Education and Learning," 72–73.

139. Kraemer, interview with Shurley.

140. Ken Kontor, "Editorial: Why a National Strength and Conditioning Foundation?"

141. McQuilkin, "'The World's Source,'" 24, 109.

142. Ken Kontor, "Editorial: Why a National Strength and Conditioning Foundation?," 80–81.

143. The group received a grant from the Massachusetts Criminal Justice Training Council (MCJTC) to develop a course for use by officers in training. The group was hopeful that the program would serve as a model for law-enforcement

training programs across the country. Gary Goranson, "Conditioning Foundation Clinic: Experience Charts the Course."

144. Like the NSCA as a whole, the foundation grew quickly. Initial membership numbered only 125, but the group grew to 500 members within a year. Likewise, *Conditioning Instructor*'s initial issue was only four pages long but had increased to sixteen pages by the group's one-year anniversary. Gary Goranson, "Conditioning Instructor Expands the Foundation's Reach"; Ken Kontor, "Editorial: 1990 Executive Director's Report."

145. Kontor, "Editorial: 1990 Executive Director's Report."

146. In the second issue Kontor claimed that "weight rooms are being invaded" by both female and male athletes in a variety of sports and that more coaches and athletes were interested in the idea of strength training for female athletes. "Join the NSCA!"; Kontor, "Editorial," 2 (quotation).

147. National Federation of State High School Associations, "Sports Participation Survey" (n.d.): http://www.nfhs.org/ParticipationStatics/PDF/Participation%20 Survey%20History%20Book.pdf (accessed May 30, 2018).

148. National Collegiate Athletic Association, "Sports Sponsorship and Participation Rates Report, 1981–1982–2010–2011" (n.d.): http://www.ncaapublications.com /productdownloads/PR2012.pdf (accessed January 3, 2018); Welch Suggs, *A Place on the Team: The Triumph and Tragedy of Title IX*, 59.

149. Michael Stone, Kyle Pierce, William Sands, and Meg Stone, "Weightlifting: A Brief Overview."

150. John Fair, *Mr. America: The Tragic History of a Bodybuilding Icon*, 259–262.

151. In interviews with women at fitness centers in the early 2000s, sociologist Shari Dworkin noted that women often pointed to the physiques of female bodybuilders and expressed "explicit fear and repulsion" in regard to developing that look. Shari L. Dworkin, "'Holding Back': Negotiating a Glass Ceiling on Women's Muscular Strength."

152. McQuilkin, "'The World's Source,'" 40.

153. Thomas Baechle, "Profile of 1985 Certified Strength and Conditioning Specialists."

154. Jean Barrett Holloway, Denise Gater, Meg Ritchie, Lori Gilstrap, Lyne Stoessel, Jan Todd, Ken Kontor, Terry Todd, David Gater, Sue Hillman, Michael H. Stone, John Garhammer, and William Kraemer, "Strength Training for Female Athletes: A Position Paper: Part I"; Mcquilkin, "'The World's Source,'" 45.

155. According to the National Federation of State High School Associations, the number of girls competing at the high school level increased from 294,000 in 1972 to just over 1.8 million at the time that the Women's Committee was formed in 1986. Vern D. Seefeldt and Martha Ewing, "Youth Sports in America: An Overview," 5.

156. Holloway et al. "Strength Training for Female Athletes," 43.

157. Ritchie held the absolute (including indoor and outdoor track) NCAA records in both the shot put and the discus from 1981 until 2016, when her shot put record was broken. Her discus record, however, still stands. McQuilkin, "'The World's Source,'" 47; Doug Gillon, "Meg Ritchie's Long-Playing Records Tell a Tale of Power and Prowess," *Sunday Herald* (Glasgow, Scotland), June 11, 2014: http:// www.heraldscotland.com/sport/13165012.Meg_Ritchie_s_long_playing _records_tell_a_tale_of_power_and_prowess/; "Collegiate Track and Field

Records"; United States Track and Field and Cross Country Coaches Association, "USTFCCCA Collegiate Track and Field Records" (January 28, 2019): http://www.ustfccca.org/records-lists/ustfccca-collegiate-records.

158. Meg Ritchie (Stone), interview with Jan Todd, Las Vegas, July 10, 2009: The Quest for Victory: A History of Weight Training for Sports, H. J. Lutcher Stark Center for Physical Culture and Sports.

159. McQuilkin, "'The World's Source,'" 45; Holloway et al., "Strength Training for Female Athletes," 44.

160. Holloway et al., "Strength Training for Female Athletes," 43–51.

161. Jean Barrett Holloway, Denise Gater, Meg Ritchie, Lori Gilstrap, Lyne Stoessel, Jan Todd, Ken Kontor, Terry Todd, David Gater, Sue Hillman, Michael H. Stone, John Garhammer, and William Kraemer, "Strength Training for Female Athletes: A Position Paper: Part II," 30.

162. William J. Kraemer, "Women in the NSCA"; William J. Kraemer, "President's Message: Some Final Thoughts and Thank You."

163. Kraemer, "Women in the NSCA," 84.

164. Jan Todd, Dorothy Lovett, and Terry Todd, "The Status of Women in the Strength and Conditioning Profession," 35.

165. As examples, see Carol Fleming Gyorgyfalvy, "Meet the Strength and Conditioning Professional"; Christine Woods, "The Female Athlete: Overcoming Concerns toward Weight Training"; Denis A. Ference, "Motivation: A Modified Awards Program for Women"; Stephanie Armitage-Johnson, L. Brandon, Vickie Cass, Meg Ritchie, Lynne Stoessel-Ross, and Beth Stringham, "Roundtable: Women Discuss Career Expectations and Experiences."

166. Armitage-Johnson et al. "Roundtable: Women Discuss Career Expectations and Experiences."

167. It is worth mentioning that the most contemporaneous survey of members holding the CSCS credential, performed in 1991, revealed that less than 10 percent of certified individuals were female. McQuilkin, "'The World's Source,'" 47 (quotation); Thomas R. Baechle and Roger W. Earle, "Survey: Does Being CSCS-Certified Make a Difference?"

168. Bruno Pauletto, "President's Message: An Association at a Crossroads."

169. Ken Kontor, "Editorial: Read Labels Carefully," 84.

170. "NSCA Leaders Share Their Vision for the Future," 2.

171. On restructuring of the national office, see Bruno Pauletto's articles: "President's Message: The 'New' NSCA"; "President's Message: What a Meeting!"; and "President's Message: Welcome Members!"

172. McQuilkin, "'The World's Source,'" 89–91.

173. At the end of 1994 Maelu Fleck, who would assume the role of NSCA executive director following Kontor's resignation, commented that "we've had a heck of a time tracking membership over the past few years, with all sorts of figures being thrown around . . . now we've reached a true 10,000+ membership." Ibid.; "NSCA Ranks Continue to Grow," 2 (quotation).

174. Bruno Pauletto, "President's Message: An Association on the Move."

175. Kraemer, interview with Shurley; "NSCA History: The 1990s" (n.d.): https://www.nsca.com/About-Us/History/ (accessed June 1, 2018).

176. "NSCA History: The 1990s."

177. Bruno Pauletto, "President's Message: Membership Has Its Privileges."

178. "NSCA Joins Forces to Serve NSCA Members: Human Kinetics to Publish *NSCA Journal.*"

179. Pauletto, "President's Message: Welcome Members!," 3.

180. Boyd Epley, "College Strength and Conditioning Coaches Committee Update," 8.

181. "Changes Ahead for Publication; NSCA, Foundation to Merge."

182. "Personal Training: A Field in Progress."

183. Ibid.; "Changes Ahead," 8.

184. A survey of 1,700 members showed that 18 percent listed their primary responsibility as "educator," with 16 percent other (including chiropractor, registered dietitian, physician, wellness coordinator, etc.), 11 percent athletic trainer, 10 percent exercise physiologist, and only 8 percent strength and conditioning coach. For secondary job responsibility, 39 percent responded strength and conditioning coach, 33 percent educator, 27 percent personal trainer, 22 percent sport coach. "Survey Results Plan 1994 Conference."

185. Weakness, Stone asserted, would be caused by factionalism among the many professions with claims inside the tent of strength and conditioning. The NSCA would be undermined if those factions put their particular interests ahead of the welfare of the organization as a whole. Mike Stone, "President's Message."

186. Mike Stone, "President's Message: Sports, Coaches and the NSCA"; "NSCA Member Profile"; "Member Profile"; "NSCA Members: A Body of Strength!"

187. Donald Chu, "President's Message: To the Membership."

188. Dan Wathen, "President's Message: Special Interests," 3.

189. "About the CSCCa," CSCCa.org (n.d.): https://www.cscca.org/about (accessed December 4, 2016).

190. McQuilkin, "'The World's Source,'" 25–26.

CHAPTER 7: STRENGTH COACHING IN THE TWENTY-FIRST CENTURY

1. Dan Wathen, "From the President: The Future," 2.

2. For example. "NSCA Leaders Share Their Vision for the Future"; Boyd Epley, "College Strength and Conditioning Coaches Committee Update"; Mike Stone, "President's Message."

3. Wathen, "From the President," 2.

4. Letter to Karri Baker from Chuck Stiggins, March 9, 2000, CSCCa archives.

5. Chuck Stiggins, letter to strength and conditioning coaches, n.d., CSCCa archives.

6. Chuck Stiggins, "23 Coaches in Attendance at CSCCa Foundation Meeting," CSCCa archives.

7. Boyd Epley, *The Path to Athletic Power: The Model Conditioning Program for Championship Performance*, 302.

8. Chuck Stiggins, "Invitation to Join the CSCCa," January 9, 2001, CSCCa archives.

9. Epley, *The Path to Athletic Power*, 302.

10. Dennis Read, "CSCC Weighs In"; Collegiate Strength and Conditioning Coaches' Association, "About the CSCCa" (n.d.): http://cscca.org/about (accessed January 10, 2017).

11. Read, "CSCC Weighs In," 12.

12. "About the CSCCa."

13. Research in the field of exercise science as a whole exploded during the last years

of the twentieth century. As an example, 655 exercise-related journal manuscripts were published in 1981; that number had risen to 3,895 by 1992. Charles Tipton, "Exercise Physiology, Part II: A Contemporary Historical Perspective," 405.

14. Read, "CSCC Weighs In," 12 (quotation), 14.

15. The average annual salary for the cohort of strength coaches was $47,416. C. Dwayne Massey, John Vincent, and Mark Maneval, "Job Analysis of College Division I-A Football Strength and Conditioning Coaches."

16. Tipton, "Exercise Physiology, Part II," 405.

17. David L. Durrell, Thomas J. Pujol, and Jeremy T. Barnes, "A Survey of the Scientific Data and Training Methods Utilized by Collegiate Strength and Conditioning Coaches."

18. The replies of the collegiate strength coaches indicated that 93 percent got information from colleagues, 77 percent cited clinics, 74 percent utilized information from strength coaches employed at the professional level, 73 percent used the NSCA's text, and 64 percent cited *Training and Conditioning*. Ibid., 370.

19. "About," (n.d.): http://training-conditioningceu.com/about (accessed January 5, 2018).

20. Jan Todd and Jason Shurley, "Building American Muscle: A Brief History of Barbells, Dumbbells, and Pulley Machines."

21. "First Nautilus Center to Open Soon," *Washington Post*, February 23, 1981, 28; Elaine Louie, "Working Out," *New York Times*, August 30, 1981, 238.

22. Candice Galik, "Link by Link: Understanding the Closed Kinetic Chain." More information on the contributions of Gary Gray are available on his Gray Institute website (n.d.): https://www.grayinstitute.com/ (accessed December 31, 2018).

23. Arthur Steindler, *Kinesiology of the Human Body under Normal and Pathological Conditions*.

24. Galik, "Link by Link," 4; Susan G. Beckham and Michael Harper, "Functional Training: Fad or Here to Stay?"

25. For example, see Michael L. Voight and Gray Cook, "Clinical Application of Closed Kinetic Chain Exercise"; Lynn Snyder-Mackler, "Scientific Rationale and Physiological Basis for the Use of Closed Kinetic Chain Exercise in the Lower Extremity"; Rod A. Harter, "Clinical Rationale for Closed Kinetic Chain Activities in Functional Testing and Rehabilitation of Ankle Pathologies"; Rebecca Kern-Steiner, Helen S. Washecheck and Douglas D. Kelsey, "Strategy of Exercise Prescription Using an Unloading Technique for Functional Rehabilitation of an Athlete with an Inversion Ankle Sprain"; Paul A. Borsa, Eric L. Sauers, and Scott M. Lephart, "Functional Training for the Restoration of Dynamic Stability in the PCL Injured Knee"; John McMullen and Timothy L. Uhl, "A Kinetic Chain Approach to Shoulder Rehabilitation."

26. Quoted in Galik, "Link by Link," 4.

27. According to Durrell et al. (A Survey of the Scientific Data, 371), by the early 2000s most strength coaches were using training methods with their teams that could be considered "functional" in that they were ground-based, performed at the speed of sport, and/or mimicked sporting movements. Their survey showed that 90 percent of strength coaches utilized plyometrics, 85 percent used variations on the Olympic lifts, and 54 percent said they used loaded exercises that "mimicked skilled movements." Less than half (43 percent) used

the cam-style Nautilus-like machines, while 81 percent used pulley machines and plate-loaded machines, like those produced by the Hammer Strength company.

28. Alan M. Klein, *Little Big Men: Bodybuilding Subculture and Gender Construction*; Bryan E. Denham, "Masculinities in Hardcore Bodybuilding"; Jesper Andreasson and Thomas Johansson, "The Fitness Revolution: Historical Transformations in the Global Gym and Fitness Culture."

29. As examples, see Dan Cipriani and Ryan Vermillion, "New Steps in Knee Rehab"; Gray Cook and Keith Fields, "Functional Training for the Torso"; Vern Gambetta and Mike Clark, "A Formula for Function"; Steven Conca and Lee Burton, "Workouts for Throw Outs."

30. Galik, "Link by Link," 8, 11; Robert A. Panariello, "The Closed Kinetic Chain in Strength Training."

31. Vern Gambetta, "Strength in Motion," 12.

32. John P. Jesse, "Misuse of Strength Development Programs in Athletic Training."

33. In that study by Rasch and Morehouse, subjects trained for six weeks on isotonic or isometric exercises, with both producing gains in hypertrophy and strength. When subjects were tested in a novel position relative to the position in which they had trained, however, little to no improvement in strength was observed. This led the authors to conclude that the strength gains observed in the familiar position were more closely associated with skill acquisition rather than with muscular adaptation. Philip J. Rasch and Laurence E. Morehouse, "Effect of Static and Dynamic Exercises on Muscular Strength and Hypertrophy."

34. Vern Gambetta and Gary Gray, "Following a Functional Path." See also Juan Carlos Santana, *Functional Training: Breaking the Bonds of Traditionalism*; Michael Boyle, *Functional Training for Sports*.

35. Daniel Kunitz, *Lift: Fitness Culture from Naked Greeks and Acrobats to Jazzercise and Ninja Warriors*; Burt Helm, "Do Not Cross CrossFit."

36. Kunitz, *Lift*, 260–261; Jessie Cameron Herz, *Learning to Breathe Fire: The Rise of CrossFit and the Primal Future of Fitness*, 20–25.

37. Rebecca Dube, "No Puke, No Pain, No Gain," *Globe and Mail* (Toronto, Ontario), January 11, 2008, https://www.theglobeandmail.com/life /no-puke-no-pain---no-gain/article666270/.

38. A thruster is a variation on the Olympic clean and jerk lift. It entails a barbell front squat from which the lifter jumps and throws the bar overhead at arms' length. Hertz, *Learning to Breathe Fire*, 21.

39. Quoted in Kunitz, *Lift*, 261.

40. The workouts listed are for April 13–15, 2017. A burpee box jump entails dropping to the floor in a push-up position, performing a push-up, and then immediately jumping onto a 24-inch-high box. The height of the box can be varied depending upon ability, as can the weight added to the run or utilized for the clean exercise. "WODs" (n.d.): https://www.crossfit.com/workout/ (accessed April 19, 2017).

41. Glassman has also gone so far as to assert: "Nature will punish the specialist. I want to be a jack of all trades and a master of none. Specialization is for insects . . . anyone who is wise at all realizes that being a specialist represents a compromised position." Grant Stoddard, "Inside the Cult of Crossfit," x; Terry Peters, "The Future of Fitness; Cross Fit Philosophy Changing the Way We Workout," *North Shore (British Columbia) News*, August 17, 2008, 15.

42. "Official Document: The National Strength and Conditioning Association Position Paper on Prepubescent Strength Training"; Lyle Michelli, "The Prepubescent Athlete: Physiological and Orthopedic Considerations for Strengthening Prepubescent Athletes"; Julie Schafer, "Prepubescent and Adolescent Weight Training: Is it Safe? Is it Beneficial?"; Paul M. Pitton, "Prepubescent Strength Training: The Effects of Resistance Training on Strength Gains in Children."

43. Grant M. Hill, "A Study of Sport Specialization in Midwest High Schools and Perceptions of Coaches regarding the Effects of Specialization on High School Athletes and Athletics Programs."

44. Grant M. Hill and Jeffrey Simons, "A Study of Sport Specialization in High School Athletics," 1.

45. Smith cites swimmers like Sylvia Ruuska, Chris von Saltza, and Donna de Varona who became specialized in swimming due to a lack of opportunities to participate in other sports. In the decades before Title IX women's interscholastic teams often did not exist, so the few opportunities that were available to those athletes came in the form of AAU competitions in swimming, gymnastics, or track and field. Maureen M. Smith, "Early Sport Specialization: A Historical Perspective."

46. Robert Pruter, *The Rise of American High School Sports and the Search for Control, 1880–1930*, 322.

47. As examples, see Michael Conroy, "The Use of Periodization in the High School Setting"; Ollie Whaley, "A High School Weight Training Curriculum Model"; Gregory J. Renfro, "Summer Plyometric Training for Football and Its Effect on Speed and Agility"; Richard B. Summers, "Complex Training at Ponderosa High."

48. Vern Gambetta, "All-Season Training."

49. According to demographic data cited by the equipment manufacturer Rally Fitness, as of 2014 nearly two-thirds of CrossFit adherents were born after 1980. "Latest CrossFit Market Research Data," November 28, 2014: https://rallyfitness .com/blogs/news/16063884-latest-crossfit-market-research-data).

50. "What Is CrossFit?" (n.d.): https://www.crossfit.com/what-is-crossfit (accessed February 2, 2017); "American College of Sports Medicine Position Stand: The Recommended Quantity and Quality of Exercise for Developing and Maintaining Cardiorespiratory and Muscular Fitness in Healthy Adults."

51. In a 2013 article in *Inc.* magazine, author Burt Helm asserted that both Berger and his social media colleague Russ Greene, as well as Glassman, believe the ACSM "has it in for CrossFit." Helm, "Do Not Cross CrossFit," 114; Russell Berger, "Prescribe What to Whom and Why?" *CrossFit Journal*, March 15, 2016: https://journal.crossfit.com/article/prescribe-what-to-whom-and-why-2; Lon Kilgore, "Exercise Is Medicine: Imprecision and Impracticality," *CrossFit Journal*, January 31, 2016: https://journal.crossfit.com/article/eim-kilgore-2; Andrea Maria Cecil, "Lines of Coke," *CrossFit Journal*, February 10, 2016, https://journal.crossfit.com/article/lines-of-coke-2.

52. "About: What Is Exercise Is Medicine?" (n.d.): http://www.exerciseismedicine .org/support_page.php/about/ (accessed April 14, 2017).

53. "Exercise Is Medicine Public Presentation" (n.d.): http://www.exerciseismedicine .org/assets/page_documents/EIM%20Public%20Presentation_2016_07_07.pdf (accessed April 14, 2017).

54. Michael M. Smith, Allan J. Sommer, Brooke E. Starkoff, and Steven T. Devor,

"CrossFit-Based High-Intensity Power Training Improves Maximal Aerobic Fitness and Body Composition."

55. Grant Davis, "Is CrossFit Killing Us?" *Outside* (November 4, 2013): https://www.outsideonline.com/1928481/crossfit-killing-us.

56. Warren Cornwall, "Crossing Swords with CrossFit," *Outside* (December 19, 2013): https://www.outsideonline.com/1928106/crossing-swords-crossfit.

57. "Erratum," *Journal of Strength and Conditioning Research* 29, no. 10 (October 2015): e1.

58. Anthony Dominic, "NSCA Article Included False Injury Data about CrossFit, Judge Rules," *Club Industry*, September 27, 2016: https://www.clubindustry.com/commercial-clubs/nsca-article-included-false-injury-data-about-crossfit-judge-rules.

59. Nina Mandell, "CrossFit Sues over Study That Alleges High Injury Rate," *USA Today*, July 11, 2014: http://ftw.usatoday.com/2014/07/crossfit-sues-over-study-that-alleges-high-injury-rate.

60. Nicole Carroll, "CrossFit Trainer Education and Certification: New Programs and a New Structure," *CrossFit Journal*, July 2014: https://library.crossfit.com/free/pdf/CFJ_2014_06_Education_13NCarroll.pdf.

61. "CrossFit Level 1 Certificate Course" (n.d.): https://training.crossfit.com/level-one (accessed February 3, 2019); "Exam Fees," in *NSCA Certification Handbook*, 18; "Exam Costs" (n.d.): https://www.acsm.org/get-stay-certified/stay-certified (accessed April 14, 2017).

62. "CrossFit Level 1 Certificate Course," (n.d.): https://training.crossfit.com/level-one (accessed February 3, 2019); "Recertification," in *NSCA Certification Handbook*, 26.

63. "Introduction," in *NSCA Certification Handbook*, 6.

64. "Summary of Certification Statistics" (n.d.): https://www.acsm.org/get-stay-certified/get-certified/cert-stats (accessed April 14, 2017).

65. The data are attributed to a Quantcast Analytics analysis of figures provided through CrossFit.com. "The Demographics of CrossFit" (October 3, 2013): http://www.everylastrep.com/fitness-for-beginners/infographic-crossfit-demographics; "Latest CrossFit Market Research Data" (November 28, 2014): https://rallyfitness.com/blogs/news/16063884-latest-crossfit-market-research-data.

66. Herz, *Learning to Breathe Fire*, 69.

67. Ibid.; Melisa Angelone, "Trading Skinny for Strong: Alexa Fourlis" (n.d.): https://games.crossfit.com/article/trading-skinny-strong-alexa-fourlis; Jamie Toland, "CrossFit Girl Power," *Box* (September 6, 2015): http://www.theboxmag.com/blog/crossfit-girl-power-11205 (accessed April 14, 2017).

68. Karisa D. Laskowski and William P. Ebben, "Profile of Women Collegiate Strength and Conditioning Coaches," 3490.

69. C. Dwayne Massey and John Vincent, "A Job Analysis of Major College Female Strength and Conditioning Coaches."

70. Laskowski and Ebben, "Profile of Women Collegiate Strength and Conditioning Coaches," 3488.

71. Marshall J. Magnusen and Deborah J. Rhea, "Division I Athletes' Attitudes toward and Preferences for Male and Female Strength and Conditioning Coaches."

72. Monica L. Reynolds, Lynda B. Ransdell, Shelly M. Lucas, Linda M. Petlichkoff,

and Yong Gao, "An Examination of Current Practices and Gender Differences in Strength and Conditioning in a Sample of Varsity High School Athletic Programs," 180.

73. Walter R. Thompson, "Worldwide Survey Reveals Fitness Trends for 2007."
74. Walter R. Thompson, "Worldwide Survey of Fitness Trends for 2018."
75. Thompson, "Worldwide Survey Reveals Fitness Trends for 2007," 10–11.
76. Walter R. Thompson, "Worldwide Survey of Fitness Trends for 2013," 12.
77. Walter R. Thompson, "Worldwide Survey of Fitness Trends for 2015"; Walter R. Thompson, "Worldwide Survey of Fitness Trends for 2018."
78. Walter R. Thompson's surveys: "Worldwide Survey, 2007," "Worldwide Survey, 2013," "Worldwide Survey, 2015," "Worldwide Survey, 2016," "Worldwide Survey Reveals Fitness Trends for 2008," "Worldwide Survey Reveals Fitness Trends for 2009," "Worldwide Study Reveals Fitness Trends for 2010," "Worldwide Study Reveals Fitness Trends for 2011," "Worldwide Study Reveals Fitness Trends for 2012," "Now Trending: Worldwide Survey of Fitness Trends for 2014," "Worldwide Survey of Fitness Trends for 2018."
79. Thompson, "Worldwide Survey, 2007," 11.
80. Thompson, "Worldwide Survey, 2018," 18.
81. Thomas S. Kuhn, *The Structure of Scientific Revolutions*.
82. "American College of Sports Medicine Position Stand: The Recommended Quantity and Quality of Exercise for Developing and Maintaining Cardiorespiratory and Muscular Fitness in Healthy Adults," 265–274. See also Carol Krucoff, "The New Iron Age: When Aerobics Is Not Enough," *Washington Post*, October 16, 1990, Z10; Sharon Peters, "Aerobics Isn't Enough, Experts Say You Have to Pump Iron," *USA Today*, July 18, 1991, 10C.
83. "Performance Enhancement Specialization" (n.d.): https://www.nasm.org/performance-training/performance-enhancement-specialization; "Strength Coach Certification" (n.d.): https://www.ncsf.org/examprep/strengthcoach/; "Strength and Conditioning Certification" (n.d.): https://www.issaonline.edu/certification/strength-and-conditioning-certification/; "Certified Functional Strength Coach" (n.d.): http://www.certifiedfsc.com/; "FAQs" (n.d.): http://www.certifiedfsc.com/faq (all accessed April 19, 2017).
84. Andrew Greif, "Multiple Ducks Football Players Hospitalized After Grueling Workouts," *Oregonian*, January 16, 2017, http://www.oregonlive.com/ducks/index.ssf/2017/01/oregon_ducks_workouts_hospital.html; Chantel Jennings, "Report: Three Oregon Football Players Hospitalized after 'Grueling' Workouts," ESPN.com, January 17, 2017, http://www.espn.com/college-football/story/_/id/18491292/three-oregon-ducks-football-players-hospitalized-strength-conditioning-workouts.
85. Jon Solomon and Dennis Dodd, "The Unregulated World of Strength Coaches and College Football's Killing Season" (CBSSports.com, March 10, 2017): http://www.cbssports.com/college-football/news/the-unregulated-world-of-strength-coaches-and-college-footballs-killing-season/.
86. Raymond Vanholder, Mehmet Sukru Sever, Ekrem Erek, and Norbert Lamiere, "Rhabdomyolysis."
87. "Strength & Conditioning Coach Certification" (USTFCCCA) (n.d.): http://www.ustfccca.org/track-and-field-academy/strength-conditioning-specialist-certification (accessed April 19, 2017).

88. Charnele Kempner and Kristen Matha, "NCAA Division I Bylaw 11 (Conduct and Employment of Athletics Personnel)" (NCAA.org), April 24, 2014: http://www.ncaa.org/sites/default/files/DI%20Conduct%20and%20Employment%20of%20Athletics%20Personnel%20ONLINE.ppt; "NCAA Division I Certification Standard for Strength and Conditioning Coaches" (NSCA.com, n.d.): https://www.nsca.com/media-room/news-and-announcements/ncaa-faq/ (accessed April 19, 2017).

89. Solomon and Dodd, "The Unregulated World," para. 42.

90. Douglas J. Casa, Scott A. Anderson, Lindsay Baker, et al., "The Inter-Association Task Force for Preventing Sudden Death in Collegiate Conditioning Sessions: Best Practice Recommendations."

91. Quoted in Solomon and Dodd, "The Unregulated World," para. 12.

92. Wes Rucker, "Butch Jones 1 on 1, Part Two" (GoVols247.com, December 22, 2012): https://247sports.com/college/tennessee/Article/govols247-1-on-1-Tennessee-Vols-Butch-Jones-Part-Two-107976/.

93. Casa et. al., "The Inter-Association Task Force," 477.

94. Stan Berkowitz, "Iowa Strength Coach Is Highest Paid and Set to Make More," *USA Today*, December 8, 2016: https://www.usatoday.com/story/sports/ncaaf/bigten/2016/12/08/iowa-strength-coach-chris-doyle/95144696/; "2016 NCAA Football Strength Coach Salaries," *USA Today* (n.d.): http://sports.usatoday.com/ncaa/salaries/football/strength (accessed April 20, 2017).

95. "Iowa Players Battling Muscle Disorder" (ESPN.com, January 26, 2011): http://www.espn.com/college-football/news/story?id=6061650; Marc Morehouse, "100 Squats, 17 Minutes, Rhabdomyolysis," *Gazette* (Cedar Rapids, Iowa), January 26, 2011: http://www.thegazette.com/2011/01/26/100-squats-17-minutes-rhabdomyolysis.

96. Athletes from other sports have also been hospitalized for performing similar workouts in recent years. As an example, in August 2016 eight volleyball players from Texas Woman's University were hospitalized after performing fitness testing that included completion of a certain number of repetitions during a specific amount of time. Azia Branson, "Texas Woman's Volleyball Coach Resigns; Move Unrelated to Ill Players," *Fort Worth Star Telegram*, August 27, 2016, http://www.star-telegram.com/news/local/article98330552.html. See also Todd Jones, "Rhabdomyolysis Laid Low Six Athletes," *Columbus (Ohio) Dispatch*, March 9, 2013, http://www.dispatch.com/content/stories/sports/2013/03/09/illness-laid-low-6-athletes.html; Tony Adame, "Six Butler Softball Players Treated for Skeletal Muscle Condition after Workouts," *Wichita (Kansas) Eagle*, August 17, 2015: http://www.kansas.com/sports/college/state-college-sports/article31327925.html; Katie Thomas, "Muscle Injuries Rattle an Oregon High School," *New York Times*, August 23, 2010.

97. "Chris Doyle: Director, Strength & Conditioning" (HawkeyeSports.com, n.d.): http://www.hawkeyesports.com/coaches.aspx?rc=1420 (accessed April 21, 2017).

98. Parker Gabriel, "Husker Football: Frost: 'Hospitalized Players My Responsibility,'" *Lincoln (NE) Journal Star*, January 30, 2018: https://journalstar.com/sports/huskers/football/frost-hospitalized-players-my-responsibility-moos-says-no-suspensions-for/article_9e604ce5-cf8e-5340-9ed2-c2e5be35c850.html.

99. "Zach Duval: Head Football Strength and Conditioning Coach" (Huskers .com, n.d.): http://www.huskers.com/ViewArticle.dbml?DB_OEM _ID=100&ATCLID=211689071 (accessed February 3, 2019).

100. Gabriel, "Husker Football."

101. Kelley King, "Wild Out West," *Sports Illustrated*, November 1, 2004.

102. S. L. Price, "Urban Meyer," *Sports Illustrated*, December 7, 2009.

103. Wright Thompson, "Urban Meyer Will Be Home for Dinner," *ESPN the Magazine*, August 20,2012: http://www.espn.com/espn/otl/story/_/id/8239451 /ohio-state-coach-urban-meyer-new-commitment-balancing-work-family-life.

104. Gabriel, "Husker Football," para. 21 (quotation); Sam McKewon, "Two Nebraska Football Players Hospitalized, Treated after Offseason Workout," *Omaha (NE) World-Herald*, January 30, 2018: https://www.omaha.com/huskers/football /two-nebraska-football-players-hospitalized-treated-after-offseason-workout /article_d5929674-53a7-5d90-803e-6b4e9205ee60.html.

105. William J. Kraemer, "The Second Journal: *Applied Sport Science Journal* Addition."

106. Gregory R. Waryasz, Alan H. Daniels, Joseph A. Gil, Vladimir Suric, and Craig P. Eberson, "NCAA Strength and Conditioning Coach Demographics, Current Practice Trends, and Common Injuries of Athletes during Strength and Conditioning Sessions," 1190–1191.

107. David L. Durrell, Thomas J. Pujol, and Jeremy T. Barnes, "A Survey of the Scientific Data and Training Methods Utilized by Collegiate Strength and Conditioning Coaches."

108. Anthony R. Anzell, Jeffrey A. Potteiger, William J. Kraemer, and Sango Otieno, "Changes in Height, Body Weight, and Body Composition in American Football Players from 1942 to 2011."

109. Ibid., 282; Cynthia L. Ogden, Cheryl D. Fryar, Margaret D. Carroll, and Katherine M. Flegal, "Mean Body Weight, Height, and Body Mass Index, United States 1960–2002."

110. John R. Olson and Gary R. Hunter, "A Comparison of 1974 and 1984 Player Sizes, and Maximal Strength and Speed Efforts for Division I NCAA Universities."

111. Tony Manfred, "One GIF That Shows How NFL Players Are Exploding in Size," BusinessInsider.com, July 29, 2014: https://www.businessinsider.com.au /nfl-player-size-over-time-2014-7.

112. Anzell et al., "Changes in Height, Body Weight, and Body Composition," 282.

113. David Epstein, *The Sports Gene: Inside the Science of Extraordinary Athletic Performance*, 117–118.

114. "Drug Schedules," DEA.gov (n.d.): https://www.dea.gov/drug-scheduling (accessed April 21, 2017); Bryan E. Denham, "*Sports Illustrated*, the 'War on Drugs,' and the Anabolic Steroid Control Act of 1990: A Study in Agenda Building and Political Timing."

BIBLIOGRAPHY

ARCHIVAL COLLECTIONS

Collegiate Strength and Conditioning Coaches Association Archives (CSCCa), Provo, UT.

H. J. Lutcher Stark Center for Physical Culture and Sports and Todd-McLean Physical Culture Collection at the University of Texas at Austin
        Robert Hoffman and Alda Ketterman Collection
        Harold Weiss Collection
        Terry and Jan Todd Collection
        Joe and Betty Weider Collection
        Ottley R. Coulter Collection
        Thomas L. DeLorme Collection

BOOKS, PAMPHLETS, ARTICLES, JOURNALS, MAGAZINES

"Abstracts from the World of Strength and Conditioning." *NSCA Journal* 2.4 (1980): 48–49.

Adams, Mark. *Mr. America: How Muscular Millionaire Bernarr Macfadden Transformed the Nation through Sex, Salad, and the Ultimate Starvation Diet.* New York: Harper, 2009.

Aden, Roger C. *Huskerville: A Story of Nebraska Football, Fans, and the Power of Place.* Jefferson, NC: McFarland, 2008.

Alexander, John F., Clare J. Drake, Peter J. Reichenbach, and James B. Haddow. "Effect of Strength Development on Speed of Shooting of Varsity Ice Hockey Players." *Research Quarterly* 35.2 (May 1964): 101–106.

Alger, Horatio. *Ragged Dick; or, Street Life in New York with the Boot Blacks.* New York: Signet Classics, 2005.

Algra, Bruce. "An In-Depth Analysis of the Bench Press." *NSCA Journal* 4.5 (1982): 6–13.

Allen, Harvey. "Weight Lifting in the Association." *Journal of Physical Education* 34.3 (January–February 1937): 48–49.

Alley, Louise E. "Barbells on Campus: State University of Iowa." *Strength & Health* (June 1960): 24–25, 52.

American Academy of Pediatrics Committee on Sports Medicine, "Weight Training and Weightlifting: Information for the Pediatrician." *Physician and Sportsmedicine* 11.3 (1983): 157–161.

American Association for Health, Physical Education, and Recreation. *Weight Training in Sports and Physical Education.* Ed. Frank Sills, Laurence E. Morehouse, and Thomas DeLorme. Washington, DC: AAHPER, 1962.

"American College of Sports Medicine Position Stand: The Recommended Quantity and Quality of Exercise for Developing and Maintaining Cardiorespiratory and Muscular Fitness in Healthy Adults." *Medicine and Science in Sports and Exercise* 22.2 (April 1990): 265–274.

Anderson, Bob. "Conditioning Report: Static Stretching for Athletes." *NSCA Journal* 1.6 (1979): 34–36.

Anderson, E. H. "Heavy Resistance, Low Repetition Exercises in the Restoration of Function in the Knee Joint." *Nova Scotia Medical Bulletin* 25.12 (December 1946): 397–400.

Andreasson, Jesper, and Thomas Johansson. "The Fitness Revolution: Historical Transformations in the Global Gym and Fitness Culture." *Sport Science Review* 23.3–4 (2014): 91–112.

Anzell, Anthony R., Jeffrey A. Potteiger, William J. Kraemer, and Sango Otieno. "Changes in Height, Body Weight, and Body Composition in American Football Players from 1942 to 2011." *Journal of Strength and Conditioning Research* 27.2 (2013): 277–284.

Armitage-Johnson, Stephanie, L. Brandon, Vickie Cass, Meg Ritchie, Lynne Stoessel-Ross, and Beth Stringham. "Roundtable: Women Discuss Career Expectations and Experiences." *NSCA Journal* 15.2 (1993): 49–58.

Armstrong, Tim. *American Bodies. Cultural Histories of the Physique.* Sheffield, UK: Sheffield Academic Press, 1996.

Artelt, Gertrude. "Is Strength Masculine and Weakness Feminine?" *Strength* 8 (December 1923): 54.

Assael, Shaun. *Steroid Nation: Juiced Home Run Totals, Anti-Aging Miracles, and a Hercules in Every High School.* New York: ESPN Books, 2007.

"Associate Editors." *NSCA Journal* 4.4 (1983): 3.

"Associate Editors—Gary Dudley and Jack Wilmore." *NSCA Journal* 4.5 (1982): 3.

Bachtell, Dick. "Weight Training in the Service." *Strength & Health* (May 1943): 20–21, 35–36.

Bacon, Jules. "What Can You Do?" *Strength & Health* (September 1941): 19, 44–46.

———. "What Can You Do?" *Strength & Health* (October 1941): 19, 39–41.

Baechle, Thomas. "An Analysis of Attitudes concerning the Topic of Establishing Certification Standards for Strength Coaches: A National Survey." *NSCA Journal* 3.1 (1981): 34–37.

———. "Certified Strength and Conditioning Specialists Program: Certification—Now and in the Future." *NSCA Journal* 8.1 (1986): 54–56.

———. "President's Message: 9000 and Climbing." *NSCA Journal* 7.2 (1985): 60.

———. "President's Message: Certification Update." *NSCA Journal* 5.6 (1984): 50.

———. "President's Message: Certified Strength and Conditioning Specialists Underway for 1985." *NSCA Journal* 6.5 (1984): 54, 66.

———. "President's Message: The *NSCA Journal* and Certification: Tools for a Stronger Association." *NSCA Journal* 5.5 (1983): 52.

———. "President's Message: Opportunities for Greater Participation: Dual Responsibility." *NSCA Journal* 6.1 (1984): 50.

———. "Profile of 1985 Certified Strength and Conditioning Specialists." *NSCA Bulletin*
8.6 (1987): 42A.

Baechle, Thomas R., and Roger W. Earle, eds. *Essentials of Strength Training and
Conditioning*. Champaign, IL: Human Kinetics, 2008.

———. "Survey: Does Being CSCS-Certified Make a Difference?" *NSCA Journal* 14.4
(1992): 23–27.

Baillie, David. "Barbells on Campus: Springfield College." *Strength & Health* (December 1959): 34–35, 51–54.

Baily, Brian, and James Gillett. "Bodybuilding and Health Work: A Life Course
Perspective." In *Critical Readings in Bodybuilding*, ed. Adam Locks and Niall
Richardson, 91–106. New York: Routledge, 2012.

Bainbridge, Francis A., Arlie V. Bock, and David B. Dill. *The Physiology of Muscular
Exercise*. London: Longmans, Green, and Co., 1931.

Baker, W. A. "The Pete Dawkins Story." *Strength & Health* (December 1959): 36–37,
55–56.

Ball, Jerry R., George O. Rich, and Earl L. Wallis. "Effect of Isometric Training on
Vertical Jump Ability." *Research Quarterly* 35.3 (October 1964): 231–235.

Bannister, E. W. "Research Report: Strength Gains from Muscle Training: Preparation for Competition." *NSCA Journal* 1.6 (1979): 24–29.

Barnes, W. S. "The Relationship of Motor Unit Activation to Isokinetic Muscular
Contraction at Different Contractile Velocities." *Physical Therapy* 60 (1980):
1152–1158.

Barney, Vermon S., and Blauer L. Bangerter. "Comparison of Three Programs of
Heavy Resistance Exercise." *Research Quarterly* 32.2 (May 1961): 138–146.

Barr, J. S., W. A. Eilliston, H. Musnick, Thomas DeLorme, J. Hanelin, and A. A.
Thibodeau. "Fracture of the Carpal Navicular (Scaphoid) Bone: An End-Results
Study in Military Personnel." *Journal of Bone and Joint Surgery*, American volume
35A.3 (1953): 609–625.

Beamish, Rob, and Ian Ritchie. "From Fixed Capacities to Performance-
Enhancement: The Paradigm Shift in the Science of 'Training' and the Use of
Performance-Enhancing Substances." *Sport in History* 25.3 (December 2005):
412–433.

———. "Totalitarian Regimes and Cold War Sport: Steroid 'Ubermenschen' and
'Ball-Bearing Females.'" In *East Plays West: Sport and the Cold War*, ed. Stephen
Wagg and David L. Andrews, 19–20. New York: Routledge, 2007.

Beck, Charles. *A Treatise on Gymnastics, Taken Chiefly from the German of F. L.
Jahn*. Northampton, MA: Simeon Butler, 1828.

Beckham, Susan G., and Michael Harper, "Functional Training: Fad or Here to Stay?"
ACSM Health and Fitness Journal 14.6 (November/December 2010): 24–30.

Beckwith, Kimberly. "Building Strength: Alan Calvert, the Milo Bar-Bell Company,
and the Modernization of American Weight Training." PhD diss., University of
Texas–Austin, 2006.

———. "Thomas Jefferson 'Stout' Jackson: Texas Strongman." *Iron Game History* 3.2
(January 1994): 8–15.

———. "Weight-Lifting 'as a Sport, as a Means of Body Building, and as a Profession':
Alan Calvert's *The Truth about Weight-Lifting*." *Iron Game History* 10.4 (January
2009): 22–33.

Beckwith, Kimberly, and Jan Todd. "George Hackenschmidt vs. Frank Gotch: Media Representations and the World Wrestling Title of 1908." *Iron Game History* 11.2 (June 2010): 14–25.

———. "Requiem for a Strongman: Reassessing the Career of Professor Louis Atilla." *Iron Game History* 7.2–3 (July 2002): 42–55.

———. "*Strength*, America's First Muscle Magazine: 1914–1935." *Iron Game History* 9.1 (August 2005): 11–28.

Benioff, Howard. "The Mike Connelly Story." *Physical Power* 3.5 (September–October 1962): 12–13, 32.

———. "Track and Field Special Feature: The Story of Bob Humphreys." *Physical Power* 3.1 (January–February 1962): 14–17.

Bennett, Bruce. "Dudley A. Sargent: A Man for All Seasons." *Quest* 29 (1978): 33–45.

Benninghoff, C. F. "Weight Lifting." *Journal of Physical Education* 35.6 (July–August 1938): 96.

Berger, Richard A. "Comparative Effects of Three Weight Training Programs." *Research Quarterly* 34.3 (October 1963): 396–398.

———. "Comparison of the Effect of Various Weight Training Loads on Strength." *Research Quarterly* 36.2 (May 1965): 141–146.

———. "Comparison of Weight Lifting Ability between Lifters." *Physical Educator* 20.2 (May 1963): 59–60.

———. "Effect of Static and Dynamic Training on Vertical Jumping Ability." *Research Quarterly* 34.4 (December 1963): 419–424.

———. "Effect of Varied Weight Training Programs on Strength." *Research Quarterly* 33.2 (May 1962): 168–181.

———. "Effects of Isometric Training." *Physical Educator* 22.2 (May 1965): 81.

———. "Optimum Repetitions for the Development of Strength." *Research Quarterly* 33.3 (October 1962): 334–338.

Berger, Richard A., and Billy Hardage. "Effect of Maximum Loads for Each of Ten Repetitions on Strength Improvement." *Research Quarterly* 38.4 (December 1967): 715–718.

Berger, Richard A., and Joe M. Henderson. "Relationship of Power to Static and Dynamic Strength." *Research Quarterly* 37.1 (March 1966): 9–13.

Berry, Mark. "The Old Standard Methods Are Best." *Your Physique* (November 1940).

———. "Physical Training Problems Simplified." *Your Physique* 1:4 (March 1941): 4–5, 13.

Berryman, Jack W. "Exercise and Medical Tradition from Hippocrates through Antebellum America: A Review Essay." In *Sport and Exercise Science: Essays in the History of Sports Medicine*, ed. Jack W. Berryman and Roberta J. Park, 1–56. Urbana: University of Illinois Press, 1992.

———. *Out of Many, One: A History of the American College of Sports Medicine*. Champaign, IL: Human Kinetics, 1995.

Bingham, Norman. *The Book of Athletics and Out-of-Door Sports*. Boston: Lothrop, 1895.

Black, Jonathan. *Making the American Body: The Remarkable Saga of the Men and Women Whose Feats, Feuds, and Passions Shaped Fitness History*. Lincoln: University of Nebraska Press, 2013.

Blaikie, William. *How to Get Strong and Stay So*. New York: Harper, 1898.

Bompa, Tudor, and Gregory Haff. *Periodization: Theory and Methodology of Training*. Champaign, IL: Human Kinetics, 2009.

Borsa, Paul A., Eric L. Sauers, and Scott M. Lephart. "Functional Training for the Restoration of Dynamic Stability in the PCL Injured Knee." *Journal of Sport Rehabilitation* 8 (1999): 362–387.

Bourne, Nicholas. "Fast Science: A History of Training Theory and Methods for Elite Runners through 1975." PhD diss. University of Texas–Austin, 2008.

Brady, Thomas A., Bernard R. Cahill, and Leslie M. Bodnar. "Weight-Training Related Injuries in the High School Athlete." *American Journal of Sports Medicine* 10.1 (1982): 1–5.

Brier, Bill. "Weight Trained College Swimmers Win Ninth Consecutive Championship." *Strength & Health* (September 1957): 17.

Bristol, Matt. "Born of Controversy: The G.I. Bill of Rights." *Vanguard* (January 2006): 23.

Brooks, George A., and L. Bruce Gladden. "The Metabolic Systems: Anaerobic Metabolism (Glycolytic and Phosphagen)." In *Exercise Physiology: People and Ideas*, ed. Charles M. Tipton, 323–352. New York: Oxford University Press, 2003.

Brose, Donald E., and Dale E. Hanson. "Effects of Overload Training on Velocity and Accuracy of Throwing." *Research Quarterly* 38.4 (December 1967): 528–533.

Brown, Eugene W., and Richard G. Kimball. "Medical History Associated with Adolescent Powerlifting." *Pediatrics* 72.5 (1983): 636–644.

Bruce, George. "Parry O'Brien—Shotput Champion." *Strength & Health* (August 1954): 10–11, 36.

Bryant, Doug. "William Blaikie and Physical Fitness in Late Nineteenth Century America." *Iron Game History* 2.3 (July 1992): 3–6.

Buck, Josh. "Louis Cyr and Charles Sampson: Archetypes of Vaudevillian Strongmen." *Iron Game History* 5.3 (1998): 18–28.

Buckiewicz, Frank A. "An Experimental Study of the Effects of Weight Training on Fine Motor Skills." MS thesis, Pennsylvania State University, 1954.

Buckley, William E., Charles E. Yesalis, Karl E. Friedl, William A. Anderson, Andrea L. Streit, and James E. Wright. "Estimated Prevalence of Anabolic Steroid Use among Male High School Seniors." *Journal of the American Medical Association* 260.23 (1988): 3441–3445.

Budd, Michael. "Heroic Bodies: Physical Culture Commerce and the Promise of the Perfected Self, 1898–1918." PhD diss., Rutgers University, 1992.

Burnham, Stan. "Better Rebounding through Weight Training." *Physical Power* 2.11 (October 1961): 10–12, 29.

———. "A Conditioning Program for Football Players." *Physical Power* 2.10 (July–August 1961): 16–17.

———. "Football Conditioning at the University of Texas." *Physical Power* (Fall 1965): 8–11, 23–24.

———. "Strength for Fitness and Competition." *Physical Power* 5.2 (March–April 1964): 10–13, 38–39.

———. "The Value of Combined Isometric and Isotonic Exercise." *Physical Power* 3.2 (May–June 1963): 14–15, 35.

Cahn, Susan K. *Coming on Strong: Gender and Sexuality in Twentieth-Century Women's Sport*. Cambridge, MA: Harvard University Press, 1994.

Caldwell, Stratton F. "Weight Training." *Physical Educator* 14.1 (March 1957): 17–18.

Calvert, Alan. *An Article on Natural Strength versus "Made" Strength, Preceded by an Explanation of Why I Abandoned the Field of Heavy Exercise*. Philadelphia: by the author, 1925.

———. *Confidential Information on Lifting and Lifters*. Philadelphia: by the author, 1925.

———. *The Truth about Weight Lifting*. Philadelphia, PA: by the author, 1911.

———. "What Does 'Muscle-Bound' Mean?" *Strength* (March 1915): 2–5.

Calvin, Sidney. "Effects of Progressive Resistance Exercises on the Motor Coordination of Boys." *Research Quarterly* 30.4 (December 1959): 387–398.

Campbell, Robert L. "Effects of Supplemental Weight Training on the Physical Fitness of Athletic Squads." *Research Quarterly* 33.3 (October 1962): 343–348.

Capen, Edward K. "The Effect of Systematic Weight Training on Power, Strength, and Endurance." MS thesis, University of Iowa, 1949.

———. "The Effect of Systematic Weight Training on Power, Strength, and Endurance." *Research Quarterly* 21.2 (May 1950): 83–93.

———. "Study of Four Programs of Heavy Resistance Exercises for Muscular Strength." *Research Quarterly* 27.2 (May 1956): 132–142.

Capretta, John. "The Condition Called Muscle-Bound." *Journal of Health and Physical Education* 3.2 (February 1932): 43, 54.

"Captain Thomas L. DeLorme Receives Legion of Merit." *Pulse*, undated clipping. Thomas DeLorme Collection, H. J. Lutcher Stark Center for Physical Culture and Sports, University of Texas at Austin.

Carse, Alan. "Barbell Training in Universities." *Strength & Health* (January 1943): 24, 36–39.

———. "Muscle Bound Frank." *Strength & Health* 4:9 (August 1936): 19, 40.

———. "The Old Athlete Tells a Secret." *Strength & Health* 3:6 (May 1935): 66.

———. "Survival of the Fittest." *Strength & Health* (November 1935): 18, 48.

———. "A Tale of Survival of the Fittest." *Strength & Health* (December 1935): 18, 44–45, 50.

Casa, Douglas J., Scott A. Anderson, Lindsay Baker, et al. "The Inter-Association Task Force for Preventing Sudden Death in Collegiate Conditioning Sessions: Best Practice Recommendations." *Journal of Athletic Training* 47.4 (2012): 477–480.

Chaikin, Tommy, and Rick Telander. "The Nightmare of Steroids." *Sports Illustrated*, October 23, 1988, 82–88, 90, 92, 94, 97–98, 101–102.

Chandler, T. Jeff, and Michael Stone. "NSCA Position Paper: The Squat Exercise in Athletic Conditioning: A Position Statement and Review of Literature." *NSCA Journal* 13.5 (1991): 51–58.

Chaney, Matt. *Spiral of Denial: Muscle Doping in American Football*. Warrensburg, MO: Four Walls Publishing, 2009.

"Changes Ahead for Publication; NSCA, Foundation to Merge." *NSCA Bulletin* 13. 6 (1992): 8.

Chapman, Carleton B. "The Long Reach of Harvard's Fatigue Laboratory, 1926–1947." *Perspectives in Biology and Medicine* 34.1 (1990): 17–33.

Chapman, David. *Sandow the Magnificent: Eugen Sandow and the Beginnings of Bodybuilding*. Urbana: University of Illinois Press, 1994.

Chu, Donald. "President's Message: to the Membership." *National NSCA Bulletin* 19.3 (1998): 3.

Chui, Edward F. "Effect of Isometric and Dynamic Weight-Training Exercises upon Strength and Speed of Movement." *Research Quarterly* 35.3 (October 1964): 246–257.

———. "The Effect of Systematic Weight Training on Athletic Power." MS thesis, University of Iowa, 1948.

———. "The Effect of Systematic Weight Training on Athletic Power." *Research Quarterly* 21.3 (October 1950): 188–194.

Cipriani, Dan, and Ryan Vermillion. "New Steps in Knee Rehab." *Training and Conditioning* 5.5 (October 1995): 15–18, 20–21, 23–24.

Clark, Mike. "A Realistic Approach for Strength and Conditioning Coaches to Deal with Steroids." *NSCA Journal* 10.2 (1988): 28–30.

Clarke, David H. "Correlation between Strength/Mass Ratio and the Speed of Arm Movement." *Research Quarterly* 31.4 (December 1960): 570–574.

Clarke, David H., and Franklin M. Henry. "Neuromuscular Specificity and Increased Speed from Strength Development." *Research Quarterly* 32.3 (October 1961): 315–325.

"Coaches' Roundtable: Off-Season Strength and Conditioning for Basketball." *NSCA Journal* 5.1 (1983): 19–22, 24, 26–29, 54–55.

"Coaches' Roundtable: Prevention of Athletic Injuries through Strength Training and Conditioning." *NSCA Journal* 5.2 (1983): 14–19.

"Coaches' Roundtable: Speed Development." *NSCA Journal* 5.6 (1983): 12–20, 72–73.

"Coaches' Roundtable: Winter Conditioning: Off-Season Training for Football." *NSCA Journal* 4.6 (1982): 15–18, 20–22, 24, 28–31.

Cohen, George. "Gary Gubner: Teen-Age Super Athlete." *Strength & Health* (June 1962): 34–35, 52–53, 55.

Cohen, Lizabeth. *A Consumer's Republic: The Politics of Mass Consumption in Post-War America*. New York: Knopf, 2003.

Colbath, H. J. "Favors Sugar Diet." *New York Times*, January 11, 1931.

Colfer, George. "Barbells on Campus: Ithaca College." *Strength & Health* (February 1967): 46–47, 75–77.

Colgate, John A. "Arm Strength Relative to Arm Speed." *Research Quarterly* 37.1 (March 1966): 14–22.

Collins, Bob. "His Fight Was against a Frail, Weak Physique." *Birmingham Post*, July 21, 1939.

Combe, Andrew. *The Principles of Physiology Applied to the Preservation of Health and to the Improvement of Physical and Mental Education*. New York: Harper Brothers, 1834.

Conca, Steven, and Lee Burton. "Workouts for Throw Outs." *Training and Conditioning* 8.6 (December 1998): 40–45, 47.

Conn, Herbert, and Caroline Holt. *Physiology and Health*. Boston: Silver, Burdett, and Co., 1921.

Conroy, Michael. "The Use of Periodization in the High School Setting." *Strength and Conditioning Journal* 21.1 (1999): 52.

Cook, Gray, and Keith Fields. "Functional Training for the Torso." *Strength and Conditioning Journal* 19.2 (1997): 14–19.

Coontz, Stephanie. *The Way We Never Were: American Families and the Nostalgia Trap*. New York: Basic Books, 1992.

Counsilman, James E. "Does Weight Training Belong in the Program?" *Journal of Health, Physical Education, and Recreation* 26.1 (January 1955): 17–18, 20.

Coyle, Edward F., David L. Costill, and G. R. Lesmes, "Leg Extension Power and Muscle Fiber Composition." *Medicine and Science in Sports and Exercise* 11:1 (1979): 12–15.

Crawford, Russ. *The Use of Sports to Promote the American Way of Life during the Cold War*. Lewiston, NY: Edwin Mellen Press, 2008.

Crouch, Larry. "Neck Injuries—Prevention to Aid Rehabilitation, Part II." *NSCA Journal* 1.6 (1979):29–31.

Crowther, Nigel. "Weightlifting in Antiquity: Achievement and Training." *Greece & Rome, Second Series* 24 (October, 1977): 112–123.

Cutter, Calvin. *First Book on Anatomy, Physiology and Hygiene for Grammar Schools and Families.* Philadelphia: J. B. Lippincott and Co., 1854.

Dalton, Kathleen. *Theodore Roosevelt: A Strenuous Life.* New York: A. A. Knopf, 2002.

Dandurand, Arthur. "I Am Young at Sixty-Two." *Your Physique* 1.1 (August 1940): 5, 18, 22.

Danna, Sammy R. "The 97 Pound Weakling . . . Who Became the 'World's Most Perfectly Developed Man.'" *Iron Game History* 4.4 (September 1996): 3–4.

———. "Charles Atlas." In *The Guide to United States Popular Culture*, ed. Ray Broadus Browne and Pat Browne, 50. Madison, WI: Popular Press, 2001.

Davidson, James West. *Nation of Nations: A Narrative History of the American Republic.* New York: McGraw-Hill, 2008.

Davis, John. "Irving Mondschein—U.S. Decathlon Champion." *Strength & Health* (June–July 1948): 18–19, 28, 30–32.

Dawson, Percy. *The Physiology of Physical Education for Physical Educators and Their Pupils.* Baltimore: Williams and Wilkins, 1935.

Degler, Carl. *In Search of Human Nature: The Decline and Revival of Darwinism in American Social Thought.* New York: Oxford University Press, 1991.

De la Pena, Carolyn. "Dudley Allen Sargent: Health Machines and the Energized Male Body." *Iron Game History* 8.2 (October 2003): 3–19.

DeLorme, Eleanor P. Telephone interview with Terry Todd, July 6, 2010. Thomas DeLorme Collection, H. J. Lutcher Stark Center for Physical Culture and Sports, University of Texas at Austin.

DeLorme, Thomas L. "Heavy Resistance Exercises." *Archives of Physical Medicine* 27.10 (1946): 607–630.

———. "Restoration of Muscle Power by Heavy Resistance Exercises." *Journal of Bone and Joint Surgery* 27.4 (1945): 645–667.

———. "Treatment of Congenital Absence of the Radius by Transepiphyseal Fixation." *Journal of Bone and Joint Surgery*, American volume 51.1 (1969): 117–129.

DeLorme, Thomas L., B. G. Ferris, and J. R. Gallagher. "The Effect of Progressive Resistance Exercise on Muscle Contraction Time." *Archives of Physical Medicine* 33.2 (1952): 86–92.

DeLorme, Thomas L., R. S. Schwab, and Arthur L. Watkins. "The Response of the Quadriceps Femoris to Progressive-Resistance Exercise in Polio Patients." *Journal of Bone and Joint Surgery*, American volume 30A.4 (1948): 834–847.

DeLorme, Thomas L., R. S. Shaw, and W. G. Austen. "A Method of Studying 'Normal' Function in the Amputated Human Limb Using Perfusion." *Journal of Bone and Joint Surgery*, American volume 46.1 (1964): 161–164.

———. "Musculoskeletal Functions in the Amputated Perfused Human Being Limb." *Surgical Forum* 15 (1964): 450–452.

DeLorme, Thomas L., and Arthur L. Watkins. *Progressive Resistance Exercise: Technic and Medical Application.* New York: Appleton-Century-Crofts, 1951.

———. "Technics of Progressive Resistance Exercise." *Archives of Physical Medicine and Rehabilitation* 29.5 (1948): 263–273.

DeLorme, Thomas L., F. E. West, and W. J. Shriber. "The Influence of Progressive

Resistance Exercise on Knee Function following Femoral Fractures." *Journal of Bone and Joint Surgery*, American volume 32.4 (1950): 910–924.

Denegar, Craig R., Ethan Saliba, and Susan Saliba. *Therapeutic Modalities for Musculoskeletal Injuries*. Champaign, IL: Human Kinetics, 2010.

Denham, Bryan E. "Masculinities in Hardcore Bodybuilding." *Men and Masculinities* 11.2 (2008): 234–242.

———. "*Sports Illustrated*, the 'War on Drugs,' and the Anabolic Steroid Control Act of 1990: A Study in Agenda Building and Political Timing." *Journal of Sport and Social Issues* 21.3 (1997): 260–273.

Denman, Elliot. "Russia Wins the Olympics." *All American Athlete* 6.10 (June 1964): 14–17, 52–61.

Dennison, J. D., M. L. Howell, and W. R. Morford. "Effect of Isometric and Isotonic Exercise Programs on Muscular Endurance." *Research Quarterly* 32.3 (October 1961): 348–352.

Denny-Brown, Derek. "The Histological Features of Striped Muscle in Relation to Its Functional Activity." *Proceedings of the Royal Society* 104.731 (March 1929): 371–411.

Dent, Jim. *The Junction Boys: How Ten Days in Hell with Bear Bryant Forged a Championship Team*. New York: Thomas Dunne Books, 2000.

Desbonnet, Edmond. "Yousouf: The Terrible Turk." *Your Physique* 11.1 (April 1949): 14–15, 36.

Deutsch, Felix, and Emil Kauf. *Heart and Athletics: Clinical Researches upon the Influence of Athletics upon the Heart*. St. Louis, MO: C. V. Mosby Co., 1927.

"Development Task Force." *Journal of Applied Sport Science Research* 1.1 (1987): 2.

Diamond, Wilf. "The Story of Jack Johnson." *Your Physique* 10.1–3 (October–December 1948): 14–15, 22–23, 26–27.

Dick, Frank. "Periodization: An Approach to the Training Year." *Track Technique* 62 (1975): 1968–1969.

Dintiman, George B. "Effects of Various Training Programs on Running Speed." *Research Quarterly* 35.4 (December 1964): 456–463.

Di Pasquale, Mauro G. "Anabolic Steroid Detection." *NSCA Journal* 10.2 (1988): 26–27.

Donaldson, Donald. "Weight Training in Relation to Strength and Muscular Coordination." M. Ed thesis, Pennsylvania State College, 1952.

Donelan, Paul. "Baseball Star Says Weight Training Helps." *Strength & Health* (August 1955): 10–11, 62, 65.

Downing, D. A. "Barbell Training in the Service." *Strength & Health* (January 1943): 22–23, 34–36.

———. "Why Are Medical Doctors Seldom Healthy?" *Strength & Health* (September 1935): 60, 84–85.

Dudley, Gary A., and Steven J. Fleck. "Research: Reading and Understanding: The Results Section: Major Concepts and Compounds." *NSCA Journal* 4.5 (1982): 22.

Durrell, David L., Thomas J. Pujol, and Jeremy T. Barnes. "A Survey of the Scientific Data and Training Methods Utilized by Collegiate Strength and Conditioning Coaches." *Journal of Strength and Conditioning Research* 17.2 (2003): 368–373.

Durso, Kent. "Letters to the Editor: Father Lange's Legacy." *Milo* 6:4 (1999): 6–7.

Dutton, Kenneth R. *The Perfectible Body: The Western Ideal of Male Physical Development*. New York: Continuum, 1995.

Dworkin, Shari L. "'Holding Back': Negotiating a Glass Ceiling on Women's Muscular Strength." *Sociological Perspectives* 44.3 (2001): 333–350.

Dyreson, Mark. *Making the American Team: Sport, Culture, and the Olympic Experience.* Urbana: University of Illinois Press, 1998.

Ebel, Richard. *Far beyond the Shoe Box: Fifty Years of the National Athletic Trainers' Association.* New York: Forbes Custom Publishing, 1999.

Ecker, Tom, ed. *Championship Track and Field by 12 Great Coaches.* Englewood Cliffs, NJ: Prentice Hall, 1961.

Edwards, Robert. "Physical Fitness through Weight-Lifting." *Journal of Health and Physical Education* 11.10 (December 1940): 606–607, 635.

Eells, Roger. "I Was Given Three Months to Live." *Strength & Health* (April 1935): 26, 44–45.

Eiferman, George. "Weight Training: The Key to Greater Athletic Ability." *Muscle Builder* (November 1957): 32–35, 65–66, 70.

Eisenman, P. A. "The Influence of Initial Strength Levels on Responses in Vertical Jump Training." *Journal of Sports Medicine and Physical Fitness* 18.3 (1978): 277–282.

Elder, George. "Letters to the Editor." *NSCA Newsletter* 1.2 (1979): 15.

———. "Viewpoint: Machines: A Viable Method for Training Athletes?" *National Strength Coaches' Association Newsletter* 1.3 (1979): 24, 28.

Elliott, Len, and Barbara Kelly. *Who's Who in Golf.* New Rochelle, NY: Arlington House, 1976.

Endres, John Paul Endres. "The Effect of Weight Training Exercise upon the Speed of Muscular Movement." MS thesis, University of Wisconsin–Madison, 1953.

English, Eleanor B. "Charles H. McCloy: The Research Professor of Physical Education." *Journal of Physical Education, Recreation and Dance* 54.4 (1983), 16–18.

———. "The Enigma of Charles H. McCloy." *Journal of Physical Education, Recreation and Dance* 54.5 (1983): 40–42.

Epley, Boyd. *Body Composition Assessment: How to Gain or Lose Bodyweight.* Lincoln, NE: Body Enterprises, 1983.

———. *Boyd Epley Workout for Football.* Lincoln, NE: Body Enterprises, 1988.

———. *Cardiovascular Fitness . . . The Nebraska Way.* Lincoln, NE: Body Enterprises, 1980.

———. "College Strength and Conditioning Coaches Committee Update." *NSCA Bulletin* 13.6 (November/December 1992): 8.

———. *Dynamic Strength Training for Athletes.* Dubuque, IA: Wm. C. Brown Co., 1985.

———. *Husker Power: Committed to Improving Performance.* Lincoln, NE: Husker Power, 1990.

———. *Husker Power for '83–'84.* Lincoln: University of Nebraska Press, 1983.

———. *Interval Sprints for Football . . . The Nebraska Way.* Lincoln, NE: Body Enterprises, 1983.

———. "Join the NSCA!" *National Strength Coaches Association Newsletter* 1.1 (1978): 1.

———. *Motivate Your Athletes . . . The Nebraska Way.* Lincoln, NE: Body Enterprises, 1983.

———. *Multi-Purpose Machine Exercises . . . The Nebraska Way.* Lincoln, NE: Body Enterprises, 1983.

——. *The National Directory of Strength Coaches*. Lincoln: University of Nebraska Printing and Duplicating, 1978.

——. *Neck Exercises . . . The Nebraska Way*. Lincoln, NE: Body Enterprises, 1983.

——. *The Path to Athletic Power: The Model Conditioning Program for Championship Performance*. Champaign, IL: Human Kinetics, 2004.

——. *The Strength of Nebraska*. Lincoln: Body Enterprises, 1979.

——. *Strength Training for Baseball and Softball . . . The Nebraska Way*. Lincoln, NE: Body Enterprises, 1983.

——. *Strength Training for Basketball . . . The Nebraska Way*. Lincoln, NE: Body Enterprises, 1983.

——. *Strength Training for Football . . . The Nebraska Way*. Lincoln, NE: Body Enterprises, 1983.

——. *Strength Training for Golf . . . The Nebraska Way*. Lincoln, NE: Body Enterprises, 1983.

——. *Strength Training for Racquet Sports . . . The Nebraska Way*. Lincoln, NE: Body Enterprises, 1983.

——. *Strength Training for Swimming . . . The Nebraska Way*. Lincoln, NE: Body Enterprises, 1983.

——. *Strength Training for Track & Field . . . The Nebraska Way*. Lincoln, NE: Body Enterprises, 1983.

——. *Strength Training for Wrestling . . . The Nebraska Way*. Lincoln, NE: Body Enterprises, 1983.

——. *Stretching . . . The Nebraska Way*. Lincoln, NE: Body Enterprises, 1983.

——. *Survivor Circuit Training . . . The Nebraska Way*. Lincoln, NE: Body Enterprises, 1983.

——. *Test Your Athletes . . . The Nebraska Way*. Lincoln, NE: AMF American Consulting Service, 1983.

——. *When How and Why to Begin Lifting Weights . . . The Nebraska Way*. Lincoln, NE: Body Enterprises, 1983.

Epley, Boyd, and Tom Wilson, *Weight Training Instruction Manual*. Lincoln, NE: Body Enterprises, 1981.

Epstein, David. *The Sports Gene: Inside the Science of Extraordinary Athletic Performance*. New York: Current, 2013.

Ernst, Robert. *Weakness Is a Crime: The Life of Bernarr Macfadden*. Syracuse, NY: Syracuse University Press, 1991.

Fair, John. "Bob Hoffman, the York Barbell Company, and the Golden Age of American Weightlifting, 1945–1960." *Journal of Sport History* 14.2 (Summer 1987): 164–188.

——. "Father Figure or Phony?: George Jowett, the ACWLA and the Milo Barbell Company, 1924–1927." *Iron Game History* 3.5 (December 1994): 13–25.

——. "From Philadelphia to York: George Jowett, Mark Berry, Bob Hoffman, and the Rebirth of American Weightlifting, 1927–1936." *Iron Game History* 4.3 (April 1996): 3–17.

——. "George Jowett, Ottley Coulter, David Willoughby, and the Organization of American Weightlifting, 1911–1924." *Iron Game History* 2:6 (May 1993): 3–15.

——. "Jimmy Payne: The Forgotten Mr. America." *Iron Game History* 11.4 (January 2012): 22–35.

——. "Katie Sandwina: 'Hercules Can Be a Lady.'" *Iron Game History* 9.2 (December 2005): 4–7.

————. "Mr. America: Idealism or Racism: Color Consciousness and the AAU Mr. America Contests, 1939–1982." *Iron Game History* 8.1 (June/July 2003): 9–30.

————. *Mr. America: The Tragic History of a Bodybuilding Icon.* Austin: University of Texas Press, 2015.

————. *Muscletown USA: Bob Hoffman and the Manly Culture of York Barbell.* University Park, PA: Pennsylvania State University Press, 1999.

————. "Searching for the Real Paul Anderson." *Iron Game History* 7.1 (June 2001): 22–29.

————. "'That Man's Just Too Strong for Words to Describe': The Weightlifting Exploits of John C. Grimek." *Iron Game History* 6.1 (April 1999): 64–71.

Faires, Randolph. "Physical Education." *Medical News* 64.7 (1894): 173.

Faul, Joseph. "Barbells on Campus: Stonehill College." *Strength & Health* (March 1961): 34–35, 61.

Faulkner, Everett W. "A Comparison of the Effectiveness of Two Methods of Exercise for the Development of Muscular Strength." MS thesis, University of Iowa, 1949.

Ference, Denis A. "Motivation: A Modified Awards Program for Women." *NSCA Journal* 14.5 (1992): 28.

Figliolino, Joseph. "Barbells on Campus: Bloomsburg State College." *Strength & Health* (March 1965): 16–18, 62.

Finkelstein, Jack. "Bama's Hercules Displays Weight-Lifting Abilities." *Crimson White*, undated clipping. Thomas DeLorme Collection, H. J. Lutcher Stark Center for Physical Culture and Sports, University of Texas at Austin.

"The First Five Years: Results and Analysis of the 1982–83 Member Survey." *NSCA Journal* 5.4 (1983): 54–55, 72.

Fitzsimmons, Robert. "Knotty Muscles of Little Value." *Fort Wayne News*, November 2, 1900.

Fleck, Steven J. "Exercise Physiology Corner: Determination of Body Fat Via Skinfold Measurements." *NSCA Journal* 3.5 (1981): 56–57, 60.

Fleck, Steven J., and William J. Kraemer. *Designing Resistance Training Programs.* Champaign, IL: Human Kinetics, 2014.

Fleishman, Alfred. "Exercise to Recovery." *Strength & Health* (February 1944): 18–19, 37.

Flint, Austin. *On the Source of Muscular Power: Arguments and Conclusions Drawn from Observations upon the Human Subject, under Conditions of Rest and Muscular Exercise.* New York: Appleton, 1878.

Folland, Jonathan, and Beth Morris. "Variable-cam Resistance Training Machines: Do They Match the Angle-Torque Relationship in Humans?" *Journal of Sport Sciences* 26.2 (2008): 163–169.

"For the Athlete in Action," *All American Athlete* 6:7 (March 1964): 98.

Foster, John. "How It All Began." *Flex* (June 1985): 90, 96.

Fournier, Joe. "Naval Academy Turns to Weightlifting." *Strength & Health* (March 1964): 16–19, 62–63.

Franklin, Martin. "Arthur Saxon's Views on Weightlifting." *Muscle Power* 4:6 (March 1948): 20, 42.

Frei, Terry. *Third Down and a War to Go.* Madison: Wisconsin Historical Society Press, 2005.

Furer, Andrew. "'The Strength of the Strong': (Re)forming the Self in 'Fin de Siècle' American Literature and Culture." PhD diss., University of California–Berkeley, 1995.

Gabriel, Parker. "Husker Football: Frost: 'Hospitalized Players My Responsibility.'" *Lincoln (NE) Journal Star*, January 30, 2018.

Galik, Candice. "Link by Link: Understanding the Closed Kinetic Chain." *Training and Conditioning* 3.2 (June 1993): 4–11.

Gallagher, J. Roswell, and Thomas L. DeLorme. "The Use of the Technique of Progressive Resistance Exercise in Adolescence." *Journal of Bone and Joint Surgery*, American volume 31A.4 (1949): 847–858.

Gambetta, Vern. "All-Season Training." *Training and Conditioning* 10.5 (July/August 2000): 12–19.

——. "Strength in Motion." *Training and Conditioning* 3.2 (June 1993): 12–16.

Gambetta, Vern, and Mike Clark. "A Formula for Function." *Training and Conditioning* 8.4 (August 1998): 24–29.

Gambetta, Vern, and Gary Gray. "Following a Functional Path." *Training and Conditioning* 5.2 (1995): 25–30.

Gammon, Spec. "The Texas A&M Weight Program for Football." *Strength & Health* (September 1968): 28–31.

Ganong, Ray. "University of Miami Baseball Strength and Conditioning." *NSCA Journal* 1.6 (1979): 32–33.

Garhammer, John. "Evaluation of Human Power Capacity through Olympic Weightlifting Analyses." PhD diss., University of California–Los Angeles, 1980.

——. "Strength Training Modes: Free Weight Equipment for the Development of Athletic Strength and Power—Part I." *NSCA Journal* 3.6 (1981): 24–26.

Garris, Rembert. "The Rise of Weightlifting in the YMCA." *Journal of Physical Education* 53.3 (January–February 1956): 77–78.

Garth, Richard L. "A Study of the Effect of Weight Training on the Jumping Ability of Basketball Players." MS thesis, University of Iowa, 1954.

Gaudreau, Leo. "Barbells for Exercise and Sport." *Muscle Power* (November 1946): 96–97, 125.

Gems, Gerald R. *Pride, Profit and Patriarchy: Football and the Incorporation of American Cultural Values.* Lanham, MD: Scarecrow, 2000.

George, Pete. "The World's Greatest Swimmer." *Strength & Health* (November 1955): 16–18, 56–57.

Gibson, A. M. "Does Exercise Harm the Heart?" *Strength & Health* (March 1959): 37, 57.

——. "Is Weightlifting Dangerous?" *Strength & Health* (October 1959): 24–25, 46–47.

Giessing, Jurgen, and Jan Todd. "The Origins of German Bodybuilding: 1790–1970." *Iron Game History* 9.2 (December 2005): 8–20.

Gilberg, Richard. "How High School Football Champions Train." *Physical Power* 3.4 (July–August 1962): 13, 33.

Gillesby, George. "The Physiologists Speak on Weight-Lifting." *Journal of Physical Education* 36.1 (September-October 1938): 16.

Glauser, Sidney. "Barbells on Campus: Temple University." *Strength & Health* (May 1960): 28–29, 52–54.

Glick, Harry. "Does Lifting Make You Muscle Bound?" *Strength* (June 1923): 40–43.

Goellner, William. "Aggie Weight Star Credits Barbells for Improvement." *Strength & Health* (March 1955): 10, 36.

Goldblatt, David. *The Games: A Global History of the Olympics.* New York: W. W. Norton, 2016.

Goldenberg, Joseph. "Barbells on Campus: New York University." *Strength & Health* (November 1959): 30–31, 55–57.

Good, Harry. "Are Strong Men Born or Made?" *Strength & Health* (April 1934): 12–13, 29.

———. "Barbells and Their Use versus Public Opinion." *Strength & Health* (March 1933), 9, 18.

———. "Facts to Disprove Time Worn Opinions." *Strength & Health* (February 1935): 17, 41–43.

———. "Gordon Venables: Weight Lifting Champion and Athlete Extraordinary." *Strength & Health* (November 1935): 20–21, 45.

Goranson, Gary. "Conditioning Foundation Clinic: Experience Charts the Course." *NSCA Journal* 1.4 (1990): 89–90.

———. "Conditioning Instructor Expands the Foundation's Reach." *NSCA Journal* 13.3 (1991): 83.

Gorn, Elliott. *The Manly Art: Bare-Knuckle Prize Fighting in America.* Ithaca, NY: Cornell University Press, 1986.

Gorn, Elliott, and Warren Goldstein. *A Brief History of American Sports.* Urbana: University of Illinois Press, 2004.

Gould, Adrian G., and Joseph A. Dye. *Exercise and Its Physiology.* New York: A. S. Barnes and Co., 1935.

Gould, Stephen Jay. *The Mismeasure of Man.* New York: W. W. Norton, 1996.

Granger, Frank Butler. *Physical Therapeutic Technic.* Philadelphia: W. B. Saunders, 1932.

Green, Harvey. *Fit for America: Health, Fitness, Sport, and American Society.* New York: Pantheon Books, 1986.

Gregor, Adrian. "Despite My Burns—Exercise Won." *Strength & Health* (March 1933): 26.

Gregory, Earl C. "Exercise Your Swimming Muscles." *Physical Culture* (July 1926): 51–52, 70, 72.

Grimek, John. "Barbells on Campus: Mt. Saint Mary's." *Strength & Health* (November 1963): 16–17, 61.

Grunberger, Lisa. "Bernarr Macfadden's 'Physical Culture': Muscles, Morals, and the Millennium." PhD diss., University of Chicago, 1997.

Gundelfinger, Phil. "Once a Cripple Now a Lifter!" *Strength & Health* (May 1945): 15, 39–40.

Guttmann, Allen. "The Cold War and the Olympics." *International Journal of Sport History* 43.4 (1988): 554–568.

———. *From Ritual to Record: The Nature of Modern Sports.* New York: Columbia University Press, 1978.

———. *Women's Sports: A History.* New York: Columbia University Press, 1991.

Gyorgyfalvy, Carol Fleming. "Meet the Strength and Conditioning Professional." *NSCA Journal* 13.3 (1991): 68–69.

Hairabedian, Ara. "Weight Training in Relation to Strength and Speed of Movement." MEd thesis, Pennsylvania State College, 1952.

Halberstam, David. *The Fifties.* New York: Villard Books, 1993.

Hale, Tudor. "History of Developments in Sport and Exercise Physiology: A. V. Hill, Maximal Oxygen Uptake, and Oxygen Debt." *Journal of Sports Sciences* 26.4 (2008): 365–400.

Hall, John R. "Citation for Legion of Merit." December 4, 1945. Thomas DeLorme Collection, H. J. Lutcher Stark Center for Physical Culture and Sports, University of Texas at Austin.

Halliwell, Martin. *American Culture in the 1950s*. Edinburgh, Scotland: Edinburgh University Press, 2007.

Hamilton, Dana. "Are Girl Athletes Masculine?" *Strength* 11 (November 1926): 31–33, 80–82.

Hanson, Bud. "In-Season Basketball Conditioning." *Physical Power* 4:6 (November–December 1963): 12–13, 36, 43.

Hanson, Nate. "A Strength and Health Boy Grows Up." *Strength & Health* (August 1952): 32–33, 45–46, 49.

Hargreaves, Jennifer. *Sporting Females: Critical Issues in the History and Sociology of Women's Sports*. New York: Routledge, 1994.

Hargreaves, Jennifer, and Patricia Vertinsky, eds. *Physical Culture, Power, and the Body*. London: Routledge, 2007.

Harmon, Everett. "Resistive Torque Analysis of Five Nautilus Exercise Machines." *Medicine and Science in Sports and Exercise* 15.2 (1983): 113.

Harter, Rod A. "Clinical Rationale for Closed Kinetic Chain Activities in Functional Testing and Rehabilitation of Ankle Pathologies." *Journal of Sport Rehabilitation* 5.1 (1996): 13–24.

Harvey, Norm. "Barbells on Campus: Villanova University." *Strength & Health* (October 1968): 24–25, 76–79.

Helfgott, Hali. "Al Wiggins, College Swimmer." *Sports Illustrated*, January 14, 2002.

Helm, Burt. "Do Not Cross Crossfit." *Inc.* (July/August 2013): 102–104, 114.

Henry, Clayton G. "Comparison of the Effectiveness of Two Methods of Exercise for the Development of Muscular Strength." MS thesis, University of Iowa, 1949.

Henry, Franklin M. "Influence of Athletic Training on the Resting Cardiovascular System." *Research Quarterly* 25.1 (March 1954): 28–41.

Herz, Jessie Cameron. *Learning to Breathe Fire: The Rise of CrossFit and the Primal Future of Fitness*. New York: Crown, 2014.

Hettinger, Theodor. *Physiology of Strength*. Springfield, IL: Thomas, 1961.

Higgins, Ace. "Football's Weightlifting All-American: Billy Cannon." *Strength & Health* (November 1959): 34–35, 57.

Higginson, Thomas Wentworth. "Gymnastics." *Atlantic Monthly* 7 (March 1861): 289.

Hill, Grant M. "A Study of Sport Specialization in Midwest High Schools and Perceptions of Coaches regarding the Effects of Specialization on High School Athletes and Athletics Programs." PhD diss., University of Iowa, 1987.

Hill, Grant M., and Jeffrey Simons. "A Study of Sport Specialization in High School Athletics." *Journal of Sport and Social Issues* 13.1 (1989): 1–13.

Hill, Harvey. "Is Heavy Exercise Necessary?" *Your Physique*, 2.2 (January–February 1942): 6–7.

Hitchcock, Edward. "Anthropometric Statistics of Amherst College." *Publications of the American Statistical Association* 3.24 (1893): 588–599.

Hoag, Dorothy G. "Physical Therapy in Orthopedics with Special Reference to Heavy Resistance, Low Repetition Exercise Program." *Physiotherapy Review* 26.6 (November–December 1946): 291–294.

Hoberman, John. *Mortal Engines: The Science of Performance and the Dehumanization of Sport*. Caldwell, NJ: Blackburn, 2002.

——. *Testosterone Dreams: Rejuvenation, Aphrodisia, Doping*. Berkeley: University of California Press, 2005.

Hoffman, Bob. "1938 National Championships—Can We Beat the Germans?" *Strength & Health* (July 1938): 28–29.

——. "1938 World's Weightlifting Championships at Vienna." *Strength & Health* (November 1938): 4, 30–31.

——. "Are the Germans Superior?" *Strength & Health* (August 1940): 10–11, 37–39.

——. "Are You a Fighter?" *Strength & Health* (April 1938): 28–29, 40.

——. "Barbells Build Winning Football Team." *Strength & Health* (May 1956): 8–9, 39–40, 42.

——. "Barbell Training in the Service." *Strength & Health* (August 1941): 22, 37–39.

——. *Bob Hoffman's Simplified System of Barbell Training*. York, PA: York Barbell Company Press, 1941.

——. "Editorial." *Strength & Health* (December 1932): 1.

——. "Editorial." *Strength & Health* (March 1934): 19.

——. "Editorial." *World Health Ecology News* 6.4 (April 1975), 1.

——. "Editorial—Barbells Build Better Athletes." *Strength & Health* (April 1955): 3–4, 63.

——. "Editorial—Living Examples." *Strength & Health* (October 1933): 2.

——. "Editorial—Millions Would Benefit." *Strength & Health* (October 1936), 5.

——. "Editorial—Weightlifters Are Successful in Other Sports." *Strength & Health* (August 1947): 3–4.

——. "Editorial—What Good Are Muscles?" *Strength & Health* (April 1949): 3, 5, 7.

——. "Especially for *Strength and Health*'s Boys." *Strength & Health* (November 1934): 20–21.

——. "Especially for *Strength and Health*'s Boys." *Strength & Health* (December 1934): 20, 48.

——. *Functional Isometric Contraction: A System of Static Contraction—Exercise without Movement*. York, PA: Strength & Health Publishing, 1964.

——. "How Many Repetitions?" *Strength & Health* (December 1940): 19, 36–39.

——. "How Much Weight Should You Use?" *Strength & Health* (May 1941): 24–25, 40–41.

——. "How to Become an Athletic Star." *Strength & Health* (January 1933): 9.

——. "How to Improve at Your Chosen Sport." *Strength & Health* (December 1932): 5–8.

——. "If You Want to Beat the Russians." *Strength and Health* (July 1958) 16–18.

——. "Improving Athletic Ability through Barbell Training." *Strength & Health* (April 1936): 19, 40.

——. *I Remember the Last War*. York, PA: Strength & Health Publishing, 1940.

——. "Muscles May Save Your Life!" *Strength & Health* (May 1952).

——. "Physical Training in the Service." *Strength & Health* (December 1941): 12, 43–44.

——. "Reaching Your Physical Goal." *Strength & Health* (October 1933).

——. "Results of the World Championships." *Strength & Health* (January 1947) 49.

——. *Secrets of Strength and Development*. York, PA: Strength & Health Publishing, 1940.

——. "Should We Prepare for War?" *Strength & Health* (November 1939): 43.

——. "The Story of the World Famous York Barbell Club." *Strength & Health* (November 1945): 15, 36–40.

——. "There Should Be a Law against It." *Strength & Health* (May 1936): 14, 36–37.

——. "'Tis Never Too Late to Start." *Strength & Health* (May 1933): 11, 26.

——. "The Way to Super Strength." *Strength & Health* (July 1933): 6–8, 28.

——. *Weight Lifting*. York, PA: Strength and Health Publishing, 1939.

——. "Weightlifting Builds Better Athletes." *Strength & Health* (October 1950): 9, 30.

——. "What Can We Believe?" *Strength & Health* (October 1943): 26–27, 42.

——. "Why You Should Be Strong." *Strength & Health* (June 1933): 5.

——. *York Advanced Methods of Weight Training*. York, PA: Strength & Health Publishing, 1951.

——. *York Barbell and Dumbbell System*. York, PA: Strength & Health Publishing, 1946.

——. "York High Wins First Football Championship." *Strength & Health* (March 1954): 12–13, 44.

——. "You Can Be a Better Athlete." *Strength & Health* (February 1953): 10–11, 52–55.

——. "Your Heart and Exercise." *Strength & Health* (March 1936): 12, 38–39.

——. "Your Training Problems." *Strength & Health* (April 1944): 8–9.

Hoffman, Rosetta. "Physical Training Builds Health, Strength and Beauty for the Ladies." *Strength & Health* (January 1937): 12, 36–38.

Hoffman, Shirl James. *Good Game: Christianity and the Culture of Sports*. Waco, TX: Baylor University Press, 2010.

Holloway, Jean Barrett, Denise Gater, Meg Ritchie, Lori Gilstrap, Lyne Stoessel, Jan Todd, Ken Kontor, Terry Todd, David Gater, Sue Hillman, Michael H. Stone, John Garhammer, and William Kraemer. "Strength Training for Female Athletes: A Position Paper: Part I." *NSCA Journal* 11.4 (1989): 43.

——. "Strength Training for Female Athletes: A Position Paper: Part II." *NSCA Journal* 11.5 (1989): 29–36.

Hooks, Eugene G. "Barbells on Campus: Wake Forest University." *Strength & Health* (November 1961): 28–29, 49–51.

——. "The Prediction of Baseball Ability through an Analysis of Selected Measures of Structure and Strength." PhD diss., Vanderbilt University, 1957.

Hoolahan, Paul. "Strength and Conditioning for Basketball: The University of North Carolina Program—Why Strength Training?" *NSCA Journal* 2.4 (1980): 20–21.

Horvath, Barton R. "Weight Training Helped Make Him a Champion." *Your Physique* 15.2 (May 1951): 18–19, 38.

——. "What Can Weight Training Do for Me Besides Build Big Muscles?" *Muscle Power* 18:9 (November 1955): 22–23, 50–52.

Horvath, Steven M., and Elizabeth Horvath. *The Harvard Fatigue Laboratory: Its History and Contributions*. Englewood Cliffs, NJ: Prentice-Hall, 1973.

Hottinger, William. "Barbells on Campus: University of Illinois." *Strength & Health* (January 1961): 36–37, 50–52.

Houtz, Sarah J., Annie M. Parrish, and F. A. Hellebrandt. "The Influence of Heavy Resistance Exercises on Strength." *Physiotherapy Review* 26.6 (November–December 1946): 299–304.

Howell, Maxwell L., Ray Kimoto, and W. R. Morford. "Effect of Isometric and Isotonic Exercise Programs upon Muscular Endurance." *Research Quarterly* 33.4 (December 1962): 536–540.

Hughes, Ellen. "Machines for Better Bodies: A Cultural History of Exercise Machines in America, 1830–1950." PhD diss., Cornell University, 1997.

Hunsicker, Paul, and George Greey. "Studies in Human Strength." *Research Quarterly* 28.2 (May 1957): 109–122.

Hunt, Thomas. *Drug Games: The International Olympic Committee and the Politics of Doping, 1960–2008*. Austin: University of Texas Press, 2012.

Huxley, A. F. "Review Lecture: Muscular Contraction." *Journal of Physiology* 243.1 (1974): 1–43.

Huxley, A. F., and R. Niedergerke. "Structural Changes in Muscle during Contraction: Interference Microscopy of Living Muscle Fibres." *Nature* 173 (1954): 971–973.

Huxley, H., and J. Hanson. "Changes in the Cross-Striations of Muscle during Contraction and Stretch and Their Structural Interpretation." *Nature* 173 (1954): 973.

"In Memoriam: Dr. Terry Todd (1938–2018) Pioneering Powerlifter, Writer, Sport Promoter and Historian Who Changed the Cultural Paradigm for Strength." *Journal of Strength and Conditioning Research* 32.11 (2018): 2995–3003.

Issurin, Vladimir B. "Periodization Training from Ancient Precursors to Structured Block Models." *Kinesiology* 46.1 (September 2014): 3–8.

Jackson Lears, T. J. "American Advertising and the Reconstruction of the Body, 1880–1930." In *Fitness in American Culture: Images of Health, Sport, and the Body, 1830–1940*, ed. Kathryn Grover, 47–66. Amherst, MA: University of Massachusetts Press, 1989.

Jaffee, Irving. "We Deserve to Lose the Olympics." *All American Athlete* 6.9 (May 1964): 20–21, 51–55.

Jahn, Friedrich Ludwig, and Ernst Eiselen. *Die Deutsche Turnkunst zur Einrichtung der Turnplatze Dargesteldt von Friedrich Ludwig Jahn und Ernst Eiselen*. Berlin: Kosten der Herausgeber, 1816.

James, Ed. *Practical Training for Running, Walking, Rowing, Wrestling, Boxing, Jumping, and All Kinds of Athletic Feats*. New York: Ed James, 1877.

James, Ronald. "Olympic Paddlers Swing to Scientific Weight Training." *All American Athlete* 6.9 (October 1964): 20–25, 60–62.

———. "You Can Make It—Build Your Own Resistance Running Sled." *All American Athlete* (October 1964): 10, 63.

Janes, Lewis G. *Health-Exercise: The Rationale and Practice of the Lifting-Cure or Health Lift*. New York: Lewis G. Janes, 1871.

Jensen, Clayne R. "Effect of Five Training Combinations of Swimming and Weight Training on Swimming the Front Crawl." *Research Quarterly* 34.4 (December 1963): 471–477.

Jesse, John P. "Misuse of Strength Development Programs in Athletic Training." *Physician and Sportsmedicine* 7.10 (October 1979): 46–50, 52.

———. "A New Look at Strength Development in Track and Field Athletes." *Physical Educator* 22.2 (May 1965): 72–75.

———. "Weight Training for Middle-Distance Runners." *Physical Power*, 4.6 (November–December 1963): 26–27, 32–3, 39, 42.

Johansson, Thomas. "What's Behind the Mask? Bodybuilding and Masculinity." In *Bending Bodies: Molding Masculinities*, vol. 2, ed. Soren Ervo and Thomas Johansson, 92–106. Burlington, VT: Ashgate Publishing, 2003.

Johnson, Andrea. "Human Performance: An Ethnographic and Historical Account of Exercise Physiology." PhD diss., University of Pennsylvania, 2009.

Johnson, William Oscar. "Steroids: A Problem of Huge Dimensions." *Sports Illustrated*, May 13, 1985, 38–61.

Jones, Arthur. "The Colorado Experiment." *Iron Man* 32.6 (1973): 34–37.

Jorgensen, N. M. "The Development of Weight Training at East Carolina College." *Physical Power* 2.12 (November 1961): 6.

Jowett, George. "How You Can Build Super Speed in Your Muscles." *Muscle Builder* 12.7 (October 1962): 29.

———. "Speedy Muscles." *Strength & Health* (September 1933): 3–5.

Judy, Roy. "Barbells on Campus: Gordon Military College." *Strength & Health* (June 1966): 24–25, 64.

Junqueira, Luiz Fernando, Jr. "Teaching Cardiac Autonomic Function Dynamics Employing the Valsalva (Valsalva-Weber) Maneuver." *Advances in Physiology Education* 32.1 (2008): 100–106.

Karpovich, Peter V. "Incidence of Injuries in Weight Lifting." *Journal of Physical Education* 48.4 (March–April 1951): 71–72.

———. *Physiology of Muscular Exercise*. Philadelphia: W. B. Saunders, 1959.

Kasson, John F. *Houdini, Tarzan, and the Perfect Man: The White Male Body and the Challenge of Modernity in America*. New York: Hill and Wang, 2001.

Kawalek, Thaddeus. Telephone interview with Terry Todd, December 5, 2003. Thomas DeLorme Collection, H. J. Lutcher Stark Center for Physical Culture and Sports, University of Texas at Austin.

Kehoe, Sim D. *The Indian Club Exercise*. New York: American News Company, 1866.

Keith, Marcia T. "Emphasis on Exercise as a Therapeutic Agent in a Naval Physical Therapy Department." *Physiotherapy Review* 27.1 (January–February 1947): 10–13.

Kempner, Kurt E. *College Football and American Culture in the Cold War Era*. Urbana: University of Illinois Press, 2009.

"Ken Kontor: Assistant Executive Director and Editor." *National Strength Coaches' Association Newsletter* 1 (1979): 9.

Kern-Steiner, Rebecca, Helen S. Washecheck, and Douglas D. Kelsey. "Strategy of Exercise Prescription Using an Unloading Technique for Functional Rehabilitation of an Athlete with an Inversion Ankle Sprain." *Journal of Orthopaedic and Sports Physical Therapy* 29. 5 (1999): 282–287.

Kerr, A. M. "Safeguarding the Heart in High School." *Journal of Health and Physical Education* 2.1 (January 1931): 16–17, 46.

Keteyian, Armen. *Big Red Confidential: Inside Nebraska Football*. Chicago: Contemporary Books, 1989.

Kimmel, Michael. "Consuming Manhood: The Feminization of American Manhood and the Recreation of the Male Body, 1832–1920." *Michigan Quarterly Review* 33.1 (1994): 7–36.

———. *Manhood in America: A Cultural History*. New York: Free Press, 1996.

Klein, Alan M. *Little Big Men: Bodybuilding Subculture and Gender Construction*. Albany, NY: State University of New York Press, 1993.

Klein, Siegmund. "Why We Need Exercise." *Strength & Health* (October 1935): 6, 50.

Knortz, Karen. "Kinesiology Corner: The Upright Row." *NSCA Journal* 2.2 (1980): 40.

Kodya, Mark. "An Exploration of the History of Weightlifting as a Reflection of the Major Socio-Political Events and Trends of the 20th Century." MS thesis, State University of New York—Empire State College, 2005.

Kolb, Joe. "Weight Training for Football: The Fort Lauderdale Story." *Strength & Health* (May 1956): 10, 42, 44.

Konig, Jason. *Athletics and Literature in the Roman Empire.* Cambridge, UK: Cambridge University Press, 2005.

Kontor, Ken. "Convention II—300 Strong." *National Strength Coaches' Association Newsletter/Journal* 1.4 (1979): 1.

——. "Editorial." *National Strength Coaches' Association Bulletin* 1.2 (1979): 2–3.

——. "Editorial: 1990 Executive Director's Report." *NSCA Journal* 13.3 (1991): 76–77.

——. "Editorial: Bridging the Gap." *NSCA Journal* 4.1 (1982): 11.

——."Editorial: Equipment Companies." *NSCA Journal* 1.6 (1979): 4.

——. "Editorial: Myths Persist." *NSCA Journal* 4.4 (1982): 5.

——. "Editorial: NSCA Five Year Plan: 1983–'88 and 1989–'94." *NSCA Journal* 10.5 (1988): 76.

——. "Editorial: The NSCA Story." *National Strength Coaches' Association Bulletin* 1.2 (1979): 2–3.

——. "Editorial: Read Labels Carefully." *NSCA Journal* 14.3 (1992): 84.

——. "Editorial: The Second Journal." *NSCA Journal* 7.6 (1985): 14.

——. "Editorial: Strength Coach Certification—The Next Step." *NSCA Journal* 3.1 (1981): 4

——. "Editorial: Why a National Strength and Conditioning Foundation?" *NSCA Journal* 13.4 (1991): 80–81.

——. "Meet America's Strongest: A Final Look at the National Strength Coaches' Association All-American Strength Team." *NSCA Journal* 1.6 (1979): 8–11.

——. "Nine Months of Progress . . . Nine Months of History." *NSCA Newsletter* 1.3 (1979): 1.

——. "President's Message: Education and Learning." *NSCA Journal* 12.2 (1990): 72–73.

Kraemer, William J. "An Introduction to Research: Reading and Understanding." *NSCA Journal* 4.2 (1982): 11.

——. "Kinesiology Corner: Wrist Curls." *NSCA Journal* 3.5 (1981): 64–65.

——. "An Open Letter to the NSCA Membership." *NSCA Journal* 7.6 (1985): 42A.

——. "President's Message: Bridging the Gap: Examining the Concept." *NSCA Journal* 11.5 (1989): 75–77.

——. "President's Message: Education and Learning." *NSCA Journal* 12.2 (1990): 72–73.

——. "President's Message: Represent Your Profession." *NSCA Journal* 11.4 (1989): 76.

——. "President's Message: Some Final Thoughts and Thank You." *NSCA Journal* 13.3 (1991): 72–74.

——. "President's Message: Time to Train." *NSCAJ* 12.3 (1990): 74–75.

——. "Research: Reading and Understanding: The Starter Steps." *NSCAJ* 4.3 (1982): 49.

——. "The Second Journal: *Applied Sport Science Journal* Addition." *NSCAJ* 8.2 (1986): 41–42.

——. "Women in the NSCA." *NSCA Journal* 12.4 (1990): 84.

Kraus, Hans, and Ruth P. Hischland, "Muscular Fitness and Health." *Journal of the American Association for Health, Physical Education, and Recreation* 24.10 (1953): 17–19.

Krause, Ted. "Trends in 'Y' Weight Lifting." *Journal of Physical Education* 36.5 (May–June 1939): 94.

Kroll, Walter. "Putting Science into Coaching: A Dilemma." *Physical Educator* 15.1 (March 1958): 13.

Kuhn, Thomas S. *The Structure of Scientific Revolutions*. Chicago, IL: University of Chicago Press, 1970.

Kunitz, Daniel. *Lift: Fitness Culture, from Naked Greeks and Acrobats to Jazzercise and Ninja Warriors*. New York: HarperCollins, 2016.

Kusinitz, Ivan, and Clifford E. Keeney. "Effects of Progressive Weight Training on Health and Physical Fitness of Adolescent Boys." *Research Quarterly* 29.3 (October 1958): 294–301.

Kutzer, William. "The History of Olympic Weightlifting in the United States." PhD diss., Brigham Young University, 1979.

Laberge, Walter. "Correct Those Little Postural Deficits." *Strength & Health* (February 1935): 12, 37.

———. "Little Known Facts concerning the Heart." *Strength & Health* (March 1935): 5, 12.

LaGrange, Ferdinand. *Physiology of Bodily Exercise*. New York: D. Appleton and Co., 1896.

Lake, Owen. "Pioneer of Physical Medicine: Dr. Thomas DeLorme." *Strength & Health* (June 1959): 22–23, 48, 50–51.

———. "Sox Sluggers' Secret of Success." *Strength & Health* (June 1958): 16–17, 48.

LaLanne, Jack. "Do You Want Strength Plus Endurance?" *Your Physique* 10.5 (February 1949): 26–27, 37–38.

Lange, Bernard H. "Build Up Your Back." *Strength* 8.2 (October 1923): 53–55, 82.

———. "Football as a Bodybuilder." *Strength* 7.2 (October 1922): 37–41, 66–69.

———. "Football as a Bodybuilder." *Strength* 7.4 (December 1922): 25–29, 72, 74, 76.

———. "How to Use the Gymnasium." *Strength* 6.6 (February 1922): 26–29, 50.

———. "How to Use the Gymnasium." *Strength* 6.7 (March 1922): 21–24, 62–63.

———. "How to Use the Gymnasium." *Strength* 6.8 (April 1922): 23–26, 58–59.

———. "The Neck and How to Develop It." *Strength* 7.9 (May 1923): 42–49.

———. "The Proven Way." *Strength & Health* (December 1947): 19, 34–37.

Larmour, David Henry James. *Stage and Stadium*. Hildesheim, Germany: Weidmann, 1999.

Laskowski, Karisa D., and William P. Ebben. "Profile of Women Collegiate Strength and Conditioning Coaches." *Journal of Strength and Conditioning Research* 30.12 (December 2016): 3481–3493.

Layden, Tim. "Power Play." *Sports Illustrated*, July 27, 1998: 60–65.

Lee, Benjamin. "The Health Lift: Is it Rational, Scientific, or Safe?" *Medical and Surgical Reporter* 38 (April 1878): 261–365.

Lee, Bob, and Jerri Lee. "Weight Training for a Mountain Marathon." *Strength & Health* (August 1960): 24–25, 45–48.

Leigh, Bob. "Barbells: A Springboard to Sports." *Muscle Power* 2.2 (December 1946): 129.

Leighton, Jack R. "Are Weight Lifters Muscle Bound?" *Strength & Health* (March 1956): 16, 44–46.

———. "Barbells on Campus: Eastern Washington College of Education." *Strength & Health* (December 1961): 34–35, 50–52.

———. *Progressive Weight Training*. New York: Ronald Press, 1961.

Leistner, Ken, and Sandy McLeod. "Alvin Roy—Fitness for Football." *Strength & Health* (November 1960): 50–51.

Lewis, Dale A. "Collegiate Tennis Conditioning." *Physical Educator* 7.3 (October 1950): 78.

Lewis, Dio. *The New Gymnastics*. London: W. Tweedie, 1864.

Liederman, Earle. "Are Large Muscles Useful?" *Muscle Power* (December 1946): 31–35, 121.

———. "Barbells and a Golf Champion!" *Muscle Power* 8.2 (July 1949): 32, 49.

———. "Editorial." *Muscle Power* (April 1951): 3.

———. "What Good Are Muscles Anyway?" *Your Physique* (August 1946): 34–35, 47, 53–54.

———. "What the Champs Are Saying." *Muscle Power* (November 1954): 7, 42.

Little, C., H. Strayhorn, and A. T. Miller. "Effect of Water Ingestion on Capacity for Exercise." *Research Quarterly* 20.4 (December 1949): 398–401.

Litwhiler, Danny. "Baseball Conditioning Secrets." *All American Athlete* (May 1964): 22–25, 56.

Locks, Adam, and Niall Richardson, eds. *Critical Readings in Bodybuilding*. New York: Routledge, 2012.

Loewendahl, Evelyn. "Muscle Development in Athletic Training." *Journal of Health, Physical Education, and Recreation* 21.6 (June 1950): 331–332.

Lowther, George. "How Johnny Weissmuller Keeps Fit." *Your Physique* 8:6 (March 1948): 8–9, 43.

Lupica, Benedict. "Muscle Power and Reflexes." *Muscle Power* (March 1949): 23, 46.

Lurie, Dan. "Heavy Exercise and Sports." *Muscle Power* 1.3 (April 1946): 61–64.

MacMahon, Charles. "Cash In on Trained Muscles." *Strength* 12 (June 1927): 25–27.

MacQueen, I. J. "Recent Advances in the Technique of Progressive Resistance Exercise." *British Medical Journal* 2.4898 (November 20, 1954): 1193–1198.

———. "Recent Advances in the Technique of Progressive Resistance Exercise." *Muscle Builder* 4.3 (April 1955): 36.

Magdalinski, Tara. *Sport, Technology, and the Body: The Nature of Performance*. New York: Routledge, 2009.

Magnusen, Marshall J., and Deborah J. Rhea. "Division I Athletes' Attitudes toward and Preferences for Male and Female Strength and Conditioning Coaches." *Journal of Strength and Conditioning Research* 23.4 (2009): 1084–1090.

Mahoney, R. J. "Barbells on Campus: Notre Dame." *Strength & Health* (October 1967): 46–48, 59.

Manis, Dub. "The Weight Trained Track Team of Abilene Christian College." *Strength & Health* (May 1965): 14–17, 69.

Mannie, Ken. "Anabolic-Androgenic Steroids in the High School: The New Drug Crisis." *NSCA Journal* 10.4 (August 1988): 64–65.

Maraniss, David. *Rome 1960: The Olympics That Changed the World*. New York: Simon & Schuster, 2008.

Marble, Sanders. *Rehabilitating the Wounded: A Historical Perspective on Army Policy*. Falls Church, VA: Office of the Surgeon General, Office of Medical History, 2008.

Marburg-Cappel, Erich Geldbach. "The Beginning of German Gymnastics in America." *Journal of Sport History* 3.3 (Fall 1976): 236–272.

Masley, John W., Ara Hairabedian, and Donald Donaldson. "Weight Training in Relation to Strength, Speed, and Coordination." *Research Quarterly* 24.3 (October 1953): 308–315.

Massengale, John, and Richard Swanson, eds. *The History of Exercise and Sport Science*. Champaign, IL: Human Kinetics, 1997.

Massey, Benjamin H. *The Kinesiology of Weightlifting*. Dubuque, IA: Wm. C. Brown Co., 1959.

Massey, Benjamin H., and Norman L. Chaudet. "Effects of Systematic, Heavy Resistive Exercise on Range of Joint Movement in Young Male Adults." *Research Quarterly* 27.1 (March 1956): 41–51.

Massey, Benjamin H., Harold W. Freeman, Frank R. Manson, and Janet A. Wessel. *The Kinesiology of Weightlifting*. Dubuque, IA: Wm. C. Brown Co., 1959.

Massey, C. Dwayne, and John Vincent. "A Job Analysis of Major College Female Strength and Conditioning Coaches." *Journal of Strength and Conditioning Research* 27.7 (July 2013): 2000–2012.

Massey, C. Dwayne, John Vincent, and Mark Maneval. "Job Analysis of College Division 1-A Football Strength and Conditioning Coaches." *Journal of Strength and Conditioning Research* 18.1 (2004): 19–25.

Matveyev, Leo Pavlovic. *Periodization of Sports Training*. Moscow: Fiskultura i Sport, 1965.

May, Elaine T. *Homeward Bound: American Families in the Cold War Era*. New York: Basic Books, 2008.

McArdle, William, Frank Katch, and Victor Katch. *Exercise Physiology: Nutrition, Energy, and Human Performance*. Baltimore, MD: Lippincott, Williams, and Wilkins, 2010.

McCallum, Jack. "Everybody's Doin' It." *Sports Illustrated*, December 3, 1984, 72–86.

McCandless, Wilbur. "Body-Building and Weightlifting." *Journal of Physical Education* 38.4 (March–April 1941): 64–65, 75–76.

McClanahan, W. J. "Strength Most Important in Football Success." *Strength & Health* (December 1945): 20, 34.

McClements, Lawrence E. "Power Relative to Strength of Leg and Thigh Muscles." *Research Quarterly* 37.1 (March 1966): 71–78.

McCloy, C. H. "Adequate Overload." *Journal of Physical Education* 42.4 (March–April 1945): 69.

———. "Endurance." *Physical Educator* 5.2 (March 1948): 9–10, 23.

———. "A Half Century in Physical Education." *Physical Educator* 17.3 (1960): 83.

———. "How about Some Muscle?" *Journal of Health and Physical Education* 7.5 (1936): 302–303, 355.

———. "Physical Reconditioning in the Army Service Forces." *Journal of Health and Physical Education* 15.7 (September 1944): 365–367, 412.

———. "Weight Training for Athletes?" *Strength & Health* (July 1955): 8–11, 39–40, 44.

———. "Weight Training Routine Used by State University of Iowa Basketball Team in the Training Season Preceding the Competitive Schedule in 1954." *Journal of Physical Education* 53.2 (November–December 1955): 50.

McComas, Alan J. "The Neuromuscular System." In *Exercise Physiology: People and Ideas*, ed. Charles M. Tipton, 39–97. New York: Oxford University Press, 2003.

McCoy, Frank. "The Way to Good Health." *San Antonio Express*, February 4, 1933.

McCraw, Lynn W., and Stan Burnham. "Resistive Exercises in the Development of Muscular Strength and Endurance." *Research Quarterly* 37.1 (March 1966): 79–88.

McCurdy, James. H., and Leonard A. Larson. *The Physiology of Exercise: A Text-Book for Students of Physical Education*. Philadelphia: Lea and Febiger, 1939.

McGovern, Art, and Edwin Goewey. "Babe Ruth Brought Back by Physical Culture." *Physical Culture* (August 1926): 38–39, 107–111.

McKenzie, R. Tait. *Exercise in Education and Medicine*. Philadelphia, W. B. Saunders, 1917 and 1924.

——. "The Influence of Exercise on the Heart." *American Journal of the Medical Sciences* 145.1 (1913): 69.

McKenzie, Shelly. *Getting Physical: The Rise of Fitness Culture in America*. Lawrence: Kansas University Press, 2013.

——. "Mass Movements: A Cultural History of Physical Fitness and Exercise, 1953–1989." PhD diss., George Washington University, 2008.

McLaughlin, Harry. "Barbells Aid Olympic Swimming Aspirants." *Strength & Health* (May 1952): 26–27, 42.

McLean, Roy J., and Karl K. Klein. "Barbells on Campus: The University of Texas." *Strength & Health* (January 1960): 34–35, 53–57.

McMullen, John, and Timothy L. Uhl. "A Kinetic Chain Approach to Shoulder Rehabilitation." *Journal of Athletic Training* 35.3 (2000): 329–337.

Meaders, H. T. "Iron Men of Georgia." *Strength & Health* (April 1949): 22–23, 31–32.

"Member Profile." *NSCA Bulletin* 18.2 (1997): 13.

"Member Spotlight: Boyd Epley, CSCS." *NSCA Bulletin* 18.3 (1997): 4.

Michelli, Lyle. "The Prepubescent Athlete: Physiological and Orthopedic Considerations for Strengthening Prepubescent Athletes." *NSCA Journal* 7.6 (1985): 26–27.

Miller, Carl. "Rotary Action of the Legs and Hips Common to Many Sports." *NSCA Journal* 1.6 (1979): 20–22.

Miller, Joe. "Joe Miller's Rise to Fame." *Strength & Health* (December 1932): 8–9.

Miller, Stephen G. *Ancient Greek Athletics*. New Haven, CT: Yale University Press, 2004.

Mills, George R. *A View from the Bench: The Story of an Ordinary Player on a Big-Time Football Team*. Urbana: University of Illinois Press, 2004.

Montez de Oca, Jeffrey. "The 'Muscle Gap': Physical Education and U.S. Fears of a Depleted Masculinity, 1954–1963." In *East Plays West: Sport and the Cold War*, ed. Stephen Wagg and David L. Andrews, 122–148. New York: Routledge, 2007.

Moore, Louis. "Black Sparring Masters, Gymnasium Owners, and the White Body, 1825–1886." *Journal of African American History* 96.4 (Fall 2011): 448–473.

Moore, Pamela, ed. *Building Bodies*. Piscataway, NJ: Rutgers University Press, 1997.

Morehouse, Laurence E., and John M. Cooper. *Kinesiology*. St Louis, MO: C. V. Mosby, 1950.

Mozee, Gene. "L. Jay Silvester." *Physical Power* 3.2 (March–April 1962): 4–6, 28.

——. "The Mighty Trojans: How They Use Weights in Training." *Physical Power* 4.3 (May–June 1963): 18–19.

——. "University of Southern California: National Football Champions." *Physical Power* 4.2 (March–April 1963): 6–8.

——. "Weight Training for Baseball: How Jim Winn Became a Pro through the Use of Weights." *Physical Power* 3.3 (May–June 1962): 8–10.

Mrozek, Donald. "The Cult and Ritual of Toughness in Cold War America." In *Sport in America: From Wicked Amusement to National Obsession*, ed. David K. Wiggins, 257–267. Champaign, IL: Human Kinetics, 1995.

——. "The Scientific Quest for Physical Culture and the Persistent Appeal of Quackery." *Journal of Sport History* 14.1 (1987): 76–86.

——. "Sport in American Life: From National Health to Personal Fulfillment." In *Fitness in American Culture: Images of Health, Sport, and the Body,*

1830–1940, ed. Kathryn Grover, 18–46. Amherst: University of Massachusetts Press, 1989.

Murphy, Michael. *Athletic Training*. Ed. Edward Bushnell. New York: Scribner's, 1914.

Murray, Jim. "British Empire Speedster Uses Weight Training." *Strength & Health* (March 1955): 11, 40.

———. "Canadian Barbelle Glamazon Seeks Olympic Games Victory." *Strength & Health* (July 1955): 12–13, 44.

———. "Do You Think You Are Too Small for Football?" *Strength & Health* (November 1953): 10–11, 42.

———. "How Weight Training Makes Basketball Giants." *All American Athlete* 6.12 (December 1964): 22–25.

———. "Isometric Exercise." *Muscle Builder* (February 1963): 40–41, 84–85, 88–89.

———. "More about Isometric Contractions." *Muscle Builder* (March 1963): 26–27, 74–75, 78.

———. "Pre-Season Football Training." *Physical Power* 3.4 (July–August 1962): 6–7.

———. "Protective Exercises in an Athletic Training Program." *Mr. America* (January 1963): 52–53, 84–85.

———. "Scientific Studies and High Quality Publications Attest to the Value of Weight Training Exercise." *Muscle Builder* 11.3 (May 1967): 26–27, 61–62.

———. "Summer Training for Football—With Barbells." *Strength & Health* (June 1955): 10, 44.

———. "Taking a Look at Isometric Exercise." *Physical Power* (March–April 1962): 18–21, 25, 28.

———. "Weightlifting's Non-Lifting Patron Saint." *Iron Game History* 4.5–6 (August 1997): 3–5.

———. "Weight Training and Football." *Physical Power* (October 1961): 6–7, 26–27.

———. "Weight Training for the Shot Put." *Mr. America* 5.12 (July 1963): 30–31, 86–88.

———. "Weight Training for Wrestlers." *Physical Power* (January–February 1962): 6–7.

Murray, Jim, and Peter Karpovich. *Weight Training in Athletics*. Englewood Cliffs, NJ: Prentice-Hall, 1956.

Muzumdar, S. "The Great Gama." *Your Physique* (January 1949): 8–9, 34.

McQuilkin, Scott. "'The World's Source for Strength and Conditioning Information': A History of the National Strength and Conditioning Association, 1978–1993." MS thesis, Pennsylvania State University, 1995.

McQuilkin, Scott, and Ronald A Smith. *A History of the National Strength and Conditioning Association, 1978–2000*. Colorado Springs, CO: NSCA, 2005.

"Member Update." *NSCA Bulletin* 12.9 (1991): 12.

Nash, Heyward. "Instructor Certification: Making Fitness Programs Safer?" *Physician and Sportsmedicine* 13.10 (October 1985): 143–143, 146, 151–155.

"National Strength and Conditioning Association: Position Statement: Use and Abuse of Anabolic Steroids." *NSCA Journal* 7.2 (April 1985): 27.

Nay, Ronald. "In-Season Weight Training for Football." *Strength & Health* (December 1969): 16–18, 61.

Needham, Dorothy. *Machina Carnis: The Biochemistry of Muscular Contraction in Its Historical Development*. Cambridge: Cambridge University Press, 1971.

Nelson, John. "Summer Football Training." *Physical Power* 3.3 (May–June 1962): 12, 29.

Nelson, Richard C., and Richard A. Fahrney. "Relationship between Strength and Speed of Elbow Flexion." *Research Quarterly* 36.4 (December 1965): 455–463.

Neumann, John. "Barbells on Campus: The University of California." *Strength & Health* (February 1962): 40–41, 56–57.

——. "Weight Training for Football Players." *Strength & Health* (October 1959): 28–29, 50, 53–56.

Nicoll, Ernest. "Principles of Exercise Therapy." *British Medical Journal* 1.4302 (June 19, 1943): 747–750.

Noverr, Douglas A., and Lawrence E Ziewacz. *The Games They Played: Sports in American History, 1865–1980*. Chicago: Nelson-Hall, 1988.

"The NSCA 15-Year Chronology." *NSCA Journal* 15.1 (1993): 7–8.

NSCA Certification Handbook. Colorado Springs, CO: NSCA, 2015.

"NSCA Joins Forces to Serve NSCA Members: Human Kinetics to Publish *NSCA Journal*." *NSCA Bulletin* 14.5 (1993): 1–2.

"NSCA Leaders Share Their Vision for the Future." *NSCA Bulletin* 13.6 (November/December 1992): 1–3.

"NSCA Member Profile." *NSCA Bulletin* 18.1 (1997): 1.

"NSCA Members: A Body of Strength!" *NSCA Bulletin* 19.3 (1998): 1–2.

"NSCA Ranks Continue to Grow." *NSCA Bulletin* 15.6 (1994): 2.

"Nutrition Report: Vitamin B-15." *NSCA Journal* 1.6 (1979): 37.

O'Brien, Booker, and John Fair. "'As the Twig Is Bent': Bob Hoffman and Youth Training in the Pre-Steroid Era." *Iron Game History* 12.1 (August 2012): 28–51.

"Official Document: Code of Ethics for the National Strength and Conditioning Association." *NSCA Journal* 7.2 (1985): 25.

"Official Document: The National Strength and Conditioning Association Position Paper on Prepubescent Strength Training." *NSCA Journal* 7.4 (1985): 27–31.

Ogden, Cynthia L., Cheryl D. Fryar, Margaret D. Carroll, and Katherine M. Flegal. "Mean Body Weight, Height, and Body Mass Index, United States 1960–2002." *Advance Data from Vital and Health Statistics* 347 (October 27, 2004): 1–20.

Olson, John R., and Gary R. Hunter. "A Comparison of 1974 and 1984 Player Sizes, and Maximal Strength and Speed Efforts for Division I NCAA Universities." *NSCA Journal* 6.6 (1985): 26–28.

Oriard, Michael. *Bowled Over: Big-Time College Football from the Sixties to the BCS Era*. Chapel Hill: University of North Carolina Press, 2009.

——. *King Football: Sport and Spectacle in the Golden Age of Radio and Newsreels, Movies and Magazines, the Weekly and Daily Press*. Chapel Hill: University of North Carolina Press, 2001.

——. *Reading Football: How the Popular Press Created an American Spectacle*. Chapel Hill: University of North Carolina Press, 1993.

Orlick, E. M. "Editorial—Let's Close the Scientific Sports Gap!" *All American Athlete* (February 1965): 5, 46.

——. "How Bodybuilding Can Make You a Better Athlete." *Muscle Builder* (June 1959): 34–35, 61.

——. "Introducing a New Scientific Strength Building Service." *All American Athlete* 6:9 (October 1964): 54.

——. "Let's Answer the Communist Sports Challenge." *All American Athlete* 6:7 (March 1964): 5, 70.

Orlick, E. M., and Joe Weider. "Barbells and Baseball." *Mr. America* 5.1 (June 1962): 38–39, 75–77.

O'Shea, Patrick. "Barbells on Campus: Oregon State University." *Strength & Health* (August 1965): 28–29, 76–77.

———. "Effects of Selected Weight Training Programs on the Development of Strength and Muscle Hypertrophy." *Research Quarterly* 37.1 (March 1966): 95–102.

———. "Oregon State University's Weight Trained Track Stars." *Strength & Health* (November 1968): 24–25, 63–65.

———. *Scientific Principles and Methods of Strength and Fitness.* Reading, MA: Addison-Wesley, 1976.

O'Shea, Patrick, and G. I. Strahl. "Barbells on Campus: Michigan State." *Strength & Health* (January 1962): 36–37, 51–53, 55.

Otott, George. "Barbells on Campus: Notre Dame." *Strength & Health* (April 1960): 36–37, 55–57.

Ove, Torseten. "Obituary: Albert M. Wiggins Jr." *Pittsburgh Post-Gazette*, July 3, 2012.

Page, Floyd. "Why Exercise?" *Muscle Power* (January 1949).

Panariello, Robert A. "The Closed Kinetic Chain in Strength Training." *NSCA Journal* 13.1 (1991): 29–33.

Park, Roberta. "Athletes and Their Training in Britain and America, 1800–1914." In *Sport and Exercise Science: Essays in the History of Sports Medicine*, ed. Jack W. Berryman and Roberta Park, 57–108. Urbana: University of Illinois Press, 1992.

———. "History of Research on Physical Activity and Health: Selected Topics, 1867 to the 1950s." *Quest* 47.3 (1995): 274–287.

———. "Muscles, Symmetry, and Action: 'Do You Measure Up?'—Defining Masculinity in Britain and America from the 1860s to the Early 1900s." *International Journal of the History of Sport* 24.12 (December 2007): 1604–1636.

———. "Physiology and Anatomy Are Destiny?!: Brains, Bodies and Exercise in Nineteenth Century American Thought." *Journal of Sport History* 18.1 (1991): 31–63.

Park, Roberta, J. A. Mangan, and Patricia Vertinsky. *Gender, Sport, and Science: Selected Writings of Roberta J. Park.* London: Routledge, 2009.

Paschall, Harry. "Barbells and Basketball." *Strength & Health* (December 1956): 15.

———. "Bosco." *Strength & Health* (March 1949): 12.

———. "Can Shelton Break the 7-Foot Barrier?" *Strength & Health* (June 1956): 10–11, 44.

———. "The Don Brag Story." *Strength & Health* (September 1956): 12–13, 50.

———. "Kansas' Bill Nieder." *Strength & Health* (November 1956): 28, 43.

———. "Weight Training for Athletics: Football." *Strength & Health* (October 1956): 10–11, 44.

Paul, Joan. "The Health Reformers: George Barker Windship and Boston's Strength Seekers." *Journal of Sports History* 10 (Winter 1983): 41–57.

Pauletto, Bruno. "President's Message: An Association at a Crossroads." *NSCA Journal* 13.6 (1991/1992): 79–80.

———. "President's Message: An Association on the Move." *NSCA Journal* 14.4 (1992): 84.

———. "President's Message: Membership Has Its Privileges." *NSCA Journal* 14.5 (1992): 5.

———. "President's Message: The 'New' NSCA." *NSCA Journal* 14, no. 1 (1992): 83.

———. "President's Message: Welcome Members!" *NSCA Journal* 15.1 (1993): 3.

———. "President's Message: What a Meeting!" *NSCA Journal* 14.2 (1992): 75.

Pearn, John. "Two Early Dynamometers: An Historical Account of the Earliest

Measurements to Study Human Muscular Strength." *Journal of the Neurological Sciences* 37 (1978): 127–134.

Pedemonte, Jimmy. "Foundations of Training Periodization Part One: Historical Outline." *NSCA Journal* 8.3 (1986): 62–66.

———. "Foundations of Training Periodization Part Two: The Objective of Periodization." *NSCA Journal* 8.4 (1986): 27.

———. "Historical Perspectives: Foundations of Training Periodization Part Two: The Objective of Periodization." *NSCA Journal* 8.4 (1986): 26–29.

———. "Training Notes: The Preparation of Soviet Throwers for the Moscow Olympics." *NSCA Journal* 5.5 (1983): 47–54.

———. "Training of General, Specific, and Special Strength: A Key to Improved Performances in Sport." *NSCA Journal* 3.6 (1981): 54–55.

———. "Updated Acquisitions about Training Periodization: Part One." *NSCA Journal* 4.5 (1982): 56–60.

———. "Updated Acquisitions about Training Periodization: Training the Young and Intermediate Athlete." *NSCAJ* 4.6 (1982): 42–44.

Pendergast, Tom. *Creating the Modern Man: American Magazines and Consumer Culture, 1900–1950.* Columbia: University of Missouri Press, 2000.

"Perceptions of High School Strength Coaches Regarding Steroid Use: A Pilot Study." *NSCA Journal* 11.3 (1989): 67–70.

"Personal Training: A Field in Progress." *NSCA Bulletin* 14.6 (1993): 3, 5.

Petro, A. T. "The Effect of Barbell Exercise on the Heart." *Muscle Power* 7.5 (April 1949): 5, 45–46.

Philostratus. "Gymnasticus." In Jeffrey Rusten and Jason Konig, eds. and trans., *Heroicus, Gymnasticus, Discourses 1 and 2.* Cambridge, MA: Harvard University Press, 2014.

Piper, Ralph A. "Values of Early Ambulation and Exercise in Surgical and Medical Treatment." *Journal of Health and Physical Education* 18.5 (May 1947): 297–299, 349–353.

Piscapo, John. "Strength." *Physical Educator* 24.2 (May 1967): 66–68.

Pitton, Paul M. "Prepubescent Strength Training: The Effects of Resistance Training on Strength Gains in Children." *NSCA Journal* 14.6 (1992): 55–57.

Plagenhoef, Stan. "Barbells on Campus: Wesleyan College of Connecticut." *Strength & Health* (December 1965): 16–17, 63–64.

Pope, Harrison, Katharine Phillips, and Roberto Olivardia. *The Adonis Complex: The Secret Crisis of Male Body Obsession.* New York: Free Press, 2000.

Portney, Leslie G., and Mary P. Watkins. *Foundations of Clinical Research: Applications to Practice.* Upper Saddle River, NJ: Pearson/Prentice Hall, 2009.

Prentice, William E. *Principles of Athletic Training.* New York: McGraw-Hill, 2011.

———. *Rehabilitation Technique for Sports Medicine and Athletic Training.* New York: McGraw-Hill, 2011.

Pruter, Robert. *The Rise of American High School Sports and the Search for Control, 1880–1930.* Syracuse, NY: Syracuse University Press, 2013.

Pullum, W. A. "Are Weightlifters Slow?" *Muscle Power* 1.6 (September 1946): 72–75.

Putney, Clifford. *Muscular Christianity: Manhood and Sports in Protestant America, 1880–1920.* Cambridge, MA: Harvard University Press, 2001.

Rabinbach, Anson. *The Human Motor: Energy, Fatigue, and the Origins of Modernity.* Berkeley: University of California Press, 1992.

Rader, Benjamin. *American Sports: From the Age of Folk Games to Televised Sports.* Upper Saddle River, NJ: Prentice-Hall, 1999.

Rader, Peary. "Weight Training at University of Nebraska for Student Body." *Iron Man* (March-April 1960): 19–20.

Rasch, Philip. "In Praise of Weight Training." *Muscle Power* 8.1 (June 1949): 12–13, 33–35.

———. "Relationship of Arm Strength, Weight, and Length to Speed of Arm Movement." *Research Quarterly* 25.3 (October 1954): 328–332.

Rasch, Philip J., and Laurence E. Morehouse. "Effect of Static and Dynamic Exercises on Muscular Strength and Hypertrophy." *Journal of Applied Physiology* 11.1 (1957): 29–34.

Rasch, Philip, Eugene O'Connell, and Gerald Gardner. "Circuit Training for the Athlete." *Strength & Health* (February 1961): 36–37, 55–57.

Ravelle, Lou. *Bodybuilding for Everyone.* New York: Emerson, 1965.

Raymond, Joe. "All That I Am, I Owe to Barbell Training." *Strength & Health* (March 1935): 22, 35.

Read, Dennis. "CSCC Weighs In." *Training and Conditioning* 11.9 (December 2001): 11–12, 14–17.

Reich, Jacqueline. "'The World's Most Perfectly Developed Man': Charles Atlas, Physical Culture, and the Inscription of American Masculinity." *Men and Masculinities* 12.4 (2010): 444–461.

Renfro, Gregory J. Renfro, "Summer Plyometric Training for Football and Its Effect on Speed and Agility." *Strength and Conditioning Journal* 21.3 (1999): 42.

"Results and Analysis of 1982–1983 Membership Survey." *NSCA Journal* 5.4 (1983): 54.

Reynolds, Monica L., Lynda B. Ransdell, Shelly M. Lucas, Linda M. Petlichkoff, and Yong Gao. "An Examination of Current Practices and Gender Differences in Strength and Conditioning in a Sample of Varsity High School Athletic Programs." *Journal of Strength and Conditioning Research* 26.1 (2012): 174–183.

Richardson, Tom, Pete Schmotzer, Jim Brandenburg, and William Kraemer. "Sports Performance Series: Improved Rebounding Performance through Strength Training." *NSCA Journal* 4.6 (1982): 6–9.

Rider, Toby C. *Cold War Games: Propaganda, the Olympics, and U.S. Foreign Policy.* Urbana: University of Illinois Press, 2016.

Riecke, Lou. "Steeler Strength the Powersafe Way." *NSCA Journal* 1.6 (1979): 12–13.

Riordan, James. "The Rise and Fall of Soviet Olympic Champions." *Olympika* 2 (1993): 25–44.

———. *Soviet Sport: Background to the Olympics.* Oxford: Basil Blackwell, 1980.

———. *Sport in Soviet Society: Development of Sport and Physical Education in Russia and the USSR.* Cambridge: Cambridge University Press, 1977.

Ritchey, George W. "Barbells on Campus: L.S.U." *Strength & Health* (July 1960): 36–37, 59–60.

Roach, Randy. *Muscle, Smoke, and Mirrors, Volume One.* Bloomington, IN: AuthorHouse, 2008.

———. *Muscle, Smoke, and Mirrors, Volume Two.* Bloomington, IN: AuthorHouse, 2011.

Roberts, Randy, and James S. Olson. *Winning Is the Only Thing: Sports in America since 1945.* Baltimore, MD: Johns Hopkins University Press, 1989.

Rosen, Daniel. *Dope: A History of Performance Enhancement in Sports from the Nineteenth Century to Today.* Westport, CT: Prager, 2008.

Ross, Clarence. "The Secret of Speed and Endurance." *Muscle Power* (June 1953): 17–18, 54–55.

Roth, Charles B. "Toughest Man on Earth." *Your Physique* 8.3 (December 1947): 16–17, 40.

"Roundtable: Determining Factors of Strength—Part One." *NSCA Journal* 7.1 (1985): 10–19, 22–23.

"Roundtable: Power Clean." *NSCA Journal* 6.6 (1984): 10–19, 22–25.

Roy, Alvin. "The Strength Program of the San Diego Chargers." *Strength & Health* (January 1965): 14–17, 62–66.

Rudd, J. L. "Medical Aspects of Weight Lifting—Its Use in Rehabilitation." *Journal of Physical Education* 46.3 (March–April 1949): 53–54.

———. "Weight Lifting—Healthful—Harmful?" *Journal of Physical Education* 46.6 (July–August 1949): 90–91.

Ruff, Wesley. "Barbells on Campus: Stanford University." *Strength & Health* (March 1960): 24–25, 59.

Sahrmann, Shirley. *Diagnosis and Treatment of Movement Impairment Syndromes.* Philadelphia: Mosby, 2002.

Sanders, M. T. "A Comparison of Two Methods of Training on the Development of Muscular Strength and Endurance." *Journal of Orthopedic Sports Physical Therapy* 1.4 (1980): 210–213.

Sansone, Tony. "A Miracle of Barbells." *Strength & Health* (July 1937): 24, 43.

Santana, Juan Carlos. *Functional Training: Breaking the Bonds of Traditionalism.* Boca Raton, FL: Optimum Performance Systems, 2000.

Sargent, Dudley Allen. *Anthropometric Apparatus with Directions for Measuring and Testing the Principal Physical Characteristics of the Human Body.* Cambridge, MA: n.p., 1887.

———. *Dudley Allen Sargent: An Autobiography.* Philadelphia: Lea & Febiger, 1927.

———. *Health, Strength & Power.* Boston, MA: H. M. Caldwell, 1904.

Saxon, Arthur. *The Development of Physical Power.* New York: Healthtex, 1931.

Schafer, Julie. "Prepubescent and Adolescent Weight Training: Is It Safe? Is It Beneficial?" *NSCA Journal* 13.1 (1991): 39–46.

Schmidt, F. A. "Opinions on Heart Exercise and Acute Heart Dilation." *Physical Educator* 14.1 (March 1957): 10–13.

Schneider, Edward, and Peter Karpovich. *Physiology of Muscular Activity.* Philadelphia: Saunders, 1959.

Schofro, Frank. "How I Got That Way." *Strength & Health* (August 1944): 20–21, 42–43.

———. "How I Got That Way—Part II." *Strength & Health,* (September 1944): 29, 7, 9.

Schuessler, Raymond. "Training for the Sprints." *All American Athlete* (April 1964): 49–53, 89.

Schultz, Gordon W. "Effect of Direct Practice, Repetitive Sprinting, and Weight Training on Selected Motor Performance Tests." *Research Quarterly* 38.1 (March 1967): 108–118.

Scott, Jim. "Who Are America's Weight Trained Athletes?" *Strength & Health* (September 1960): 30–31, 59–60.

Scranton, Sheila, and Anne Flintoff, eds. *Gender and Sport: A Reader*. London: Routledge, 2001.

Seaver, Jay W. *Anthropometry and Physical Examination: A Book for Practical Use in Connection with Gymnastic Work and Physical Education*. Meriden, CT: Curtiss-Way Co., 1909.

Secora, Craig A., Richard W. Latin, Kris E. Berg, and John M. Noble. "Comparison of Physical and Performance Characteristics of NCAA Division I Football Players: 1987 and 2000." *Journal of Strength and Conditioning Research* 18.2 (2004): 286–291.

Seefeldt, Vern D., and Martha Ewing, "Youth Sports in America: An Overview." *President's Council on Physical Fitness and Sports: Research Digest* 2.11 (September 1997): 3–14.

Segurson, Jack. "Weights and Winning Tennis—Weight Training Keeps Jim Dye a Top Notch Net Star." *Strength & Health* (December 1958): 20–21.

Seida, Lowell M. *William Buckingham "Father Bill" Curtis: Father of American Amateur Athletics*. Westchester, IL: by the author, 2001.

Shaw, Gary. *Meat on the Hoof: The Hidden World of Texas Football*. New York: St. Martin's Press, 1972.

Shelton, Herbert. "Medicine Discovers Weight Lifting." *Your Physique* (August 1944): 14–15, 59.

Shelton, Robert E. "Responsibilities of the Athletic Trainer." *Physical Educator* 15.4 (1958): 140.

Sherrington, Charles. "Some Functional Problems Attaching to Convergence." *Proceedings of the Royal Society* 105.737 (September 1929): 332–362.

Shurley, Jason. "Strength for Sport: The Development of the Professional Strength and Conditioning Coach." PhD diss., University of Texas–Austin, 2013.

Shurley, Jason, and Jan Todd. "'If Anyone Gets Slower You're Fired': Boyd Epley and the Formation of the Strength Coaching Profession." *Iron Game History* 11.3 (2011): 4–18.

———. "Joe Weider, All American Athlete, and the Promotion of Strength Training for Sport: 1940–1969." *Iron Game History* 12.1 (August 2012): 4–26.

———. "'The Strength of Nebraska': Boyd Epley, Husker Power, and the Formation of the Strength Coaching Profession." *Journal of Strength and Conditioning Research* 26.12 (2012): 3177–3188.

Shurley, Jason, Jan Todd, and Terry Todd. "The Science of Strength: Reflections on the NSCA and the Emergence of Research-Based Strength and Conditioning." *Journal of Strength and Conditioning Research* 31.2 (2017): 517–530.

Siff, Mel. *Supertraining: A Scientific Method for Strength, Endurance, and Weight Training*. Denver: Supertraining Institute, 2004.

Sifft, Josie. "Reading and Understanding Research: Guidelines for Selecting a Sample." *NSCA Journal* 6.1 (1984): 26–27.

———."Research: Reading and Understanding: Utilizing Descriptive Statistics in Sport Performance." *NSCA Journal* 5.5 (1983): 26–28.

Sifft, Josie, and William J. Kraemer. "Research: Reading and Understanding: Introduction, Review of Literature, Methods." *NSCA Journal* 4.4 (1982): 24–25.

Sipes, Charles. "How I Use Weider Power Methods to Build Championship Football Teams." *Mr. America* (February 1960): 32–33, 64–65.

———. "Misconceptions about Weight Training." *Mr. America* (April 1962): 36–37, 64.

Smith, Charles. "Jack Delinger—From Rheumatic Fever to the World's Perfect Man." *Muscle Builder* 2.3 (April 1954): 5, 64.

Smith, G. Malcolm. "You Can Build a Powerful Physique." *Your Physique* (January 1942): 12–13.

Smith, Gordon C. "Barbells on Campus: Weightlifting at Michigan State U." *Strength & Health* (May 1959): 36–37, 60–61.

Smith, Leon E. "Influence of Strength Training on Pre-Tensed and Free-Arm Speed." *Research Quarterly* 35.4 (December 1964): 554–561.

Smith, Leon E., and Jim D. Whitley. "Relation between Muscular Force of a Limb, under Different Starting Conditions, and Speed of Movement." *Research Quarterly* 34.4 (December 1963): 489–496.

Smith, Maureen M. "Early Sport Specialization: A Historical Perspective." *Kinesiology Review* 4.3 (2015): 220–229.

Smith, Michael M., Allan J. Sommer, Brooke E. Starkoff, and Steven T. Devor. "CrossFit-Based High-Intensity Power Training Improves Maximal Aerobic Fitness and Body Composition." *Journal of Strength and Conditioning Research* 27.11 (2013): 3159–3172.

Smith, Ronald A. "Far More Than Commercialism: Stadium Building from Harvard's Innovations to Stanford's 'Dirt Bowl.'" *International Journal of the History of Sport* 25.11 (2008): 1453–1474.

———. *Sports & Freedom: The Rise of Big-Time College Athletics*. New York: Oxford University Press, 1988.

Smith, Steve. *Forever Red: Confessions of a Cornhusker Football Fan*. Lincoln: University of Nebraska Press, 2005.

Snyder-Mackler, Lynn. "Scientific Rationale and Physiological Basis for the Use of Closed Kinetic Chain Exercise in the Lower Extremity." *Journal of Sport Rehabilitation* 5.1 (1996): 2 12.

Sperber, Murray. *Beer and Circus: How Big-Time College Sports Is Crippling Undergraduate Education*. New York, Henry Holt & Company, 2000.

———. *Onward to Victory: The Crises That Shaped College Sports*. New York: Henry Holt, 1998.

Sport in Los Angeles. Little Rock: University of Arkansas Press, 2017.

Stafford, George, and Oscar Duncan. *Physical Conditioning: Exercises for Sports and Healthful Living*. New York: Barnes, 1942.

Stanko, Steve. "Strength Most Important in Football Success." *Strength & Health* (November 1945): 20–21, 43.

Starck, Al, and Steven J. Fleck. "Research: Reading and Understanding: The Discussion Section." *NSCA Journal* 4.6 (1982): 40–41.

Starling, E. H., and M. B. Visscher, "The Regulation of the Energy Output of the Heart." *Journal of Physiology* 62 (1926): 243–261.

Steindler, Arthur. *Kinesiology of the Human Body under Normal and Pathological Conditions*. Springfield, IL: Thomas, 1955.

Steinhaus, Arthur. "Chronic Effects of Exercise." *Physiological Reviews* 13.1 (January 1933): 103–147.

———. "Physiology at the Service of Physical Education." *Journal of Health and Physical Education* 18 (October 1930): 34.

———. "Physiology at the Service of Physical Education: Chemical Changes in Muscle Due to Training." *Journal of Health and Physical Education* 3.7 (September 1932): 52, 54.

———. "Physiology at the Service of Physical Education: Muscle Hypertrophy." *Journal of Health and Physical Education* 3.6 (June 1932): 36–37.

——. "Physiology at the Service of Physical Education: The Heart Size—Effects of Training." *Journal of Health and Physical Education* 2.10 (December 1931): 42.

——. "Physiology at the Service of Physical Education: The Theory of Muscular Contraction Is Being Renovated." *Journal of Health and Physical Education* 3.1 (1932): 44–45.

——. "Why Exercise?" *Journal of Health and Physical Education* 5.5 (May 1934): 5–6.

Steinhaus, Arthur, Alma Hawkins, Charles Giauque, and Edward Thomas. *How to Keep Fit and Like It: A Manual for Civilians and a Plan for a Community Approach to Physical Fitness*. Chicago: Consolidated Book Publishers, 1943.

Stern, Leo. "How Frank Stranahan Trains for Golf." *Strength & Health* (April 1958): 26.

Stern, Marc. "The Fitness Movement and the Fitness Center Industry, 1960–2000." *Business and Economic History Online* 6 (2008): 11.

"Steroid Education: What the Coach, Athlete, and Parent Need to Know about Anabolic Drugs: A Fact Sheet." *NSCA Journal* 11.6 (1989): 10–13.

Stevens, Ernest. "The Importance of Breath Control." *Strength & Health* (February 1935): 13, 38–40.

Stiggins, Chuck. "23 Coaches in Attendance at CSCCa Foundation Meeting." CSCCa Archives, n.d.

——. "Invitation to Join the CSCCa." CSCCa Archives, January 9, 2001.

——. Letter to Karri Baker. CSCCa Archives, March 9, 2000.

——. Letter to Strength and Conditioning Coaches. CSCCa Archives, n.d.

Stockton, Pudgy. "Barbelles." *Strength & Health* (May 1946): 21.

——. "Barbelles." *Strength & Health* (May 1950): 24–25, 46.

——. "Barbelles." *Strength & Health* (October 1950): 14.

Stoddard, Grant. "Inside the Cult of Crossfit." *Men's Health* (November 2011): 130–175.

Stone, Mike. "President's Message." *NSCA Bulletin* 15.6 (November/December 1994): 3.

——. "President's Message: Sports, Coaches and the NSCA." *NSCA Bulletin* 17.3 (1996): 3.

——. "Strength Training Modes: Free Weights—Part II: Considerations in Gaining a Strength–Power Training Effect (Machines vs. Free Weights)." *NSCA Journal* 4.1 (1982): 22–24.

Stone, Mike, and John Garhammer. "Viewpoint: Some Thoughts on Strength and Power." *NSCA Journal* 3.5 (October 1981): 24–25, 47.

Stone, Mike, Robert L. Johnson, and David R. Carter. "A Short Term Comparison of Two Different Methods of Resistance Training on Leg Strength and Power." *Athletic Training* 14.3 (1979): 158–160.

Stone, Mike, Harold O'Bryant, and John Garhammer. "A Hypothetical Model for Strength Training." *Journal of Sports Medicine and Physical Fitness* 21.4 (1981): 342–351.

Stone, Mike, Harold O'Bryant, John Garhammer, Jim McMillan, and Ralph Rozenek. "A Theoretical Model of Strength Training." *NSCA Journal* 4.4 (1982): 36–39.

Stone, Mike, Kyle Pierce, William Sands, and Meg Stone. "Weightlifting: A Brief Overview." *Strength and Conditioning Journal* 28.1 (2006): 50–66.

Stowers, Tim, Jim McMillan, Dwight Scala, Voris Davis, Dennis Wilson, and Mike

Stone. "The Short-Term Effects of Three Different Strength-Power Training Methods." *NSCA Journal* 5.3 (1983): 24–27.

Strain, D. E. "Body Building with Weights." *Journal of Physical Education* 42.4 (March–April 1945): 76–77.

"Strength Training Modes: Nautilus: The Concept of Variable Resistance." *NSCA Journal* 3.4 (1981): 48–50.

Suggs, Welch. *A Place on the Team: The Triumph and Tragedy of Title IX*. Princeton, NJ: Princeton University Press, 2005.

Summers, Richard B. "Complex Training at Ponderosa High." *Strength and Conditioning Journal* 21.4 (1999): 46.

"Survey Results Plan 1994 Conference." *NSCA Bulletin* 14.6 (1993): 6–7, 9.

Swetz, Frank. "Barbells on Campus: Marist College." *Strength & Health* (December 1964): 24–25, 68, 70.

Taft, William H. "Bernarr Macfadden." *Missouri Historical Review* 63:1 (October 1968): 71–89.

Tanny, Armand. "George Frenn—Power Lifter." *Muscle Builder* (July 1966): 40–41, 58–59.

———. "The Man on the Surfboard." *All American Athlete* 6.4 (November 1963): 53–56, 98.

Taylor, Frederick Winslow. *The Principles of Scientific Management* (1919). Mineola, NY: Dover Publications, 1988.

Telander, Rick. *The Hundred Yard Lie: The Corruption of College Football and What We Can Do to Stop It*. New York: Fireside, 1989.

Terlazzo, Tony. "Barbell Men in the Service." *Strength & Health* (August 1943): 12–14.

———. "Barbell Men in the Service." *Strength & Health* (June 1944): 12–13, 46.

Terpak, John. "You Can Improve Your Athletic Ability." *Strength & Health* (June 1944): 24, 38–39.

Terrell, Roy. "All-Star Who Can Do without Glory." *Sports Illustrated*, June 23, 1958.

Teufel, William F. "A Comparison of the Effectiveness of Two Methods of Exercise for the Development of Muscular Strength." MS thesis, University of Iowa, 1952.

Theriault, Ed. "Barbells and Running." *Mr. America* 5.3 (August–September 1962): 38–39, 76, 78–79.

Thomas, Al. "Reflections on Musclebinding." *Iron Game History* 2.2 (1992): 1–2.

———. "Where Are They Now? Bill Curry and the Gospel of Physical Fitness." *Iron Game History* 2.6 (May 1993): 18.

Thomas, Zenta. "Britain's Weight-Trained Lady Jumper." *Strength & Health* (February 1964): 50–52.

Thompson, Hugh L., and G. Alan Stull. "Effects of Various Training Programs on Speed of Swimming." *Research Quarterly* 30.4 (December 1959): 479–485.

Thompson, Paul. "Historical Concepts of the Athlete's Heart." *Medicine and Science in Sports and Exercise* 36.3 (2004): 363–370.

Thompson, Walter R. "Now Trending: Worldwide Survey of Fitness Trends for 2014." *ACSM's Health and Fitness Journal* 17.6 (2013): 10–20.

———. "Worldwide Survey Reveals Fitness Trends for 2007." *ACSM's Health and Fitness Journal* 10.6 (2006): 8–14.

———. "Worldwide Survey Reveals Fitness Trends for 2008." *ACSM's Health and Fitness Journal* 11.6 (2007): 7–13.

——. "Worldwide Survey Reveals Fitness Trends for 2009." *ACSM's Health and Fitness Journal* 12.6 (2008): 7–14.

——. "Worldwide Study Reveals Fitness Trends for 2010." *ACSM's Health and Fitness Journal* 13.6 (2009): 9–16.

——. "Worldwide Study Reveals Fitness Trends for 2011." *ACSM's Health and Fitness Journal* 14.6 (2010): 8–17.

——. "Worldwide Study Reveals Fitness Trends for 2012." *ACSM's Health and Fitness Journal* 15.6 (2011): 9–18.

——. "Worldwide Survey of Fitness Trends for 2013." *ACSM's Health and Fitness Journal* 16.6 (2012): 8–17.

——. "Worldwide Survey of Fitness Trends for 2015." *ACSM's Health and Fitness Journal* 18.6 (2014): 8–17.

——. "Worldwide Survey of Fitness Trends for 2016: 10th Anniversary Edition." *ACSM's Health and Fitness Journal* 19.6 (2015): 9–18.

——. "Worldwide Survey of Fitness Trends for 2018." *ACSM's Health and Fitness Journal* 21.6 (2017): 10–19.

Thune, John B. "Defense of Weight Training." *Journal of Physical Education* 44.3 (January–February 1945): 58.

——. "Personality of Weightlifters." *Research Quarterly* 20.3 (October 1949): 296–306.

Tilney, Frederick. "Getting Acquainted with Your Editor-in-Chief Joseph E. Weider." *Your Physique* 4.4 (October 1944): 8–9.

——. "Re-Energize Yourself." *Strength & Health* (May 1936): 6–7, 42.

Tipton, Charles M. "Exercise Physiology, Part II: A Contemporary Historical Perspective." In *The History of Exercise and Sport Science*, ed. John D. Massengale and Richard A. Swanson, 396–438. Champaign, IL: Human Kinetics, 1997.

——, ed. *Exercise Physiology: People and Ideas*. New York: Oxford University Press, 2003.

Todd, Jan. "'As Men Do Walk a Mile, Women Should Talk an Hour . . . Tis Their Exercise,' and Other Pre-Enlightenment Thought on Women and Purposive Exercise." *Iron Game History* 7.2–3 (July 2002): 56–70.

——. "Bernarr Macfadden: Reformer of the Feminine Form." *Journal of Sport History* 14.1 (Spring 1987): 61–75.

——. "'Chaos Can Have Gentle Beginnings': The Early History of the Quest for Drug Testing in American Powerlifting: 1964-1984." *Iron Game History* 8.3 (May-June 2004): 3–22.

——. "The Classical Idea and Its Impact on the Search for Suitable Exercise: 1774–1830." *Iron Game History* 2.4 (November 1992): 6–16.

——. "From Milo to Milo: A History of Barbells, Dumbbells, and Indian Clubs." *Iron Game History* 3.6 (December 1995): 4–16.

——. "Legacy of Iron: A History of the Men, Women and Implements That Created the 'Iron Game.'" In *Resistance Training: The Total Approach*, ed. Lewis Bowling, 183–185. Durham, NC: Carolina Academic Press, 2007.

——. "The Legacy of Pudgy Stockton." *Iron Game History* 2.1 (January 1992): 5–7.

——. "The Mystery of Minerva." *Iron Game History* 1.2 (April 1990): 14–17.

——. "The Origins of Weight Training for Female Athletes in North America." *Iron Game History* 2.2 (April 1992): 4–14.

——. "Physical Culture and the Body Beautiful: An Examination of the Role of

Purposive Exercise in the Lives of American Women, 1800–1870." PhD diss., University of Texas at Austin, 1995.

———. *Physical Culture and the Body Beautiful: Purposive Exercise in the Lives of American Women, 1800–1870*. Macon, GA: Mercer University Press, 1998.

———. "Size Matters: Muscle, Drugs, and Sport." *Iron Game History* 10.3 (August 2008): 3–22.

———. "'Strength Is Health': George Barker Windship and the First American Weight Training Boom." *Iron Game History* 3.1 (September 1993): 3–14.

Todd, Jan, Dorothy Lovett, and Terry Todd. "The Status of Women in the Strength and Conditioning Profession." *NSCA Journal* 13.6 (1991–1992): 35–38.

Todd, Jan, Joe Roark, and Terry Todd. "A Briefly Annotated Bibliography of English Language Serial Publications in the Field of Physical Culture." *Iron Game History* 1.4 (1991): 25–40.

Todd, Jan, and Jason Shurley. "Building American Muscle: A Brief History of Barbells, Dumbbells, and Pulley Machines." In *The Routledge History of American Sport*, ed. Linda J. Borish, David K. Wiggins, and Gerald R. Gems, 343–356. New York: Routledge, 2017.

Todd, Jan, Jason Shurley, and Terry Todd. "Science from Strength: Thomas L. DeLorme and the Medical Acceptance of Progressive Resistance Exercise." *Iron Game History* 12.4 (August 2014): 68–80.

———. "Thomas L. DeLorme and the Science of Progressive Resistance Exercise." *Journal of Strength and Conditioning Research* 26.11 (2012): 2913–2923.

Todd, Jan, and Terry Todd. "The Conversion of Dr. Peter Karpovich." *Iron Game History* 8.4 (March 2005): 4–12.

———. "Legacy of Iron. A History of the Men, Women, and Implements That Created the 'Iron Game.'" In *Resistance Training: The Total Approach*, ed. Lewis Bowling, 165–215. Durham, NC: Carolina Academic Press, 2007.

———. "Peter V. Karpovich: Transforming the Strength Paradigm." *Journal of Strength and Conditioning Research* 17.2 (May 2003): 213–220.

Todd, Terry. "Al Roy: Mythbreaker." *Iron Game History* 2.1 (January 1992): 12–16.

———. "Al Roy: The First Modern Strength Coach." *Journal of Physical Education, Recreation, and Dance* 79.8 (2008): 14–16.

———. "Anabolic Steroids: The Gremlins of Sport." *Journal of Sport History* 14.1 (1987): 87–107.

———. "The Expansion of Resistance Training in U.S. Higher Education through the Mid-1960s." *Iron Game History* 3.4 (August 1994): 11–16.

———. "The History of Resistance Exercise and Its Role in United States Education." PhD diss., University of Texas—Austin, 1966.

———. "The History of Strength Training for Athletes at the University of Texas." *Iron Game History* 2.5 (January 1993): 6–13.

———. "A History of the Use of Anabolic Steroids in Sport." In *Sport and Exercise Science: Essays in the History of Sports Medicine*, ed. Jack W. Berryman and Roberta J. Park, 319–350. Urbana: University of Illinois Press, 1992.

———. "A Man of Heft Who's Also Deft." *Sports Illustrated*, November 8, 1982, 40–42, 44–45.

———. "The Myth of the Muscle-Bound Lifter." *NSCA Journal* 7.3 (1985): 37–41.

———. "The PGA Tour's Traveling Gym: How It All Began." *Iron Game History* 3.3 (April 1994): 14–19.

———. "A Pioneer of Physical Training: C. H. McCloy." *Iron Game History* 1.6 (August 1991): 1–2.

———. "Progressive Resistance for Football at the University of Texas." *Strength & Health* (September 1964): 18–19, 52, 54, 56.

———. "Remembering Bob Hoffman." *Iron Game History* 3.1 (1993): 18–23.

———. "Steroids: An Historical Perspective." *Iron Game History* 1.2 (April 1990): 1–3.

———. "The Steroid Predicament." *Sports Illustrated*, August 1, 1983, 70–73.

———. "Steroids: A Problem of Huge Dimensions." *Sports Illustrated*, May 13, 1985, 38–61.

Todd, Terry, and John Hoberman. "Yearning for Muscular Power." *Iron Game History* 9.3 (January/February 2007): 20–32.

Todd, Terry, and Jan Todd. "Dr. Patrick O'Shea: A Man for All Seasons." *Journal of Strength and Conditioning Research* 15.4 (2001): 401–404.

———. "Herbert A. deVries: 60 Years of Exercise and Science." *Journal of Strength and Conditioning Research* 16.1 (2002): 5–8.

———. "Pioneers of Strength Research: Herbert A deVries: 60 Years of Exercise and Science." *Journal of Strength and Conditioning Research* 16.1 (2001): 5–8.

———. "Pioneers of Strength Research: John Patrick O'Shea: A Man for All Seasons." *Journal of Strength and Conditioning Research* 15.4 (2001): 401–404.

———. "Pioneers of Strength Research: The Legacy of Dr. Richard A. Berger." *Journal of Strength and Conditioning Research* 15.3 (2001): 275–278.

———. "Professor Pat O'Shea: Strength Science Pioneer." *Iron Game History* 7.4 (2003): 26–29.

———. "The Science of Reps: The Strength Training Contributions of Dr. Richard A. Berger." *Iron Game History* 12.2 (February/March 2013): 12–15.

"Topics of the Times." *New York Times*, August 22, 1913.

Tracey, Allen. "You Can Make It: Strength Building Device for Swimmers." *All American Athlete* (September 1964): 10, 63.

Trall, Russell. *The Illustrated Family Gymnasium: Containing the Most Improved Methods of Applying Gymnastic, Calisthenic, Kinesipathic, and Vocal Exercises to the Development of the Bodily Organs, the Invigoration of Their Functions, the Preservation of Health, and the Cure of Diseases and Deformities*. New York: Fowler and Wells, 1857.

Triplett, N. Travis, Chat Williams, Patrick McHenry, and Michael Doscher. "Strength and Conditioning Professional Standards and Guidelines." *Strength and Conditioning Journal* 31.5 (2009): 14–38.

Tuppeny, James P. "Barbells on Campus: Weight Training for Track and Field Men at Villanova." *Strength & Health* (March 1959): 28–29, 54–56.

Uhls, Joe. "Football + F.I.C. = Stronger Football Players." *Strength & Health* (October 1963): 28–29, 50, 53.

———. "Weight Training for Basketball: SEMO State Hoopsters Use Weights in and out of Cage Season." *Strength & Health* (November 1960): 28–29, 47–48.

Underwood, John. "The Desperate Coach." *Sports Illustrated*, August 25, 1969, 66–68, 70–71, 73–76.

Van Cleef, Raymond. "Barbells on Campus: Weight Training at San Jose State." *Strength & Health* (March 1963): 28–29, 45–46.

———. "Baseball's Top Twirler Is Barbell Enthusiast." *Strength & Health* (June 1962): 22–23, 46.

——. "Winning Tennis via Weights." *Strength & Health* (July 1958): 14–15, 44–45.

Vanholder, Raymond, Mehmet Sukru Sever, Ekrem Erek, and Norbert Lamiere. "Rhabdomyolysis." *Journal of the American Society of Nephrology* 11.8 (2000): 1553–1561.

Vaughan, Victor. "Hygiene and Public Health." *American Journal of Medical Sciences* 140.5 (1910): 778.

Vertinsky, Patricia. *The Eternally Wounded Woman: Women, Doctors, and Exercise in the Late Nineteenth Century*. New York: St. Martin's Press, 1990.

"Viewpoint: Nautilus—A Statement of Purpose." *National Strength Coaches' Association Newsletter* 1.4 (June 1979): 21–23.

Vogel, E. E., M. S. Lawrence, and P. R. Strobel. "Professional Service of Physical Therapists in World War II." In *AMEDD History: Army Medical Specialist Corps*. 16–24. Washington, D.C.: Department of the Army, Office of the Surgeon General, 1968.

Vogel, Steven. *Prime Mover: A Natural History of Muscle*. New York: Norton, 2001.

Voight, Michael L., and Gray Cook, "Clinical Application of Closed Kinetic Chain Exercise." *Journal of Sport Rehabilitation* 5 (1996): 25–44.

Wackenhut, George. "The Cardiovascular System—What You Should Know about It." *Journal of Health, Physical Education, and Recreation* 21.7 (September 1950): 41–42.

Walsh, Larry. "Barbells on Campus: The University of Maryland." *Strength & Health* (April 1966): 20–21, 61–62.

Walters, Bernard Ross. "The Relative Effectiveness of High and Low Repetitions in Weight Training Exercises on Strength and Endurance of the Arms." MS thesis, University of Iowa, 1949.

Ward, Bob, and Mac Engel. *Building the Perfect Star: Changing the Trajectory of Sports and the People in Them*. Olathe, KS: Ascend Books, 2015.

Waryasz, Gregory R., Alan H. Daniels, Joseph A. Gil, Vladimir Suric, and Craig P. Eberson. "NCAA Strength and Conditioning Coach Demographics, Current Practice Trends, and Common Injuries of Athletes during Strength and Conditioning Sessions." *Journal of Sports Medicine and Physical Fitness* 56.10 (2016): 1188–1197.

Wathen, Dan. "A Comparison of the Effects of Isotonic and Isokinetic Exercises, Modalities, and Programs on Vertical Jump in College Football Players." *National Strength Coaches' Association Journal* 2.5 (1980): 46–48.

——. "From the President: The Future." *NSCA Bulletin* 21.1 (January/February 2000): 2.

——. "President's Message: Special Interests." *NSCA Bulletin* 20.5 (1999): 3.

——. "Stopping Anabolic Steroid Abuse on a Zero Dollar Budget." *NSCA Journal* 10.6 (1988): 56–60.

Watterson, John Sayle. *College Football: History, Spectacle, Controversy*. Baltimore, MD: Johns Hopkins University Press, 2000.

Waugh, Clifford. "Bernarr Macfadden: The Muscular Prophet." PhD diss., State University of New York—Buffalo, 1979.

Wayne, David. "The Greatest of Them All." *Strength* (December 1922): 47–48, 78.

Weaver, George. "The One Way to Physical Perfection." *Muscle Power* (September 1945): 43–45.

——. "What's Wrong with Strength?" *Muscle Power* (October 1950): 9, 31–32.

Webster, David. "A Chronology of Significant Events in the Life of Eugen Sandow." *Iron Game History* 2.4 (November 1992): 17–18.

———. "The Flemish Hercules." *Iron Game History* 6.2 (January 2000): 26–30.

———. "Giovanni Belzoni: Strongman Archaeologist." *Iron Game History* 1.2 (April 1990): 10–11.

———. *The Iron Game: An Illustrated History of Weight-Lifting.* Irvine, Scotland: John Geddes Printers, 1976.

———. "Monte Saldo." *Iron Game History* 2.1 (January 1992): 17–19.

———. "Oscar Heidenstam." *Iron Game History* 1:6 (August 1991): 14–15.

———. "William Pagel: Circus Strongman." *Iron Game History* 4.1 (July 1995): 11.

Weider, Ben. "Barbells and the Decathlon." *Mr. America* 5.10 (April 1963): 24–25, 67–68, 72.

———. "Helpful Hints for Athletes." *All American Athlete* 7.2 (February 1965): 66.

Weider, Joe. "Alex Aronis Makes Good." *Muscle Builder* 2.4 (May 1954): 28–29, 50.

———. "Barbells and Basketball." *Mr. America* 3.7 (December 1962): 40–41, 86, 88.

———. "Barbells and Bowling." *Mr. America* 5.8 (February 1963): 30–31, 73, 76.

———. "Barbells and Boxing." *Mr. America* 5.7 (January 1963): 18–19, 86–87.

———. "Barbells and Football." *Mr. America* 5.4 (October 1962): 22–23, 53, 55.

———. "Barbells and Shot-Putting." *Mr. America* 5.5 (November 1962): 42–43, 88, 90.

———. "Barbells and Swimming." *Mr. America* 5.3 (July 1962): 24–25, 62, 64, 67.

———. "Barbells and Wrestling." *Mr. America* 5:9 (March 1963): 28–29, 75.

———. "Debunking the Opponents of Weight Training." *Your Physique* (October 1949): 16–17, 30–31.

———. "Editorial." *Your Physique* 1.1: (August 1940): 21–22.

———. "Editorial—Bring Out Your Reserve Power!" *Your Physique* 2.5 (August 1942): 3.

———. "Editorial—I Predict." *Your Physique* 13.4 (July 1950): 5.

———. "Here's Why You Need Scientific Training." *Your Physique* 3.1 (March 1943): 18–19, 32.

———. "Our Teachings Have Been Proven Best after All." *Your Physique* 3.5 (November 1943): 6–7, 33.

———. "Sports and Lifting." *Muscle Power* 10.5 (October 1950): 8–9.

———. "You Can Be Strong and Muscular!" *Muscle Builder* 1.6 (January 1954): 10–13, 58–60.

———. "Weight Training Made Frank Stranahan a Champion." *Muscle Builder* 6.1 (March 1956): 18–19, 48–50.

Weider, Joe, Ben Weider, and Mike Steere. *Brothers of Iron: How the Weider Brothers Created the Fitness Movement and Built a Business Empire.* Champaign, IL: Sports Publishing, 2006.

"Weights Don't Hurt Knees." *NSCA Journal* 2.4 (1980): 28B.

Weingarten, Jack. "Barbells on Campus: Franklin and Marshall College." *Strength & Health* (May 1968): 22–23, 58, 61.

Welch, Edmund. "Edward Hitchcock, M.D., Founder of Physical Education in the College Curriculum." In *A History of Physical Education & Sport in the United States and Canada*, ed. Earle F. Zeigler, 121–127. Champaign, IL: Stipes, 1975.

Wellard, Ian. *Sport, Masculinities and the Body.* London: Routledge, 2009.

Werblow, Joan, Alice Hennemen, and Hazel Fox. "Women's Report: Nutrition for Women in Sports." *NSCA Journal* 1.6 (1979):40–41.

Wettan, Richard G., and Joe D. Willis. "William Buckingham Curtis: The Founding

Father of American Amateur Athletics, 1837–1900." *Quest* 27 (Winter 1977): 28–37.

Whaley, Ollie. "A High School Weight Training Curriculum Model." *Strength and Conditioning Journal* 21.2 (1999): 25.

Whitley, Jim D., and Leon E. Smith. "Influence of Three Different Training Programs on Strength and Speed of Limb Movement." *Research Quarterly* 37.1 (March 1966): 132–142.

Whorton, James C. "'Athlete's Heart': The Medical Debate over Athleticism, 1870–1920." In *Sport and Exercise Science: Essays in the History of Sports Medicine*, ed. Jack W. Berryman and Roberta Park, 109–136. Urbana: University of Illinois Press, 1992.

———. *Crusaders for Fitness: The History of American Health Reformers*. Princeton, NJ: Princeton University Press, 1982.

"Why You Should Advertise in *All American Athlete*." *All American Athlete* 6:4 (November 1963): 114.

Wiggins, David K., ed. *Sport in America: From Wicked Amusement to National Obsession*. Champaign, IL: Human Kinetics, 1995.

Wilkin, Bruce M. "The Effect of Weight Training on Speed of Movement." MA thesis, University of California–Berkeley, 1951.

———. "The Effect of Weight Training on Speed of Movement." *Research Quarterly* 23.3 (October 1952): 361–369.

Williams, Bill. "Barbells Build Winning Football Team." *Strength & Health* (May 1956): 8–9, 39–40, 42.

Wilson, Howard. "Uplifting Weight-Lifting." *Journal of Physical Education* 34.5 (May–June 1937): 86–87.

Windship, George Barker. "Autobiographical Sketches of a Strength Seeker." *Atlantic Monthly 9* (January 1862): 102–115.

Wolf, Michael. "The Nautilus Controversy: Continued Response to a Continuing Critique." *NSCA Journal* 3.4 (1981): 38–39.

———. "Viewpoint: A Response to the Yessis Critique of Nautilus." *NSCA Journal* 2.4 (August 1980): 39.

Wolffe, Joseph, and Victor A. Diglio. "The Heart in the Athlete: A Study of the Effects of Vigorous Physical Activity on the Heart." *Journal of Health, Physical Education, and Recreation* 20.1 (January 1949): 8–9, 62–63.

Wolffe, Joseph, and Grover Mueller. "The Heart of the Athlete." *Physical Educator* 6.2 (May 1949): 3–5.

Woods, Christine. "The Female Athlete: Overcoming Concerns toward Weight Training." *NSCA Journal* 14.4 (1992): 34.

Wright, James E., and Michael H. Stone. "NSCA Statement on Anabolic Drug Use: Literature Review." *NSCA Journal* 7.5 (1985): 45–59.

———. "Position Statement: Literature Review: Anabolic-Androgenic Steroid Use by Athletes." *NSCA Journal* 15.2 (1993): 10–28.

Wyatt, Cynthia (as told to Tommy Kono). "Cindy Wyatt Wants to Be a Champion." *Strength & Health* (November 1962): 28–29, 56, 57, 58.

Wyle, Ken. "Barbells on Campus: Kendall College." *Strength & Health* (August 1968): 22–23, 65, 67.

Yessis, Michael. "The Athlete Defined: A Soviet System of Rank." *NSCA Journal* 3.4 (1981): 20–21.

———. "If the Soviets Had Football." *NSCA Journal* 4.1 (1982): 4–7.

———. "A Response to the Reaction of Dr. Wolf to the Yessis Critique of Nautilus." *NSCA Journal* 3.2 (1981): 32–35.

———. "Trends in Soviet Strength and Conditioning: From Macro to Meso to Micro-cycles." *NSCA Journal* 4.4 (1982): 45–47.

———. "Trends in Soviet Strength and Conditioning: The Competitive Period in the Multiyear and Yearly Training Programs." *NSCA Journal* 5.1 (1983): 45–46.

———. "Trends in Soviet Strength and Conditioning: The Role of All-Around General Preparation in the Multiyear and Yearly Training Programs." *NSCA Journal* 4.5 (1982): 48–50.

———. "Trends in Soviet Strength and Conditioning: The Role of Specificity in Strength Training for Track, Gymnastics, and Other Sports." *NSCA Journal* 3.5 (1981): 20–21.

———. "Trends in Soviet Strength and Conditioning: The Soviet Sports Training System: The Yearly Cycle." *NSCA Journal* 3.6 (1981): 20–22.

———. "Trends in Soviet Strength and Conditioning: The Transitional (Post-Competitive) Period." *NSCA Journal* 5.2 (1983): 64–65.

———. "Viewpoint: A Response to Nautilus." *NSCA Journal* 2.3 (June 1980): 42–43.

Zang, David W. *Sports Wars: Athletes in the Age of Aquarius*. Fayetteville: University of Arkansas Press, 2001.

Zatsiorsky, Vladimir M. *Science and Practice of Strength Training*. Champaign, IL: Human Kinetics, 1995.

Zimmerman, Dick. "Best Weightlifters Are Best Athletes." *Strength & Health* (June 1942): 18–19, 35.

Zorbas, William S., and Peter V. Karpovich. "The Effect of Weight Lifting upon the Speed of Muscular Contractions." *Research Quarterly* 22.2 (May 1951): 145–148.

INDEX